9·13

Hit
List

✳ ✳ ✳

Hit List

An In-Depth Investigation into the Mysterious
Deaths of Witnesses to the JFK Assassination

Richard Belzer and
David Wayne

Skyhorse Publishing

Skyhorse Publishing books may be purchased in bulk at special discounts for sales promotion, corporate gifts, fund-raising, or educational purposes. Special editions can also be created to specifications. For details, contact the Special Sales Department, Skyhorse Publishing, 307 West 36th Street, 11th Floor, New York, NY 10018 or info@skyhorsepublishing.com.

Skyhorse® and Skyhorse Publishing® are registered trademarks of Skyhorse Publishing, Inc.®, a Delaware corporation.

Visit our website at www.skyhorsepublishing.com.

10 9 8 7 6 5 4 3 2 1

Library of Congress Cataloging-in-Publication Data
Belzer, Richard.
 Hit list : an in-depth investigation into the mysterious deaths of witnesses to the JFK assassination / Richard Belzer and David Wayne.
    pages cm
  ISBN 978-1-62087-807-1 (hardcover : alk. paper) 1.   Kennedy, John F. (John Fitzgerald), 1917-1963--Assassination. 2.   Witnesses--Death--United States. 3.   Witnesses--Texas--Dallas-- Biography. I. Wayne, David, 1963- II. Title.
  E842.9.B444 2013
  973.922092--dc23
                              2013001767

History will not absolve us if we do not, once and for all,
reveal all that is known about the greatest, most tragic murder mystery
in American History. After all, 90 percent of the American people believe
that there was a conspiracy to assassinate John F. Kennedy. The other 10 percent
work for the government or the media. This book is dedicated to
the 90 percent: May you forever question, hold accountable, and improve,
the great gift from our forebears; what historians have called our
"Experiment in Democracy." Let us all join in this quest to
preserve the very soul of our nation.

Anybody can commit a murder, but it takes an expert to commit a suicide.[1]

> —Legendary CIA asset, Bill Corson, who held a uniquely close position to the highest and darkest echelons of the Central Intelligence Agency.

People are eliminated. Honey, you don't know how many people are just eliminated, just on the operating table alone. They just need to be disposed of. And don't ever believe what you read in the papers. It's all made up.[2]

> —Joe Shimon, a professional assassin and deep cover operative who, for decades, did the dirty work for the "permanent Government" of U.S. military and intelligence—and who finally divulged the above facts to his daughter, late in his life.

Someday you will read that I have been killed in an accident, but don't believe it, I've been murdered.[3]

> —William Sullivan, high-ranking member of FBI, head of Division 5, Counterespionage and Domestic Intelligence, who was *officially* killed "in a hunting accident" shortly thereafter.

All I know is that witnesses with vital evidence in the case are bad insurance risks.[4]

> —New Orleans District Attorney Jim Garrison, when asked about all the deaths of witnesses who had been sought for testimony.

---

[1] Peter Janney, *Mary's Mosaic: The CIA Conspiracy to Murder John F. Kennedy, Mary Pinchot Meyer, and Their Vision For World Peace* (Skyhorse Publishing: 2012), 267.

[2] Janney, *Mary's Mosaic* (Shimon interview, February 15, 2007), 384.

[3] John Hawkins, "Right Wing News," 20 Aug 2007. Robert D. Novak, *The Prince of Darkness: 50 Years Reporting in Washington* (Crown Forum: 2007).

[4] Donald W. Miller, Jr., MD, "Pursuing Truth on the Kennedy Assassinations," 2012: http://lewrockwell.com/miller/miller40.1.html

TABLE OF CONTENTS

IMPORTANT BACKGROUND INFORMATION

In the three-year period which followed the murder of President Kennedy and Lee Harvey Oswald, 18 material witnesses died: six by gunfire, three in motor accidents, two by suicide, one from a cut throat, one from a karate chop to the neck, three from heart attacks and two from natural causes. An actuary engaged by the London Times calculated the probability that at least 18 witnesses would die of any cause within 3 years of the JFK assassination as **1 in 100,000 trillion.**[5]

Thus began the promotion of the 1973 film *Executive Action,* and a controversy that became legendary.

It's important to note that, during the exact same time period that this plethora of suspicious deaths occurred, President Lyndon Johnson and FBI Director J. Edgar Hoover were in the process of slamming the door on any and all evidence that implied a conspiracy in the JFK assassination. As historian Walt Brown grimly notes:

> Johnson's "actions were a virtual guarantee that the truth would be buried and" furthermore, "the assassination would not have been carried out if those behind it did not have the full acquiescence of the incoming President and the FBI Director.
>
> They controlled *everything* once the shots ended.
>
> They controlled *everything* but they did *nothing.*"[6]

For those unfamiliar with the historical context, the chain of events was extremely unnerving:

- First, President Kennedy was gunned down in broad daylight on a Dallas street during a parade;
- Minutes later, in a somehow related crime, Dallas Officer J. D. Tippit was murdered on the street in a hail of bullets in a different section of town;
- Two days later, the accused assassin of President Kennedy was murdered while in Dallas police custody, with the event being captured on national television;
- Then, a seemingly endless list of witnesses started dying, many from obviously unnatural causes.

---

[5] Jim Marrs, *Crossfire: The Plot That Killed Kennedy* (New York: Carroll & Graf, 1989).

[6] "Actions Speak Much Louder than Words—what, exactly, did Johnson and Hoover do?," Walt Brown, Ph.D., *JFK Deep Politics Quarterly,* Vol. 17, #4, July, 2012 (emphasis in original).

Body Count

Author Kent Heiner did an excellent job of detailing the alarming rise in the "convenient deaths" of JFK witnesses:

> The weekend of November 22, 1963, was a bloody one. But these three deaths—Kennedy, Tippit, and Oswald—were only the beginning. There would be dozens of suspicious deaths to follow over the years.
>
> - "Dorothy Kilgallen, the nationally-famous reporter who interviewed Jack Ruby in prison, died of unexplained causes after hinting at an explosive breakthrough in the Kennedy story.
> - A panicked intelligence professional named Gary Underhill reportedly came to a friend's home in fear of his life on the night after the assassination, raving about the (CIA) Agency's Southeast Asian drug traffickers having killed the President, and committed 'suicide' days later.
> - A railroad worker who saw a shooter on the 'grassy knoll' died in an automobile accident.
> - Strippers employed by Ruby had reported having seen him with Oswald before the assassination; they too were soon dead.
> - Sheriff's deputies who talked too much about what they saw were killed on duty or driven to suicide.
> - A witness who saw men other than Oswald fleeing the TSBD (Texas School Book Depository building) after the shooting received several telephoned threats and survived multiple attempts on his life.
> - And, of course, there is the Pitzer case."[7] Lieutenant Commander Pitzer was at the Kennedy autopsy and then was killed under very suspicious circumstances.
> - Just to top it off, even *President Kennedy's mistress*, Mary Pinchot Meyer, was silenced forever in an assassination so professional that one CIA insider said it "had all the markings of an in-house rubout."[8]

---

[7] Kent Heiner, *Without Smoking Gun: Was the Death of Lieutenant Commander William Pitzer Part of the JFK Assassination Cover-Up Conspiracy?* (TrineDay: 2004), 113.
[8] Janney, *Mary's Mosaic*, 346-347.

The observation that it was numerically impossible for so many witness deaths to simply be coincidence had dramatic implications: Witnesses who "knew something" were being systematically eliminated. On the other side of the coin, government pundits have, for decades, dismissed the "myth" as an "urban legend" and countered that the math was all wrong (and they even got that newspaper cited above to say so, too).

Like most people, we were initially unsure what to make of it all. After all, events don't "consult the odds" prior to happening; they simply *happen*. Then someone comes along later and figures out what the odds of it happening were. Some of the deaths seemed purely coincidental; heart attacks, hunting accidents, etc. Others clearly seemed noteworthy; witnesses who *did* seem to know something and *did* seem to die mysteriously.

When we embarked upon this study, we initially viewed statements such as the one which follows with an appropriate sense of caution.

> When Congress established the House Select Committee on Assassinations (HSCA) it gave the committee the mandate to investigate any relevant murder or mysterious death, specifically President Kennedy and Martin Luther King.
>
> But there were three murders that weekend in Dallas – the President, police officer J. D. Tippit and Lee Harvey Oswald. During the following years many other witnesses and suspects in the assassination of the president were murdered or died under strange and unusual circumstances.
>
> Many witnesses died or were brutally murdered during the course of the committee's investigation, some shortly before they were to testify under oath.
>
> Most of those who died violently had knowledge of Lee Harvey Oswald's activities or had knowledge of the CIA/Mafia plots to kill Fidel Castro.[9]

As researcher William Kelly aptly notes, the would-be "investigation" was flawed from the start:

> Rather than address each of the deaths individually, or conduct a proper investigation into any one death or murder, they had the Congressional Research Service at the Library of Congress compile all newspaper and magazine articles "... concerning those deaths," and evaluate only the known facts.

As a result, naturally, they found very little. There was little to no detail in the very vague news coverage of those deaths; in fact, it was almost as though someone had made sure that there was little to find and that those "facts" were intentionally vague. Therefore, it became clear that the many coincidental deaths were <u>never properly investigated</u>.

So *we* investigated, case-by-case. We also checked on the math. We examined the facts and re-examined the odds. We learned that more important than the number of witness deaths occurring in the first year after the JFK assassination is the fact that most of the convenient deaths of witnesses occurred at precisely the time of the two major investigations into the assassination: During 1964, for the Warren Commission investigation, and then again in 1977, when witnesses were being called for the Congressional investigation by the HSCA.

---

[9] William Kelly, "STRANGE DEATHS STUDY," 27 Aug 2007, "Deaths of Witnesses," *The Education Forum*: http://educationforum.ipbhost.com/index.php?showtopic=603&st=105

We will answer the immediately imperative question first: The experts, whom we worked with, determined that the initial estimate above was wrong. The correct odds are *not* 1 in 100,000 trillion. The correct odds are lower. However, lest one presume that there is not substantial cause for concern, the correct odds are "only" 1 in 167 trillion; and you read that correctly, that's trillion with a t. To be exact, it's 1 chance in 167,145,910,421,722. They even "show their work" in case you're interested:

> The correct equation *should* read: Probability of at least 15 unnatural deaths among 1,400 witnesses within a 1-year period:
>
> "The probability is equal to 1—the sum of the probabilities for 0 to 14 deaths:
> $P(X > 14) = 1 - [\,prob\,(0) + prob\,(1) + prob\,(2) \ldots + prob\,(14)]$
> $P(X > 14) = 1 - \Sigma P\,(i)$ where i=0, 14
> $P(X > 14) = 5.98E\text{-}15$
> P= 1 in 167,145,910,421,722 = 1 in 167 trillion"[10]

The odds against "exactly 15 unnatural deaths among 1,400 witnesses in a 1-year period" are actually quite a bit higher: They are 175 trillion-to-1.[11] But 167 trillion-to-1 is sufficiently substantial for us. We think it's safe to call a 167 trillion-to-1 shot quite unlikely; a tad *suspicious*, even . . .

The obvious counter-attack to that will be that there weren't really 15 "true" deaths of witnesses due to unnatural causes. And they're right, there weren't—we have verified that there were actually *more* than 15.[12]

The numbers get even worse, moving forward, because witness deaths increased dramatically at the time of the 1977 Congressional investigation:

> In the 14 years following the JFK assassination, there were a minimum of 70 unnatural deaths out of approximately 1,400 witnesses. The probability is 1.40E-33 or 1 in 714,705,498,316,173,300,000,000,000,000,000.[13]

That's over 714 *million trillion trillion*. Just to put that in perspective, try this on for size:

> That number is greater than all of the stars in the universe and grains of sand on earth. There are an estimated 300 billion trillion (3E23) stars in the universe. That's 3 followed by 23 zeros: 300,000,000,000,000,000,000, 000. There are an estimated 700 thousand trillion (7E17) grains of sand on earth or 7 followed by 17 zeros: 700,000,000,000,000,000.[14]

---

[10] Richard Charnin, "JFK Assassination: A Probability Analysis of Unnatural Witness Deaths," 18 May, 2012: http://richardcharnin.com/jfkprob.htm

[11] Ibid.

[12] See the Appendix for the original list and updates to it..

[13] Richard Charnin, "JFK-Related Deaths," (accessed 10 Sept. 2012): https://docs.google.com/spreadsheet/ccc?key=0AjAk1JUWDMyRdDFSU3NVd29xWWNyekd2X1ZJYllKTnc#gid=1 and Richard Charnin, "JFK Calc Spreadsheet," (accessed 10 Sept. 2012): https://docs.google.com/spreadsheet/ccc?key=0AjAk1JUWDMyRdDFSU3NVd29xWWNyekd2X1ZJYllKTnc#gid=0 and Richard Charnin, email to author 9 Sept. 2012

[14] Richard Charnin, "JFK Assassination: A Probability Analysis of Unnatural Witness Deaths," 18 May, 2012: http://richardcharnin.com/jfkprob.htm

Richard Charnin is an author and quantitative software developer with advanced degrees in applied mathematics and operations research. He paints a very clear portrait of the JFK witness deaths in the context of the mathematical landscape:

> **I have proved mathematically what many have long suspected: The scores of convenient JFK unnatural witness deaths cannot be coincidental.**[15]

Another huge increase in the amount of witnesses dying in a short period of time occurred just around the time that witnesses were being called in the nationally observed testimony for the HSCA from 1976–1978, which was re-investigating the JFK assassination (due to the obvious fact that it had never *really* been investigated the first time). It's not possible to determine the exact number of witnesses slated to testify before the Committee, because much of their work was conducted in secret, records were sealed, and what they did divulge was largely obscure and confusing—historians are still sorting through it all. Some of the documents are still sealed; scheduled to be released at a future date. It was basically what is known in intelligence parlance as a "limited hangout"; they admitted it was a conspiracy but slammed the door on delving deeper into it. Historian Walt Brown, Ph.D., observed that the witness testimony is still difficult to access because:

> **The HSCA published everything they published "butt-backwards."**[16]

Historian John Simkin notes further that:

> **The House Select Committee on Assassinations refused to publish all the documents obtained during the investigation. The CIA forced all members of the committee, all staff members, all consultants to the committee, and several independent researchers involved in the investigation, to sign a Nondisclosure Agreement.**[17]

Rising Body Count

▶ *(The Beat Goes On...)*
And just when everyone thought the whole thing was too impossible to believe but at least was finally over and done with: *The beat went on...*

---

[15] Richard Charnin, email to author, 4 Dec. 2011.
[16] Walt Brown, Ph.D., email to author, 27 Nov. 2011.
[17] John Simkin, "House Select Committee on Assassinations", *Spartacus Educational*, http://www.spartacus.schoolnet.co.uk/JFKassassinationsC.htm (accessed 14 May 2012).

- "CIA and Mafia-connected smugglers Eladio del Valle and David Ferrie, both implicated in the assassination, were sought in 1967 by the New Orleans District Attorney's office; they were murdered on the same day in separate locations.
- . . . high-profile gangsters such as Sam Giancana and Johnny Roselli had been brutally murdered.
- Jimmy Hoffa simply disappeared.
- Rolando 'el Tigre' Masferrer, the financial middleman for Carlos Marcello and his favorite Cuban exile terrorist faction, died in 1976 when his car exploded.
- On March 28, 1977, the HSCA made telephone calls attempting to locate Chicago hitman Charles Nicoletti; the following day he was shot to death in his car."[18]
- On the very same day that Nicoletti was eliminated—and at the very time that the investigator for the Congressional committee was on his way to meet him—George de Mohrenschildt, a businessman with clear links to the CIA who had been overseeing Oswald in Dallas for the Agency, received a shotgun blast to the face. His burglar alarm had gone off shortly before he was killed, but they labeled it a suicide anyway.

[18] Heiner, *Without Smoking Gun*, 113.

But by their own admission, in their own published findings in the *Final Report of the House Select Committee on Assassinations*—it clearly states the following, for the year 1977:[19]

Number of Witnesses:	35
Number of Subpoenas Issued:	103
Number of Immunity Grants:	5

Now consider this—six high-level FBI officials—all connected to the investigation of the JFK assassination—died during a six-month period in 1977, right when they were scheduled to testify before the Congressional committee. Coincidence? Not likely.

If we take the number of witnesses for that year—35—the fact that 6, who were all from the FBI, met their deaths in a six-month time period is astonishingly implausible. Mathematicians use the term *order of magnitude*, which is defined as "An estimate of size or magnitude expressed as a power of ten."[20] In this case, as Richard Charnin puts it:

> The order of magnitude is essentially **ZERO**, meaning prohibitive—the odds of such a bizarre series of events occurring are simply mathematically impossible.[21]

---

[19] House Select Committee on Assassinations, *HSCA Final Report: Appendices*, 1979: http://www.history-matters.com/archive/jfk/hsca/report/pdf/HSCA_Report_5_Appendices.pdf
[20] Editors of The American Heritage Dictionaries, Houghton Mifflin Company, *The American Heritage Dictionary of the English Language, Fourth Edition*, 2006.
[21] Richard Charnin, email to author, 4 Dec. 2011, emphasis in original.

The same held true during the same time period for a long list of mobsters who were apparently involved in one way or another with the JFK assassination and were also scheduled to appear before that same Congressional committee. These guys started getting bumped off like there was no tomorrow. So it's glaringly obvious that somebody didn't want a lot of these people going on the official record at that particular point in time.

The public's interest on this point was not lost on the CIA; their "Damage-Control" unit jumped right to work.

In a 1967 memo to Central Intelligence Agency Chiefs of Station transmitted by CIA headquarters at Langley, the initiator writes:

> **Such vague accusations as that "more than 10 people have died mysteriously" can always be explained in some rational way: e.g., the individuals concerned have for the most part died of natural causes; the (Warren) Commission staff questioned 418 witnesses—the FBI interviewed far more people, conducting 25,000 interviews and reinterviews—and in such a large group, a certain number of deaths are to be expected.[22]**

An astute observation was made by authors Craig Roberts and John Armstrong:

> **If the CIA was not involved with any of the deaths, then it seems a mystery why such a memo would have to be disseminated.[23]**

Suffice to say that it's also probably no coincidence that the deaths spiked up dramatically at the points where there was testimony being sought by witnesses:

> **Of particular interest is the fact that the greatest number of deaths coincided with the four main investigations conducted by government entities: The Warren Commission (1964–65); the Jim Garrison investigation of the New Orleans connection, and later, Clay Shaw (1965–69); the Senate Committee investigation (1974–76), and the House Committee on Assassinations investigation (1976–79). By graphing out the dates of death, the authors discovered that they peaked in the months leading up to, and during, the above named inquiries—sometimes with an important witness being killed, or "committing suicide" only days or hours prior to their scheduled testimony.[24]**

DEATH BY MEDICAL "ACCIDENT"

We also determined from our research that sometimes deaths from "complications from surgery" are actually assassinations. As long-time high-level professional assassin Joe Shimon divulged, late in his life, to his querying daughter:

> **People are eliminated. Honey, you don't know how many people are just eliminated, just on the operating table alone.[25]**

---

[22] Craig Roberts & John Armstrong, *JFK: The Dead Witnesses* (Consolidated Press International, 1995).
[23] Roberts & Armstrong, *The Dead Witnesses*
[24] Ibid.
[25] Janney, *Mary's Mosaic* (Shimon interview, February 15, 2007), 384.

Several of the conveniently timely JFK-related deaths, such as William Harvey, were from post-surgery complications; so that is, at the very least, a possibility that has to be considered. Combine that with the fact that "Wild Bill" Harvey was in charge of hiring assassins for the deep cover ZR/RIFLE Project and was removed from that position by the Kennedys, whom he despised—and one can certainly see adequate reason to include that death in any expansive investigation.[26] Other deaths could have been the result of poisoning, so that possibility should also be kept in mind when investigating the specific cases.

The next matter we investigated was every bit as chilling:

WHETHER OR NOT THE U.S. INTELLIGENCE COMMUNITY HAD THE CAPABILITY TO MAKE ASSASSINATIONS APPEAR TO BE FROM "NATURAL CAUSES," SUCH AS HEART ATTACKS OR CANCER

The research regarding the feasibility of "medical assassination" is quite shocking. It turns out that what many view as marginal capabilities are actually quite real; such as inducing heart attacks and causing cancer in a victim. In reality, they are actual capabilities based on valid, existing science. The CIA, for example, has had the capability of inducing heart attacks for many years; it's considered very concrete technology in the world of the professional assassin.[27]

So we learned that not only is it *possible*, it's a capability that they've had for a long time and have worked on with tremendous emphasis. It may sound like a James Bond movie, but CIA technicians have actually testified to Congress about TWEP (Terminate with Extreme Prejudice) weapons. Many of these TWEP weapons were the result of the CIA's active pursuit of finding ways to kill people that would not look like murder and would leave "no postmortem residue."[28]

Here's what one memo said:

> I think the gross divisions in presenting this subject might be:
>
> 1. bodies left with no hope of the cause of death being determined by the most complete autopsy and chemical examinations;
> 2. bodies left in such circumstances as to simulate accidental death;
> 3. bodies left in such circumstances as to simulate suicidal death;
> 4. bodies left with residue that simulate those caused by natural death . . .[29]

There you have it, folks—your tax dollars at work! Killing people without trial, at a crime scene near you—and it won't even look like any funny business was involved.

U.S. Intelligence Examiner Fred Burks of Berkeley, California, has investigated whether the CIA is capable of inducing heart attacks as a method of assassination, and based on the evidence, concluded that they have had that capability for many decades.

---

[26] John Simkin, "Biography: William K. Harvey," *Spartacus Educational* (accessed 26 Sept 2012): http://www.spartacus.schoolnet.co.uk/JFKharvey.htm

[27] "Congressional testimony: CIA secret weapon causes heart attack," *Public Education and Empowerment Resource Service (PEERS)*, (accessed 11 Sept. 2012): http://www.personalgrowthcourses.net/video/cia_secret_weapon

[28] "CIA secret weapon causes heart attack," *PEERS*

[29] Jim Marrs & Ralph Schuster, "A Look at the Deaths of Those Involved," 2002: http://www.assassinationresearch.com/v1n2/deaths.html

The point is actually confirmed in Congressional testimony. Furthermore, unless there is an autopsy within a few hours—which is extremely unlikely in the case of a heart attack—and the medical examiner knows precisely what he or she is looking for, the method is virtually undetectable because the drug denatures very quickly in the body.[30] And it gets even better. Congressional hearings in 1975 were conducted at the behest of an extremely progressive Senator Frank Church, who proved the exact same point. They even held up the gun during the hearing, and you can watch it online: http://www.personalgrowthcourses.net/video/cia_secret_weapon

Here's what they testified to in that Congressional hearing:

Senator Church:

(Holding up pistol)
Does this pistol fire the dart?

CIA Director Colby:

Yes, it does, Mr. Chairman, and a special one was developed which, potentially, would be able to enter the target without perception.

Senator Church:

But also, the toxin itself would not appear in the autopsy?

CIA Director Colby:

Yes, so that there was no way of perceiving that the target was hit.[31]

And what, you may ask, did Senator Church get for bringing this important information into the light of day for the American public? They ruined him, that's what. They did a big "hatchet job" on his life, and his prolific public career suddenly came to a screeching end.

Mary Embree, a former CIA employee in a division at CIA Headquarters which included poison research, further explains the method of CIA assassination by heart attack:

One time they wanted me to find out if there was such a thing as a poison that was undetectable; especially one that seemed to mimic a heart attack that would kill someone but it would appear that they had a heart attack. I did find such a thing.[32]

---

[30] Fred Burks, Email to author, 5 Dec., 2011

[31] "CIA secret weapon causes heart attack," *PEERS*: http://www.personalgrowthcourses.net/video/cia_secret_weapon

[32] PEERS Websites, "Secrets of the CIA" Five courageous former CIA agents reveal deep secrets of the CIA," (accessed 9 Sept. 2012): http://personalgrowthcourses.net/video/secrets_cia

Ms. Embree also detailed how the poison was employed and its special properties:

> The poison was frozen into some sort of dart and then it was shot at very high speed into the person, so when it reached the person it would melt inside them and the only thing would be like one little tiny red dot on their body, which was hard to detect. There wouldn't be a needle left or anything like that in the person.[33]

Author Peter Janney spent many years researching the death of JFK's mistress, Mary Pinchot Meyer. He concluded that even deaths which were related to that murder were government-sponsored and that the deaths of two authors researching that case "along with former Washington Post publisher Philip Graham's purported suicide, all attest to the CIA's MKULTRA and other long-running, secret programs in mind control: Its ability to administer powerful, undetected poisons that can induce cancerous tumors, heart attacks, or suicidal depression."[34]

The research of Vietnam veteran Lieutenant Colonel Craig Roberts and co-author John Armstrong led to this conclusion:

> Regarding deaths that could be simulated to appear as "natural causes," the various assassination experts within the intelligence communities of the world knew quite well of the effects of such chemical agents as sodium morphate, which caused heart attacks; thyon phosphate, which is a solution that can suspend sodium morphate and provide a vehicle to penetrate the surface of the skin with the chemical (which is used to coat something the victim might touch); and beryllium, which is an extremely toxic element that causes cancer and fibrotic tumors.[35]

Well, well, well . . . isn't that reassuring?

Therefore, as noted historian John Simkin points out:

> It is of course true that Florence Pritchett died of cancer. However, that does not mean she was not murdered.
>
> Research by Dr. Bernice Eddy and Dr. Sarah Stewart at the National Cancer Institute in 1959 showed that it was possible to inject someone with cancer. . . . The research of Eddy and Stewart was backed up by that of Laurella McClelland working in Philadelphia. As McClelland was working for a vaccine manufacturer, this information was covered up at the time . . .
>
> As early as 1961 the CIA knew that it was possible to kill someone with a rapid growing cancer virus. Florence Pritchett was not the only one to die this way. This is the way that they got rid of Jack Ruby in 1967.

---

[33] Ibid.

[34] *"MARY'S MOSAIC: The Conspiracy to Murder John F. Kennedy, Mary Pinchot Meyer, And Their Vision For World Peace, By Peter Janney,* Joan Ullman, *JFK Deep Politics Quarterly,* Vol. 17, #4, July, 2012

[35] Roberts & Armstrong, *The Dead Witnesses*

> Is it a coincidence that JFK's two long-term mistresses, Florence Pritch-
> ett (November, 1965) and Mary Pinchot Meyer (October 1964) both died
> within two years of JFK? If you add to this the fact that Dorothy Kilgallen,
> who was using Pritchett as a source for her investigation into the JFK as-
> sassination, also died in November, 1965, one cannot help to get suspi-
> cious about these "cancer" deaths.[36]

It has been clearly established that cancer cells *were* indeed injected into hundreds of non-consensual patients in the United States for the purpose of medical experimentation.[37] Jack Ruby firmly believed that he'd been injected with cancer cells; and that he even knew when.

> It is widely known that Ruby believed injections he was being given, were
> cancer cells. He truly believed he was being murdered in this most un-
> usual manner.[38]

And Ruby may have been correct. His jailhouse doctor was none other than CIA psychiatrist Louis Jolyon "Jolly" West, reportedly a top expert in the CIA's MKULTRA program, a project involving special drugging and mind-control techniques that included programming individuals to kill.[39] Dr. West was one of the foremost experts in the world on brainwashing and mind control.[40] Veteran Jack Ruby researcher Greg Parker examined the timeline in detail and concluded that "it is feasible that the onset of cancer coincided with Dr Jolyon West's visit in April, 1964 to administer hypnosis and drugs."[41]

Also consider this: Ruby was conclusively linked to research taking place in New Orleans on the development of a fast-acting "super-cancer" to be used as a bioweapon.[42] Then he just *happens* to be the guy who forever silences the key witness, Lee Harvey Oswald, live on national television, convincing about 90 percent of the viewing audience that something was very obviously rotten in Denmark.

The District Attorney of New Orleans was also apparently convinced that Ruby had been injected with cancer cells.[43] Note the observation of New Orleans District Attorney Jim Garrison:

> . . . I do find it interesting that Jack Ruby died of cancer a few weeks after
> his conviction for murder had been overruled in Appeals Court and he
> was ordered to stand trial outside of Dallas—thus allowing him to speak
> freely if he so desired.[44]

---

[36] John Simkin, "Florence Pritchett: The Forgotten Witness," 11 Sept. 2007, *The Education Forum*: http://educationforum.ipbhost.com/index.php?showtopic=2358&st=15

[37] Ronald B. Standler, "Nonconsensual Medical Experiments on Human Beings," revised 18 June, 2000: http://www.rbs2.com/humres.htm

[38] Greg Parker, "Jack Ruby Timeline" (note 12), 23 Nov. 2004, *The Education Forum*, http://educationforum.ipbhost.com/index.php?showtopic=2342

[39] "A Clockwork Orange Career: The maestro of 'mind-control' continues to haunt America," *Freedom Magazine* (accessed 9 Sept. 2012): http://www.freedommag.org/english/LA/issue02/page12.htm

[40] Ronald K. Siegel; Louis Jolyan West (1975). *Hallucinations: Behavior, Experience, and Theory*.

[41] Greg Parker, "Jack Ruby Timeline" (note 12), 23 Nov. 2004, *The Education Forum*, http://educationforum.ipbhost.com/index.php?showtopic=2342

[42] Edward T. Haslam, *Dr. Mary's Monkey: How the unsolved murder of a doctor, a secret laboratory in New Orleans and cancer-causing monkey viruses are linked to Lee Harvey Oswald, the JFK assassination and emerging global epidemics* (TrineDay: 2007).

[43] Ibid, 46.

[44] Ibid, 60.

And as you will see in the Jack Ruby chapter which soon follows, he so desired.

Also, please bear in mind the specific contexts of some of the other so-called "coincidences" in contemporary history as you read about the individual cases. For example, writer and researcher Kathleen Collins posits that the murder of Karyn Kupcinet, the daughter of super-popular Chicago newspaper columnist Irv Kupcinet, may have been a "shock murder" to draw attention away from the links that "Kup" was investigating between the Chicago Mob and Jack Ruby's "muting by murder" of Lee Harvey Oswald, which happened shortly before the Kupcinet murder. Whether intended as such or not, that was the effect achieved: The murder of Karyn Kupcinet took over the headlines and eliminated any would-be discussion of Jack Ruby's very extensive links to the Chicago Mob.[45] So the possibility of it having been a shock crime is certainly plausible.

Ms. Collins also established that shortly after Ruby silenced Oswald, Irv Kupcinet telephoned a fellow Chicagoan, long-time Mob-connected Paul "Red" Dorfman, who was vacationing in Palm Springs, California, at the same time as Karyn, Irv's daughter. Kupcinet specifically asked Dorfman what he thought about Ruby's silencing of Oswald.[46] As veteran JFK researcher Tom Scully notes, whether it was distraction by design or not, the same result was achieved: Kup's columns never mentioned Jack Ruby's links to the Chicago Mob. He didn't write about the assassination until being infuriated by Oliver Stone's film, *JFK*. Kupcinet simply stuck to the scripted story that it was Oswald who shot Kennedy—period.

> **If Paul Dorfman was giving Irv Kupcinet a message in reaction to Kupcinet's call to him about Ruby, by killing Karyn Kupcinet, it worked because Kupcinet stopped asking questions or including any mention of Ruby in his columns after November 25, 1963.[47]**

Likewise, it's been speculated that the kidnapping of Frank Sinatra Jr. in early December of 1963 may have been another "shock crime" to take the heat off of "Chicago," just as one victim had warned.[48] Casino owner Jack Zangetty predicted to friends that Ruby would kill Oswald and that Sinatra's son would later be "kidnapped" in order to distract attention. Both of those events actually occurred shortly after his prediction, so Zangetty clearly appeared to have pre-knowledge of those events. He was also brutally murdered shortly after making those uncannily accurate predictions.[49]

---

[45] Kathleen Collins, "Irving Kupcinet and Karyn Kupcinet," 11 Nov 2011, *The Ducation Forum*: http://educationforum.ipbhost.com/index.php?showtopic=18151

[46] Kathleen Collins, "Deaths of Witnesses," 11 Dec. 2005, *The Education Forum*: http://educationforum.ipbhost.com/index.php?showtopic=603&st=120

[47] Tom Scully, "Deaths of Witnesses," 3 January 2009, *The Education Forum*: http://educationforum.ipbhost.com/index.php?showtopic=603

[48] Craig Roberts & John Armstrong, *JFK: The Dead Witnesses* (Consolidated Press International: 1995), 16. Kathleen Collins, "Deaths of Witnesses, 21 Oct 2007, *The Education Forum*: http://educationforum.ipbhost.com/index.php?showtopic=603&st=105

[49] Roberts & Armstrong, *The Dead Witnesses*, 16.

There were a number of things that people—even at the time it grabbed headlines—felt were "fishy" about the Sinatra kidnapping in much the same way that the public felt the televised murder of Oswald was very fishy:

- Sinatra's son disappeared from a casino hotel linked to the Mob;
- He loaned gas money to his kidnappers;
- The kidnappers only asked for a $240,000 ransom even though Sinatra had publicly offered a million dollars for his son's safe return.[50]

It was another case of "something rotten in Denmark." The money was paid and his son was released, unharmed. But things seemed so out of kilter that, even at the time, a lot of people speculated that it was possibly all a publicity stunt. Ruby's bizarre assassination of Oswald, right on live TV, had been a topic on everyone's minds and lips at that strange moment in history, and it's not at all outrageous to suspect that *other* events may have taken place to spin off the public's attention on those matters.

The cases in this book basically appear in the chronological order in which they impacted the case; i.e., the police officer shot right after the President's assassination, the murder of the President's alleged killer, the man who murdered the President's alleged killer, the man who correctly predicted the murder of the alleged killer, etc. However, it's also very interesting to note that the numerous "coincidental" deaths linked to the JFK assassination can also be successfully separated into only four categories:

- Witnesses to the crime;
- Reporters investigating the case;
- U.S. Intelligence linked to the matter;
- Mafia linked to the crime and/or to U.S. Intelligence.

An examination of the evidence in the primary cases follows, leading to (necessarily) different conclusions; some cases are clearly linked to a "clean-up operation" after the murder of President Kennedy (and were even "national security assassinations"). Others clearly were the result of other forces. We detail the differences of the cases and delineate their broader implications.

It is very noteworthy that several of the witnesses eliminated were among those who were operating *closest* to Lee Harvey Oswald and were intricately involved in that strange nexus that enabled the assassination of President Kennedy: David Ferrie, Dr. Mary Sherman, George de Mohrenshchildt (who appears to have had considerable "assistance" with his so-called suicide), as well as Jack Ruby, were all directly linked.

Many of the murdered witnesses were also mobsters and we were not oblivious to the point that mobsters often die violent deaths; in fact, we concluded that some of those mobster deaths indeed were simply the result of inner Mob workings. However, some were clearly related to extremely sensitive information they possessed regarding the JFK assassination and were *not* the result of common machinations within the Mafia.

Put simply, we followed the *evidence*, not the rumors.

On a final note, bear in mind that whatever "hits" may have been ordered by representatives of the U.S. government in a damage control or clean-up operation headed

---

50 Kara Kovalchik, "TRUE CRIME: The Incompetent Kidnapping of Frank Sinatra, Jr.," 20 Aug 2008, http://www.mentalfloss.com/blogs/archives/17723

by President Johnson after the JFK assassination, the Mafia may have had their own "hit list" for the purpose of ensuring the Sicilian code of silence known as omertà. That would certainly seem to be the obvious case, inasmuch as mobsters like Sam Giancana, Chuck Nicoletti, and Johnny Roselli, who all had vital information pertaining to the anti-Cuba intelligence links to the JFK assassination, were murdered as they were slated to testify as witnesses. The HSCA was specifically investigating the evidence that the assassination plot was hatched from anti-Castro U.S. intelligence operations in Florida. It became evident that, in an attempt to assassinate Fidel Castro, the CIA had employed members of the Chicago Crime Family—specifically, Roselli, Giancana and hitman Nicoletti—and that operation was reportedly "hijacked" and re-targeted at JFK. Roselli told Senator Frank Church's House Select Committee on Intelligence Activities that "a CIA hit team had been 'turned' and used to kill Kennedy."[51] That investigation led to the formation of the HSCA, which was actively seeking testimony from Roselli and the other mobsters involved. Roselli was then warned by a friend that Florida Mob boss Santo Trafficante had put out a murder contract on him and, in July of 1976, Roselli's body was found floating in an oil drum off the coast of Florida—his throat had been garroted, his legs sawn off, and stuffed into a barrel.[52] Then, after the murder of Sam "The Man" Giancana in his suburban Chicago home, an FBI wiretap picked up Santo Trafficante, saying "Now there are only two people who know who shot Kennedy. And they aren't talking."[53] Trafficante's statement was quite apparently in reference to himself and New Orleans Mob boss, Carlos Marcello. Omertà.

Columnist Jack Anderson of the *Washington Post* printed a story on September 7, 1976 in which he revealed that, shortly before his death, Roselli had told him:

> **When Oswald was picked up, the underworld conspirators feared he would crack and disclose information that might lead to them. This almost certainly would have brought a massive U.S. crackdown on the Mafia. So Jack Ruby was ordered to eliminate Oswald.[54]**

---

[51] John Simkin, "John Roselli: Biography," *Spartacus Educational*, (accessed 10 Sept. 2012): http://www.spartacus.schoolnet.co.uk/JFKroselli.htm

[52] Ibid.

[53] Spoken telephonically on FBI wiretap, 1975: Jerome A. Kroth, *Conspiracy in Camelot: A Complete History of the John Fitzgerald Kennedy Assassination* (Algora Publishing, 2003), 190.

[54] John Simkin, "John Roselli: Biography," *Spartacus Educational*, (accessed 10 Sept. 2012): http://www.spartacus.schoolnet.co.uk/JFKroselli.htm

Officer J. D. Tippit,
November 22, 1963

Dallas police department Officer J. D. Tippit

Victim	**J. D. Tippit, veteran officer, Dallas police department**
Cause of Death	Multiple Gunshots
Official Verdict	While on patrol shortly after the assassination of President Kennedy, Officer Tippit stopped a suspect who fit the description of JFK's killer that was being broadcast over the police radio. That suspect was Lee Harvey Oswald, who shot and killed Officer Tippit.
Actual Circumstances	Officer Tippit was out of his assigned patrol area and behaving in an extremely erratic manner, which some have even described as frantic.

1. Officer Tippit was not where he was directed to be after the assassination of President Kennedy, and he even lied about his whereabouts when asked his exact location by police dispatch. He was not just a *little* bit out of his area, either—he was in a dramatically different location.
2. Mere minutes after the assassination of the President, a Dallas police car pulled up and stopped in front of Oswald's apartment window, honked twice, and then left. Right after the police car honked, Oswald left his apartment. If it was an authentic Dallas police car, the only car in that area was Tippit's.
3. In the minutes before his death, Officer Tippit behaved in a wild, seemingly erratic manner, as though he was frantically searching for something.
4. The "suspect" Officer Tippit stopped did *not* match even the very broad description of the President's assailant broadcast on the police radio.
5. According to eyewitnesses, Officer Tippit conversed amiably with the "suspect" for about a minute. Witnesses assumed they were friends and that there was nothing out of the ordinary taking place.
6. Due to a timing issue which we cover in detail below, it is virtually impossible that Oswald could have been in the location where Tippit stopped the suspect at the time that the incident took place.
7. Officers at the scene described the murder weapon at the Tippit crime scene as an "automatic"; Oswald was found with a revolver and there are dramatic ballistics differences between the two different types of pistols.
8. Officers also found a wallet at the Tippit crime scene containing IDs with the names "Lee Harvey Oswald" and "Alek Hiddel." The name "Alek Hiddel" was a well-known "floating alias" used by military intelligence covert operatives at that time.
9. The great majority of eyewitness descriptions at the crime scene identified Officer Tippit's assailant as very *unlike* Lee Harvey Oswald. Some witnesses also saw two men involved in shooting Officer Tippit.
10. Witness testimony that did not fit the official version that Oswald shot Tippit was roundly rejected by would-be investigators. Witnesses were threatened, intimidated, and, in some cases, even shot at. It is little wonder, under those circumstances, that some witnesses eventually changed their testimony to fit the official version of events.

People tend to forget that the first mysterious death associated with the JFK assassination was actually that of Dallas police officer, J. D. Tippit, which occurred very shortly after the shots were fired at President Kennedy.

Officer Tippit was one of the few Dallas police officers not assigned to the area of the President's motorcade. He was patrolling the Oak Cliff area of Dallas, in accordance with his orders for that day. Shortly after 1:00 p.m., Tippit, alone in his patrol car, was seen stopping his car near an individual who was walking along East 10th Street. Witnesses who clearly observed the incident reported that there did not seem to be any trouble. To the contrary, Officer Tippit simply seemed to be chatting amiably with the man; in fact, the unidentified man was standing near the curb and leaning down with his hands on the passenger side door of the car, which apparently had the passenger window down, as the two conversed. As further evidence that it did not appear to be a confrontational situation, witnesses observed that at no time did Officer Tippit draw his weapon, nor did he direct the individual to adopt a less casual position; i.e., there was no "Hands on the car, feet back and spread them," or anything of that nature. For all intents and purposes, the two simply seemed to be talking amiably.[55]

At that point, Officer Tippit got out of the car and began walking toward the front of his squad car toward the man on the other side, with his hand placed on the butt of his gun. Before Officer Tippit even reached the front of the car, the man fired three shots into Tippit's chest, then walked around the back of the car and fired a fourth shot directly into his head, killing him instantly. The suspect appeared to be very professional and confident: He calmly walked away "and he took the shells up in his hand, and as he took off, he threw them in the bushes more or less like nothing really . . ."[56]

That was the way an eyewitnesses reported the event. It later became "scripted" in the official version that Officer Tippit had stopped a suspect who fit the description going over the police radio of President Kennedy's assassin and that the individual was Lee Harvey Oswald, and that Oswald shot Tippit. Evidence not fitting what became that official version of the event was basically tossed aside. However, that official version simply does not stand up to scrutiny:

> In the commission's account, J. D. Tippit, who was a "fine, dedicated officer," was driving his patrol car when he saw a man who fit the general description of the suspect wanted in the murder of President Kennedy. This "fine, dedicated officer," who had the chance to make the arrest of a lifetime, did not try to arrest this dangerous suspect, nor did he draw his gun (according to the wanted description broadcast over the police radio, the suspect was carrying a 30.06 rifle). Instead, he called the man over to his car and began having a casual conversation.[57]

---

[55] John Simkin, "Biography: J. D. Tippit," *The Education Forum* (accessed 13 Sept. 2012) http://www.spartacus.schoolnet.co.uk/JFKtippit.htm

[56] Domingo Benavides (eyewitness) , "The Warren Report: Part 3," 27 Jun 1967, *CBS Television*

[57] Michael L. Kurtz, *Crime of the Century: The Kennedy Assassination from a Historian's Perspective* (University of Tennessee Press: 1993)

Timeline: The Shooting of Officer J. D. Tippit

"On the morning of November 22, J. D. Tippit hugged his oldest son Allen and said, 'No matter what happens today, I want you to know that I love you.' Such overt signs of affection toward his son were uncharacteristic of Tippit. This was the last time young Allen Tippit saw his father alive. Sometime later, Lee Harvey Oswald was seen at the Top Ten Record Store—a block from the Texas Theater. Oswald returned a short time later and was in the small record shop at the same time J. D. Tippit was there."[58]

There are, in fact, many dramatic inconsistencies in the scripted version that Lee Harvey Oswald shot Officer J. D. Tippit:

- Contrary to the conclusions of the Warren Commission, it has been established that Officer Tippit was friends with both Jack Ruby and Lee Harvey Oswald; the three were often seen having breakfast together.[59]
- Tippit's police unit was officially assigned to be patrolling the central Oak Cliff area of Dallas on the day of the assassination. Instead, Tippit's police unit was seen in North Oak Cliff all that afternoon, a district to which he was not assigned.[60] Additional to that point is that Tippit was not a little bit out of his assigned area;

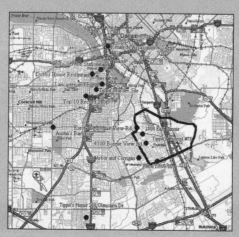

Although Officer J. D. Tippit was ordered to patrol in District 78 (the area outlined), his actual locations on the afternoon of the assassination were far to the northwest.

---

58   John Armstrong, "Harvey, Lee and Tippit: A New Look at the Tippit Shooting," *Probe Magazine*, January-February 1998 (Vol. 5 No. 2): http://www.ctka.net/pr198-jfk.html

59   Harrison E. Livingstone, *The Radical Right and the Murder of John F. Kennedy: Stunning Evidence in the Assassination of the President* (Trafford: 2006) and Dixie Dea, "J. D. Tippit: Was he part of the conspiracy?," 11 Jan 2005: http://educationforum.ipbhost.com/index.php?showtopic=2862

60   Ibid.

he was way out of it. As the previous map clearly delineates, central Oak Cliff and far North Oak Cliff are distinctly different areas.[61]

- The actions of Officer Tippit in relation to the assassination of President Kennedy also bear noting. At 12:20 p.m., he reported on his police radio: "78 Clear"; which meant that he was done with lunch and back on patrol.[62] At 12:45 p.m. (note that this is only fifteen minutes after the President of the United States had been shot), Officer Tippit was clearly seen in his car, sitting at the Good Luck Gas Station (also known as the GLO-CO Station, acronym for Good Luck Oil Company) in North Oak Cliff. His car was parked on the south end of the Houston Street Viaduct, and he was observing the cars coming off the ramp of the Houston Street Viaduct from downtown Dallas (where the assassination had taken place). Several gas station employees saw him sitting there: "Tippit stayed at the station 'for about ten minutes, somewhere between 12:45 and 1:00, then he went tearing off down Lancaster at high speed . . .'" Oswald's cab driver, William Whaley, testified that he took the ramp down from the Houston Street Viaduct when he drove Oswald, and that was during the time period that Tippit was watching the ramp.[63]

- Also at about 12:45, Tippit was asked by dispatch on his police radio to report his location. Tippit responded: "I'm about Keist and Bonnie View" which, if the multiple eyewitness testimony is accurate, could not have been true.[64]

- It was apparently shortly after 12:50 p.m. that witnesses saw Tippit take off rapidly in his car, heading south. That is further established by a radio call he placed at 12:54 p.m., telling police dispatch that he was at "Eighth and Lancaster," which was several blocks south of the gas station.[65]

- Then, at around 1:00 p.m., Tippit parked his car, went into a record store, Top Ten Records, on Jefferson Street, and placed a phone call using the store's phone. Witnesses reported that the call was apparently unanswered and that Tippit then left the store abruptly, appearing agitated.[66]

---

[61] William M. Drenas, "Tippit Locations 11/22/63," October 1998: http://mcadams.posc.mu.edu/tippit1.gif and William M. Drenas, "Car #10 Where Are You?," October 1998: http://mcadams.posc.mu.edu/car10.htm

[62] William M. Drenas, "Car #10 Where Are You?," October 1998: http://mcadams.posc.mu.edu/car10.htm

[63] Ibid.

[64] Ibid.

[65] Ibid.

[66] David Welsh, "In the Shadow of Dallas: The Legacy of Penn Jones, Jr.," *Ramparts Magazine*, November 1966, pp 39-50: http://www.unz.org/Pub/Ramparts-1966nov-00039 and Livingstone, *The Radical Right and the Murder of John F. Kennedy* and Dixie Dea, "J. D. Tippit: Was he part of the conspiracy?," 11 Jan 2005: http://educationforum.ipbhost.com/index.php?showtopic=2862

- At 1:03 p.m., Officer Tippit received a call from dispatch over his police radio, to which he did not respond.[67]
- Rather than reporting to the Triple Underpass in downtown Dallas as most Dallas police units did (even, in some cases, in direct violation of their orders), Officer Tippit was quite apparently looking for some*one* or some*thing*. As Professor William Pulte summarized the evidence regarding Tippit's actions at this point:

. . . Tippit's movements are consistent with the actions of a man frantically looking for someone.[68]

- He got back in his police car and, traveling west on Tenth Street, passed a car being driven by an insurance salesman, James Andrews. Contrary to police procedure, Tippit did not put on his siren and pull the car over from behind. He passed Andrews' car, cut in front of him, and stopped on an angle, blocking the car. He got out of his police car and rushed to the driver's side of Andrews' car, reportedly directing his attention to the floor area between the seats. Not seeing whatever it was that he was apparently looking for, he then rushed back into his car, reversed directions, and sped away quickly to the east.[69]
- According to a witness who was driving behind Tippit's police car at that point, Tippit slammed on the brakes of his car, stopping so rapidly that the driver behind him was unable to stop in time and hit the rear bumper of Tippit's police unit. Tippit was completely unconcerned with the matter and, rather than attending to the collision, instead backed up rapidly toward the curb near Tenth and Patton Streets.[70]
- Officer Tippit was then observed by several witnesses—in his car at the curb near Tenth and Patton Streets—talking to a pedestrian through the passenger side of the police car. According to witnesses, the two conversed amiably and casually, for about a minute. According to the Warren Commission, that pedestrian was Lee Harvey Oswald. According to many eyewitnesses to the incident, however, that man did *not* fit Oswald's description.[71]
- Also, after the shooting of President Kennedy, the landlady at Oswald's rooming house, Earlene Roberts, observed Oswald

[67] William M. Drenas, "Car #10 Where Are You?," October 1998: http://mcadams.posc.mu.edu/car10.htm

[68] Ibid.

[69] Livingstone, *The Radical Right and the Murder of John F. Kennedy* and Dixie Dea, "J. D. Tippit: Was he part of the conspiracy?," 11 Jan 2005: http://educationforum.ipbhost.com/index.php?showtopic=2862

[70] William M. Drenas, "Car #10 Where Are You?," October 1998: http://mcadams.posc.mu.edu/car10.htm

[71] John Armstrong, *Harvey and Lee: Just the Facts, Please,* 1998 (accessed 21 Sept 2012): http://www.acorn.net/jfkplace/09/fp.back_issues/25th_issue/facts.html

going into his room. Shortly afterwards, she saw a Dallas police car stop in front of the rooming house. Two honks came from the driver of the police car, who then drove away, and Oswald soon left the rooming house.[72] If the car was actually a unit from the Dallas police, it had to be Tippit's, because he was the only unit assigned to the Oak Cliff area of Dallas that day.[73]

It is intriguing, to say the least, that Oswald's departure from the rooming house occurred only moments after the strange appearance and horn-blowing of the patrol car from the Dallas Police Department. Exhaustive investigations have virtually established that the only police car officially in the vicinity was that of Officer J. D. Tippit. Less than fifteen minutes after this incident, Officer Tippit was savagely murdered and left dead in the street, about a mile from Oswald's rooming house.[74]

- Oswald's whereabouts at 1:04 p.m. were pinpointed by his landlady, who looked out of the window and saw Oswald standing at the bus stop at that time.[75] At 1:06 p.m., only two minutes later, Officer Tippit, by some reports, had already been shot and lay dead on the ground. Witness Domingo Benavides, spoke the following into the police radio of Tippit's unit: "Hello police operator—we've had a shooting here, it's a police officer. Somebody shot him." The police report stated that the call came from witness Benavides over the police radio at 1:16 p.m. But that was quite some time after the shooting. Benavides made that call *after* he waited a while to ensure that the killer was gone from the scene and he would not be attacked by him. Benavides' exact words were:

...I sat there for just a few minutes...I thought maybe he [the killer] had lived in there (the house where he last saw the gunman) and I didn't want to get out and rush right up. He might start shooting again....That is when I got out of the truck and walked over to the policeman...The policeman, I believe, was dead when he hit the ground...[76]

Another eyewitness, T. F. Bowley, certified in his legal Affidavit that he arrived at the Tippit crime scene and saw Officer Tippit lying dead on the ground. He looked at his watch and it was 1:10 p.m. The assailants were long gone and there were already several bystanders looking

---

[72] John Simkin, "Earlene Roberts: Biography," *Spartacus Educational*, accessed 17 Sept 2012: http://www.spartacus.schoolnet.co.uk/JFKrobertsE2.htm

[73] Henry Hurt, *Reasonable Doubt: An Investigation into the Assassination of John F. Kennedy* (Holt, Rinehart & Winston: 1986).

[74] Ibid.

[75] Jim Garrison, *On the Trail of the Assassins: My Investigation and Prosecution of the Murder of President Kennedy* (Sheridan Square: 1988), cited at *Lee Harvey Oswald's "Murder" of Policeman JD Tippit*: http://scribblguy.50megs.com/tippit.htm

[76] Jim Marrs, *Crossfire*: http://spot.acorn.net/jfkplace/03/JDT/brundage.tippit

at the crime scene, so the shooting had to have happened at least a couple minutes before that.[77]

Therefore, when the facts are examined closely, 1:08 p.m. appears to be the accurate approximation of the latest possible time of the shooting.

- That crime scene was at Tenth and Patton streets, over a mile away from the bus stop where Oswald was placed at 1:04, and the bus that came by during that time span was traveling in the opposite direction of Tenth and Patton. There would not have been time for Oswald to walk one mile and then converse with Officer Tippit for about a minute, prior to his murder at 1:08 p.m.[78] That point was hammered home by Jim Garrison, the only man to officially pursue and prosecute the assassination of President Kennedy; District Attorney Garrison put the time of the shooting at 1:06 p.m.:

First of all, given what was known about Oswald's movements, it was highly improbable that he could have been physically present at the time of Tippit's murder. According to several eyewitnesses at the scene, Tippit was shot anywhere from 1:06 p.m. to 1:10 p.m. Deputy Sheriff Roger Craig, who was at the Book Depository at the time, confirmed this. When he heard the report of Tippit's death on the radio, he looked at his watch; it was 1:06 p.m.

And yet Oswald, it was generally acknowledged, had returned to his rooming house at around 1:00 p.m. He left quickly and Earlene Roberts, the housekeeper, observed him standing by the northbound Beckley Avenue bus stop at 1:04. The area where Tippit was killed was in the opposite direction, a mile to the south. Using the broadest interpretation of the time element, even if Oswald had changed his mind about the bus and run southward, it was virtually impossible for him to have arrived at the scene before the shooting of the police officer.[79]

- The Warren Commission officially placed the time of Tippit's death at 1:16 p.m., solving the aforementioned timing problem that was apparent after it became known that Oswald was waiting at the bus stop at 1:04 p.m.[80]
- The Warren Commission also concluded that Tippit stopped Oswald because he fit the description of the President's assassin which had been broadcast over the police radio. That was an extremely irrational conclusion. The official version, that

---

[77] "Affidávit of T.F. Bowley," 2 Dec 1963, *JFK Assassination Forum*: http://www.jfkassassinationforum .com/index.php?topic=4004.45;wap2

[78] Roberts & Armstrong, *The Dead Witnesses*, 30-31.

[79] Jim Garrison, *On the Trail of the Assassins: My Investigation and Prosecution of the Murder of President Kennedy* (Sheridan Square: 1988), cited at *Lee Harvey Oswald's "Murder" of Policeman JD Tippit*: http://scribblguy.50megs.com/tippit.htm

[80] Jim Marrs, Crossfire: http://spot.acorn.net/jfkplace/03/JDT/brundage.tippit

Officer Tippit stopped a man who fit the description of President Kennedy's assassin, simply makes no sense. The description over the police radio was so general that it could have fit half the male population and it also described the subject as carrying a rifle, which Oswald was not. Tippit did not approach the individual as if he were a suspect.

The verbatim broadcast was:

'Attention, all squads, the suspect is believed to be a white male, age 30, 5 feet 10 inches, slender build, 165 pounds, armed with what is thought to be a 30-30 rifle. No further description or information at this time.'

Thus the broadcast description was for a suspect that was neither short nor tall, a man that was neither large nor small, and neither young nor old. It was a description for the average white guy, while Oswald, a slight young man at 24 years of age and only 131 pounds, was not a good fit for the description. And thus, while there was no known reason in his appearance or behavior to arouse suspicions, the same cannot be said of Tippit. Aside from there being no adequate explanation why Tippit stopped Oswald, the fact is that Tippit was not on his routine patrol as the Warren Commission claimed. For reasons that remain suspicious Tippit had left his assigned patrol area in District 78 in south Dallas and had driven to Oswald's neighborhood.[81]

- The eyewitness testimony regarding the man who shot Officer Tippit also *did not* match the description of Lee Harvey Oswald.[82] In fact, numerous eyewitness accounts described an assailant quite unlike Oswald. As was a constant and disturbing pattern in the aftermath of the JFK assassination, witness testimony which did not align with the official version of events was systematically ignored or marginalized. In fact, at least six eyewitnesses—all ignored by the Warren Commission—saw not one, but two men involved in the shooting of Officer Tippit.[83]

Put plainly:

The descriptions of Tippit's killer by several witnesses and police broadcasts are reasonably consistent with each other, but not with the Oswald arrested minutes later at the Texas Theater.[84]

---

[81] Donald Byron Thomas, *Hear No Evil: Social Constructivism and the Forensic Evidence in the Kennedy Assassination* (Mary Ferrell Foundation Press: 2010) 493. http://www.maryferrell.org/mffweb/archive/viewer/showDoc.do?docId=145592&relPageId=519

[82] Armstrong, *Harvey and Lee: Just the Facts, Please*

[83] Richard E. Sprague, *The Taking of America, 1-2-3* (Richard Sprague: 1976): http://www.ratical.org/ratville/JFK/ToA/

[84] John Armstrong, "Harvey, Lee and Tippit: A New Look at the Tippit Shooting," *Probe Magazine*, January-February 1998 (Vol. 5 No. 2): http://www.ctka.net/pr198-jfk.html

Federal investigators summarily rejected the testimony of Acquilla Clemons and stated the reason was "because of her poor health."[85] Although Ms. Clemons suffered from diabetes, it was obviously insufficient cause to reject her very valid testimony. Witness intimidation was obvious and, in several cases, after a stubborn witness was shot at or otherwise intimidated, they changed their story to conform to the official version.[86]

- Officer Tippit was reportedly shot with an automatic and Oswald was carrying a revolver. Two very experienced witnesses (a police Sergeant and a combat-experienced former Marine) testified they were certain that the crime scene gun was an automatic.[87]

Mr. Myers: After the shooting, police found shells at the scene. They went on the radio and said they were .38 automatics. Later Oswald's arrested with a revolver that fires .38 specials, a shell that's clearly about a quarter inch longer. Besides, they're clearly stamped on the bottom. One says, ".38 special," one says, ".38 automatic."

Narrator: Automatic shells would mean Oswald was not there and that the evidence could have been planted.[88]

District Attorney Jim Garrison saw that matter as a huge red flag:

As I continued my research, I discovered that beyond the eyewitnesses there was other evidence gathered and altered by the Dallas homicide unit showing that Lee Oswald had been framed in the Tippit murder. For instance, I read transcripts of the messages sent over the Dallas police radio shortly after the murder. These were recorded automatically on a log. Just minutes after a citizen first reported the murder on Tippit's radio, Patrolman H.W. Summers in Dallas police unit number 221 (the designation for the squad car) reported that an "eyeball witness to the getaway man" had been located. The suspect was described as having black wavy hair, wearing an Eisenhower jacket of light color, with dark trousers and a white shirt. He was "apparently armed with a .32, dark finish, automatic pistol," which he had in his right hand. Moments later, Sergeant G. Hill reported that "the shell at the scene indicates that the suspect is armed with an automatic .38 rather than a pistol."

---

[85] Ibid.

[86] John Simkin, "Biography: Warren Reynolds," accessed 20 Sept 2012: http://www.spartacus .schoolnet.co.uk/JFKreynolds.htm and David Welsh, "In the Shadow of Dallas: The Legacy of Penn Jones, Jr.," *Ramparts Magazine*, November 1966, pp 39-50: http://www.unz.org/Pub/Ramparts-1966nov-00039 and Gil Jesus, "Re; Oswald's Sole Guilt – Point By Point," *JFK Lancer Forums*, 31 Dec 1969: http://www.jfklancerforum.com/dc/dcboard.php?az=printer_friendly&forum=3&topic_id=17758&mesg_id=17855

[87] Michael T. Griffith, "Did Oswald Shoot Tippit?: A Review of Dale Myers' Book *With Malice: Lee Harvey Oswald and the Murder of Officer J. D. Tippit*," 2002: http://www.kenrahn.com/jfk/the_critics/griffith/With_Malice.html

[88] *PBS FRONTLINE: Who Was Lee Harvey Oswald?* 20 November 2003: http://www.pbs.org/wgbh/pages/frontline/shows/oswald/etc/script.html

It seemed clear to me from this that the hand gun used to shoot Tippit was an automatic. But the gun allegedly taken from Lee Oswald when Dallas police later arrested him at the Texas Theatre was a revolver. Unless Oswald had stopped and changed guns, which no one had ever suggested, this fact alone put a severe hole in the government's case.[89]

> There is no more serious matter on this planet to a police officer than a radio call of "Officer down"— if there is ever a time that another officer will make sure to "get it right," it is when one of their own has been mortally wounded. So if the officer on the scene made the point of saying over the radio that the assailant was armed with an automatic, then you can pretty much bet the ranch that he was sure on that specific point.

- "In a 1986 interview, Hill said he knew the shells were .38-caliber shells because he picked one up and examined it. This is significant because .38 automatic shells are marked '.38 AUTO' on the bottom. Hill specifically said he looked at the bottom of the shell that he examined. It is no wonder, then, that Hill got on the radio and said: 'The shells at the scene indicate that the suspect is armed with an automatic .38.'"[90]
- The bullets in Oswald's revolver were <u>never conclusively linked</u> to the four bullets in Officer Tippit. District Attorney Garrison:

When a homicide occurs, it is standard operating procedure for the police homicide division to send off the bullets and cartridges to the FBI laboratory in Washington, D.C. for study and possible identification of the gun that fired them. In this case, the homicide unit, understandably shy about advertising the coroner's discovery, sent only one bullet to the FBI lab, informing the Bureau that this was the only bullet found in Tippit's body.

To everyone's surprise, the Bureau lab found that the bullet did not match Oswald's revolver. When it discovered this oddity, the Warren Commission was inspired to look for other bullets that might match up better. Although the Commission never received a copy of Tippit's autopsy report, somehow it found out that four bullets rather than merely one had been found in Tippit's body. The ordinarily incurious Commission asked the FBI to inquire about the three missing bullets, and they were found after four months gathering dust in the files of the Dallas homicide division.

---

[89] Jim Garrison, *On the Trail of the Assassins: My Investigation and Prosecution of the Murder of President Kennedy* (Sheridan Square: 1988), cited at *Lee Harvey Oswald's "Murder" of Policeman JD Tippit*: http://scribblguy.50megs.com/tippit.htm

[90] Griffith, "Did Oswald Shoot Tippit?," emphasis in original.

These bullets were sent to the FBI lab. But Special Agent Courtlandt Cunningham, the ballistics expert from the lab, testified before the Commission that the lab was unable to conclude that any of the four bullets found in Tippit's body had been fired by the revolver taken from Lee Oswald."[91]

One government witness later concluded: "I am satisfied that the two projectiles came from the same weapon," implying that a bullet from Oswald's gun had conclusively matched the ballistics of a bullet found in Officer Tippit. However, that testimony is "clarified" by J. Raymond Carroll, a research expert on the shooting of J. D. Tippit:

For the benefit of anyone who is still confused about the ballistics evidence in the Tippit murder, the FBI experts told the Warren Commission that the bullets found in Tippit's body could not be traced to the Oswald revolver, although it was certainly possible that they were fired from that weapon.

The Commission then hired an outside expert, Mr. Nicol, who gave the opinion cited above. This was the only time the Warren Commission rejected the opinion of FBI experts. The House Select Committee on Assassinations hired a whole team of ballistic experts, and every single expert agreed with the FBI and said that it is scientifically impossible to match the Tippit bullets to the Oswald revolver, although the Tippit bullets COULD have come from that revolver.

I respectfully submit that citing Nicol's opinion as though it was authoritative shows a lack of objectivity. Nicol's opinion has been thoroughly and completely debunked, as even Dale Myers admits in his book, *With Malice*.

As Myers concedes on Page 251 of WM, "[N]one of the other eight ballistics experts who have examined the bullets agree with Nicol's positive identification."[92]

District Attorney Garrison basically caught on to the "funny business" with the bullets:

The FBI lab found that *two* of the cartridge cases had been manufactured by Western and *two* by Remington. Since the lab had already concluded that *three* of the bullets found in Tippit's body were copper-coated Westerns and *one* was a lead Remington, these numbers simply did not add up.[93]

[91] Garrison, *On the Trail of the Assassins*
[92] J. Raymond Carroll, "The J. D. Tippit Shooting Evidence," 12 May 2006: http://educationforum.ipbhost.com/index.php?showtopic=6722
[93] Jim Garrison, *On the Trail of the Assassins: My Investigation and Prosecution of the Murder of President Kennedy* (Sheridan Square: 1988), cited at *Lee Harvey Oswald's "Murder" of Policeman JD Tippit*: http://scribblguy.50megs.com/tippit.htm

There were other evidentiary inconsistencies as well. The jacket discarded by the suspect at the Tippit crime scene was not Oswald's jacket, per the testimony of his wife, who knew that he only had two jackets and that was not one of them. The "crime scene jacket" was also a size "Medium" jacket and Oswald wore a "Small."[94]

And to further confound the possibility that Oswald shot Tippit, it has also been established that Oswald's revolver had a defective firing pin which completely prevented it from firing a bullet.[95]

If you'd like to see the simple conclusion of all that info, the "bottom line" of the matter is this:

The revolver taken from Oswald at the Texas Theater was not the gun used to kill Tippit.[96]

---

[94] Armstrong, "Harvey, Lee and Tippit: A New Look at the Tippit Shooting": http://www.ctka.net/pr198-jfk.html
[95] Ibid.
[96] Ibid.

As the evidence clearly mandates at this point, the official version of Officer Tippit's murder simply does not stand up to scrutiny:

If Oswald had been tried for the murder of Officer Tippit, the eyewitness testimony against him would have been destroyed under competent cross-examination. The Commission's star witness in the case, Helen Markham, markedly contradicted herself and made false statements, not to mention the fact that she initially described the killer in terms that did NOT resemble Oswald. None of the Commission's other witnesses actually saw the shooting.[97]

Even the Warren Commission's senior counsel later admitted that their star witness had zero credibility.

The star witness in the Tippit shooting was best summed up by Joseph Ball senior counsel to the Warren Commission itself. In 1964, he referred in a public debate to her testimony as being "full of mistakes," and to Mrs. Markham as an "utter screwball." He dismissed her as "utterly unreliable," the exact opposite of the Report's verdict.[98]

Unlike Helen Markham, Acquilla Clemons and Frank Wright were very credible witnesses who had excellent views of the crime. Ms. Clemons was sitting on her front porch when she observed the murder of Officer Tippit.

Acquilla Clemons lived on the north side of Tenth Street in Dallas. On November 22, 1963, Clemons was sitting on the porch of her house when

---

[97] Griffith, "Five Myths," emphasis in original.
[98] Anthony Summers, *Not in Your Lifetime: The Definitive Book on the JFK Assassination* (Marlowe & Co.: 1980)

she saw Officer J. D. Tippit killed. Afterwards she claimed that there were two men involved in the attack on Tippit. She later testified that the gunman was a "short guy and kind of heavy". . . The Dallas police warned her not to repeat this story to others or "she might get hurt." Clemons was not called to give evidence to the Warren Commission.[99]

Mrs. Acquilla Clemons, who was in a house close to the spot where Tippit was killed, told independent investigators she saw two men near the policeman's car just before the shooting. She said she ran out after the shots and saw a man with a gun. But she described him as "kind of chunky . . . kind of heavy," a description which does not fit Oswald at all. Much more disturbing, this was not the only man she saw.

Obviously, Mrs. Clemons should have been questioned more thoroughly than in a television interview. She said she had been visited by the FBI, who decided not to take a statement because of her poor health. Mrs. Clemons suffered from diabetes, hardly a condition to deter efficient investigators from taking a statement. According to two reporters who visited Mrs. Clemons several years after the assassination, she and her family still spoke with conviction of seeing two men at the scene of the Tippit shooting. Mrs. Clemons' story finds corroboration from another witness, and he too was ignored.[100]

Ms. Clemons was an excellent witness who was certain of what she saw and describes it clearly and unerringly; her video statement is available online at: http://www.youtube .com/watch?v=zTjq7jz8b5g&feature=related

The fact that the testimony of a high-quality witness like Acquilla Clemons was completely ignored by the Warren Commission is further indication that the Commission actually sought to close the case, not to investigate it.

Frank Wright was another eyewitness whose testimony, it seems, was intentionally ignored.

Frank Wright lived along the street from the spot where Tippit was killed, and heard the shots as he sat in his living room. While his wife telephoned for help, Wright went straight to his front door. He later told researchers: "I was the first person out," and caught sight of Tippit in time to see him roll over once and then lie still. Wright also said, "I saw a man standing in front of the car. He was looking toward the man on the ground. I couldn't tell who the man was on the ground. The man who was standing in front of him was about medium height. He had on a long coat. It ended just above his hands. I didn't see any gun. He ran around on the passenger side of the police car. He ran as fast as he could go, and he got into his car. . . . He got in that car and he drove away as fast as you could see. . . . After that a whole lot of police came up. I tried to tell two or three people what I saw. They didn't pay any attention. I've seen what came out on television and in the

[99] John Simkin, "Acquilla Clemons: Biography," *Spartacus Educational*, accessed 30 Sept 2012: http://www .spartacus.schoolnet.co.uk/JFKclemons.htm
[100] Summers, *Not in Your Lifetime*

newspaper but I know that's not what happened. I know a man drove off in a gray car. Nothing in the world's going to change my opinion.[101]

Eyewitness testimony also revealed that whoever Tippit's killer was, he was walking towards the police car, not away from it as Oswald would have been if he was walking toward the movie theater from his rooming house as the Warren Commission indicated.[102]

> **William Scoggins, a cab driver who was an eyewitness, testified that the gunman was walking west toward Tippit's car prior to the shooting. Another witness [Jim Burt] reported similarly. Reports from the Dallas police as well as the first reports of the Secret Service reflect the same impression. Despite the preponderance of evidence that the killer and Tippit's car were moving TOWARD each other, the Warren Report concluded the killer was walking in the opposite direction. The commission version held that Tippit's car overtook the pedestrian killer.[103]**

Witnesses who were clearly intimidated by authorities into changing their testimony include Acquilla Clemons, Warren Reynolds, and Domingo Benavides.

- "Warren Reynolds did not see the shooting but saw the gunman running from the scene of the crime. He claimed that the man was not Oswald. After he survived an attempt to kill him, he changed his mind and identified Oswald as the man he had seen."[104]

Domingo Benavides changed his testimony after his brother was murdered.

- "Domingo Benevides, a dark, slim auto mechanic, was a witness to the murder of Officer Tippit who testified that he 'really got a good view' of the slayer. He was not asked to see the police lineup in which Oswald appeared. Although he later said the killer resembled newspaper pictures of Oswald, he described the man differently: 'I remember the back of his head seemed like his hairline sort of went square instead of tapered off . . . it kind of went down and squared off and made his head look flat in back.' Domingo reports that he has been repeatedly threatened by police, and advised not to talk about what he saw."[105]

After his brother was shot in the back of the head and killed, Domingo told the authorities what they wanted to hear, and it's pretty hard to blame him for that. There was also a highly suspicious break in the evidentiary chain:

- "Officer J. M. Poe marked two of the empty shells found at the crime scene with his initials, a standard chain-of-evidence procedure, but none of the shells produced by the FBI and the Dallas police as evidence of Oswald's

---

101 Ibid.
102 Michael T. Griffith, "Why Would Tippit Have Stopped Oswald?," 1997: http://www.kenrahn.com/jfk/the_critics/griffith/Why_Tippit_stopped_Oswald.html
103 Griffith, "Five Myths," citing Henry Hurt, *Reasonable Doubt: An Investigation into the Assassination of John F. Kennedy* (Holt, Rinehart & Winston: 1986), 149-150, emphasis in original.
104 John Simkin, "Primary Sources: Murder of J. D. Tippit," *The Education Forum*, accessed 3 Oct 2012: http://www.spartacus.schoolnet.co.uk/JFKStippit.htm
105 Welsh, "In the Shadow of Dallas".

guilt had Poe's markings on them. WC apologists claim Officer Poe was "mistaken," but Poe initially told the Secret Service he was positive he had marked the shells, and even under tough questioning from the WC, Poe said he believed he had marked the shells. Moreover, one of Poe's superior officers testified he ordered Poe to mark some of the shells."[106]

Yet the Warren Commission ignored the obvious and concentrated on what was necessary in order to convict the assigned individual in the public mind to keep the lid on the cover-up for reasons of national security.

- "As far as the witnesses who did not support the "Oswald did it" scenario—they weren't even scrutinized—wary eye or not. In fact, the witnesses that reported that the gunman was someone other than Oswald (Acquilla Clemons and Mr. and Mrs. Wright in particular) were never called before the Warren Commission. In addition, Ms. Clemons was told to keep her "mouth shut" about what she had seen."[107]

Jim Garrison arrived at the conclusion that the murder of Officer J. D. Tippit was a component of the plan to kill the "patsy" and wipe out the evidence trail.

- "The reason for Officer Tippit's murder is simply this: It was necessary for them to get rid of the decoy in the case, Lee Oswald. . . . Now, in order to get rid of him—so that he would not later describe the people involved in this, they had what I think is a rather clever plan. It's well known that police officers react violently to the murder of a police officer. All they did was arrange for an officer to be sent out to Tenth Street, and when Officer Tippit arrived there he was murdered, with no other reason than that. Now, after he was murdered, Oswald was pointed to, sitting in the back of the Texas Theater where he'd been told to wait, obviously. . . He was arrested. This left a problem, because if Lee Oswald stayed alive long enough, obviously he would name names and talk about this thing that he'd been drawn into. It was necessary to kill him."[108]

Note the very important point here: That if Oswald *had* been killed immediately after the assassination, very few Americans would have even questioned the composition of the crime; rather, they would have shared a sense of relief that the President's assassin had indeed been apprehended.

The testimony of James Files further supports the notion that Oswald had to be silenced and that the conspirators were keenly intent on that point. Here's the way that Files described it:

Question:	But the Tippit killing is related to the murder of Kennedy?
J. Files:	No, the Tippit killing is not related to the murder of Kennedy. If you want to get right down to it.

---

[106] Griffith, "Five Myths About the JFK Assassination"
[107] Jesus, "Re: Oswald's Sole Guilt – Point By Point".
[108] Simkin, "Primary Sources: Murder of J. D. Tippit," citing Garrison, *CBS Television*; June 27, 1967

The Tippit killing is related to Oswald. Because Oswald is the one that was supposed to die. Not Tippit. Tippit was just one of those people that stopped the wrong person, that got called into the wrong place . . .

Question: So the party that killed Tippit though, was actually after-

J. Files: He was after Lee Harvey Oswald. . . . The party that killed J. D. Tippit, he wasn't there to kill J. D. Tippit. He had parked a little ways from Oswald's boarding house. They went down there to kill Oswald. They wanted to kill Oswald. They didn't want to make a big spectacle out of it. They wanted to silence him at that point of the game. Before anybody could get to him. But I guess- I don't know if Lee got spooked or whatever it was, but then he went to the theater. . . . My understanding was that Lee, that he was gonna meet his controller, which is David Phillips, who was my controller. He was gonna meet him. I didn't know it was gonna be at the theatre. I have no knowledge of that at that point. But if Lee Harvey Oswald ran to a theatre, which had to be where the meeting was going to take place. Lee must have left his house earlier or for whatever reason, I don't really know, but the party that went there, didn't find Lee there. And when he started to leave, he was stopped by the police. This is when he shot Tippit. What transpired there I can't tell you, who saw this guy there, I can't tell you whether he ran, I can't tell you whether he walked, I don't know. All I understand is this: A party that I know, that had come by my motel room, told me he had to burn a cop. The cop he burned was J. D. Tippit. That was the only cop killed in Dallas that day, it had to be the one that he burned. At this point he says: "Here, do you want to get rid of that?" I said: "Hell no, you take care and get rid of your own weapon! I've got my own problems, Get out of here. Go!"[109]

---

[109] Wim Dankbaar, "James Files Interview," November 19, 2003: http://www.jfkmurdersolved.com/tip.htm

Some researchers have assaulted the veracity of James Files, a witness who was in Dallas that day. However, veteran former FBI Special Agent Zack Shelton is the man who investigated that case more thoroughly than any other law enforcement official; and Zack concluded that Files' story holds up. Files was the driver and bodyguard to Chuck Nicoletti, Chicago's most infamous hitman. Zack checked his story thoroughly and his story checks out.[110] James Files said that, shortly after the assassination, a killer, whom he knew, came to his motel room and told him that he had just "burned a cop"—killed a police officer.[111] That man's identity has since been reportedly established as Gary Marlow, a friend of James Files', going back to their school days.[112]

So there is a simple answer to the question: Who shot Officer Tippit? Gary Marlow, not Lee Harvey Oswald. Marlow was a highly professional cold-blooded killer. In pursuit of his prey, which apparently was Oswald, he was approached by a police officer. He calmly chatted with Officer Tippit. Then, when Tippit must have figured he had his man and got out of the driver's side of his police car, the shooter calmly put three bullets in his chest.[113] According to eyewitnesses at the scene, just to make sure, he calmly walked up to the body and fired a fourth coup de grâce shot, killing him instantly.[114] Then, also according to the best witnesses, he calmly walked away, unloading his shells, and tossing them in the bushes.[115] His photo is below; note that his "bushy hair" also matches the eyewitness descriptions of the pedestrian who was speaking to Officer Tippit that day. The photograph was taken in New Orleans in 1962.[116]

Photo courtesy of Wim Dankbaar and JFKMurderSolved.com

This is a photo of the man (on right) who apparently murdered Officer J. D. Tippit. He told James Files (pictured at left) that "things got messed up today" "—"I didn't get Oswald" and that "he had to burn a cop." His name was reportedly Gary Eugene Marlow, a lifelong friend of Files. He died in 2007.

The intention to eliminate Oswald is further supported by some obvious "funny business" with Oswald's ID. A highly reliable FBI agent, Robert M. Barrett, maintained

---

[110] Belzer & Wayne, *Dead Wrong* (Skyhorse: 2012), 131-136.

[111] Dankbaar, "James Files Interview"

[112] Joe Lanier, "Part One: Who Shot President John F. Kennedy?," *The Conspiracy Zone*, accessed 25 Sept 2012: http://www.theconspiracyzone.org/posts/28151

[113] Earl F. Rose, M.D. & Coroner, Judge Joe B. Brown, Jr., "Autopsy Report: J. D. Tippit," 22 Nov 1963: http://www.acorn.net/jfkplace/03/JDT/jdtaut.txt

[114] Dale K. Myers, *With Malice: Lee Harvey Oswald and the Murder of Officer J. D. Tippit* (Oak Cliff Press: 1998)

[115] Donald E. Wilkes Jr., Professor of Law, "The Rosetta Stone of the JFK Assassination?," 20 Nov 2002, *Flagpole Magazine*: http://digitalcommons.law.uga.edu/cgi/viewcontent.cgi?article=1145&context=fac_pm

[116] Wim Dankbaar, Email to author, 24 Sept 2012.

with certainty that Oswald's ID was found at the Tippit murder scene. Special Agent Barrett testified that he was at the Tippit crime scene when a wallet was found there and that he was then asked by Dallas Police Captain Westbrook if he knew the names "Lee Harvey Oswald" or "Alek Hidell"; Special Agent Barrett therefore logically assumed that those two IDs were in the wallet, and he always confidently maintained that belief even when it was politely suggested that he might possibly be mistaken.[117] Here is the photo of law enforcement officials looking at the wallet at the Tippit crime scene:

At the crime scene of Officer Tippit's murder, FBI Special Agent Robert M. Barrett testified that when a wallet was found, Dallas police Captain W. R. Westbrook asked him if he knew the names "Lee Harvey Oswald" or "Alek Hiddel" because those IDs were in the wallet.

The problem with that is simply a matter of "too many wallets." Oswald's wallet was in his pants pocket when he was arrested at the Texas Theater. So why would a wallet containing his ID be found at the Tippit crime scene? In fact, there is even a much more obvious point that should be made here:

Here's a Question for You: What kind of an idiot would shoot a cop and then leave a wallet containing his own ID right there at the murder scene?

Answer: He wouldn't. *Not even an idiot would.*

The apparent fact of the matter is that, just like most men at the time, Oswald had his wallet right in his back pants pocket. The wallet at the Tippit crime scene, just like the discarded jacket that was found there, did not actually belong to Oswald; they were left there by the man who murdered Tippit, whom was not Lee Harvey Oswald, in an obvious attempt to frame Oswald for that murder.

Some researchers have speculated that J. D. Tippit was a "dirty" cop who was somehow involved in the JFK assassination himself.[118] We looked into that possibility very seriously and here's what we concluded from examining the available research:

---

[117] John Armstrong, "Harvey and Lee: November 22, 1963," 1998: http://www.mindserpent.com/American_History/books/Armstrong/November/November_22.htm

[118] "J. D. Tippit: Was he part of the conspiracy?," *The Education Forum: JFK Assassination Debate*, accessed 18 Sept 2012: http://educationforum.ipbhost.com/index.php?showtopic=2862&st=15

Not likely.

We checked with our "Black Ops" friend, Tosh Plumlee, a former pilot for the CIA and a Military Intelligence veteran with over fifty years experience in undercover intelligence operations. His intelligence bonafides can be verified at: http://toshplumlee.info/

It was Tosh Plumlee's affidavit in our book, *Dead Wrong*, which substantiated the historical record that Lee Harvey Oswald was operational with U.S. Military Intelligence.[119]

From checking on the covert side of things, we uncovered information which sheds new light on the matter of Officer Tippit's death. We learned that, far from being suspect, Officer Tippit was known to be involved in and aware of ongoing covert Military Intelligence operations in Dallas. Officer Tippit, along with other select members of the Dallas Police Department, would operate in support of those Intel operations as part of a special tactical team from the Dallas police.[120]

In his Congressional testimony, Mr. Plumlee also stated that certain members of the Dallas Police Department were part of an elite team that operated in support of broader U.S. intelligence operations. That special unit of the Dallas police was "hooked up" with the 112th Military Intelligence Group in Texas. That special unit was "DPD and their tactical team which was operating INTEL in and around Oak Cliff with MI associations from Fourth Army, Dallas Love Field, as well as other connections at Redbird Airport and the near-by 'Oak Cliff' Country Club often used by ONI personnel from Hensley Field." Bear in mind also that, as Plumlee observed, "Dallas Oak Cliff is where 'Oswald' was hanging out at the Beckley rooming house."[121]

It has also been vaguely insinuated that Officer Tippit was out of his assigned area that afternoon because of his "womanizing." But Mr. Plumlee also revealed that J. D. Tippit, and fellow Dallas police officer Roscoe White, were both members of that special tactical team and that their function on the afternoon of November 22, 1963, was to escort members of the Abort Team to Redbird Airport.[122] *That* would certainly put a different perspective on what a frantic Officer J. D. Tippit was doing in Oak Cliff that afternoon.

In that respect, it makes a great deal of sense that Officer Tippit's desperate actions in his last moments were actually in attempted support of Oswald's actions. Plumlee's personal speculation on Oswald (and bear in mind that Plumlee was in Dealey Plaza operationally as a component of the Military Intelligence Abort Team that attempted to stop the assassination), is that Oswald was operational in Dallas. Others with direct knowledge have also confirmed that Oswald was "working an Intel mission" in Dallas.[123]

---

[119] Belzer & Wayne, *Dead Wrong*, 111-115.
[120] William Robert "Tosh" Plumlee, Email to author, 18 Sept 2012
[121] William Robert "Tosh" Plumlee, email to author, 3 Oct 2012.
[122] "J. D. Tippit: Was he part of the conspiracy?," *The Education Forum: JFK Assassination Debate*, accessed 18 Sept 2012: http://educationforum.ipbhost.com/index.php?showtopic=2862&st=15
[123] William Robert "Tosh" Plumlee, Email to author, 21 Sept 2012. Others who indicated that Oswald was working an Intel mission in Dallas were: Captain Edward G. Seiwell, Military Intelligence, Fourth Army, Dallas Love Field, Captain Gilbert C. Cook , special unit of 49th Armored Division, 156th Tank Battalion, connected to the 112th MIG (Military Intelligence Group), Dallas, Texas and San Marcos, Texas, Military Intelligence operative Richard Case Nagell, Jay Harrison, Dallas Police Department, Charles Plumlee, Dallas Police Department; Tommy Pugh, Dallas Police Department, Judyth Vary Baker, Billy Sol Estes, Clint Murchison and Gordon McClinton. Also see Russell, *The Man Who Knew Too Much*, Belzer & Wayne, *Dead Wrong*: "Affidavit of William R. Plumlee" and "eighteen U.S. intelligence veterans with direct and pertinent knowledge concluded that Lee Harvey Oswald was operational with U.S. Intelligence."

The Navy's ONI (Office of Naval Intelligence) operations at Bachman Lake, at the time, were working a special operation in conjunction with the 112th (112th Military Intelligence Group), Fourth Army, Dallas Love Field, concerning the Alpha 66, Miami Dallas Cubans, and weapons that were being pilfered, perhaps stolen from National Guard Armories in the Dallas and southwest Texas areas.

This, I believe, ONI, was Oswald's assigned "cut out", and the 112th, as well as the 49th Armored Div., Dallas Love Field were his prime contacts for the Dallas P.D. UC (undercover) operations. This was not a federal operation, but a local law enforcement investigation launched toward Intel on the KKK (Ku Klux Klan) and the Texas Minutemen. Oswald was acting as a "paid informant", a CI (confidential informant) for the Dallas police, as well as the Dallas FBI. Marina almost let this slip on national TV some years ago. This timeline started shortly after Oswald came back to the USA from Russia with Marina. This was about a year or so before that day in Dallas.[124]

And lest one think that is not a serious claim, just consider this: Remember that *other* name that the Dallas police Captain asked the FBI agent about at the Tippit murder scene because they had found a wallet? It was *Alek Hidell.* "Alek Hiddell" was well-established as an operational cover name used by multiple covert operatives of U.S. Military Intelligence.[125]

Oswald possessed a false ID when he was arrested. Identification in the same false name, Alek Hiddell, was also found at the crime scene of Officer Tippit's death, as well as an ID in Oswald's real name. The name "Alek Hiddell" was a well-known operational cover name in Military Intelligence that was used by many operatives. It was what is known in Intelligence parlance as a "floating alias"; other operatives could even recognize by the name that the person using it was also operational.

---

[124] William Robert "Tosh" Plumlee, Email to author, 21 Sept 2012
[125] Russell, *The Man Who Knew Too Much.*

So that changes the landscape of the event dramatically: One of the Military Intelligence operatives who used the Alek Hidell cover name was Lee Harvey Oswald. When we observe the events of the murder of Officer Tippit from the perspective that both he and Lee Harvey Oswald were acting in concert with U.S. Military Intelligence, it is like putting on a pair of eyeglasses of the proper prescription and viewing the event properly for the first time.

Here is a noteworthy portion of Tosh Plumlee's Congressional testimony, much of which is still, to this day, classified as "Sealed: Top Secret, Committee Sensitive":

> **The team was to meet at Redbird Airport, or at the safe house near the Oak Cliff Country Club southeast of Redbird. Officers from the Dallas Police Department would escort most of the abort team to the location for departure from Redbird.**[126]

As far as what happened "in Dallas that day," Plumlee pulls no punches as far as his knowledge of what was taking place on his end of events:

> **Tippit and White both had Military Intel and CIA fingerprints all over Dallas and Fort Worth before the assassination of Kennedy. They both knew about the "Abort Team" and why and how they were dispatched to Dallas that day.**[127]

When you go back and look at our Timeline of J. D. Tippit's last day with *that* in mind, it then suddenly makes a great deal more sense.

So, as you look at the shooting of Officer Tippit, bear in mind that, only minutes before, the President of the United States was assassinated and that a Military Intelligence Abort Team was, at that precise moment, ex-filtrating Dealey Plaza en route to Redbird Airport in the Oak Cliff section of Dallas; part of the extraction team were select Dallas police officers who were supposed to be escorting the Abort Team members to Redbird. If you look at the map of Officer Tippit's locations with that perspective in mind, he's not "out of his area" at all; from an operational intelligence standpoint, he's *right at the optimum location*: Watching the down ramp from Dealey Plaza traffic at the Houston Street Viaduct, from which it is a straight shot south through Oak Cliff to Redbird Airport.

Obviously, a lot of things went wrong that day; the Abort Team made it to Dealey Plaza, but communications were difficult, they couldn't intervene and the President was killed.[128] Some critics have made the simplistic argument that the whole assassination could have been avoided if someone had just called the Secret Service and told them not to go through Dealey Plaza. Aside from the fact that it's pretty easy to quarterback Sunday's football game on Monday morning, for problematic reasons, that apparently was simply not feasible. The President's trip to Chicago had been altered dramatically for security purposes, and then the same types of security alterations to planned

---

[126] "Testimony of William Robert Plumlee to House Select Committee on Assassinations," Email to author, 18 Sept 2012

[127] William Robert "Tosh" Plumlee, Email to author, 18 Sept 2012

[128] Belzer & Wayne, *Dead Wrong*, 110-128.

appearances occurred in Florida, as well, immediately prior to the trip to Texas.[129] For various considerations at that time, which may have been more bureaucratic than anything else, it was not deemed feasible to simply tell the Secret Service to "call it all off." It may sound logical in retrospect, but in "Boots-on-the-ground in real-time" it obviously wasn't.

Something also obviously went wrong during the ex-filtration of the Abort Team. J. D. Tippit apparently figured something out—possibly that Oswald was supposed to be eliminated as the coup de grâce of the conspiracy—and his last actions, which were frantic in nature, were apparently intervening to accomplish some component of the best interests of the intel team or its ex-filtration. It's not clear what he was specifically doing, but it is clear that he must have been acting operationally. Whatever he figured out culminated in the intense focusing of his attention on suspicious individuals near Oswald and/or others and he did indeed locate one. Confronting that individual, however, quickly ended in his own murder.

Simplified, Oswald was on the same team as "the good guys" and Officer Tippit ("the good guys" also) was apparently intervening on his behalf. That intervention cost him his life.

CONCLUSIONS BASED ON EVIDENTIARY INDICATIONS

The man whom Officer Tippit stopped was NOT Lee Harvey Oswald.

The man who shot Officer Tippit was NOT Lee Harvey Oswald.

Whatever it was that Officer Tippit was so desperately searching for in his final moments, it appears that those acts were clearly linked to some aspect of his liaison with Military Intelligence and/or the extraction of the Military Intelligence Abort Team from Dallas on November 22, as a direct result of his being part of a tactical team from the Dallas Police Department being used as support in sensitive intelligence operations.

---

[129] Lamar Waldron & Thom Hartmann, *Ultimate Sacrifice* (New York: Carroll & Graf, 2005).

Lee Harvey Oswald,
November 24, 1963

Oswald joined the Marines in 1956, and by 1957 was in specialized intelligence training in Nags Head, North Carolina. Veteran undercover operative, Tosh Plumlee, who remembers seeing Oswald there, said it was for training, prior to "going international," in false identities, maintenance of cover stories, etc. CIA veteran Victor Marchetti confirmed that the "false defector" operation was being run out of Nags Head at that time.

Victim	Lee Harvey Oswald
Cause of Death	Single Gunshot
Official Verdict	Murdered by a Dallas nightclub operator, Jack Ruby, for the purpose of not forcing President Kennedy's widow to endure a criminal trial of the accused.
Actual Circumstances	Even though the accused assassin of the President of the United States was the most prominent suspect in American history, Jack Ruby walked right through an unlocked door at the Dallas Police Department, approached the Nags suspect without challenge from any of the army of police

officers guarding Oswald, then drew his weapon, also without challenge, pointed it at Oswald, also without challenge, and then fired—all captured on live television to a stunned audience of millions of Americans who literally could not believe the implausibility of the event they had just witnessed.

Inconsistencies

1. Oswald could not have been at the so-called "sniper's nest" on the sixth floor because his verified actual location a couple minutes later completely precluded that possibility.[130]
2. Oswald was operational with U.S. Military Intelligence, as we established in *Dead Wrong*.[131]
3. Voice Stress Analysis on Oswald's recorded voice revealed that he was actually telling the truth when he made the statements "I'm a patsy" and "I didn't kill anybody."[132]
4. Never in American history has an important criminal been so poorly protected. It would be dramatic understatement to say that security was "very lax." The ease with which Ruby executed the guarded prisoner, and the complete absence of police intervention, made it seem as though the event was scripted that way before it happened, a point which was not lost on the viewing audience.
5. It has been conclusively established that Jack Ruby knew Oswald well, even though would-be investigations like the Warren Commission went to great lengths and did everything in their considerable power to minimize that fact. Jack Ruby's very clear connections to the Mafia and to U.S. Intelligence via its anti-Castro operations in which Ruby participated were minimized in exactly the same manner.
6. As has been speculated, part of the original assassination plan was probably to eliminate Oswald right after the President was shot. That would have made it a nice neat package with no loose ends. Oswald, however, temporarily escaped that fate. But once in custody, he was a "sitting duck" for that eventuality. It befell upon Jack Ruby to finish the job.[133]
7. Oswald never got his "day in court," and the silencing of a key witness was never more obvious.

[130] Richard Belzer, "Defaming History or, Who Didn't Kill JFK," August 13, 2007, *Huffington Post*: http://www.huffingtonpost.com/richard-belzer/defaming-history-or-who-d_b_60188.html
[131] Belzer & Wayne, *Dead Wrong*, 110-128.
[132] Belzer & Wayne, *Dead Wrong*, 127-128.
[133] Simkin, *John Roselli: Biography*

Two days after the assassination of President Kennedy, a national television audience watched incredulously as mobster Jack Ruby easily approached and murdered the accused assassin, Lee Harvey Oswald—live on TV—as the prisoner was being transported by the Dallas Police Department (with whom Ruby had well-established ties). Never has the silencing of a crucial witness been more obvious or suspect.

In the most obvious case of witness elimination in history, the accused assassin—there was never a trial or eyewitnesses—of President Kennedy was gunned down in broad daylight, even though he was surrounded by a bevy of law enforcement officers, as the prisoner was being transferred to another jail. A stunned nation watched in silent disbelief because the event had been televised and everyone had wanted to get a look at the accused killer. We all got much more than a look. We got a taste of incredulity because people literally could not believe the obviousness of a crucial witness being eliminated before their eyes.

Oswald's "defection" to Russia was part of an ongoing intelligence operation, the False Defector Program of ONI (Office of Naval Intelligence). But the KGB (Russian Intelligence) were no fools and disbelieved the authenticity of his actions.

Here's how one of the millions of witnesses to it described the incredible event. As you read it, keep in mind that the President of the United States had just been brutally slaughtered in broad daylight about forty-eight hours previous:

> Two days later, in one of the most bizarre, phantasmagorical events ever witnessed on national television, Oswald was fatally shot by a man identified as Jack Ruby, adding to the bewilderment of an already stunned audience of viewers. So unprecedented had been the spectacle of horror, Agnes Meyer, mother of *Washington Post* publisher Katharine Graham, reportedly seethed, "What is this, some kind of goddamn banana republic?" The American media struggled to sustain a semblance of calm and order, still insistent

Lee Harvey Oswald had been the lone crackpot assassin and had acted uni-laterally. But observers and journalists in other countries had already start-ed speculating Oswald had been killed to keep him from talking.[134]

In addition to the substantial evidence we provided in *Dead Wrong* conclusively docu-menting that Oswald was a component of an intelligence operation known as the False Defector Program, we found even further substantiation. U.S. Senator Richard Sch-weiker, a veteran Republican Senator from Pennsylvania, was Co-Chairman of a U.S. Senate Subcommittee to investigate the JFK assassination in 1975. In 2007, after retire-ment, Senator Schweiker was specific that Oswald's phony defection to the Soviet Union in 1959 was actually part of an intelligence operation, the False Defector Program:

Oswald "was the product of a fake defector program run by the CIA."[135]

As we noted in *Dead Wrong*, CIA officer Victor Marchetti confirmed the existence of the top-secret CIA/ONI False Defector Program in Nags Head, North Carolina in the late 1950s, during an interview with author Anthony Summers. Marchetti confirmed that account on October 4, 2007, in an interview with Peter Janney, in the book *Mary's Mosaic*. Author Joan Mellen also reconfirmed that "the ONI program was overseen by the CIA's counterintelligence chief, James Jesus Angleton. Upon Oswald's return to the U.S. in 1962, he was, in fact, 'debriefed' by a CIA officer named Aldrin ('Andy') Anderson. The debriefing report was read by CIA officer Donald Deneselya, who confirmed this in an interview for this book on May 25, 2007, as well as in the 1993 PBS *Frontline* program, 'Who Was Lee Harvey Oswald?' "[136]

The CIA suspected that Oswald's Russian wife, Marina Prusakova, was KGB: How could a Russian teenager manage to meet the 2nd and 3rd U.S. defectors to the Soviet Union, in cities hundreds of miles apart, speak to them in English, and marry one of them (Oswald) within days of their first meeting, then leave the Soviet Union without any exit difficulties, at the height of the Cold War? Marina's uncle, Ilya Prusakova, a Colonel in the MVD (Ministry of Internal Affairs, a.k.a. Soviet Secret Police), approved the very sudden marriage between his niece and the American defector. So U.S. Intelligence utilized George de Mohrenschildt, a Russian émigré and CIA asset who befriended Oswald in Dallas, to try to monitor the Oswald-Marina Prusakova situation. Mohrenschildt died under very suspicious circumstances, just before he was scheduled to testify about what he knew.

---

[134] Janney, *Mary's Mosaic*, 282.
[135] David Talbot, *Brothers: The Hidden History of the Kennedy Years* (Free Press, 2007), 381.
[136] Janney, *Mary's Mosaic*, 430.

Quite unlike the well-established actions of political assassins throughout history, Oswald continually professed his innocence, telling anyone who would listen that he had been set up as the "patsy" to take the fall for the crime. There's a pretty good reason for that too; the man was stating a fact.

When Oswald returned from Russia, his actions were clearly calculated to create a "legend" for a sophisticated intelligence operation. He was intentionally arrested in New Orleans, for "disturbing the peace," as part of that process. He was simultaneously pro-Castro/anti-Castro, infiltrated the Fair Play for Cuba Committee, and was involved with Alpha 66 anti-Castro Cubans at CIA "safe houses" in the Oak Cliff section of Dallas and government-sanctioned gunrunning operations.

Rather than taking credit for the shooting, as political assassins have done throughout history, Oswald vehemently denied shooting Kennedy or anybody else, and politely but forcefully maintained that he was "a patsy." His recorded words were subjected to new voice analysis technologies which determined that he was actually telling the truth when he made those statements.

The cover story for the murder of Oswald was one of the most transparent fabrications in contemporary history— his killer, Jack Ruby, said he wanted to "spare the President's widow of a trial," which is about as likely as the moon really being made of green cheese. Jack Ruby killed Oswald live on television and a national audience immediately sensed that something clearly stunk about the whole scenario. There were cops all over the place—it was the Dallas jail, for heaven's sakes—but nobody made the slightest move to stop Ruby and the gun he brazenly displayed, even though they were supposedly "guarding" the most important prisoner in American history.

To add further fuel to the whole fiasco, Jack Ruby was seriously hooked up with just about everybody suspected of playing a major role in the assassination, from the Mafia to U.S. Intelligence and its (and Ruby's) involvement in ongoing anti-Cuban intelligence operations. It's absolutely preposterous to presume for even a second that those connections weren't directly linked to the real reasons that he murdered Oswald.

After his arrest, even Oswald's expressions seemed to capture a man completely perplexed by the untenable situation in which he found himself.

As far as Lee Harvey Oswald, his recorded voice stands up to the technological scrutiny of modern voice analysis. According to the VSA testing, it clearly determined that Oswald was telling the truth when he said that he hadn't killed anybody and that he was a patsy.[137] Wouldn't it be nice if we could use that voice testing technology on our politicians who tell us what supposedly happened and swear it's the truth?

---

[137] George O'Toole, *The Assassination Tapes: An electronic probe into the Murder of John F. Kennedy and the Dallas cover-up* (Penthouse Press, 1975).

3 | Jack Ruby,
January 3, 1967

Victim	Jack Ruby
Cause of Death	Cancer
Official Verdict	Natural Causes
Actual Circumstances	Ruby maintained throughout his incarceration that he had been injected with cancer cells. Although that claim seems odd, it is much more relevant than first meets the eye. It is now known that a rapid onset "super-cancer" was being developed for use as a bioweapon to be deployed

Actual Circumstances	against Fidel Castro. Ruby was in the same nexus as those developing the bioweapon and would have had knowledge of its development. Ruby's cancer was rapid onset and occurred shortly after he was granted a new trial, at which time he would have been able to present evidence; an opportunity he had long sought, because he maintained that he would be murdered if he ever revealed what had really happened.
Inconsistencies	1. There was NO MOTIVE for Ruby to have killed Oswald other than Ruby's extensive links to the Mafia and to U.S. Intelligence via anti-Cuba gunrunning operations with which Ruby was heavily involved. 2. Jack Ruby clearly knew all the players in the assassination drama, from the Chicago mobsters, to the anti-Castro CIA agents, to the Dallas police officers, to Lee Harvey Oswald himself. 3. Ruby was clearly in fear for his life, both before and after the shooting of Oswald. Police officers reported that he was actually very relieved when told that Oswald had died from his wounds. His fear then manifested in the fact that he was not safe in a Dallas jail. He pleaded with Chief Justice Earl Warren to take him to Washington, D.C., where he would then be able to explain what had actually happened. They denied his request. 4. The occurrence of Ruby's rapid-onset cancer coincided with medical visits to him in jail from a well-known MKULTRA expert. (MKULTRA was the top-secret CIA program, part of which was aimed at using drugs, hypnotism and anything else available to control an individual's will, even to the extent of making them perform murder.)

The case is closed, is it? Well I'd like to know how in a big smart town like Dallas, a man like Jack Ruby—operator of a striptease honky tonk—could stroll in and out of police headquarters as if it were a health club at a time when a small army of law enforcers was keeping a "tight security guard" on Oswald.

Security! What a word for it.

I wouldn't try to speak for Dallas, but around here, the people I talk to really believe that a man has the right to be tried in court.

When that right is taken away from any man by the incredible combination of Jack Ruby and insufficient security, we feel chilled.[138]

With those words, columnist Dorothy Kilgallen openly stated what had been on millions of Americans' minds ever since Jack Ruby casually strolled up to the most wanted criminal in history and forever eliminated his possible testimony.

Frankly, mobster Johnny Roselli's version of the event sounds a lot easier to buy. Shortly before he was murdered, Roselli also told the *Washington Post* reporter, Jack Anderson:

When Oswald was picked up, the underworld conspirators feared he would crack and disclose information that might lead to them. This almost certainly would have brought a massive US crackdown on the Mafia. So Jack Ruby was ordered to eliminate Oswald.[139]

Few Americans are aware of some dramatic conclusions reached—very officially—by the investigation and *Final Report of the House Select Committee on Assassinations* in 1979:

. . . Ruby's shooting of Oswald was not a spontaneous act, in that it involved at least some premeditation. Similarly, the committee believed it was less likely that Ruby entered the police basement without assistance, even though the assistance may have been provided with no knowledge of Ruby's intentions. . . . The committee was troubled by the apparently unlocked doors along the stairway route and the removal of security guards from the area of the garage nearest the stairway shortly before the shooting. . . . There is also evidence that the Dallas Police Department withheld relevant information from the Warren Commission concerning Ruby's entry to the scene of the Oswald transfer.[140]

In other words, it was a <u>set-up</u>; they had to let Ruby shoot Oswald because Oswald had to be taken out of the equation.

Whatever we may think about it, we should take serious note of what Jack Ruby himself thought—and he clearly believed that he had been injected with cancer cells. Dallas Deputy Sherriff Al Maddox stated the following:

Ruby told me, "Well, they injected me for a cold." He said it was cancer cells. That's what he told me, Ruby did. I said you don't believe that bullshit. He said, "I damn sure do!" (And then) one day when I started to leave, Ruby shook hands with me and I could feel a piece of paper in his palm . . . (in the note that he handed to him) he said it was a conspiracy and he said . . . if you will keep your eyes open and your mouth shut, you're gonna learn a lot. And that was the last letter I ever got from him.[141]

Ruby also made it very clear that he blamed the new President, Lyndon Johnson, for the assassination of President Kennedy—specifically implicating him in its planning.

---

[138] Dorothy Kilgallen, 29 November 1963, *New York Journal American.*
[139] Richard Mahoney, *Sons and Brothers*, 418.
[140] "HSCA Final Assassinations Report," House Select Committee on Assassinations, 157-158.
[141] Marrs, *Crossfire*, 431-432; Gil Jesus, "Video: Ruby's Letter from Prison," 2 July 2007: http://educationforum. ipbhost.com/index.php?showtopic=10399

He spells it out very clearly in video interviews that can be accessed on YouTube: http://www.youtube.com/watch?v=FDDxYOqyqlc

> Ruby: "When I mentioned about Adlai Stevenson, if he was Vice President there never would have been an assassination of our beloved President Kennedy." (JFK almost chose Stevenson as Vice President instead of Johnson)
>
> Reporter: "What do you mean by that, Jack?"
>
> Ruby: "Well, your answer is the man in office now (Lyndon Johnson)."

Here was another one:

> Ruby: "Everything pertaining to what's happening has never come to the surface. The world will never know the true facts of what occurred—my motives. The people who had so much to gain, and had such an ulterior motive for putting me in the position I'm in, will never let the true facts come above board to the world."
>
> Reporter: "Are these people in very high positions Jack?"
>
> Ruby: "Yes."[142]

Ruby also seemed certain of his fate and, for a man clearly facing death, would seem to have little reason to lie at that point:

> Not long before Ruby died, according to an article in the London Sunday Times, he told psychiatrist Werner Teuter that the assassination was "an act of overthrowing the government" and that he knew "who had President Kennedy killed." He added: "I am doomed. I do not want to die. But I am not insane. I was framed to kill Oswald."[143]

Ruby also said:

> . . . I want to tell you this, I am used as a scapegoat . . .[144]

It's one thing to sound a bit despondent due to trials and confinement—it's another thing entirely to be so fatalistic that you sound as if your fate has been sealed; Ruby was the latter, not the former.

---

[142] "Jack Ruby Press Conference," *YouTube*, 7 May 2006: http://www.youtube.com/watch?v=we2eucWXqjg

[143] "Jack Ruby," citing: Martin Shackelford, "Warren Commission Errors," 22, Sept. 1999, http://www.jfklancer.com/LNE/report35.html; Marrs, *Crossfire*, 431-432.

[144] Wim Dankbaar, "Jack Ruby," *JFK Murder Solved*, accessed 24 Nov. 2012: http://www.jfkmurdersolved.com/ruby.htm

Ruby: But I won't be around, Chief Justice. I won't be around to verify these things you are going to tell the President.

Attorney: Who do you think is going to eliminate you, Jack?

Ruby: I have been used for a purpose, and there will be a certain tragic occurrence happening if you don't take my testimony . . .[145]

The written record from Jack Ruby is quite illuminating. He told it straight out to the former Chief Justice of the Supreme Court and to a United States Congressman:

Gentlemen, I want to tell the truth, but I cannot tell it here. If you want a fair shake out of me, you have to take me to Washington.[146]

He also told the Warren Commission that he not only feared for his own life, but had been warned of reprisals against his family, especially his brother. Notice the constant fatalism—he sounds as if he's *already dead* and speaking from the grave:

Well, you won't see me again. I tell you that a whole new form of government is going to take over the country, and I know I won't live to see you another time.[147]

Here's more, from a letter that he wrote in jail, to someone he trusted:

. . . you must believe me that I know what is taking place, so please with all my heart, you must believe me, because I am counting on you to save this country a lot of blood-shed. As soon as you get out you must read Texan looks at Lyndon (*A Texan Looks at Lyndon* by J. Evetts Haley), and it may open your eyes to a lot of things. This man is a Nazi in the worst order.[148]

Unlike most Americans during the 1960s, the above reference exemplifies that Jack Ruby clearly knew the vast trail of corruption for which Lyndon Johnson was responsible. That trail included several murders, as we documented in *Dead Wrong*. The book, *A Texan Looks at Lyndon: A Study in Illegitimate Power*, was the first to openly address the ruthless and even deadly tactics of the Lyndon Johnson political machine; it had just come out in March of 1964, and Ruby was already familiar with its contents. Of course, Ruby had probably witnessed the ruthlessness of Johnson firsthand, because Ruby was familiar himself with the dark underside of Texas and its melding of Organized Crime and cold-blooded politics. Ruby's letter to his friend also included the following passage:

Isn't it strange that Oswald who hasn't worked a lick most of his life, should be fortunate enough to get a job at the Book Building two weeks before the president himself didn't know as to when he was to visit Dallas,

---

[145] Ibid.
[146] Ibid.
[147] Ibid.
[148] Ibid.

now where would a jerk like Oswald get the information that the president was coming to Dallas? Only one person could have had that information, and that man was Johnson who knew weeks in advance as to what was going to happen, because he is the one who was going to arrange the trip for the president, this had been planned long before the president himself knew about, so you can figure that one out. The only one who gained by the shooting of the president was Johnson, and he was in a car in the rear and safe when the shooting took place. What would the Russians, Castro or anyone else have to gain by eliminating the president? If Johnson was so heartbroken over Kennedy, why didn't he do something for Robert Kennedy? All he did was snub him.[149]

This is how Ruby's testimony before the Warren Commission concluded:

Ruby:	You have lost me though. You have lost me, Chief Justice Warren.
Chief Justice Warren:	Lost you in what sense?
Ruby:	I won't be around for you to come and question me again.
Chief Justice Warren:	Well, it is very hard for me to believe that. I am sure that everybody would want to protect you to the very limit.
Ruby:	All I want is a lie detector test, and you refuse to give it to me.
	Because as it stands now—and the truth serum, and any other—Pentothal—how do you pronounce it, whatever it is. And they will not give it to me, because I want to tell the truth.
	And then I want to leave this world. But I don't want my people to be blamed for something that is untrue, that they claim has happened.
Chief Justice Warren:	Mr. Ruby, I promise you that you will be able to take such a test.

Ruby was eventually given a polygraph examination, but the results were deemed void of interpretation. The results—questions and answers included—can be accessed online.[150]

---

[149] Ibid.

[150] Report of the House Select Committee on Assassinations, Appendix 17: Polygraph Examination of Jack Ruby," page 807.http://history-matters.com/archive/jfk/wc/wr/pdf/WR_A17_PolygraphExamRuby.pdf

As the document notes, Ruby himself refers to the process of "brainwashing" which some think he was also victim to:

> I would like to be able to get a lie detector test or truth serum, of what motivated me to do what I did at that particular time, and it seems as you get further into something, even though you know what you did, it operates against you somehow, brain washes you, that you are weak in what you want to tell the truth about and what you want to say which is the truth.[151]

The efforts of Ruby and his attorneys then focused on legally establishing Ruby's basis for a new trial:

> Eventually, the appellate court agreed with Ruby's lawyers for a new trial, and on October 5, 1966, ruled that his motion for a change of venue before the original trial court should have been granted. Ruby's conviction and death sentence were overturned. Arrangements were underway for a new trial to be held in February 1967, in Wichita Falls, Texas, when on December 9, 1966, Ruby was admitted to Parkland Hospital in Dallas, suffering from pneumonia. A day later, doctors realized he had cancer in his liver, lungs, and brain. Three weeks later, he died.[152]

Gee, wasn't *that* convenient!

> And so Jack Ruby, on December 9, 1966, exactly one day after he had learned that his new trial was going to be held in February or March of 1967, at Wichita Falls, about 140 miles from Dallas, was stricken with a mysterious disease first diagnosed as a common cold, then as pneumonia and finally as generalized cancer.
>
> For more than three years, with a death sentence hanging over his head for most of the time, Ruby had been as fit as a fiddle in the custody of Dallas Sheriff Bill Decker. At no time before December 9 had the prison doctor who visited him regularly detected any flaw in Ruby's splendid health. But now, with a new trial in prospect in a different place, death quickly overtook the man who knew perhaps more than any other living person (with the possible exception of David Ferrie, then still totally unknown to the public at large) about the real background to the assassination. He passed away in the morning of January 3, 1967—and another inconvenient trial was happily averted.[153]

Put it all together, folks, and the one thing that it clearly does <u>not</u> spell out is a man who silenced a key witness for personal reasons, as the official version would have us believe.

And Jack Ruby knew what he was talking about. He was the man to whom *all* the dots connected:

---

[151] Ibid.

[152] "A Last Wish," *Time*, December 30, 1966.

[153] Joachim Joesten, *How Kennedy Was Killed* (Tandem-Daynay: 1968): http://www.spartacus.schoolnet.co.uk/JFKSruby.htm

- He was hooked up big-time with the Chicago and New Orleans Mob and, specifically, with the three top Mafia bosses linked to the assassination: Santo Trafficante, Sam "The Man" Giancana, and Carlos Marcello.
- Ruby had established links to the CIA and was involved extensively in the CIA's anti-Castro "covert operations."[154]
- Senator Richard Schweiker, who investigated the assassination, acknowledged that Ruby must have—at the very least—been working with the CIA during his gun-running activities to Cuba.[155]
- The FBI admitted he was one of their informants.[156]
- He was the Mob's connection to the Dallas Police Department and knew the entire Department very well.
- He was also connected to the covert New Orleans research project on creating a new fast-acting "super cancer" to be used as a secret bioweapon against Fidel Castro.

On the Trail of the JFK Assassins by Dick Russell examines the many links between the Mob, the intelligence community, Ruby, Oswald, David Ferrie, Guy Banister, and Clay Shaw. Ruby was deeply entrenched in the anti-Castro efforts in Cuba. He was a frequent visitor of Florida Godfather Santo Trafficante while Trafficante was imprisoned in Cuba. Ruby was not only deeply involved in the Mob's gambling operations, but also in extensive gunrunning to Cuba, which was done in conjunction with U.S. intelligence.[157]

> Where Ruby is concerned, as with Oswald, a lot of people may have had a lot of secrets to protect. He had been, the FBI admitted in 1975, a bureau informant. He was no stranger to labor, the mob, and Cuban affairs. He was a most convenient fellow, for anyone who wanted a quick "case closed."[158]

Furthermore, Jack Ruby is the common denominator with dozens of deaths related to the assassination. Many of the witness deaths early on were people who had been in some form of contact with Jack Ruby.

It seems the one thing they had in common was that they knew Ruby. Oswald and Ferrie knew him, the Dallas cops and sheriffs knew him, the reporters who were killed all knew him. As JFK researcher Tom Scully observed:

> Too many who approached Jack Ruby's role in an inquisitive way. . . . Kupcinet, through his daughter, Karyn, Kilgallen, and the 11/24/63 "guests" of George Senator at Jack Ruby's apartment, Hunter, Koethe and Howard… met a soon and untimely death.[159]

---

[154] Dick Russell, *On the Trail of the JFK Assassins: A Groundbreaking Look at America's Most Infamous Conspiracy* (Skyhorse Publishing, 2008) 92-93, 106.

[155] Russell, *On the Trail of the JFK Assassins*, 45.

[156] Russell, *On the Trail of the JFK Assassins*, 84.

[157] Ibid.

[158] Ibid.

[159] Tom Scully, "Deaths of Witnesses," 3 Jan 2009, *The Education Forum*: http://educationforum.ipbhost.com/index.php?showtopic=603&st=105

To convey the extent to which these folks did not fully investigate these matters, consider that the official version and interpretation of events is *still* that Jack Ruby did not have links to organized crime; which is a totally indefensible claim from all standpoints of knowledge, logic, and anything else you may care to throw in. Historian John Simkin quite humorously alludes to that point here:

> In October 1964, the Warren Commission reported that it "found no evidence that either Lee Harvey Oswald or Jack Ruby was part of any conspiracy, domestic or foreign, to assassinate President Kennedy." It also stated that there was "no significant link between Ruby and organized crime." This information came from friends of Ruby, including Dave Yaras, a Mafia hitman.[160]

That pretty much sums up the credibility of the Warren Commission right there, folks. Maybe if someone a bit more astute, like Bobby Kennedy, had been asking the questions. You think? It sounds as if Chief Justice Earl Warren was almost as intent on denying the existence of the Mafia as FBI Director J. Edgar Hoover was. No wonder organized crime has been so effective in this country. Just take a good look at the people who've been entrusted with fighting it—we can't even get them to admit that it exists!

But we digress.

Here's how author James DiEugenio described the fiasco, commenting on a so-called "documentary" that failed to include some very basic facts which he detailed in his review:

> All one needs to know about the latest Gary Mack fiasco is this: Almost none of the above is included in the hour. Nothing about the involvement of Ruby and Oswald in the Cuban conflict through the CIA and the Mafia; virtually none of the plentiful and multi-leveled connections of Ruby to the DPD; and none of the witnesses who indicate Oswald and Ruby knew each other.
>
> This, of course, is ridiculous. For if a program is trying to explore whether or not Ruby shot Oswald to conceal a plot to kill Kennedy, then it is fundamentally dishonest not to tell the viewer about the above. Because clearly those three areas of evidence would suggest the following:
>
> 1. Ruby and Oswald shared connections to the CIA and the Mafia
> 2. Ruby and Oswald knew each other through their experience in the Cuban crisis as extended into the USA
> 3. Ruby used his police contacts to enter the basement of City Hall and kill Oswald[161]

As has been reported, Ruby did indeed request to be sent to Washington, D.C. for his own safety, so that he could testify without fear for his life—which he quite apparently feared for while in Texas—and he made that request directly and personally

---

[160] John Simkin, "Jack Ruby: Biography," *Spartacus Educational*: http://www.spartacus.schoolnet.co.uk/JFKruby.htm
[161] James DiEugenio, "JFK: The Ruby Connection, Gary Mack's Follies-Part One," *Citizens for Truth about the Kennedy Assassination*, accessed 12 Nov. 21012: http://www.ctka.net/2009/ruby_mack.html

to former Supreme Court Chief Justice Earl Warren, no less. And guess what?— Request *Denied*.

> During the six months following the Kennedy assassination, Ruby repeat-
> edly asked, orally and in writing, to speak to the members of the Warren
> Commission, the commission initially showed no interest. Only after
> Ruby's sister Eileen wrote letters to the commission (and her letters be-
> came public) did the Warren Commission agree to talk to Ruby. In June
> 1964, Chief Justice Earl Warren, then-Representative Gerald R. Ford of
> Michigan and other commission members went to Dallas to see Ruby.

If you find that somewhat depressing, well, you might as well cheer up, because it gets even worse:

> "Ruby told Earl Warren that he would 'come clean' if he was moved from
> Dallas and allowed to testify in Washington. He told Warren 'my life is in
> danger here.' He added: 'I want to tell the truth, and I can't tell it here.' War-
> ren refused to have Ruby moved and so he refused to tell what he knew
> about the assassination of John F. Kennedy."[162]

For the real story, take a good look at the words of a man who ran in the exact same circles at the exact same time—the deathbed statements of Mafia hitman, Frank "The Irishman" Sheeran. Sheeran was *very* close with some very big-time mobsters of the era, especially Russell Bufalino and Jimmy Hoffa, as well as many in Chicago. Sheeran said that everybody in the Mob knew that Ruby screwed up and didn't do his job in Dallas when Oswald got away and that's why he personally had to take care of Oswald. The Giancana family states the same thing in *Double Cross*.

Sheeran, true to form, put the matter in some very blunt terms:

> Jack Ruby's cops were supposed to take care of Oswald, but Ruby bun-
> gled it. If he didn't take care of Oswald, what do you think they would
> have done to him—put Ruby on a meat hook.

The meat hook reference was something the Chicago Mob had recently done, quite infa-mously, to a loan shark named William "Action" Jackson, who was suspected of talking to the FBI. It was a vicious torture killing and one that was supposedly meant to send a message to gangsters across the country of what was waiting for them if they snitched or crossed the big boys. The message was heard loud and clear.

So, no matter how others may characterize the matter, Jack Ruby was convinced about the fact that he "was being killed" before his new trial: He was absolutely certain that he'd been injected with cancer cells. And when we get to the deaths of David Ferrie and Dr. Mary Sherman, some additional reasons for Ruby's certainty will become quite apparent: affiliates of Ruby's were deeply involved in criminally "off-the-charts" cancer

---

[162] Simkin, "Jack Ruby: Biography"

research, developing a "bioweapon" of fast-acting cancer, to be used as an assassination device against Fidel Castro. Sound crazy? Just keep reading.

The "funny business"—with Jack Ruby walking right into the middle of a police station, going straight up to Lee Harvey Oswald, who was surrounded by a bevy of armed officers, pulling out a gun, holding it out in the air and aiming it right at the center of Oswald's body and firing it, *totally* unchallenged—stretched even the imagination of observing Dallas police officers. Note the "interesting" testimony of Dallas police Captain Frank M. Martin, testifying before the Warren Commission about the security situation at the Dallas Police Department on the day of Oswald's murder:

Warren Commission: Now, Captain Martin, is there anything else you would like to say concerning any aspect of this matter at all?

Captain Martin: I—don't take this down.

Warren Commission: Well, if you don't want to say it on the record, you'd better not say it at all.

Captain Martin: There is a lot to be said, but probably be better if I don't say it.[163]

The Commission was apparently relieved to hear that. They constantly discouraged, ignored or obfuscated real matters of substance; the above is just one example of hundreds.

[163] "Testimony of Capt. Frank M. Martin," Warren Commission Hearings, Vol. XII, page 284: http://www.jfk-assassination.de/warren/wch/vol12/page284.php

An attorney in Texas who has researched the matter for decades; Dawn Meredith, highlighted the time sequence of Ruby's demise:

December 7, 1966, Ruby's trial was ordered moved from Dallas to Wichita Falls.

December 9, Ruby was moved from Dallas County Jail to Parkland Hospital, complaining of persistent coughing and nausea.

He was dead January 3, 1967.

Ruby wanted to spare Jackie a trial; someone returned the favor.

They could ill afford to allow Ruby to have a new trial. He had already said enough.

That he told Earl Warren and Gerry Ford that "a whole new form of government" was about to occur following JFK's assassination must have shaken the conspirators to the bone. Imagine what he could have said in trial. Whatever he knew, Dorthy Kilgallen would lose her life over as well.[164]

Here is the whole sordid story "in a nutshell"; summarized succinctly, and leading to a place where none but the brave dare tread:

Ruby desperately wanted away from the prison in Dallas, and he pleaded with the Warren Commission to have him transferred to Washington. Ruby said he would tell the whole story if they would get him to a safe facility. This was refused. Ruby told Earl Warren, "Well, you won't see me again. I tell you that a whole new form of government is going to take over the country, and I know I won't live to see you another time."

While awaiting a second trial, Ruby suddenly became ill and was diagnosed with lung cancer. Ruby maintained he had been injected with a cancer bioweapon in prison. He died within one month of the diagnosis, an extremely rapid progression. Ruby was a non-smoker.

The theme of a cancer bioweapon comes up again in the story of Judyth Baker. She claimed to have worked on developing such a weapon for the CIA in the early 60's. She also claimed to have been involved with Lee Oswald, who introduced her to CIA contacts in New Orleans.[165]

To continue with the story, the development of that bioweapon will be explored in the upcoming chapters on the deaths of David Ferrie and Dr. Mary Sherman whom, it has been established, were intricately involved in the project.

---

[164] Dawn Meredith, Esq., 2 Oct. 2010, "Ruby Injected with Mercury Thallium," *Deep Politics Forum*, emphasis in original: https://deeppoliticsforum.com/forums/archive/index.php/t-4388.html?s=984c061d304653e8db413aaf2cdbe772

[165] "If Adlai Stevenson Had Been Vice President...," pm247, accessed 23 Nov. 2012: http://my.firedoglake.com/pm247/tag/jack-ruby/

4 | Jack Zangetty, Late November, 1963

Victim	**Jack Zangetty, mobster with links to Chicago Mob, managed a high-end casino in Oklahoma that was popular with high-rollers and, due to its safe and remote nature, was also used to host high-level national Mafia meetings.**
Cause of Death	Multiple Gunshots
Official Verdict	Unsolved Murder
Actual Circumstances	Victim was found dead in swimming pool, multiple gunshots to chest, and appeared to have been dead in the water for one-to-two weeks.
Inconsistencies	1. Victim made one of the uncanny predictions in history. Right before the virtually unknown nightclub operator, Jack Ruby, killed Oswald, Zangetty specifically told friends (on November 23, 1963) the following: **A man named Ruby will kill Oswald tomorrow, and in a few days, a member of Frank Sinatra's family will be kidnapped just to take some of the attention away from the assassination.**[166]

[166] Penn Jones, Jr., "Disappearing Witnesses," Jan 1984, *The Rebel* magazine: http://www.maebrussell.com/ Disappearing%20Witnesses/Disappearing%20Witnesses.html

Ruby did indeed shoot Oswald the following day—and Frank Sinatra's son was kidnapped a few days later. So Zangetty apparently had obvious foreknowledge that he must have picked up via his connections.

2. Working backwards from the one-to-two week estimate of being dead in the swimming pool, Zangetty's murder would have taken place shortly after making the above statements.[167]

3. A further confidence to friends from Zangetty was that "three other men—not Oswald—killed the President."[168]

Jack Zangetty was the manager of a very popular and very high-end casino in Oklahoma called *The Red Lobster*. It was known as a safe hangout for "high-rollers," and was often used for high-level Mob meetings for "wise guys" from all over the country.[169]

The day after the assassination, Zangetty told friends that Oswald would be killed by Ruby *and also* that Frank Sinatra's son would be kidnapped "just to take some of the attention away from the assassination." Zangetty was murdered shortly after making those statements.[170]

Just like Jack Ruby's nightclub in Dallas, *The Carousel Club*, and Frank Sinatra's casino hotel in Nevada, *The Cal-Neva Lodge*, Zangetty's swank casino hotel in Oklahoma, *The Red Lobster*, was apparently a "front" for the Mob. They no doubt had hidden interests in the operation, just as they did in the aforementioned—that's the way that they operated. These guys don't go to a bank to start a business operation—they go to their benefactors because that's where they know they can get the money. It comes, however, with a price.

CONCLUSIONS BASED ON EVIDENTIARY INDICATIONS

Zangetty's predictions indeed came true; in fact, he was apparently so confident of his statements that they should properly be termed "prior knowledge" rather than "predictions."

- Jack Ruby shot and killed Lee Harvey Oswald, as a live TV audience and a roomful of cops silently watched it take place (the cops didn't move a muscle, or even flinch, until *after* Oswald was hit at very close range);

- Frank Sinatra, Jr. was indeed "kidnapped"; though, even at the time, many suspected that the whole thing was staged, due to some odd circumstances. Things like loaning gas money to his kidnappers, who had casually waltzed into Sinatra's hotel room at a Nevada casino, struck a false chord in the public perception.

---

[167] Ibid.
[168] Ibid.
[169] Roberts & Armstrong, *The Dead Witnesses*
[170] Penn Jones, "Disappearing Witnesses"

CONCLUSION

Murdered

High probability that his killing was directly linked to his "talking out of turn" regarding knowledge of post-assassination facts.

In any event, his "predictions" came true: Just as Zangetty had termed it, Ruby killed Oswald and then the Sinatra kidnapping was headline material and a major distraction that took national attention away from the Ruby/Oswald fiasco.

5 | Melba Christine Marcades, September 4, 1965

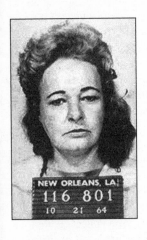

NEW ORLEANS, LA.
116 801
10 21 64

Victim	**Melba Christine Marcades (also known as Rose Cheramie, Rose Cheramie)**
Cause of Death	Hit-and-run auto accident
Official Verdict	Accidental
Actual Circumstances	Rose was part of a heroin-smuggling ring in which she was forced to participate. (They threatened to harm her child, whom they were holding until she finished performing as drug courier for the heroin network.)

	It has been substantiated by multiple parties that she actually correctly predicted how, where, and when President Kennedy would be assassinated.
Inconsistencies	1. Although the victim died from a head wound after being run over by a car, she also had a large round wound in her head, leading to speculation she may have been shot first and then run over to make the death appear as accidental. However, faced with very limited information at the scene—or people of influential means, as we describe further in the material that follows—police ruled the death was apparently accidental.[171] 2. Autopsy report disappeared.[172] 3. Our additional research revealed that evidence of the gunshot wound was blatant. See below.

Like Jack Zangetty, Rose Cheramie was another clearly established case of a person possessing obvious foreknowledge of important events related to the JFK assassination.

Her story was selected as the opening sequence for the film *JFK*, and readers will likely remember its ominous overtones of conspiracy and intrigue.

From the victim's standpoint, it's a sordid story. Rose was a dope runner associated with Jack Ruby and other mobsters. The Mob guys held her child as "insurance" that she'd complete her work. She was a courier for the dope ring; she brought the money to pay for a large heroin shipment that was coming into the port of Galveston, Texas in late 1963. She was to pick up the money from the man who was holding her child, pay for the drugs, and then take the heroin shipment. En route to the transaction, an argument apparently broke out between her and the two men who were transporting her. They threw her out of the car and she was run over by another car and then taken to a hospital, where police were then called.[173]

Her story was then told to a Lieutenant Fruge of the Louisiana State Police. Lieutenant Fruge verified the story, learning that Rose was a courier for the drug and prostitution ring that was known to be operating in the Southeastern U.S. He was amazed to also find out that, before throwing her out of the car, the two men had discussed a conspiracy plan to assassinate President Kennedy in Dallas. Now here's the amazing part: This all took place on November 20, 1963, two days *before* the assassination.

As Lieutenant Fruge testified to a Congressional committee, Rose's itinerary was to:

. . . pick up some money, pick up her baby, and to kill Kennedy.[174]

[171] J. Gary Shaw, *Dateline: Dallas*, November, 1993.
[172] J. Gary Shaw, *Conspiracy of Silence*
[173] James DiEugenio & Lisa Pease, *The Assassinations*, 225-228.
[174] Deposition of Francis Fruge, April 18, 1978, House Select Committee on Assassinations

So that was *before* the assassination of President Kennedy, and Lieutenant Fruge had dismissed it as the rambling talk of a drug user. *Two days later*, when Kennedy was assassinated in Dallas; Lieutenant Fruge felt like he'd been hit by a bolt of lightning:

> Fruge dismissed this all as the ranting of a drug user. But after Kennedy was killed, he went to the hospital to question her and also turn her over to the authorities. He later learned that she had also predicted at the hospital that the assassination was going to happen. Rose also told two men at the hospital, Doctors Weiss and Owen, that Ruby was involved in the Kennedy plot. And she told both Weiss and Fruge that she had seen Oswald at Ruby's club.[175]

It gets even weirder.

> At the hospital, Cheramie again predicted the assassination. On November 22, several nurses were watching television with Cheramie. According to these witnesses, ". . . during the telecast moments before Kennedy was shot, Rose Cheramie stated to them: 'This is when it is going to happen' and at that moment Kennedy was assassinated. The nurses, in turn, told others of Cheramie's prognostication." (Memo of Frank Meloche to Louis Ivon, 5/22/67. Although the Dallas motorcade was not broadcast live on the major networks, the nurses were likely referring to the spot reports that circulated through local channels in the vicinity of the trip. Of course, the assassination itself was reported on by network television almost immediately after it happened.)

> Furthermore, according to a psychiatrist there, Dr. Victor Weiss, Rose ". . . told him that she knew both Ruby and Oswald and had seen them sitting together on occasions at Ruby's club."[176]

> In fact, Fruge later confirmed the fact that she had worked as a stripper for Ruby.[177] (Louisiana State Police report of 4/4/67.)

> When she came out with the Kennedy business, I just said, wait a minute, wait a minute, something wrong here somewhere.[178]

> Assassination researcher James DiEugenio has documented the facts of this case conclusively:

> The word spread throughout the hospital that she had predicted Kennedy's murder in advance. Dr. Wayne Owen, who had been interning

---

[175] DiEugenio & Pease, *The Assassinations*, 225-228.
[176] Jim DiEugenio, "Rose Cheramie: How She Predicted the JFK Assassination," July-August 1999, *Probe Magazine*, Vol. 6 No. 5: http://the-puzzle-palace.com/files/pr799-rose.html
[177] Ibid.
[178] Deposition of Francis Fruge, April 18, 1978, House Select Committee on Assassinations

from LSU at the time, later told the *Madison Capital Times* that he and other interns were told of the plot in advance of the assassination. Amazingly, Cheramie even predicted the role of her former boss, Jack Ruby, because Owen was quoted as saying that one of the interns was told ". . . that one of the men involved in the plot was a man named Jack Rubinstein." Owen said that they shrugged it off at the time. But when they learned that Rubinstein was Ruby, they grew quite concerned. "We were all assured that something would be done about it by the FBI or someone. Yet we never heard anything."[179] In fact, Cheramie's association with Ruby was also revealed to Dr. Weiss. For in an interview with him after the assassination, Rose revealed that she had worked as a drug courier for Jack Ruby.[180]

How reliable a witness was Cheramie? Extremely. Fruge decided to have the drug deal aspect of her story checked out by the state troopers and U. S. Customs. The officers confirmed the name of the seaman on board the correct ship coming into Galveston. The customs people checked the Rice Hotel and the reservations had been made for her under an assumed name. The contact that had the money and her baby was checked and his name showed that he was an underworld, suspected narcotics dealer. Fruge checked Cheramie's baggage and found that one box had baby clothes and shoes inside.[181]

Lieutenant Fruge thought that the Dallas Police Department would be extremely interested in the witness he had found. They told him, in no uncertain terms, they were not interested. Fruge then thought that the Warren Commission would be interested. They too, were not. But when New Orleans District Attorney Jim Garrison mounted an authentic investigation a few years later, he found out about the story, hired Lieutenant Fruge as an investigator and sent him to find Rose Cheramie. However, she was now dead. She had been run over by a car on an extremely remote area of Highway 155 at around two o'clock in the morning, a mile and a half east of Big Sandy, Texas. It was reported that she had been hitchhiking on the road.[182]

District Attorney Garrison was so suspicious of the circumstances of her death that he attempted to have her body exhumed. That request was denied, somehow precluded by local authorities.[183]

Lieutenant Fruge went to Texas and located the investigating officer:

But in Fruge's written summary of his interview with the investigating officer, one J. A. Andrews, Fruge writes that although Moore attempted to avoid Cheramie, "he ran over the top of her skull." After a rather cursory investigation, due to the reluctance of Cheramie's family to pursue it, Andrews reluctantly closed the probe as an accidental death.[184]

---

[179] Ibid.
[180] DiEugenio, "Rose Cheramie: How She Predicted the JFK Assassination"
[181] Ibid.
[182] Ibid.
[183] Ibid.
[184] Ibid.

Author Jim DiEugenio investigated the death of Rose Cheramie in detail and was left with many questions:

> Furthermore, there are oddities in the extant medical records at Gladewater Hospital. Moore states that Rose was still alive at the scene. So he drove her to Big Sandy and asked for the nearest doctor. The doctor gave her a few shots before the ambulance arrived to take her to Gladewater. On Cheramie's death certificate, in 3 different places, she is listed as DOA (dead on arrival). Yet also on this document, we are informed that a period of eight hours elapsed between the onset of injury and her death. This eight-hour time period would coincide with the time of death, which is listed as 11:00 AM. So what happened at the hospital in the intervening hours?[185]

We also uncovered some virtually heretofore unknown evidence that is extremely relevant. Longtime JFK researcher and historian, Walt Brown, came up with this noteworthy addition:

> Rose Cheramie, on the other hand, is always listed as "Big Sandys" Texas. It is never taken far enough to state that she was found on the easement to the property of either Jerome Ragsdale or Paul Rothermel, whom I can never keep apart. Either way, she wasn't found in the street.[186]

Well, as it turns out, a key witness turning up dead very near the property of Paul Rothermel (and otherwise in the middle of nowhere on a remote Texas highway), is actually very noteworthy indeed. Paul Rothermel was the Security Chief for billionaire H. L. Hunt, who has often been linked to the JFK assassination. (It was Hunt to whom Lee Harvey Oswald wrote the cryptic note asking for more information before he proceeded with the plan.) Rothermel was an ex-FBI agent and, as Hunt's chief of security, obviously should have raised some red flags if the dead body of a crucial witness was found on the easement to his property.

As far as Rose's death, things got even weirder, and then they ended there too:

> According to researcher J. Gary Shaw in the book *Conspiracy of Silence*, the official autopsy of Cheramie has now disappeared. But in the records he *did* find, he discovered that in addition to her other injuries, she had suffered a "deep punctate stellate wound above her right forehead" (*Dateline Dallas*, 1993). Shaw researched this type of injury and found out that, according to medical textbooks, it often occurs as the result of a contact gunshot wound. When a gun is fired in contact with flesh, the resultant gasses, trapped between a layer of skin and the underlying bone, can cause a bursting, tearing effect on the surrounding tissue leaving a star-shaped wound. (Punctate stellate means a star-shaped puncture.) Whatever the true facts of Cheramie's passage, she certainly does qualify as one of the mysterious deaths that surround the JFK murder.[187]

---

[185] Ibid.
[186] Walt Brown, Ph.D., 26 Oct 2012, email to author.
[187] DiEugenio, "Rose Cheramie: How She Predicted the JFK Assassination"

Our research uncovered evidence of a gunshot wound that was far more blatant.

Jay Harrison was a member of the Dallas Police Department and, in the years following the JFK assassination, a veteran JFK researcher. He was *also* a member of that special tactical Intelligence unit which we covered in the opening chapter on J.D. Tippit.

> **Jay was a Dallas police officer and member, for a short time, assigned to one of these Dallas Special Intel units (reserve).[188]**

And here's the *clincher* on the case, folks. Get a load of this little gem:

> **Somehow, J. Harrison got the original death certificate--a certified blue copy, and he investigated "where" it happened, and the address turned out to be Rothermel's; the body, if memory serves, had been moved, just as Henry Marshall's body was moved from where he "committed suicide." Left in the street, Melba was run over, but the bullet wound in the forehead was obvious and the blood stains were on the property.[189]**

And if that sounds sinister, it *darn well should!*

CONCLUSIONS BASED ON EVIDENTIARY INDICATIONS

- Victim clearly possessed accurate foreknowledge of the JFK assassination;
- The fact that the victim was found on the property of the Chief of Security for H. L. Hunt is extremely noteworthy;
- The bullet wound in the head and blood on the property are clearly indicative of murder, not accidental death.

CONCLUSION

Murder; Directly linked to the JFK assassination.

---

[188] Tosh Plumlee, email to author, 6 Nov. 2012.
[189] Walt Brown, Ph.D., email to author, 5 Nov. 2012.

Victim	**Karyn Kupcinet, actress**
Cause of Death	Broken Neck
Official Verdict	Murder
Actual Circumstances	The Medical Examiner in the case had a sick habit of breaking the necks of corpses in his care, making the initial assumptions suspect.
Inconsistencies	1. Rumored to have made a phone call predicting JFK's murder (*didn't* happen); 2. Various inconsistencies concerning death; see below

Overview

▶ **Karyn Kupcinet**

Karyn was the daughter of famous Chicagoan, Irv Kupcinet, one of the most popular newspaper columnists in the country and a huge celebrity in his own right. She moved to Hollywood to establish an acting career and was fairly successful in that pursuit, making appearances on popular TV shows and, to a lesser extent, movies.

- Found dead in her Hollywood apartment on November 30, 1963.
- It was medically approximated by the advanced state of decomposition that she had been dead for two-to-three days and, therefore, died on November 28, 1963.
- In addition to a large amount of drugs in her body, it was determined that her neck had been broken by manual strangulation, therefore it was presumed she'd been murdered.
- Key suspect was popular Hollywood actor, Andrew Prine, who was Karyn's boyfriend. The two had been having problems, mainly insofar as Karyn had wanted a very serious relationship with him and he was not obliging. There were, apparently, no fingerprints of either Andrew Prine or David Lange (a neighbor who was also a suspect) found at her apartment. Two sets of fingerprints that went unidentified *were* found at the crime scene, however.[190] Karyn had spoken to Andrew Prine at midnight and was dead thirty minutes later.[191]
- The evidence was considered insufficient to indict Mr. Prine, or anyone else.
- Still listed as an unsolved murder.

▶ **Linkage to JFK assassination:**

It was initially reported by author Penn Jones, Jr. that Karyn had screamed into a telephone to an operator that President Kennedy was going to be killed; *prior* to his assassination:

"The woman, who dialed her local operator approximately 20 minutes before the shooting in Dallas, stated that he was going to be shot. Jones alleged that the caller was Kupcinet, attempting to warn someone of the impending assassination. Jones claimed that Kupcinet was told of the assassination by her father (who was allegedly told by Jack Ruby, whom he met in Chicago in the 1940s). Jones speculated that her death was a result of a mob hit to silence her and to send a message to Irv Kupcinet to remain silent about his knowledge."[192]

---

[190] Kathleen Collins, email to author, 6 August 2012.
[191] Kathleen Collins, email to author, 15 December 2011.
[192] Paul Fecteau, "Zapruder's Stepchildren: The Most Fascinating People in J.F.K. Assassination Lore," 2005.

Karyn was an actress in Hollywood and the daughter of one of the most popular newspaper columnists in the country: Irv Kupcinet, who was based in Chicago. "Kup", as he was fondly called, also had a nationally televised talk show. It was initially reported that Karyn "was overheard telling of JFK's death prior to 11/22/63."[193] Apparently, that is *not* correct.

Karyn had been dead for at least two-to-three days before she was found, thereby making the autopsy somewhat difficult to determine what had actually happened due to the advanced state of decomposition of her body. She was found totally nude and face down on the couch in the living room of her Hollywood apartment. The television was on and her front door was unlocked. There were specks of blood on her face and also blood that had exuded from her mouth.

The fact that it was later medically determined that Karyn had a broken hyoid bone due to manual strangulation initially made it appear that she had been murdered. The first suspect was her boyfriend and fellow actor, Andrew Prine. A neighbor of Karyn's later became the prime suspect and the Kupcinet family in Chicago was convinced of his guilt.

However, bizarre facts unfolding over the years have revealed that the medical examiner charged with Karyn's autopsy clearly suffered from a serious mental malady—it was determined that he "enjoyed" doing strange deeds to the recently deceased. Apparently, other corpses recently in his "care" that were not strangled were later found to have the exact same broken neck bone found in Karyn. To posit that it smells of foul play is a dramatic understatement—apparently he criminally assaulted the dead.

It has also since been learned that Karyn was suicidal, was obsessively "over-the-top" regarding her relationship with Mr. Prine—she actually cut out words from magazines and composed threatening letters that she apparently mailed to him (sounds like scenes from a scary movie), was anorexic and a regular user of (or addicted to) amphetamines as a dietary method. Her own mother reportedly condoned the use of amphetamines for her for the purpose of keeping her weight down—a topic which unfortunately seems to have become yet another problem for Karyn to suffer through, i.e., dealing with a mother who was obsessively belittling and controlling her life.

No one has investigated the death of Karyn Kupcinet harder than veteran researcher and writer Kathleen Collins. So rather than "re-inventing the wheel," we went straight to Kathleen, who reconstructed the crime scene.

CRIME SCENE
Let's look over the facts.

On the crime scene, here it is, point-by-point:

- Karyn's body was found in her Hollywood apartment, in an advanced state of decomposition. She had obviously been dead for a few days.
- She was found in the living room.
- She was totally nude.
- She was laying "stomach down" on the couch with her face on a pillow.
- The television set was on.
- There was no vomit present.

---
[193] Penn Jones, Jr.

- There was a lamp and other household items that had been knocked over, many cigarette butts on the floor in the living room.
- There were a lot of disturbances throughout the house; the whole home had been ransacked and was a mess, except for the bathroom where Karyn had apparently showered.
- There was a towel on the floor of her bathroom that was determined to have been recently wet.
- There was a bathrobe on a chair in the living room.
- A hairbrush and her nightgown had been neatly placed on her bed.

But basically, her apartment had been thoroughly trashed:

Her apartment was messed up: cigarettes on the floor, clothes falling from drawers, closets open (showing a mink stole), the bed clothes torn from the bed revealing two twin beds shoved together.[194]

Bear that in mind as it relates to the topic of suicide:

Was she such a bad housekeeper that she left closet doors open, drawers with their contents trailing on the floor, bed clothes pulled halfway off the bed, revealing two twin beds pushed together; and 100 methamphetamines missing?[195]

Then there's the point about the perversions of the sicko medical examiner with the fondness for broken necks. But, upon examination of the circumstances, he knew this was a high-profile murder case. Karyn was an actress from a big celebrity family, her boyfriend (the key suspect) was an extremely popular actor and her friends were actors as well. It was an extremely high-profile case, followed nationally, especially by everyone in Chicago and Hollywood. It's highly doubtful—whatever his perversions were with lesser known corpses—that the medical examiner would actually risk his entire career in molesting the corpse in such a high-profile case that was very much the talk of the town and the epicenter of a huge and very public police investigation.

And if the case was so high-profile that our depraved medical examiner didn't dare molest the corpse, then one would have to say that the broken hyoid bone effectively eliminates suicide.

But burglary would not appear to be a motive either really; because they left the mink stole furs, which were very expensive, hanging from the open closet (so they were visible to an intruder). It was determined that all that was apparently missing were about 100 pills from a container in the bathroom—the container had been left and was apparently a fresh prescription.

You sure can't swallow 100 pills without one heck of a lot of liquid. So we investigated what liquids *were* available. And get a load of this:

[194] Kathleen Collins, 19 Oct. 2010, *Spartacus Educational:* http://educationforum.ipbhost.com/index.php?showtopic=16754
[195] Kathleen Collins, 13 May 2007, *Spartacus Educational:* http://educationforum.ipbhost.com/index.php?showtopic=603&st=45

The only thing in the room that was liquid was a sour cup of coffee on the other side of the room.[196]

As far as what was "possible"; a person could conceivably have just taken water directly from the faucet in the bathroom or kitchen. But it is certainly not likely; especially with 100 pills.

It's also an acknowledged fact that female suicides are rarely found naked; Most suicide victims actually make a dramatic point of looking "presentable"—former soldiers, for example, even put on their "dress blues" or the dress uniform of their particular service. So that presents a strong reason that Karyn did *not* commit suicide.

Therefore, the failure to put on her robe and laying down nude on the couch does not add up as far as suicide.

There are other factors as well: The note she left was officially *misinterpreted* as a "suicide note." She was actually listing the things she felt were wrong in her life—it was *not* a suicide note—she was *not* saying goodbye.

Nor does the evidence at the scene conform with the possibility of accidental death.

In light of the above facts and combined with the fact that a high-profile would keep our depraved medical examiner from any funny business, leads us logically to the point that suicide can be ruled out, and natural causes can be ruled out as well, which means that she was murdered.

So let's walk through the apparent last moments of Karyn's life.

She apparently laid out her red bathrobe on a chair prior to taking a shower. She then apparently showered and dried herself off—the way we know is because a "once-wet" towel was found on the bathroom floor, which is indicative that she had dried after showering. But she never put on her waiting bathrobe, which certainly would have been the next logical step. *That* is the precise point where there is a break in the logical progression of events. Something, therefore, apparently happened to break that chain of logic and distracted her attention between the time that she dried herself off with the towel and *would have* put on her bathrobe.

Let's look at what that "something" could have been:

- A phone call?
  No, because had she answered the phone, she could have just pulled the bathrobe on while conversing.
- A knock at the door?
  No, because had there been a knock at the door, she certainly would have put on her robe on the way to answering the door.
- Dancing?
  Some have speculated that she may have been dancing nude, fallen, and broken her neck; there was a book in her home that reportedly included the topic of nude dancing and led to that speculation. But the book wasn't found in the same room as Karyn's body, and with all the difficulties she was quite apparently experiencing, it's highly dubious that she would have been in a mood for naked joyful dancing. Above and beyond that, the television was on—and was still on days later when her body was finally discovered—and that wouldn't seem conducive to some ritual type nude dancing.

---

[196] Kathleen Collins, 12/20/11, email to author

There was also *no* vomiting, but 100 pills were missing—so it would appear that her killer emptied the pill bottle perhaps to stage it as a suicide, which—accompanied with the note that many have mistakenly termed a suicide note, effectively *does* look like one. To most, a suicide note and an empty pill bottle are sufficient in their minds to term it suicide. And the room was so messed up, with clothes scattered around, yet the bathroom was neat. That seems like staging with something amiss, as well.

If she laid out her robe but did not put it on, that alerts us to the potential of an intruder in apartment.

The only thing that *does* easily explain those actions is if there was someone in the apartment—if she realized that there was an intruder in the home, which would then explain why and how:

1. She did not take the time to put on her bathrobe;
2. Her neck was broken in a struggle with the intruder. That scenario is about the only one that adequately accounts for her totally nude body on the couch in her living room. Granted, it could be something else—but that's the scenario of events that fits the evidence at the crime scene.

Kathleen Collins, a specialist on the Kupcinet case, posits the following scenario:

> There was a once-dampened towel on the floor beside the bed. Her hairbrush was on the bed and a nightgown. She possibly went to the door or the living room. Someone came in, killed her, and then ransacked the house. The only room the cops found orderly was the bathroom. Inside the medicine chest the guy stole 100 Desoxyn methamphetamine pills and left the bottle. I believe he turned on the TV for light, in case someone thought KK was still awake. The state of her bedroom was different before than after. Before the murder she had neatly put her nightgown on the bed and a hairbrush. Would she ransack the bed while she was trying to go to bed? After her death, I believe, the house was ransacked, including the bed.[197]

As Ms. Collins observed, both the manner of her broken neck and the blood evidence are consistent with the above scenario:

> There's a way of killing people by grabbing them from behind, getting them in a choke hold in which they die in a few moments, as the brain is denied oxygen. She had flecks of blood on her face and a pillow—to me it sounds like she suffered some injury to her throat.[198]

So, in all likelihood, Karyn *was* murdered. Then the question is: By whom? And the answer: We do not know. The next question: Is it connected to the JFK assassination? The answer to that one: We know the story about the mystery phone call having been made by Karyn is bogus. "Researcher Greg Parker figured out about the Oxnard call. It was not Karyn Kupcinet but a Rosicrucian ritual performed using the phone, called

[197] Kathleen Collins, 16 Sept. 2012, email to author.
[198] Ibid.

radionics."[199] But—other very valid points remain. Her father was a very famous columnist who had very strong links to the Chicago Mob.

Kathleen Collins also established that Karyn's father knew Jack Ruby:

> **Irv Kupcinet knew Ruby and worked closely with Jimmy Colitz, one of Ruby's oldest and closest Chicago friends.[200]**

And, shortly after Ruby killed Oswald, Irv Kupcinet telephoned Mob-connected Paul "Red" Dorfman in Palm Springs:

> **"Kupcinet was acquainted with Ruby and called up a mutual friend, Paul Dorfman (Mob connected), asking him questions about Ruby.[201]**

Irv Kupcinet was not just Chicago's biggest newspaper columnist; he was an institution, an icon, Chicago's most popular person; he knew everyone there was to know. He was also as tough a customer as there ever was; he grew up on the same tough streets that Jack Ruby did, running with gangs, getting into trouble, and using his fists. He was great at football, making it all the way to the NFL, where he starred for the Philadelphia Eagles until a serious injury abruptly ended his career.

Then he went into his next love, which was journalism. . . . And he was just as tough as a reporter. He developed a reputation for getting to the facts and getting them to the people, come what may. And Chicago loved him for it. They loved him so much that the city built him a monument: A huge bronze statue of Irv Kupcinet welcomes everyone to Chicago.

So he was very clearly not one to back off of a story. In fact, that was sort of a part of his legend: That Kup was afraid of no story. So that professional toughness was part of his reputation, a component of his popularity. But that changed after Jack Ruby shot Oswald and then his daughter, Karyn, was killed shortly afterwards:

> **. . . Irv's behavior after Karyn's death and for the rest of his life seems that of a prominent yet incurious newspaper gossip and society columnist behaving as if he was under control by intimidation or other coercive influence.[202]**

Karyn was in Palm Springs the same weekend that Paul "Red" Dorfman was there. Karyn had gone with friends to sort of escape the madness following the death of President Kennedy. Dorfman was a big-time mobster with national connections and someone that Irv Kupcinet knew well:

> **Recently, I found out that on the Assassination weekend, Karyn Kupcinet with friends and mobster Paul "Red" Dorfman were both in Palm Springs.**

---

[199] Kathleen Collins, "Was Irv Kupcinet's Role Obscured As A Consequence of Penn Jones's Writing?," 13 Oct. 2010, *The Education Forum*: http://educationforum.iphost.com/index.php?showtopic=16754

[200] Kathleen Collins, "Deaths of Witnesses," *The Education Forum*: http://educationforum.ipbhost.com/index.php?showtopic=603&st=135

[201] Kathleen Collins, "Deaths of Witnesses," 11 Dec 2005, *The Education Forum*: http://educationforum.ipbhost.com/index.php?showtopic=603&st=120

[202] Collins, "Deaths of Witnesses," http://educationforum.ipbhost.com/index.php?showtopic=603&st=135

> While there, Dorfman was tracked down by Irv Kupcinet who asked about Ruby shooting Oswald.[203]

Irv Kupcinet had called Dorfman so quickly after Ruby shot Oswald that Dorfman was not even aware yet that it had happened and even questioned Kup's information:

> This call came so quick, Dorfman didn't even know Oswald had been shot. "'Sparky' would never do that," he said.[204]

"Sparky" was the Mob's nickname for Jack Ruby:

> Dorfman said, "Sparky is the last guy you'd expect to do this. He was a nebbish sort of guy."[205]

So there may very well be some "fire" somewhere near all that smoke. Here's how our "Kupcinet expert" explains the theory:

> I think Dorfman was unnerved a bit by Irv's tenaciousness and eagerness. I think possibly Dorfman saw Karyn in Palm Springs that weekend. And maybe an idea sprung to mind about keeping Irv Kupcinet away from Ruby and the Chicago angle of the assassination. To kill Kupcinet would be too obvious. But to kill his daughter, whom every Chicagoan knew, would take away any interest Irv would have about Ruby. He would be in no condition to investigate the Chicago Mob. Possibly, a plan was afoot to commit an outrageous crime in Chicago, sometime after the assassination, to get the heat off the Mob. And Dorfman decided to kill Karyn to shock all of Chicago. Possibly, there'd be talk of nothing else. I myself was shocked when I looked at the microfilmed Chicago Tribune and saw the awful, large black headline (from memory): KUPCINET GIRL DEAD. My stomach knotted.[206]

Looking at the context of the issue in its totality, the "shock crime" theory makes even *more* sense:

1. Just prior to his murder, casino owner and well-connected mobster, Jack Zangetty, told friends *quite specifically* that a man named Jack Ruby would kill Oswald, and then Frank Sinatra's son would be kidnapped to take attention away (so somebody was obviously concerned with diverting attention before the event even took place).

---

[203] Kathleen Collins, "Deaths of Witnesses," 20 Oct. 2007, *The Education Forum*: http://educationforum.ipbhost.com/index.php?showtopic=603&st=105
[204] Collins, "Deaths of Witnesses," 11 Dec. 2005
[205] Collins, "Deaths of Witnesses," 20 Oct. 2007, citing: Irv Kupcinet, *Kup: A Man, an Era, a City* (Bonus Books: 1988), 176.
[206] Collins, "Deaths of Witnesses," 20 Oct. 2007, emphasis in original.

2. Both of the above events transpired, precisely as Zangetty had "predicted." Then Zangetty was found murdered.

3. In the excellent book *I Heard You Paint Houses,* which is basically a death-bed confession by longtime hitman Frank "The Irishman" Sheeran, Sheeran says everybody high up in the Mob (and Sheeran was *very* close with Russell Bufalino, Jimmy Hoffa, and others) knew that Ruby screwed up on November 22, and that's why he personally had to take care of Oswald. The Giancana family states the same thing in *Double Cross.* Sheeran said: "Jack Ruby's cops were supposed to take care of Oswald, but Ruby bungled it. If he didn't take care of Oswald, what do you think they would have done to him—put Ruby on a meat hook." The meat hook reference was something the Chicago Mob had just done, quite infamously, to a loan shark named Action Jackson, who was suspected of talking to the FBI; it was a vicious torture killing—one that everyone in Chicago knew about, certainly Kup and Korshak among them.

4. Kup not only was on a first-name basis with leaders of the Chicago Mob, traveling in same circles socially, but;

5. Kup's very close friend was Mob lawyer Sidney Korshack, who probably would have had pertinent knowledge about Ruby.

6. Kup refused the Mob's offer to "investigate" Karyn's death on behalf of the family, always assuming he knew who did it and that it was not a suicide. He was so adamant about leaving it all alone that friends knew well that it was a subject they were never to breach with him.

7. Kup quite obviously backed off from his typically thorough investigative reporting concerning Ruby's connections to the Chicago Mob and the silencing of Oswald. (Others, such as Dorothy Kilgallen, found it so obvious and abhorrent that they vowed to keep investigating it to the end.)

8. Many people at least suspected that the Sinatra Jr. kidnapping had been staged in some way. They were much the same as the obvious suspicions of something being "rotten in Denmark" when they had witnessed how easily Ruby assassinated Oswald on live television as the Dallas cops stood by and watched.

9. Whether or not it actually was a planned "shock crime" to divert attention away from Jack Ruby's Mafia connections, the same effect was achieved: Karyn's death completely took over the headlines and was the primary topic of conversation for a long time to follow.

Then—exactly as predicted—Frank Sinatra's son was kidnapped, on December 8, 1963, before Karyn's murder had completely faded from the headlines:

> Irv was the most popular man in Chicago, yet the mob may have killed his daughter. His best friend was Sidney Korshack—a mafia lawyer—who was investigated so many times, yet they never found anything that he had done was illegal. If the hit came from Chicago, I'm sure he would know. He met Irv at the airport and later identified the remains of Irv's daughter.
>
> Then Frank Sinatra Jr. was kidnapped. Who worked harder to get Kennedy in as President than Sinatra? That was another smokescreen, a way to distract the public.[207]

So, in conclusion, it can be put this way: If it *was* a shock crime, it certainly worked. Karyn's death took over the headlines and—especially in Chicago—any focus that would have been placed on Jack Ruby's Chicago Mob connections quickly evaporated.

> If she was killed to hurt Kup, no one could do a better job.[208]

There's also no reason that Karyn's family couldn't have had a second—and more professional—autopsy done. With their wealth and influence, that could have been easily accomplished. With the obviously totally botched first autopsy, performed by a man who himself had broken the necks of bodies entrusted to his care, and with all the rape and murder accusations swirling around about the case, why was a second, professional autopsy, not performed?

CONCLUSIONS BASED ON EVIDENTIARY INDICATIONS

- Necks of other corpses were apparently broken by the mentally disturbed medical examiner, initially making the ruling of murder seem very open to scrutiny.
- Many have noted that Karyn may have committed suicide; she was depressed, there was a note left, and friends reported she had been deeply disturbed and overwhelmed by events. It looked like she may have taken the contents of the empty pill bottle that was found.
- But the fact that she dried off with a towel after taking a shower and then neglected to put on the bathrobe which she had laid out before her shower is an indication of foul play, not suicide. She died very quickly, nude on her couch.
- As far as we know, no one has ever formally apologized to actor Andrew Prine for ruining a large portion of his life with a false accusal of murder; so we will, right here and right now—

---

[207] Kathleen Collins, "Deaths of Witnesses," 29 July 2011, *The Education Forum*: http://educationforum.ipbhost.com/index.php?showtopic=603&st=135
[208] Kathleen Collins, "Deaths of Witnesses," 12 May 2007, *The Education Forum*: http://educationforum.ipbhost.com/index.php?showtopic=603&st=45

Apologies, Mr. Prine.

- The "mystery call" foretelling of the assassination of President Kennedy was not placed by Karyn.[209]
- The *real story* here is that everything links back to Chicago and Jack Ruby. Therefore, one theory exists that—whatever Karyn's personal problems were—the Chicago Mob ended them and did so as a vehicle with which to attempt to draw attention away from the recent nationally-televised assassination of the President's killer, hosted by the Chicago Mob's Jack Ruby. It did indeed serve that purpose, planned or otherwise, at least in Chicago, where the Kupcinets were like a royal family. There is a large amount of circumstantial evidence supporting that thesis.
- Jack Ruby was closely affiliated with the Chicago "Boys," and was soon to murder Oswald right in the middle of a police station and on national television. The heat on "Chicago" was already tremendous and was expected to increase exponentially very quickly.

Irv Kupcinet knew Ruby and worked closely with Jimmy Colitz, one of Ruby's oldest and closest Chicago friends.

- As a Chicago celebrity, Irv Kupcinet ran in the same circles as the leaders of the Mob there, was friendly with them, and was known to obtain information from them.
- Kup's very good friend was the elite Mob attorney, Sidney Korshak (topic of the book *Supermob: How Sidney Korshak and His Criminal Associates Became America's Hidden Power Brokers*, by Gus Russo).
- Kup, therefore, certainly would have known about Jack Ruby's affiliations with "The Boys," and might have been inclined to report precisely that, as he was—when push came to shove—a very solid guy and excellent reporter.

Unlike fellow columnist Dorothy Kilgallen, who vowed publicly to get to the truth and uncover the obvious conspiracy in Ruby's silencing of Oswald—Kup remained virtually silent on the subject, never publicly divulging the secret, but highly pertinent knowledge, of Ruby's strong linkage to the Chicago Mob.

- In the context above, Kup's "silence was deafening", as the old saying goes.
- In conclusion, it bears noting from a standpoint of scientific logic, that simply because the story about Karyn making the mystery phone call is false, does not at all negate the possibility that her death is related to the Jack Ruby/Chicago Mob connection.

CONCLUSION
Probable Murder

Linkage to the JFK Assassination
Yes, the alleged linkage of the mystery phone call is false. However, Karyn's death being a "shock crime" to dominate media attention and divert focus from Jack Ruby's links to the Chicago Mob (as it clearly did in Chicago), remains a very strong possibility.

---

[209] Kathleen Collins, "Was Irv Kupcinet's Role Obscured As A Consequence of Penn Jones's Writing?," 13 Oct. 2010, *The Education Forum*: http://educationforum.iphost.com/index.php?showtopic=16754

Grant Stockdale,
close friend of JFK,
December 2, 1963

Victim	**Grant Stockdale, a wheeler-dealer in the highest echelons of the Democratic Party, former Ambassador to Ireland, and close friend of the recently assassinated President Kennedy.**
Cause of Death	Fell, or was pushed, from his office window on the 13th floor of the DuPont Building in midtown Miami.
Official Verdict	Suicide
Actual Circumstances	Victim's behavior was normal. He came into his office for work on a Monday morning, was very pleasant, conversed amiably, and did not seem suicidal. Police placed the time of

death at 10:17 a.m.[210] The only other person in the victim's office at that precise moment would have been his killer, who, due to circumstances described below, could easily have entered the office.

1. No suicide note was found.
2. Stockdale was apparently mixed up with some very serious political shenanigans. He was "a big wheel in the Democratic Party and a person of considerable influence in Washington," who was also mixed up in the corruption of the Bobby Baker scandal.[211] Stockdale was also involved in matters related to another brewing caldron of corruption involving the seven-billion-dollar F-111 contract to Texas' General Dynamics Corporation, and both scandals had threatened to ruin Lyndon Johnson politically.[212]

Inconsistencies

3. The "official line" that Stockdale committed suicide because he was depressed about the murder of his friend, JFK, seems an incredibly weak supposition. As one author notes: "Hardheaded businessmen—and Stockdale was certainly hardheaded, as his record shows—don't kill themselves because a friend has been murdered, be it the President of the United States."[213]
4. Research has established that, on November 26, 1963, Stockdale flew to Washington, D.C. and met with JFK's brothers, Robert and Edward Kennedy.

> On his return, Stockdale told several of his friends that "the world was closing in."

> On December 1, 1963, he talked to his attorney, William Frates, who summarized their conversation as follows:

> He started talking. It didn't make much sense. He said something about "those guys" trying to get him. Then about the assassination. [214]

[210] Adele Edison, "E. Grant Stockdale," 14 June 2004, ("Information taken from newspaper articles in the *Miami Herald* and *Miami News*") *The Education Forum*: http://educationforum.ipbhost.com/index.php?showtopic=943
[211] Joachim Joesten, *The Dark Side of Lyndon Baines Johnson* (Peter Dawnay: 1968): http://www.spartacus.schoolnet.co.uk/JFKstockdale.ht
[212] John Simkin, "JFK Assassination Forum," 14 June 2004, *Spartacus Educational*: http://www.spartacus.schoolnet.co.uk/JFKstockdale.htm
[213] Joesten, *The Dark Side of Lyndon Baines Johnson*
[214] John Simkin, "Grant Stockdale: Biography," *Spartacus Educational*: http://www.spartacus.schoolnet.co.uk/JFKstockdale.htm

That was <u>the day before</u> he went flying through the window of his 13th floor office.

5. Stockdale's daughter has stated publicly that her father knew he was being followed, that he had told her mother that some people were out to get him, that she herself had an attempt on her life several days after her father's funeral, and that she believed the attempt on her life was a way to coerce her mother into remaining silent—which, as she stated, actually worked (see below).

6. For the above reasons, some researchers have speculated that Stockdale figured out that an anti-Castro intelligence operation had been "hijacked" and turned against President Kennedy instead and, for that reason, Stockdale had to be killed.[215]

Grant Stockdale was a close friend of President Kennedy.[216] He was also former Ambassador to Ireland. JFK even visited Grant Stockdale at Stockdale's home in Coral Gables, Florida.[217] Stockdale was also friends with U.S. Senator George Smathers, also of Florida, who was another close friend of President Kennedy's.

President Kennedy socializing with Florida Senator, George Smathers. Stockwell was a close friend of both and also a business partner of Smathers and key political aide for JFK.

Stockdale headed the Kennedy campaign in Florida. After JFK won the Democratic nomination for President, Stockdale was the Kennedy campaign finance chairman for eleven Southern states.[218]

---

[215] John Simkin, "JFK Assassination Forum," 14 June 2004, *Spartacus Educational*: http://www.spartacus.schoolnet.co.uk/JFKstockdale.htm

[216] *The Evening Independent* (St. Petersburg, Florida), December 2, 1963, page one, "Grant Stockdale Killed in Miami": http://news.google.com/newspapers?nid=950&dat=19631202&id=VFdQAAAAIBAJ&sjid=7FYDAAAAIBAJ&pg=4173,26000

[217] *The Tucson Daily Citizen*, 3 Dec 1963: http://www.spartacus.schoolnet.co.uk/JFKstockdale.htm

[218] *The Evening Independent* (St. Petersburg, Florida), December 2, 1963, page one, "Grant Stockdale Killed in Miami": http://news.google.com/newspapers?nid=950&dat=19631202&id=VFdQAAAAIBAJ&sjid=7FYDAAAAIBAJ&pg=4173,26000

So the man certainly knew his way around, was very well-connected, and had a reputation as a very tough politician and businessman. By most accounts, Grant Stockdale was one tough cookie. It seems highly implausible, therefore, that being depressed over President Kennedy's death would be sufficient cause for Mr. Stockdale to leap to his death out of his office window without even leaving a note for his wife, five children, mother, and friends.

Researcher Adele Edison investigated the evidence and wrote the following:

> At 10:00 a.m., on Monday, December 2, 1963, Grant Stockdale came to his office on the 13th floor of the Alfred I. DuPont Building, 169 Flagler Street in Miami. His secretary, LaVerne Weingartner, who usually opened the office was not there, but at a dentist's office and would not arrive until 10:30. Stockdale went into a law office across the hall from his and asked Mrs. Mary Ruth Hauser how he could get a key to unlock his office door. She offered to call the building manager to send someone to open it.

> Mrs. Hauser stated, "He followed me into my office and stood there while I called down for a key. He stood there very calmly. He didn't seem at all agitated. . . . Somehow the subject of the President's death came up. . . . He told me he was in his office when his wife called to tell him the President had been shot. He said he just got down on his knees and prayed."

> Stockdale and Mrs. Hauser were still talking when someone came to unlock his door. She started to follow him across the hall, but just then her office phone started ringing and she returned to answer it. Mrs. Hauser said, "It couldn't have been five minutes later that there was this terrible thud . . . I just wonder if I had gone right behind him . . . I don't know, I guess it wouldn't have made any difference. The whole world has just gone mad."[219]

Now, please read the following, and see if you think it sounds like someone who is about to jump out of a 13th floor window and kill themselves a few minutes later:

> All of the people who saw and spoke to Stockdale on his way to work said he had been in good spirits, waving and saying hello. He stopped for a shoe shine, spoke to the elevator operator, and exchanged words with the parking garage attendant.[220]

That just doesn't sound like a suicidal individual, does it? And in the below quote when it states "Monday," please bear in mind that Monday is the *same* day of Mr. Stockdale's death:

> One newspaper report states that Mrs. Stockdale had urged her husband to seek help for his depression after the assassination, but she called the doctor on Monday to inform him that he was so much better.[221]

---

[219] Adele Edison, "E. Grant Stockdale," 14 June 2004, ("Information taken from newspaper articles in the *Miami Herald* and *Miami News*") *The Education Forum*: http://educationforum.ipbhost.com/index.php?showtopic=943
[220] Ibid.
[221] Ibid.

Furthermore, Grant Stockdale's own daughter, Ann Stockdale, provided us with this amazing information concerning her father's murder. Get a load of this little gem:

> One thing I do know is that Kennedy asked Daddy to go to the Air Force Base south of Miami to see if (against Kennedy's orders) bombs were being loaded on the planes. Bombs WERE being loaded on the planes!! I believe one of the reasons Daddy was killed was because he knew that the Government was being run by the Military Complex.
>
> The Military Complex didn't want the American people to realize (and still don't) that they were calling the shots. Daddy knew he was being followed . . . and he told Mom that THEY were going to get him . . . and THEY did. There was an attempt on my life also several days after Daddy's funeral. I realize now that this was a scare tactic to silence my mother . . . i.e., if you speak about anything, your kids are DEAD. It worked!![222]

CONCLUSIONS BASED ON EVIDENTIARY INDICATIONS

The simple facts that the victim was clearly:

- An intimate friend of JFK;
- A man with a reputation as a tough businessman;
- Known to be very well-connected in Washington, privy to high-level information and very capable of "connecting the dots";
- Was involved in two major scandals that were brewing that had seriously threatened the entire political career of the new President, Lyndon Johnson;
- Left no suicide note or any other indications that he was facing the end;
- Confided to friends and his attorney, on the day before his death, that people were "trying to get him" and that it was linked to the assassination:

Make it advisable to include his death in the category of "Highly Suspicious."

CONCLUSION

Probable Murder; directly linked to the JFK assassination

---

[222] "Message from Ann Stockdale received June 16, 2004," Emphasis in original, in: Adele Edison, "E. Grant Stockdale," 14 June 2004, *The Education Forum*: http://educationforum.ipbhost.com/index.php?showtopic=943

8–9

Jim Koethe,
September 21, 1964
Bill Hunter,
April 23, 1964

Victim	**Jim Koethe, Newspaper Reporter** **Bill Hunter, Newspaper Reporter**
Cause of Death	Koethe: Karate chop to neck Hunter: Shot by a policeman
Official Verdict	Koethe: Victim surprised a burglar and burglar killed victim. Hunter: Accidental Shooting
Actual Circumstances	Koethe: One of the things the burglar took was all of Koethe's notes on the JFK assassination for his planned book. Hunter: In a bizarre event, a policeman was reportedly playing around at "quick-drawing" his weapon from its holster and, pointing a loaded gun at Hunter, it accidentally went off, killing him.

Karyn Kupcinet wasn't the only JFK witness victim to die of a broken neck. Reporter Jim Koethe was killed by a karate chop to the neck as he was emerging from the shower in his bathroom—the striking similarities to the death of Karyn described in the preceding chapter are quite obvious.

Jim Koethe was a young reporter for the *Dallas Times Herald* who was actively investigating the assassination of President Kennedy and, reportedly, was in the process of writing a book about it. In an occurrence that continued repeating well beyond the odds of probability, Jim's notes on the assassination for his planned book were never found.

> Robbery appeared to be the motive, although Koethe's parents believe he was killed for other reasons. Whoever ransacked his apartment, they point out, was careful to remove his notes for a book he was preparing, in collaboration with two other journalists, on the Kennedy assassination.[223]

Jim was one of the few reporters who gained access to Jack Ruby's apartment on the night of the same day that Ruby shot Oswald. Another reporter present in Ruby's apartment that night was Bill Hunter. Both would soon be killed.

> Another reporter who was there that night, Bill Hunter, was later to be shot to death in a California police station. His death was ruled to be accidental, the result of a police officer who was just horsing around pointing a loaded gun at him and pulling the trigger.[224]

Bill Hunter had also been a newspaper reporter. He worked for the *Long Beach Independent Press Telegram*, and was also covering the assassination story. Bill had come out to Dallas to work the story and met up with Jim Koethe, an old friend with whom he had worked before. It is not known if the two discovered anything noteworthy in Jack Ruby's Dallas apartment—and the police had already been there earlier that day. But it is, at the very least, a bizarre coincidence that both were reporters, both were working on the assassination story, both were examining the story of Jack Ruby shooting Oswald, both were in Ruby's apartment on the night of the same day that he murdered Oswald, and both were soon thereafter themselves murdered.

Bill Hunter was accidentally shot by a policeman; right in a California police station. The police officer stated that he had been horsing around, playing "quick-draw" with another officer, when his gun inadvertently went off, killing Hunter. Both officers involved in the incident were sentenced to three years probation.

Here's how author, Bill Sloan, described the bizarre event:

> "At approximately 2:00 a.m., on the morning of April 23, 1964, Hunter was sitting at his desk in the press room of the Long Beach police station and reading a mystery novel entitled *Stop This Man*, when two detectives— both of whom were later described as 'friends' of Hunter—came into the room."

---

223 David Welsh, "In the Shadow of Dallas: The Legacy of Penn Jones, Jr.," *Ramparts Magazine*, November 1966, pp 39-50: http://www.unz.org/Pub/Ramparts-1966nov-00039
224 Gary Richard Schoener, "A Legacy of Fear," May, 2000, *Fair Play Magazine*.

Initially, there was considerable confusion over exactly what happened next. One officer was first quoted as saying he dropped his gun, causing it to discharge as it struck the floor. Later, he changed his story to say that he and the other detective were engaged in 'horseplay' with their loaded weapons when the tragedy occurred.

Whatever the case, a single shot suddenly rang out, striking Hunter where he sat. An autopsy later showed that the .38 caliber bullet plowed straight through Hunter's heart.

He died instantly, without ever moving or saying a word."[225]

Some wondered whether *that* story might get changed too.

"My boss called me at 2:00 a.m., and told me Bill Hunter had been shot," Bill Shelton recalls. "He wasn't satisfied with the story that the cop had dropped his gun, and as it turned out, that wasn't what happened at all."

The newspaper charged police with covering up the facts in the case, which Long Beach Police Chief William Mooney vigorously denied.[226]

But the city editor at the Long Beach newspaper Hunter worked at stated that he was "still not satisfied" with the official verdict. When asked if he thought there was a connection between Hunter's death and the JFK assassination, he declined to comment, adding the cryptic comment, "But I'd believe anything."[227]

One can call it coincidence if one so chooses. But, as we covered mathematically in the Introduction, there comes a point where coincidence occurs so frequently that it actually becomes numerically prohibitive.

The brother of that same City Editor who said "But I'd believe anything," was one of many Dallas news reporters who had covered the assassination and then left the news profession. Of those many reporters, one who had been asked to resign, characterized it this way:

It looks like a studied effort to remove all the knowledgeable newsmen who covered the assassination.[228]

So both Hunter and Koethe had been at Jack Ruby's Dallas apartment the same day that Ruby had shot Oswald. They were there with George Senator, Ruby's roommate, who blatantly perjured himself in testimony to the Warren Commission, stating that he had no memory of the event. Ruby's attorney, Tom Howard, was the other person at Ruby's apartment. In fact, it was Tom Howard who put forward the preposterous story for why

---

[225] Bill Sloan, *Breaking the Silence* (Taylor Publishing: 1993)
[226] Ibid.
[227] Welsh, "In the Shadow of Dallas"
[228] Ibid.

Ruby had shot Oswald: Because he "couldn't bear the idea of the President's widow being subjected to testifying at the trial of Oswald."[229]

> On November 24, 1963, Bill Hunter and Jim Koethe interviewed George Senator. Also, there was the attorney Tom Howard. Earlier that day, Senator and Howard had both visited Jack Ruby in jail. That evening Senator arranged for Koethe, Hunter and Howard to search Ruby's apartment.[230]

It would seem something of importance must have transpired at Jack Ruby's apartment that evening, because strange events immediately followed:

- George Senator lied about the meeting having ever taken place;
- Koethe was karate-chopped to death and his JFK notes disappeared;
- Hunter was shot because a cop played around and pointed a loaded gun at him, which cops know they're not supposed to do;
- Tom Howard, the fourth and last person who was at Ruby's apartment that night, also died, he of a heart attack on March 27, 1965 at the age of 48.

As JFK researcher Tom Scully thoughtfully observed:

> Too many who approached Jack Ruby's role in an inquisitive way. . . . Kupcinet, through his daughter, Karyn, Kilgallen, and the 11/24/63 "guests" of George Senator at Jack Ruby's apartment, Hunter, Koethe and Howard . . . met a soon and untimely death.[231]

[229] John Simkin, "Tom Howard: Biography," *Spartacus Educational*, accessed 18 Nov. 2012: www.spartacus. schoolnet.co.uk/JFKhowardT.htm

[230] Ibid.

[231] Tom Scully, "Deaths of Witnesses," 3 Jan 2009, *The Education Forum*: http://educationforum.ipbhost.com/index. php?showtopic=603&st=105

Dorothy Kilgallen,
November 8, 1965

Victim	**Dorothy Kilgallen, Nationally Syndicated Columnist**
Cause of Death	High level of barbiturates, combined with alcohol
Official Verdict	Suicide or Accidental Overdose
Actual Circumstances	Dorothy had told friends that she had obtained information regarding the JFK assassination that would "bust this case wide open," and had vowed that she would "crack this case." She was the only reporter who had a private interview with Jack Ruby after he shot Oswald, and after that interview

told friends that she was "about to blow the JFK case sky high."[232] She implied she was saving important information garnered from that interview and from her investigation to include in a book that she was working on, which she felt certain would be a blockbuster, entitled *Murder One*. She was aware of the untimely and suspicious deaths of reporters Bill Hunter and Jim Koethe, and she gave a backup copy of her JFK chapter to her close friend, the journalist Florence Pritchett Smith.[233] The death scene was obviously staged (the details follow) and Dorothy's book notes disappeared. Florence Pritchett Smith died the next day, and the backup notes which Dorothy had given her friend were never located either.

Inconsistencies	Dramatic, in both number and content, primarily related to crime scene staging (see text below).

Whoever staged the crime scene at Dorothy Kilgallen's home made a lot of mistakes. . . . But we'll get to that in a moment.

Dorothy Kilgallen was a very famous news reporter whose "gossip" column was read by millions of people on almost a daily basis. She was so famous, in fact, that she herself had become a Hollywood-type celebrity, appearing as a regular guest on the extremely popular TV show, *What's My Line?*

But what made her famous as far as the JFK assassination was a far different matter. It was the fact that she had been trusted with highly confidential information by Jack Ruby, the man who had forever silenced President Kennedy's assassin, Lee Harvey Oswald.

Dorothy was, in fact, the *only* reporter allowed an exclusive private interview with Jack Ruby at the Dallas jail, apparently at Ruby's request. What transpired during that interview is still unknown, due to Dorothy's quite premature death. However, right after that interview had taken place, Dorothy promised that she would break the JFK case wide open and that her new upcoming book would include information of a startling nature. Her information, apparently in reference to one of her upcoming columns that may have contained an important excerpt from her book, was specific and her exact words to a friend were:

"In five more days I'm going to bust this case wide open."

That was the scenario immediately prior to her untimely death.

---

[232] Carl Oglesby, *The Yankee and Cowboy War: Conspiracies from Dallas to Watergate* (Andrews McMeel: 1976).
[233] John Simkin, "Dorothy Kilgallen: Biography," accessed 15 Nov 2012: http://www.spartacus.schoolnet.co.uk/JFKkilgallen.htm

Overview

▶ ### Dorothy Kilgallen

One of the most popular newspaper columnists in the country who had been using her column to attack the gaping holes in the "official version" of the JFK assassination and the obvious cover-up taking place, which she urged her readers to question.

- Found dead on the third floor of her posh 5-story Manhattan apartment home, just off Park Avenue.
- The Medical Examiner determined that she died from "acute ethanol and barbiturate intoxication" and also noted "circumstances undetermined."[234]
- Linked directly to the JFK assassination by:
- She openly attacked the cover-up and whitewash in her very prominent newspaper column.
- She was the only reporter who was granted a private interview with Jack Ruby after he murdered Oswald. She took many notes but had not yet publicly divulged their contents.
- Dorothy was apparently saving all her info on the JFK assassination for her upcoming book, *Murder One*, which she was sure would be a blockbuster (it probably would have been) and would blow the lid off the cover-up surrounding the assassination (a version of that book not containing her JFK material was later published posthumously). Therefore, it was known that Dorothy had extensive notes, from her research as well as her private interview with Jack Ruby. In fact, it was known to some of her friends that she typically carried those notes around on her person because that's how important they were to her. Yet the search of her apartment after her death yielded no notes, no material on JFK for her upcoming book.
- It was rumored that Dorothy's friend of many years, fellow journalist Flo Pritchett, had a torrid affair with Jack Kennedy, both before and after he became President. Friends reported that their romance lasted many years and was one of only two such affairs of the President that were serious and long-lasting (the other was Mary Meyer). Dorothy reportedly gave a "backup copy" of her notes on the JFK case to Flo Pritchett (who died of leukemia—on November 9, 1965,[235] one day after Dorothy's death)—and the JFK material was not located at her Manhattan apartment either.

---

[234] Cassie Parnau, "Archive/Medical Reports," *The Kilgallen Files*, accessed 16 Nov 2012: http://kilgallenfiles.wordpress.com/category/official-reports/medical-reports/
[235] "Obituary: Mrs. Earl E.T. Smith," November 9, 1965, *New York Journal American*.

First, let's talk a little bit about the fascinating Dorothy Kilgallen's life, not death. She became one of the most revered reporters in the country. Her column was read by most people in Hollywood, most people in government, and most people in general.

Her information pipeline was incredible—she seemed to know everything about everybody—and her style was gossipy and bold, which made her column utterly fascinating and required reading for millions of Americans. Probably more than any other reporter at the time, she had her finger right on the pulse of what the public wanted to find out about. She was the only reporter who broke a story about the hot romantic affair between Marilyn Monroe and a Kennedy. The next day, Marilyn was murdered . . . well, suicide, officially . . . and Dorothy believed she had been set up by the person who tipped her off to the affair by someone who was trying to implicate the Kennedys in Marilyn's death. From what we know now, those fears were very well-placed.

Furthermore, by 1964, she seemed to be on top of something about the JFK assassination and she kept giving hints about the matter—and in print.

> Ruby, himself a TV fan of Dorothy Kilgallen, had taken a liking to her during the trial. According to Israel, he respected her more than any other reporter. She had gained his confidence and had several conversations with him in the courtroom.[236]

Dorothy took a lot of notes at that meeting and she bragged to friends that she was about to break the case "wide open" and prove a conspiracy. No one ever learned the contents of her notes because she died soon afterwards, under very mysterious circumstances, on November 8, 1965, at the age of fifty-two.

She had a reputation as a steely, high-integrity, incredibly astute reporter who could not be "bought" at any price:

> Throughout her career she consistently refused to identify any of her sources whenever a government agency questioned her, and that might have posed a threat to the alleged JFK conspirators.[237]

If you look at Dorothy's comments and columns in their totality, she seems to have put together some very important points which were highly pertinent to the JFK assassination. She makes some extremely prescient points:

- That there was a connection between Jack Ruby, Dallas police officer J. D. Tippit (reportedly shot by Oswald) and a "Texas oil millionaire" (presumably H. L. Hunt, whom many place as playing a role in organizing the assassination);
- That "Oswald" was in too many places at too many times and by too many differing descriptions to be the movements of one individual;

---

[236] Robert D. Morningstar, *Justice For JFK*, 1994: http://robalini.blogspot.com/2010/04/death-of-dorothy-kilgallen.html
[237] Lee Israel, *Kilgallen* (Delacorte: 1979), 389, 390, 440.

- That Oswald had linkage to U.S. intelligence and U.S. intelligence was nervous about it and covering something up about their relationship with him;
- That Marina Oswald (herself suspected by the CIA as being a KGB asset) knew "the truth about Oswald," and if she ever told it then it would dramatically alter public perceptions of the assassination, writing in one of her columns, regarding Marina, that if people knew the "whole story of her life with President Kennedy's alleged assassin, it would split open the front pages of newspapers all over the world"[238]—Something was rotten in Denmark, and Dorothy Kilgallen knew it. Get a load of this little gem from one of her columns:
- "Even if Marina (Oswald's wife) explained why her late husband looked so different in an official police photo and the widely-printed full-length picture featured on the cover of *Life* magazine, it would cause a sensation. This story isn't going to die as long as there's a real reporter alive—and there are a lot of them."[239]
- She also knew that the "real Oswald" story was being suppressed. . . . Here is a specific excerpt from another column of Dorothy's:
- "It appears that Washington knows or suspects something about Lee Harvey Oswald that it does not want Dallas and the rest of the world to know or suspect. . . Lee Harvey Oswald has passed on not only to his shuddery reward, but to the mysterious realm of 'classified' persons whose whole story is known only to a few government agents. . . . Why is Oswald being kept in the shadows, as dim a figure as they can make him, while the defense tries to rescue his alleged killer with the help of information from the FBI? Who was Oswald, anyway?"[240]

---

[238] Dorothy Kilgallen, September 3, 1965, *New York Journal American*
[239] Ibid.
[240] Dorothy Kilgallen, February 21, 1964, *New York Journal American*

Dorothy clearly knew a lot of things about a lot of things:

- Kilgallen herself had strong links to the anti-Castro community (it was rumored that she was a CIA media asset, which would make sense) and they regularly fed her information for her columns which originated from the same anti-Castro camps that Oswald was immersed in.
- She expressed foreknowledge in her column that Marilyn had been having affairs with President Kennedy, then with Attorney

General Robert Kennedy, and realized that it may have been linked to Marilyn's death;

- Dorothy told friends whom she trusted that she was very close to discovering who had really killed JFK;[241]
- She also explained to friends that the reason that she hadn't gone public yet on her private interview with Jack Ruby (she had never written or uttered a word about it publicly) was because she was marshalling all her forces into her new book, which she was very excited about and confident would be a bestseller (she was experiencing financial problems and saw the book as the answer to them). So the rumor was that she had a lot of information that she had not yet divulged;
- Dorothy said that she also knew that she was "under surveillance"[242];
- She gave a copy of her JFK notes to a friend as a backup for protection;
- She had explained to close friends that she had received death threats and that if certain individuals found out what information she possessed, it may get her killed;
- Had planned a trip to New Orleans that was very cloak-and-dagger and told friends she would "break the case" within the next five days;
- She was found dead immediately before that trip to New Orleans.

---

[241] Simkin, "Dorothy Kilgallen: Biography"
[242] Israel, *Kilgallen*, 393.

Dorothy had pieced together some of the main players whom she believed played key roles in the JFK assassination, including David Ferrie and Texas billionaire, H. L. Hunt. She realized that Jack Ruby had also been involved and she was investigating Ruby's connections to the Texas Mafia, run by Carlos Marcello, and Dallas police officers, including J. D. Tippit. She obviously had noted that it was far too coincidental that Ruby, prior to the assassination, had known Oswald, Ferrie, and Tippit.

On November 8, 1965, Dorothy Kilgallen was found dead in her apartment shortly after returning from Dallas where she had interviewed Jack Ruby and had conducted her own investigation of the JFK murder during several trips to cover the Ruby trial.

She had revealed secret transcripts of Ruby's testimony in her column. Kilgallen had met with Ruby. She had learned of a meeting three weeks before the assassination at Ruby's "Carousel", the Dallas underworld's merry-go-round where the "Big D" mobsters wheeled around.

Present at the meeting were Ruby, Officer J. D. Tippit, Bernard Weissman and, she would later learn, a fourth party.[243]

"It is a fact that when Dorothy returned to New York, she told friends that she had discovered that Ruby and the slain Officer J. D. Tippit had been friends. They had been seen together in Ruby's Carousel Club at a meeting two weeks before the assassination in the company of Bernard Weissman, who had placed the "JFK-Wanted for Treason" newspaper ad in Dallas newspapers on November 22, 1963. Studying the Warren Commission Report, Killgallen deduced that the meeting had also been reported to Chief Justice Warren AND that the identity of "the fourth man," which she had been unable to ascertain, had been reported to Warren as "a rich Texas oil man", as Earl Warren described him in the official transcript. She told Israel that she had discovered something that was going to break the whole JFK assassination mystery wide open. She told the same story to her next door neighbor, her hairdresser, her agent, her publisher, and the producer and host of 'Nightlife'."[244]

Many researchers have suggested that a suspicious individual named Ron Pataky, a young, debonair man who had become very close with Dorothy, may have been involved in her death. Mr. Pataky has been accused of having links to the CIA and of attending assassination training; the implication being that his sudden friendship with Dorothy was insincere and actually just a means to gain means to "suicide" her.

Well, that's all very interesting and leads to some explosive connections. Now we'd like to suggest that you do your darnedest to at least temporarily ignore that. Contrary to the common currents of human nature, which tend to tackle a crime by finding the killer and "marrying" them to the act, that's not really the way to actually solve a crime. As we note in our previous book, it is *first* necessary and proper to correctly *identify* the crime—and that's why we believe that this book is important, because so many of these deaths have apparently been intentionally misinterpreted. So let's get back to the crime scene and answer that question. Was Dorothy Kilgallen murdered? It certainly seems so, and we will lay out the case.

The official version is that Dorothy accidentally mixed too much booze with her barbiturates, which killed her. In most of the cases in this book, we simply explore the facts of each death and carefully take you to where that logically leads. As a reviewer of a book on Dorothy's death once noted, these cases are important, but each one needs to be looked at closely and fairly. Here's that important statement—it's important because it sums up simply how to look at these cases correctly:

So posterity needs to evaluate each mysterious death according to how plausible the murder theory is.[245]

But this case is so blatant that we will come right out and tell you up front and early that the official version is simply a bunch of hogwash. Not only was Dorothy Kilgallen too

[243] Robert D. Morningstar, *Justice For JFK* ,1994: http://robalini.blogspot.com/2010/04/death-of-dorothy-kilgallen.html

[244] Ibid, emphasis in original.

[245] Donald Nolen, "Review of *Killgallen*, by Lee Israel," 14 Jan 2004, *Amazon.com*

intelligent and too cautious to be as recklessly silly as the official version implies, there are huge problems with the official story. Here's a pertinent question for purveyors of that ludicrously logic-lacking official version: If Dorothy accidentally mixed too much booze with too many barbiturates, then please explain to us who spent the hours after she died carefully staging the crime scene and making some very amateurish mistakes? How 'bout that one, huh? *Hell-O?* Sorry. We digress. Back to the facts.

CRIME SCENE STAGING

The many incongruities present at the death scene immediately bring to mind the words of the Chief of the Investigative Support Unit at the FBI Academy whose excellent work we cited in our chapter of Marilyn Monroe in *Dead Wrong*:

> **Red Flags: Offenders who stage crime scenes usually make mistakes because they arrange the scene to resemble what they believe it should look like. In so doing, offenders experience a great deal of stress and do not have the time to fit all the pieces together logically.**
>
> **As a result, inconsistencies in forensic findings and in the overall "big picture" of the crime scene will begin to appear. These inconsistencies can serve as the "red flags" of staging . . .[246]**

Now, in answer to the question: Were there many of the above-referenced red flags present at the Dorothy Kilgallen crime scene? Answer: Yes, there were *tons of them*.

Even if one ignores the fact that a famous reporter working on the biggest story of their career is very unlikely to commit suicide or otherwise overdose, there are some *extremely* bizarre oddities in the death of Dorothy Kilgallen:

- Her body was found in a bed that friends and family knew she never slept in. Lest one underestimate the gravity of that point, consider this: Dorothy's hairdresser, who discovered her body, explained it this way to his friend: "When I tell you the bed she was found in, and how I found her, you're going to know she was murdered."[247]
- She was found wearing what has alternately been described as a "peignoir" or a "bolero-type blouse over a nightgown," a thing which those who knew her best stated with certainty that "she would never wear to go to bed."[248] So if you don't know what a peignoir is, here's the answer—it's a thing that Dorothy Kilgallen would never *ever* wear to bed. Actually, it's a blue bed jacket, in this case. But apparently something horrid and not even imaginably "Dorothy." And that's straight from her hairdresser and, as the saying goes, you can bet that her hairdresser knows for sure.

---

[246] John E. Douglas, Ed.D., Special Agent & Chief, Investigative Support Unit, FBI Academy, & Corinne Munn, Honors Intern, FBI Academy, *Violent Crime Scene Analysis: Modus Operandi, Signature, and Staging*, February 1992, FBI Law Enforcement Bulletin.

[247] Sara Jordan, "Who Killed Dorothy Kilgallen?," October 21, 2007, *Midwest Today*: http://www.midtod.com/new/articles/7_14_07_Dorothy.html

[248] Simkin, "Dorothy Kilgallen: Biography"

- She was in bed with makeup and her false eyelashes, which friends and family knew that she would never go to sleep wearing;
- There was a book placed on her bed, as though she were reading it before she passed out. But it was a book which, as she had told friends, she'd already read;
- She used a set of reading glasses to read books, and there were no reading glasses near her;
- Laboratory testing on the glass found near her revealed traces of one barbiturate. But the autopsy revealed that she was killed by a "cocktail" of small doses of three different barbiturates forming a lethal combination with alcohol.[249] It was made to look as though she had simply taken some pills and gone to bed and quietly passed away. So how, when and where did the other two barbiturates enter her?
- The air conditioning had been left on, which she never did at night, because the home got unbearably cold (and *was* when her hairdresser arrived).
- A casual investigation, if any at all, was done on her death; it was a "soft-pedal," rather than the serious investigation one would rightfully expect from the sudden death of a nationally-respected news personality.

LIVIDITY

There is not nearly as much forensic information on Dorothy's death as there should be, for even a typical "non-celebrity" death; and what *does* exist is often vague or self-contradictory.[250]

However, we did obtain some information on the recording of the lividity markings present in Dorothy's body and they also indicate that the body was moved post-mortem.

Cassie Parnau is the author of *The Kilgallen Files*, an online educational site dedicated to learning more about Dorothy's life and sudden death. Cassie also has a special investigator's zeal and dedication that lends well to years of specific research focused on one topic. Also having a forensic background—having "seen a lot of bodies come across the table"[251]—made her very keen to learn about the lividity markings in the case, and she unearthed whatever information was discernible. Here's what she concluded about the lividity markings on Dorothy's body:

> The scene was staged. The autopsy findings: "lividity posterior involving the left neck and face" versus how she was discovered: propped up in bed, her head tilted, prove that she died in a different position than she was "found" in—a position that promoted an accidental death.[252]

The medical implications of the lividity markings on the back of "the left neck and face" imply that the body of the victim was actually not in a propped up position at the time

[249] Parnau, *The Kilgallen Files*
[250] Ibid.
[251] Cassie Parnau, email to author, 16 November 2012.
[252] Cassie Parnau, email to author, 16 November 2012.

of death and is *highly indicative* that the body of the victim was moved after they were already dead.

> Knowing that she was moved/propped brings into question *everything* that was found at the scene.[253]

AUTOPSY & DRUG LEVELS

Dorothy's blood alcohol concentration (BAC) was 0.15, which—although legally intoxicated—by contextual standards was pretty much just a normal late night after work in 1965 for a very sociable celebrity who was known to be a regular drinker. She was not, by any means, excessively inebriated, as was attested by the witnesses who saw and heard her in the time period close to her final moments.

Much more noteworthy was the exotic combination of drugs that killed her. Three distinctly different barbiturates were found in relation to Dorothy's death.

> Amobarbital: Commonly known as "Tuinal"
> Pentobarbital: Commonly known as "Nembutal"
> Secobarbital: Commonly known as "Seconal"[254]

> An overdose of any of those drugs will cause unconsciousness in 5–15 minutes and death anywhere between 20–50 minutes.[255]

But in combination, they are particularly lethal . . . and quite interestingly, it was the *exact right amount and combination* to kill her. There was a level of only about five pills of each of the three drugs. As Kilgallen researcher Cassie Parnau notes:

> It is interesting to see that the approximation of the amount of pills in Dorothy's system at the time she died is in line with the relatively precise amount needed to cause death. The amount of pills estimated in her system do not lean toward incredibly more pills than the MLD (Minimum Lethal Dose), as most suicides by pills do. (For instance her husband Richard—when he killed himself, he practically swallowed everything in reach.)[256]

In other words, the fact that the exact amount of drugs found in Dorothy—the equivalent to 15–20 pills, although bear in mind that they may not have necessarily been in pill form—*barely* were enough to kill her; only the fact that they had been combined with some alcohol made them a fatal dose.

That presents a huge problem: If she was trying to commit suicide, then she didn't take nearly enough pills. Several doctors who studied the case agreed that the dosage was not in the range medically expected for suicide:

---

[253] Ibid, emphasis in original.
[254] Parnau, *The Kilgallen Files*
[255] Ibid.
[256] Ibid.

The suicide theory presents one nettlesome problem. If she was stood up by, spurned, or in any way emotionally ravaged by the out-of-towner (Ron Pataky, the man she had been seeing), and thereby driven to suicidal rage, she did not take the kind of massive dose consistent with that rage.[257]

She knew that there were plenty of pills at the house.

Had she returned home resolute and seething, she could have availed herself of a virtual pharmacopoeia. Kerry Kolmar recalled that his father had vats of pills around, containers of Tuinal large enough to pickle mice.[258]

So she didn't take pills to commit suicide; but it isn't possible that she took that many pills accidentally either.

Also, it appears as if it would be more difficult to ingest 15 to 20 pills accidentally. Since Dorothy was seen in the 1:00 a.m. hour—and appeared to be in control of herself but "a little high"—and her time of death was estimated at around 2:00 a.m., it would not seem feasible for her to have been so stoned out of her gourd to have accidentally taken five pills three times.[259]

And therein the problem lies.

The pills were in a perplexingly moderate range. Too many of them for accident, too few for suicide. But enough to kill her.[260]

Most of Dorothy's medical records and many medical studies related to her death are available for study online at KilgallenFiles.com.

In short, Dorothy overdosed—but the number of pills that were approximated in her system fall within a window of suspicion. It is just about a *perfect* amount. Seemingly too many for accident but far too few for intentional suicide.

Because she had been drinking, the effect of the drugs was multiplied.

She most likely died quickly, however she would have had trouble breathing—which may have been stressful to her body.[261]

One necessarily needs to look at *availability* (access to the drugs themselves), *presence* of those same drugs (quantity), the *actions* of the drugs (the time that it takes them to

---

[257] Israel, *Kilgallen*, 422.
[258] Ibid.
[259] Parnau, *The Kilgallen Files*
[260] Israel, *Kilgallen*, 422.
[261] Parnau, *The Kilgallen Files*

work), and the *effects* of the drugs (such as automatic regurgitation whence the body attempts to reject the toxins). **All of those factors point to foul play in Dorothy's death.**

As far as *access* to the drugs that were found in her body, Seconal was definitely available to Dorothy. Tuinal was located in the home, as her husband had a prescription for it, but was not a drug typically taken by Dorothy. The third drug, Nembutal, was *not* readily available to Dorothy and, oddly enough, was *also* the drug of which contents were found in the drinking glass that was placed near her. It should be noted that Seconal and Tuinol were *not* found in the drinking glass.

> The real question is how/why on the Tuinal and why the Nembutal in the glass?[262]

An even larger issue than availability is the *quantity* in the time frame that they would *have* to have been taken.

> Even more suspicious than the drugs themselves is the quantity of pills.[263]

It was medically estimated that Dorothy had the equivalent of 15 to 20 pills in her body, in a triple combination of Nembutal, Seconal, and Tuinol, combined with alcohol, which supercharged their effects.

Yet it has been established that she was observed in a fine, coherent state a short time before her death occurred. She could *not* have taken that many pills—accidentally or otherwise—and still been walking around in a coherent state. Therefore, whatever did happen must therefore have happened very quickly.

And an even larger issue is the sterility of the crime scene. There was no vomit or mess of any kind. That would simply not be possible if she had swallowed 15 to 20 pills and combined them with alcohol.

> Also worth considering is the nature of a drug overdose death, especially a barbiturate overdose. If Dorothy were drunk and had actually taken 15-20 pills, her body would have probably attempted to reject the toxins. If she didn't vomit, it is likely she would have either foamed or purged. Barbiturate overdoses aren't necessarily calm, quiet and pretty deaths. There's a CNS (central nervous system) shutdown—lungs, gasping for air or perhaps coughing. Maybe some thrashing about. Rarely do people die with their eyes closed and their mouths neatly shut. . . . Yet she was found in bed, tucked in, her eyes closed and her face peaceful, powdered and made-up.[264]

Therefore, we know that she *did not* take them accidentally or intentionally without the crime scene having been cleaned up considerably. In fact, they may not have been taken by her at all. We know that she could not have taken that many accidentally, and nor can it be explained that they were taken intentionally. And we know that the crime

[262] Cassie Parnau, emails to author, 23 Nov. 2012.
[263] Ibid.
[264] Ibid.

scene was staged, including considerable cleaning up of both the body's state—the inevitable vomiting—and the body's position—the fact that rather than being in the typically twisted or contorted position of a human body that had endured involuntary spasms, she was found propped up neatly in her bed. *Or so her killers thought*—because we know it was actually a bed that she never used, even to read.[265] That room was simply a "showcase"; to convince showbiz visitors that she and her husband were still sleeping together, and it was actually kept in a constant pristine state, but never used.

CONCLUSIONS BASED ON EVIDENTIARY INDICATIONS

We can utilize the same "Rule out method (R/O)" that we used in *Dead Wrong* to determine the true cause of death for Marilyn Monroe. In Dorothy's case:

- We can R/O Natural Causes: Although she had some substance abuse issues, the autopsy revealed that she had <u>no</u> cirrhosis of the liver; she was a healthy fifty-two-year-old woman.
- We can R/O Suicide: On the night she died, she performed live on television and was great. As was customary, she went out for cocktails afterwards with people from the show. She socialized and was not depressed. She was also very excited about her upcoming book and told friends she had information that would "shock the world." A friend, who said he talked to her earlier on the night that she died, was asked if she sounded suicidal: "No! No! The last time I talked to her, she was just normal." She telephoned Western Union at 2:20 a.m. to arrange pickup of her column for the next day's newspaper. The manager of Western Union stated: "Miss Kilgallen called me at 2:20 in the morning. She sounded great, as usual. She said 'Good morning, Mr. Spiegel, this is Dorothy Kilgallen. Would you send a messenger over to the house to pick up my column and take it to the Journal-American? I'll leave it in the regular place, in the door.' I said 'It's always a pleasure' and sent the messenger. It was there, as usual."[266]

  She also had insufficient drug levels for an attempted suicide. It was literally just enough to kill her when combined with some alcohol. Had she actually wanted to commit suicide, there were many drugs in the home that had been prescribed to her husband, which easily could have taken.
- We can R/O Accident: The exotic combination of fast-acting barbiturates found in Dorothy's body (three separate drugs which form a lethal combination) ensures that she could not have taken them accidentally or absentmindedly. It is established that, <u>at least</u> as late as 2:20 a.m., she was her usual self and completely coherent. Yet she was dead by 4:00 a.m. In order to have been an accident, she would have had to mistakenly take at least five capsules of each of three different drugs in one hour. A mistake of 3 x 5 is not even within the realm of possibility.
- It bears noting that it was common knowledge among her crowd that Dorothy's regular drink was Vodka-Tonic. Tonic contains Quinine, which

---

[265] Ibid.
[266] Sara Jordan, "Who Killed Dorothy Kilgallen?," October 21, 2007, *Midwest Today*: http://www.midtod.com/new/articles/7_14_07_Dorothy.html

is known for its ability to mask the bitterness of barbiturates when someone slips a person a lethal combination of drugs known colloquially as a "Mickey Finn" or "Knockout Drops."

Examination of the drinking glass contents found in her room revealed only *one* of the three drugs that killed her. The death scene was staged to look like she had gone to bed and died after taking medication, but there is no plausible explanation for how the other two drugs entered body.[267]

Dorothy's death had many signs of obvious crime scene staging:

- Lividity markings that were "posterior involving the left neck and face" are a strong indication that Dorothy <u>did not</u> die in the position that she was found in, sitting propped up in bed as though she had been reading a book.[268]

- Her body was found in a bed in which her close friends knew that she <u>never</u> slept. The master bedroom was strictly for the false pretense that she and her husband had a happy marriage; a fact which her killers had no way of knowing. If her family had acted to protect her reputation, as some have speculated, why would they place her in the wrong bed?

- Typical death scenes in drug overdoses reveal unnatural body positions due to the involuntary muscle spasms. They also have vomit on the victim, as the body attempts to reject the toxins. Dorothy reportedly had neither.

- Like Marilyn Monroe, the pristine condition was far too neat. A blanket had been pulled up to her neck. Here's how the friend who discovered her body described it:

- "The bed was spotless. She was dressed very peculiarly like I've never seen her before. She always (was) in pajamas and old socks and her make-up (would be) off and her hair (would be) off."

- But "she was completely dressed like she was going out, the hair was in place, the make-up was on, the false eyelashes were on."

- She was dressed in a blue "matching peignoir and robe" which was something "she would never wear to go to bed."

- Her friend also noted that "a book (was) laid out on the bed. (But it) was turned upside down; it wasn't in the right position for if she'd been reading . . . and it was laid down so perfectly."

- The home was very cold because the air-conditioner was on. That was completely unnecessary because it was cold outside and speaks to the fact that if the victim had simply gone to bed and died of too much medication, she obviously would have turned off the air conditioning first, just as she normally did.

- Another mistake in the staging was that it was a book she had already read. Her friend remembered that Dorothy had told him that she had finished that particular book several weeks ago and she had then discussed the book with him.

[267] Parnau, *The Kilgallen Files*
[268] Cassie Parnau, email to author, 16 November 2012.

- Although Dorothy needed and always used reading glasses to read a book, none were found in the room (another point that the death-scene stagers would have had no way of knowing).[269]
- Dorothy was befriended during her last months by one Ron Pataky and the two became very close and "quite an item." Some claim Pataky had links to U.S. intelligence. Lee Israel, author of the biography, *Kilgallen*, writes that prior to meeting Dorothy, Pataky "enrolled in a training school for assassins in Panama or thereabouts." Pataky is believed to be one of the last to see Dorothy alive; the two would often rendezvous late at night to share drinks together. Israel paints a mysterious portrait of Pataky, although she acknowledges she found no direct links between him and the CIA. But when asked:

  "Do you believe that Ron Pataky murdered Dorothy Kilgallen?"
  Israel responded: "He had something to do with it."[270]
- Other sources have apparently verified that Pataky ". . . did graduate from one of the schools for assassins that later became the U.S. Army School of the Americas."[271]
- Three sources claimed:

  "...that Kilgallen went from the television studio for *What's My Line?* (West 54th and Broadway) to P. J. Clarke's (Third Avenue and East 50th Street) to the Regency Hotel (Park Avenue between 61st and 62nd). Her house was on East 68th between Madison and Park. Ms. Israel could not find a driver for Carey Cadillac—the limo company Kilgallen always used—to verify that Kilgallen was alive when she voluntarily entered her house.

  The three sources cited by Ms. Israel agreed that the only reason Kilgallen would go to the Regency was for a romantic rendezvous or a private conversation with a close friend. The Regency did *not* have one of those trendy nightclubs in 1965. It had a lounge where a celebrity would go for privacy—*not* to show off or be seen. Kilgallen knew the chances of finding an actor showing off there were slim to none. Remember, in that era actors wanted their names in her column.

  Then you have something that's *not* in the Israel book. One of the *What's My Line?* contestants that night was a Kentucky woman who saw Kilgallen with a man at a banquette table in the Regency Hotel lounge. A cocktail party was going on in the lounge. That's why the Kentucky woman was there. Kilgallen and her male companion paid no attention to the cocktail party. They were not affectionate or romantic, either. 'They were talking serious business of some kind,' said the tourist from Kentucky in 1999."[272]

---

[269] Sara Jordan, "Who Killed Dorothy Kilgallen?," October 21, 2007, *Midwest Today*: http://www.midtod.com/new/articles/7_14_07_Dorothy.html

[270] John Simkin, 20 December 2005, *Spartacus Educational*: http://www.spartacus.schoolnet.co.uk/JFKpataky.htm

[271] Jonathan Wendland, "Florence Pritchett: The Forgotten Witness," March 14, 2005, *The Education Forum*: http://educationforum.iphost.com/index.php?showtopic=2358&st=15

[272] Jonathan Wendland, Florence Pritchett: The Forgotten Witness, March 16, 2005, The Education Forum http://educationforum.ipbhost.com/index.php?showtopic=2358&st=15

Although it's also possible that the staging was an attempt to cover-up a suicide or accident, it certainly does not appear likely. The job was very professional.

CONCLUSION

Dorothy Kilgallen was murdered; probably done as a National Security Assassination. Notes for her upcoming JFK book, including the backup copy she had reportedly entrusted to a friend, completely disappeared from the face of the earth (her book *was* eventually published—but notably absent was her "breakthrough" on JFK).

RESOURCES FOR FURTHER STUDY

There are two incredibly valuable resources in the case of Dorothy Kilgallen, available online:

The Kilgallen Files, an ongoing study group led by author and researcher, Cassie Parnou, at: http://kilgallenfiles.wordpress.com

Sara Jordan's "Who Killed Dorothy Kilgallen?" in *Midwest Today*, at:

http://www.midtod.com/new/articles/7_14_07_Dorothy.html

11 | Florence Pritchett Smith (also known as Mrs. Earl E. T. Smith), November 9, 1965

Victim	Florence Pritchett Smith
Cause of Death	Cerebral Hemorrhage
Official Verdict	Natural Causes
Inconsistencies	None apparent, except for the unfathomable "coincidence" that: 1. She had reportedly been entrusted with Dorothy Kilgallen's highly confidential notes for her upcoming book on the JFK assassination; 2. She died the day after Dorothy. 3. The JFK notes (of both) disappeared.

The evidence appears to support the point that Florence Pritchett Smith suffered from leukemia.

Little is known about her death, except that she died of a cerebral hemorrhage, apparently as a result of leukemia. However, the fact that it was known to several people that she had been entrusted with a "back-up copy" of Kilgallen's notes—actually the chapter of her book that focused on the JFK assassination—and, just like Kilgallen's entire manuscript, they suddenly vanished, speaks very loudly of foul play afoot. If Kilgallen's death was accidental and Smith's death was natural, there is no adequate explanation for one very important thing—why did all of Kilgallen's work she'd been doing on the JFK cover-up completely disappear?

12 | **Betty McDonald (a.k.a. Nancy Jane Mooney),** February 13, 1964

Betty McDonald worked as a dancer in Jack Ruby's night club and provided the alibi for a man accused of shooting a key witness to the JFK assassination.

Victim	**Betty McDonald**
Cause of Death	Strangulation
Official Verdict	Suicide
Actual Circumstances	Found hanging in her jail cell, at 4:45 a.m., about two hours after her arrest for fighting with another woman. She was hung by use of her own trousers around her neck.
Inconsistencies	None apparent

As far as it concerns the events surrounding the JFK assassination, the facts on the death of Betty McDonald are actually more about the facts concerning a man named Warren Reynolds. We'll explain.

When Dallas Police Officer J. D. Tippit was shot and killed in the Oak Cliff section of Dallas very shortly after the assassination of President Kennedy, a Dallas resident named Warren Reynolds was standing right in the path of the fleeing gunman leaving the Tippit crime scene. Mr. Reynolds chased after the gunman for at least a block and saw his face up close. He got a good look at the guy but, to put it plainly, it wasn't what the authorities wanted to hear.

Jack Ruby at his nightclub, *The Carousel Club* in Dallas, with three of his strippers.

Reynolds told police that the man who shot Tippit was **not** Lee Harvey Oswald. He was subsequently shot at, harassed, and almost had his ten-year-old daughter kidnapped. Finally, he changed his story and told the authorities what they wanted to hear—and who could blame him at that point?

Betty McDonald, also known as Nancy Mooney, was a stripper at Jack Ruby's night club. When police arrested the man accused of shooting Mr. Reynolds, Betty McDonald gave the man an alibi, saying she had been with him at the time of the shooting. McDonald was arrested a short time later on a different matter, and was found dead in her jail cell, apparently having either hung herself or having had some assistance in the process. It was ruled suicide, but it could have been murder. In any case, its linkage to the JFK assassination seems peripheral.

Warren Reynolds witnessed the shooting of Officer J. D. Tippit and ID'd the shooter as looking nothing like Lee Harvey Oswald. But after being threatened repeatedly and even shot at, he was coerced into changing his testimony to fit the official version.

Our thanks go to writer Gary Richard Schoener, who summed up the whole sordid story very succinctly in his article for *Fair Play Magazine*:

> Mr. Warren Reynolds, who was employed in a car lot one block from the scene of the shooting of police officer Tippit, told the FBI on January 21, 1964 that he had seen a man carrying a pistol fleeing from the scene of the killing. He also told them that he could not identify the man as Oswald, despite the fact that he had followed the man for a block and seen him at close range. Two days after this FBI interview, he was shot through the head in the basement of his office. Since nothing was stolen, there was no obvious motive.
>
> Reynolds was hospitalized and miraculously recovered from his head wound. He had been out of the hospital for about three weeks when, late in February of 1964, an attempt was allegedly made to kidnap his ten-year-old daughter. He and his family received telephone threats. Reynolds' growing fear brought about major changes in his everyday life including continuous worry, the end to night walks, and the presence of a friend at the car lot after dark. He owned a watchdog and surrounded his house with floodlights which could be instantly turned on. . . .

But the story is not over. Darrell Wayne Garner, the "prime suspect" arrested after the shooting of Reynolds, was released on the strength of an alibi provided by his girlfriend, Nancy Jane Mooney, a.k.a. Betty McDonald. Ms. Mooney had worked as a stripper at Jack Ruby's Carousel Club. Eight days after providing an alibi for Garner, Ms. Mooney was herself arrested. The charge was "disturbing the peace." She had allegedly been fighting with her roommate on a street corner, although the roommate was not arrested. Two hours later she was dead, allegedly having hung herself in her jail cell.

As with many of the cases in this book, we will never know what information Ms. McDonald may have provided, because she didn't live long enough to tell us.

Had she lived, Mooney might have rescinded her previous alibi testimony. As a former employee of the Carousel Club, she could also affirm—as did others—that both Tippit and Oswald patronized the establishment.[273]

CONCLUSIONS BASED ON EVIDENTIARY INDICATIONS

- Although the case relates to the JFK assassination, its linkage is via Warren Reynolds, which was a very clear case of the "Powers That Be" intimidating and harassing a key witness into involuntarily changing his testimony to fit the official version of events.
- As far as Betty McDonald, her death appears to either have actually been suicide, or murder for reasons unknown, by persons unknown.
- It does not appear that her death had anything to do with her "knowing too much" or any other apparent linkage to the JFK assassination.

CONCLUSION

Suicide or murder, but her death does not appear to have been a "professional" job or linked to JFK assassination.

Her story reveals, however, a clear case of witness intimidation regarding Warren Reynolds.

---

[273] *The X Spot*, "More Death by JFK Assassination, Pt. II," November 22, 2009: http://xdell.blogspot.com/2009/11/more-death-by-jfk-assassination-pt-ii.html

13 | Eddy Benavides, February, 1964

Victim	**Eddy Benavides**
Cause of Death	Gunshot
Official Verdict	Unsolved Murder
Actual Circumstances	In another odd series of events, the brother of an eyewitness was murdered (shot in the back of the head in a bar in Dallas) and, since the two looked a lot alike, it has been suggested that the murder was actually a case of mistaken identity.

Domingo "Dom" Benavides witnessed the escape of the actual killer of Officer J. D. Tippit. He got a very close look at the man and he explained to police very clearly that he could simply not identify that man as Lee Harvey Oswald.

Dom Benavides was an intelligent, well-versed, and thoughtful young man who was very confident in what he had and had not seen. He can be viewed online in interviews which convey his intelligence and presence of mind.[274]

Benavides testified that he "really got a good view of the slayer"[275] and was highly specific in his descriptions of how the killer differed from Oswald:

---

[274] An excellent video interview of the witness can be seen at: "JFK assassination JD Tippit murder witness interviews," accessed 11 Oct 2012: http://www.youtube.com/watch?v=HbcnV9cPL_w

[275] David Welsh, "In the Shadow of Dallas: The Legacy of Penn Jones, Jr.," *Ramparts Magazine*, November 1966, pp 39-50: http://www.unz.org/Pub/Ramparts-1966nov-00039

I remember the back of his head seemed like his hairline went square instead of tapered off . . . it kind of went down and squared off and made
his head look flat in back.[276]

Then things got very tricky in Dom's life. He was "repeatedly threatened by police, and advised not to talk about what he saw."[277]

No one sums up his story more clearly and concisely than author Monty Cook:

Domingo Benavides said that the killer did not resemble Oswald. Soon
afterward, Benavides received death threats, his look-alike brother was
killed in a bar fight. Suddenly, he reversed his testimony and agreed that
the killer was Oswald. The death threats stopped.[278]

So there it is! Another case of: "Who can really blame him?"

Whatever we and other people who came along, after the fact, may think of the matter, it's very important to consider what Dom Benavides himself thought:

---

[276] Ibid.
[277] Ibid.
[278] Monty Cook, *The Skeptic's Guide to Conspiracies: From the Knights Templar to the JFK Assassination: Uncovering the (Real) Truth Behind the World's Most Controversial Conspiracy Theories* (Adams Media: 2009), citing Doug Moench, *The Big Book of Conspiracies* (Paradox Press: 1995).

Domingo Benavides was convinced that Eddy's murder was a case of mistaken identity and that he was the intended victim.[279]

CONCLUSIONS BASED ON EVIDENTIARY INDICATIONS

Clear case of witness intimidation: The murder of Eddy Benavides may or may not have actually been related to the intimidation of Domingo Benavides.

---

[279] John Simkin, "Domingo Benavides: Biography," accessed 11 Oct 2012: http://www.spartacus.schoolnet.co.uk/JFKbenavides.htm

14 | Bill Chesher, March 31, 1964

Victim	Bill Chesher
Cause of Death	Heart attack
Official Verdict	Natural Causes
Inconsistencies	None apparent

Author and researcher, Sylvia Meagher, reported that Mr. Chesher was "believed to have information about a Ruby/Oswald link."[280] That seems highly plausible because, as has been established in the preceding chapters, there clearly were links between Oswald and Ruby—many reported having seen the two together.

Bill Chesher clearly did have information about an Oswald link to Ruby. Chesher was an auto mechanic who had worked on Jack Ruby's car. He and another mechanic at the garage where he worked, Robert Roy, reported that they had seen Lee Harvey Oswald driving Jack Ruby's car.[281]

However, little is also known about the death of Mr. Chesher and, thus far, there is nothing out of the ordinary that can be said about it.

CONCLUSIONS BASED ON EVIDENTIARY INDICATIONS

Death, most probably, from natural causes. In this particular case, critics appear to be correct that there is nothing innately suspicious.

---

[280] Sylvia Meagher, *Accessories After the Fact: The Warren Commission, The Authorities & The Report* (Vintage: 1992).
[281] James DiEugenio, "JFK: The Ruby Connection, Gary Mack's Follies – Part One," *CTKA (Citizens for Truth about the Kennedy Assassination)*, accessed 11 Oct 2012: http://www.ctka.net/2009/ruby_mack.html

15 | Hank Killam,
March 17, 1964

Victim	**Hank Killam**
Cause of Death	Blood loss from severed throat; deep three-inch cut through jugular vein; carotid artery.
Official Verdict	The police made a determination of "Suicide." The local medical authorities also initially concluded it as a suicide, but apparently later changed that finding to "Accident."
Actual Circumstances	The police finding of suicide only makes sense if some extremely serious government people told police it was suicide. Otherwise, no sane person would conclude that a man intentionally jumped through a ground floor plate-glass window for the purpose of committing suicide. No one commits suicide by jumping through a department store window at 4:30 in the morning. As we explain below, some serious dark forces were hot on Hank Killam's trail, and no one knew that better than he. It's a highly pertinent observation that a suicide verdict precludes a serious murder investigation and, quite apparently, the "Powers That Be" didn't want anyone investigating the murder of Hank Killam. But we did anyway.
Inconsistencies	Numerous; see text below.

The following is a verbatim excerpt from an official *Library of Congress* investigation by the *Congressional Research Service* entitled "Analysis Of Reports And Data Bearing On Circumstances Of Death Of Twenty-One Individuals Connected With The Assassination Of President John F. Kennedy":

Name:	Thomas Henry (Hank) Killam
Assassination Connection:	Hank Killam worked as a house painter in Dallas at the time of President Kennedy's assassination. Penn Jones maintains, in Volume II of *Forgive My Grief*, that Killam was connected with both Lee Harvey Oswald and his murderer. First, his wife, Wanda Joyce Killam, worked for Jack Ruby as an exotic dancer in one of his clubs for two years prior to the assassination. Second, Killam was acquainted with and occasionally worked on painting assignments with a man named John Carter, who resided in a rooming house located at 1026 North Beckley, in Dallas, where Lee Harvey Oswald also lived.
Date of Death:	March 17, 1964
Circumstances of Death:	Penn Jones gives a detailed account of Killam's death in Volume II of *Forgive My Grief*: Hank had moved from town to town after the assassination and then from state to state in an effort to avoid the continual questioning of "federal agents." According to Hank's wife. . . . Hank was "hounded from job to job" by these federal agents. Before his death in Florida, Hank told his brother, Earl Killam: "I am a dead man, but I have run as far as I am going to run." At 4:00 a.m. on March 17, 1974, while asleep in his mother's home, Hank was called to the phone. He dressed and left the house. A car door was heard to slam, according to his mother, although Hank did not own a car. A few hours later he was found dead on the street in Pensacola, Florida, with his throat cut. Since he was lying near a pile of broken glass, the papers said he either jumped or fell into a plate glass window.

> The Pensacola police ruled the death suicide. The local coroner ruled the death accidental. Neither of these parties knew of the conflict in their rulings until early 1967 when his brother, Earl Killam, asked that the body be exhumed in an effort to determine the exact cause. [282]

Believe it or not, the reasons stated by the *Congressional Research Service* for not being able to investigate the bizarre death of Hank Killam, were that "this death has proved difficult to pursue from Washington, due to the fact that the Library of Congress does not permanently retain issues of the *Pensacola Journal*." We kid you not—that was really the reason stated. Wow—what a thorough and capable group of investigators our tax dollars fund at the Congressional Research Service.

Well, we don't "permanently retain issues of the *Pensacola Journal*" either, but you know what?—we got off our duffs and researched it anyway! We thought old Hank deserved that much, at the very least. Here's what we found out:

Hank was found dead, near a broken plate glass window, in Pensacola, Florida. His jugular vein was severely cut and he bled to death before they could get him to the hospital.

Police ruled the death a suicide. The local coroner ruled it an accident. Now take a look at what the research of authors Craig Roberts and John Armstrong revealed:

> He was found dead, his throat cut wide open, his body thrown through a department store window in Pensacola, Florida, less than four months after the assassination.

> Killam's death aroused suspicions in County Solicitor Carl Harper's mind, which in 1967, began a nationally publicized investigation. During the investigation, Harper discovered that Killam had fled Dallas, moved to Pensacola, then Tampa, and then back to Pensacola to escape "agents" that were after him. [283]

Hank Killam told his brother, Earl:

> I'm a dead man. They're going to get me—but I've run as far as I'm going to run. [284]

---

[282] Congressional Research Service, Library of Congress, ""Analysis Of Reports And Data Bearing On Circumstances Of Death Of Twenty-One Individuals Connected With The Assassination Of President John F. Kennedy," June 5, 1978, Thomas H. Neale, Analyst, American National Government Division, citing Penn Jones, Jr., *Forgive My Grief II* (Midlothian Mirror: 1967): http://mcadams.posc.mu.edu/crs.htm

[283] Roberts & Armstrong, *The Dead Witnesses*, 8.

[284] Thomas Porter, "Officials Blast Theory of Suicide in Death of Man Who Claimed He Knew Too Much," April 16, 1967, *National Enquirer*, cited in "The Death of Hank Killam – The Ultimate Cold Case," *The Education Forum*: http://educationforum.ipbhost.com/index.php?showtopic=9053

Harper wasn't the only one who questioned the finding:

> Three key figures have ripped apart the police theory of "probable sui-
> cide" in the death of a man who claimed that he knew too much about the
> Kennedy assassination—and was afraid that he would be killed because
> of it.[285]

The article then goes on to delineate a number of valid reasons why the evidence is actually indicative of murder, not suicide. Pay close attention to the findings in the report of
insurance investigator, Jim Harper, who apparently did more "police work" on the case
than the police actually did:

> I was working the case as a claim against liability and didn't think too
> much about the mystery aspects of it at the time. The window of the store
> was broken. Blood went way back inside—4 to 5 feet. To me, this means
> Killam went through the window with tremendous force. Because if he
> had slipped or had staggered into the glass, the blood would have been
> right at the window. And if he had fallen through he would have landed
> real close to the edge.[286]

Even County Coroner, Dr. A. H. Northup, was shocked at the determination made by
authorities:

> I didn't know until now that police had listed the death as a probable sui-
> cide. In ten years as a medical examiner, I've never heard of a man trying
> to kill himself in that way.[287]

Hank Killam, with wife, Wanda, who worked as a dancer in Jack Ruby's nightclub.

---

285 Ibid.
286 Ibid.
287 Ibid.

It gets worse:

> Hank Killam would also have had to jump up and over a two-foot high section of brick wall even to get into the plate-glass window. And the mystery is deepened by the fact that his body was discovered on the pavement—50 feet from the window.

> "That is sure no way to commit suicide," the insurance investigator theorized. "If he had been cut anywhere else except on the jugular vein, he would never have bled to death. There were no other marks, no bruises, in any way, shape or form, on Killam's body."[288]

His brother, Earl, recalled this event, shortly prior to the incident:

> He remembered the weekend his brother died; how Hank had seen a strange man wearing the collar of a priest, several times near 316 West Romana Street, where Killam was staying with his mother, Mary. No Catholic priests or Episcopal clergymen ever visited the area. Hank Killam was frightened of the stranger who seemed to be shadowing him and told his own Baptist minister: "Be careful they don't put a knife in your back after being seen talking to me."

> The minister, the Reverend George Blue, also said Killam hinted in those last days of his life that his special knowledge of "that thing in Dallas" would lead to his death.[289]

So Hank Killam was a man on the run. It is very clear that he knew of an Oswald connection to Jack Ruby, because he was apparently a **key part** of that connection. He was not just very worried, but was in constant and acute fear for his life, and those fears turned out to be very well founded.

> According to his wife, Killam came home the night of the assassination "as white as a sheet." She said he stayed up all night watching television reports. Later, Killam began to keep a file of newspaper clippings on the Kennedy and Oswald slayings.

> After the assassination, agents—identified as "federal" by his wife and as "plotters" by Killam—began to hound her husband, Wanda said. They quizzed him about Ruby and Carter—and when one crew stopped, another began.

> Finally Killam ran. "Then they browbeat me into telling them where he had gone," Wanda said. And again the "agents" and "plotters" tracked him down in Tampa where he was working as a used car salesman. They chased him from one lot to another, then to his home and death.[290]

---

[288] Ibid.
[289] Ibid.
[290] Ibid.

And Hank was a big, confident man who didn't shy away from a problem. He was over six feet tall, over two hundred pounds, and one tough customer, by all accounts. His wife was absolutely certain he would never have committed suicide, because he just wasn't that type of a guy. The way his wife put it was that she didn't know who killed him, but "I know he wouldn't have jumped through any window."[291]

Earl Killam also related the bizarre events in the middle of that night which led to Hank's murder:

> I know my mother said he got a phone call at 4:00 a.m. the night he died, went out of the house, and a car door was heard to slam.
>
> I know he didn't have a car, and less than thirty minutes later, he was found dead.
>
> I know too, that it is possible that someone picked him up, slit his jugular vein, threw him into the window to make it look like an accident.
>
> Then, as everyone else who comes in close contact with the case, Earl Killam popped the poser: "Who would have thought of suicide? You don't commit suicide by jumping through a ground floor window."[292]

And get a load of *this*:

> But earlier that same evening, Officer Reeves had answered another call concerning Killam. Reeves was summoned to 316 West Romana Street, where he had found Killam waiting in front of the house. There was fear showing in Killam's eyes and he claimed that he was going to be killed."[293]

So let's walk through this crime scene.

- It's <u>four-thirty in the morning</u>. The victim has a slit jugular vein, carotid artery, and a three-inch gash on his neck.
- There's a trail of blood leading from the broken window, into the department store—a trail about four-feet-long; which would mean that the victim's body necessarily must have struck the window with a tremendous force, in order to propel the lost blood an additional four feet from the point of impact.
- Plus, there's a two-foot high ledge that our victim would have had to leap-frog over, in order to get into the proper position to go through the window.
- And the victim's body is found 50-feet away from the window.

So, it doesn't take Sherlock Holmes to figure out this one, folks. Our victim obviously had a lot of "help" going through that plate-glass window at high speed; help in the form, most

---

[291] Gene Bell, "Widow of Mystery Suicide Links 4 Key Figures in JFK Assassination Plot," April 16, 1967, *National Enquirer*, cited in "The Death of Hank Killam – The Ultimate Cold Case," *The Education Forum*: http://educationforum.ipbhost.com/index.php?showtopic=9053

[292] Thomas Porter, "Officials Blast Theory of Suicide in Death of Man Who Claimed He Knew Too Much," April 16, 1967, *National Enquirer*, cited in "The Death of Hank Killam – The Ultimate Cold Case," *The Education Forum*: http://educationforum.ipbhost.com/index.php?showtopic=9053

[293] Ibid.

likely, of at least one guy on each arm, propelling him through that window, probably for the purpose of disguising the manner in which his already slashed throat had been slashed.

We also found out what the victim may have been running from. While researching another death, we came across this important link back to Hank Killam:

William "Bill" Waters died on May 20, 1967. Police said he died of a drug overdose (Demerol). No autopsy was performed. His mother said Oswald and Killam came to her home before the assassination and her son tried to talk Oswald and Killam out of being involved. Waters called FBI agents after the assassination. The FBI told him he knew too much and to keep his mouth shut.[294]

And Killam has been traced to New Orleans where DA Jim Garrison contended that three men, including Lee Harvey Oswald, planned the Kennedy killing.

Hank Killam was in and out of New Orleans during September, October, and November of 1963.

He is also listed in police files there.[295]

CONCLUSIONS BASED ON EVIDENTIARY INDICATIONS

Murder: Definitely linked to JFK assassination. Victim's fears were very realistic and he even correctly predicted his own murder.

More than any other death we investigated in this book, the death of Hank Killam was not only suspicious, but was rather a blatant case of harassment and then murder, due to some extremely sensitive information which the victim quite obviously possessed. Hank actually <u>knew</u> that he was going to be killed as a result of certain knowledge he possessed about individuals, related to the JFK assassination. He didn't think he was going to be killed; he knew he was. He was even aware that there was nothing he could do about it, presumably due to the "high nature" of the people who wanted him dead. At the end, he gave up running. Shortly afterward, he received a three-inch gash on his neck that severed his jugular vein and was then apparently thrown through a plate-glass window to make that appear to be the cause of death.

Hank Killam's brother deserves and gets the last word on this case:

My brother was scared.

He may not have been important to the Warren Commission but he sure was important to someone.[296]

---

[294] Penn Jones, Jr., "Disappearing Witnesses," Jan 1984, *The Rebel* magazine: http://www.maebrussell.com/Disappearing%20Witnesses/Disappearing%20Witnesses.html
[295] Thomas Porter, "Officials Blast Theory of Suicide in Death of Man Who Claimed He Knew Too Much," April 16, 1967, *National Enquirer*, cited in "The Death of Hank Killam – The Ultimate Cold Case," *The Education Forum*: http://educationforum.ipbhost.com/index.php?showtopic=9053
[296] Roberts & Armstrong, *The Dead Witnesses*, 9.

Victim	**Veteran CIA agent, Gary Underhill**
Cause of Death	Gunshot behind left ear
Official Verdict	Suicide
Actual Circumstances	Like Hank Killam, Underhill was clearly running for his life. *Also* like Killam, his fears were very well-founded; he predicted his own murder, and he was murdered very soon after.
Inconsistencies	1. Underhill was right-handed and it would be extremely awkward—not to mention totally pointless—for a right-handed person to commit suicide by shooting themselves behind the left ear. 2. As an experienced CIA operative, if Underhill expressed concerns that his life was in danger, there are concrete reasons to believe those fears were valid. 3. Immediately after the assassination of President Kennedy, Underhill "put two and two together;" he knew exactly "who did it" and he also even knew that "they knew he knew." Therefore, hours after the assassination, he fled Washington in fear of his life. When he got to New York, he was very specific in the reasons and warnings he gave to a close friend (see text below). He knew he would be killed—and was.

Like Hank Killam, Gary Underhill seemed to be acutely aware—"certain" would actually be the correct word—that people were trying to kill him as a direct result of knowledge he possessed about the JFK assassination.

As Underhill succinctly summarized his situation to a close friend:

I know who they are.

That's the problem.

They know I know.[297]

For the above reason, Underhill firmly believed he was a "loose end" who needed to be "taken care of." And then he was.

There's very good reason to believe that Underhill knew *exactly* what he was talking about. He had a long career as a covert agent with U.S. Intelligence which is very well documented. Some of the "official version" backers have tried to paint the picture that there's no evidence that Underhill was a CIA agent,[298] but experienced researchers and JFK authors like James DiEugenio have thoroughly disproven those bogus attempts. Gary Underhill was indeed a veteran U.S. Intelligence agent.

Here are the facts of the matter:

> Posner writes that there is no source for the claim that Gary Underhill was a former CIA agent, and "no corroboration that he ever said there was CIA complicity in the assassination." I hate to plug my own work, but in *Destiny Betrayed*, Posner would have learned there are several sources for Underhill's wartime OSS career and his later CIA consulting status, including Underhill himself. As for his accusations about the CIA and the murder of JFK, he related them quite vividly to his friend Charlene Fitsimmons within twenty-four hours of the shooting. She then forwarded a letter to Jim Garrison relating the incident in detail.[299]

So, the pertinent question here would be whom exactly was Underhill talking about when he used the word "they" in "I know who they are" and "They know I know." Well, not to put words in someone else's mouth, this is exactly the way that Gary Underhill described his problem to his friend, Charlene Fitsimmons, after he fled Washington, D.C. in imminent fear for his life. And keep in mind that this was *mere hours* after the assassination of President Kennedy—Underhill immediately panicked, got into a car, and feeling he had to immediately get out of Washington, drove to the home of a friend whom he knew he could trust in Long Island, New York.

This is exactly what he told her:

> This country is too dangerous for me. I've got to get on a boat. Oswald is a patsy. They set him up. It's too much. The bastards have done something

[297] Paul Golais, April 8, 2001, *The Citizen's Voice*: http://www.spartacus.schoolnet.co.uk/JFKunderhillG.htm
[298] Gerald Posner, *Case Closed* (: 1993).
[299] James DiEugenio, "Review of Gerald Posner's book, *Case Closed*": http://www.spartacus.schoolnet.co.uk/JFKunderhillG.htm

outrageous. They've killed the president! I've been listening and hearing things. I couldn't believe they'd get away with it, but they did. They've gone mad! They're a bunch of drug runners and gun runners—a real violence group. I know who they are. That's the problem. They know I know. That's why I'm here.'[300]

Veteran CIA agent, Gary Underhill, told his friends that he was running for his life because he knew who conspired against JFK and "They know I know."

What Underhill was specifically describing was a special group within the CIA that was involved in drugs and gunrunning to Southeast Asia. He *really did* know who they were.

Underhill also said that "the Kennedy murder wasn't as cut and dried as it might appear." According to the friend, "Underhill said that he knew the people involved (and that they knew he knew) and he fled Washington for his life." He indicated that "A small clique in the CIA were responsible" who "were conducting a lucrative business in the Far East" in "gunrunning and other contraband, manipulating political intrigue to serve their ends." Underhill told his friend "Kennedy had gotten wind of something going on so he was killed before he could blow the whistle."[301]

Historian John Simkin summarized the key point that Underhill had put together:

Underhill believed there was a connection between Executive Action, Fidel Castro, and the death of Kennedy: "They tried it in Cuba and they couldn't

---

300 Paul Golais, April 8, 2001, *The Citizen's Voice*: http://www.spartacus.schoolnet.co.uk/JFKunderhillG.htm
301 Gary Richard Schoener, "A Legacy of Fear," May 2000, *Fair Play Magazine*: http://www.spartacus.schoolnet.co.uk/JFKunderhillG.htm

get away with it. Right after the Bay of Pigs, but Kennedy wouldn't let them do it. And now he'd gotten wind of this and he was really going to blow the whistle on them. And they killed him![302]

Executive Action was a special highly secret CIA and Military Intelligence unit that was attempting assassinate Cuban leader Fidel Castro. It has been suggested that President Kennedy was actually killed by a "turnaround" operation from that unit.

CONCLUSIONS BASED ON EVIDENTIARY INDICATIONS
Murder: Definitely linked to JFK assassination. Victim's fears were very realistic and he even correctly predicted his own murder.

---

[302] John Simkin, "Gary Underhill: Biography," http://www.spartacus.schoolnet.co.uk/JFKunderhillG.htm

Guy Banister,
June 6, 1964

Victim	**Guy Banister, Private Investigator**
Cause of Death	Heart Attack
Official Verdict	Natural Causes
Inconsistencies	Banister, former head of the FBI Chicago office, was a rabid anti-communist in general and anti-Castroist in particular. He developed a huge and intricate filing system on Communist activities and all his files disappeared after his death, apparently having been seized by authorities unknown.

> No inconsistencies in his death are apparent, except for the virtually impossible coincidence that every witness connected to the Guy Banister aspect of the case—including Guy Banister himself—suddenly died just prior to their being sought in the investigation of their connections to Lee Harvey Oswald; see text below, as well as the following entries for Hugh Ward, Deslesseps Morrison, Maurice Gatlin, and David Ferrie.

As historian John Simkin observed, Banister is a key link in the JFK assassination, and closely associated with two other key players, David Ferrie and New Orleans Mafia Boss Carlos Marcello, for whom Ferrie worked as pilot and private investigator:

> In 1963, Banister and David Ferrie began working for the lawyer G. Wray Gill and his client, Carlos Marcello. Later, Banister was linked to the plot to assassinate John F. Kennedy. On August 9, 1963, Lee Harvey Oswald distributed leaflets that supported Fidel Castro and his government in Cuba. On these leaflets was the address 544 Camp Street, New Orleans. This was also the office of Carlos Bringuier, an anti-Castro exile.[303]

The office referenced above led investigators to Guy Banister, because his detective agency was virtually part of the same office; technically around the corner at a different street address but, realistically, in the same building and right next door.

> Around the corner from 544 Camp Street, located in the same building, was 531 Lafayette Street, which housed the detective agency run by Banister. This raised suspicions that Oswald had been involved in a right-wing conspiracy to kill Kennedy.[304]

Jack Martin was a private investigator employed by Banister, who eventually confided in District Attorney Garrison:

> ...Martin told friends that Banister and David Ferrie had been involved in the assassination of John F. Kennedy. According to Martin, Ferrie was the getaway man whose job it was to fly the assassin out of Texas. He also claimed that Ferrie knew Lee Harvey Oswald from their days in the New Orleans Civil Air Patrol and had given him lessons on how to use a rifle with a telescopic sight.[305]

Ferrie became a very popular witness, sought for interviews, first, by the FBI, and then very seriously investigated by Jim Garrison.

---

[303] John Simkin, "Guy Banister: Biography," *Spartacus Educational*, accessed 17 Oct. 2012: http://www.spartacus.schoolnet.co.uk/JFKbannister.htm

[304] Ibid.

[305] John Simkin, "Jack Martin: Biography," *Spartacus Educational*, accessed 25 Nov. 2012: http://www.spartacus.schoolnet.co.uk/JFKmartinJ.htm

On November 25 (three days after the assassination), Martin was contacted by the Federal Bureau of Investigation. He told them that he thought Ferrie had hypnotized Oswald into assassinating Kennedy.[306]

David Ferrie was indeed a highly accomplished hypnotist, and that has been established.

This information eventually reached Jim Garrison, the district attorney of New Orleans. He interviewed Martin about these accusations. Martin claimed that during the summer of 1963, Jim Garrison now became convinced that a group of right-wing activists, including Banister, David Ferrie, Carlos Bringuier, and Clay Shaw, were involved in a conspiracy with the CIA to kill John F. Kennedy. Garrison claimed this was in retaliation for his attempts to obtain a peace settlement with Cuba and Vietnam.[307]

The links between Oswald and Banister have been established. They weren't just the matter of Oswald's pamphlets having been stored in Banister's office, as some apologists for the Warren Commission have made it out to be.[308] Oswald had been in Banister's office and had also been seen in Banister's company, and the two quite obviously knew each other.

Delphine Roberts worked for Banister and later became his mistress. Roberts told Anthony Summers that during the summer of 1963 Lee Harvey Oswald worked for Banister. She said she was in the office when Banister suggested that Oswald should establish a local *Fair Play for Cuba Committee*. This story was supported by her daughter, who met Oswald during this period.[309]

Former FBI agent and author, William Turner, being a cautious investigator, was at first skeptical of those who noted the convenient deaths associated with the JFK assassination witnesses. But he was eventually swayed by the impossible series of "coincidences":

As I sat in Garrison's office discussing the fates of Banister, Ward, and Gatlin, my mind flashed back to the previous November when *Ramparts* had run a story on the "mysterious deaths" theory of doughty Texas editor Penn Jones Jr. . . . The mysterious-deaths article so fascinated Walter Cronkite that he sent a film crew to Midlothian for a CBS News series on Jones. Although the theory caught on as "evidence" of a conspiracy, I was bemusedly skeptical.

But the untimely deaths of Banister, Ward and Gatlin gave me pause that there might in fact have been systematic elimination of people who knew too much.[310]

---

[306] Ibid.
[307] Ibid.
[308] "The 'Sinister' Stack of Leaflets Found in Guy Banister's Files" and other articles at the website of John McAdams are obvious attempts to minimize the impact of strong conspiratorial evidence in the JFK assassination: Accessed 12 Oct 2012: http://mcadams.posc.mu.edu/jimlie8.htm
[309] Simkin, "Guy Banister: Biography"
[310] William W. Turner, *Rearview Mirror: Looking Back at the FBI, the CIA and Other Tails* (Penmarin Books: 2001).

After Banister, Ward, and Gatlin, Turner then went on to note the extremely convenient death of David Ferrie, two months earlier. Ferrie was considered a key piece of the whole JFK assassination puzzle by District Attorney Garrison.

So Banister was already dead by the time that Garrison figured out the Oswald-Banister connections, but it's very interesting to note that right after Banister died, his office was ransacked after his death and that his files were also missing.

After Banister's death, Jack Martin, who had been one of Banister's private investigators, was visibly nervous when District Attorney Jim Garrison asked about the connections to the assassination.

The following is straight from Garrison himself, regarding his interview of Jack Martin about the goings-on at Banister's office in the period prior to the JFK assassination:

Martin: There was Dave Ferrie—you know about him by now.

Garrison: Was he there very often?

Martin: Often? He practically lived there.

Garrison: And Lee Harvey Oswald?

Martin: Yeah, he was there too. Sometimes he'd be meeting with Guy Banister with the door shut. Other times he'd be shooting the bull with Dave Ferrie. But he was there all right.

Garrison: What was Guy Banister doing while all this was going on?

Martin: Hell, he was the one running the circus.

Garrison: What about his private detective work?

Martin: Not much of that came in, but when it did, I handled it. That's why I was there.

Garrison: So, Jack. Just what was going on at Banister's office?

Martin: I can't answer that. I can't go into that stuff at all. I think I'd better go.

Garrison: Hold on, Jack. What's the problem with our going into what was happening at Banister's office?

Martin: *What's the problem? What's the problem?* The *problem* is that we're going to bring the goddamned federal government down on our backs. Do I need to spell it out? I could get killed—and so could you.[311]

---

[311] Jim Garrison, *On the Trail of the Assassins: My Investigation and Prosecution of the Murder of President Kennedy* (Sheridan Square: 1988)

In yet another incredibly convenient coincidence, the sudden deaths of everyone linked to Guy Banister—as well as Guy Banister *himself*—made it impossible for investigators to determine the extent of his obvious involvement in matters pertaining to the assassination of President Kennedy, especially the process of setting up Lee Harvey Oswald.

According to some investigators:

> **Banister's office was ransacked and some files went missing after his death.**[312]

Not only was Banister dead but, as Garrison quickly learned—and as the next entries in this book will show—everyone who was sought in relation to Banister and his affiliations were *also* the victims of recent sudden death: Hugh Ward, who was Banister's private investigator; Deslesseps Morrison, who was the Mayor of New Orleans; and Maurice Gatlin, an attorney who was Legal Counsel to the far right-wing "Minutemen" group with which Banister was closely associated.

As we shall soon see, yet another key witness, David Ferrie, died suddenly at the exact same time that he was being sought as an extremely important witness by the Jim Garrison investigation. So at the very first serious post-Warren Commission look at the circumstances surrounding the JFK assassination, all the key witnesses died very suddenly.

---

[312] John Beckam, "Unusual Deaths," 2 Jan. 2009, *JFK Murder Solved Forum*: http://forum.jfkmurdersolved.com/viewtopic.php?f=1&t=983

18–19

Hugh Ward,
May 22, 1964
Deslesseps Morrison,
May 22, 1964

Victims	Deslesseps Morrison, Mayor of New Orleans and Hugh Ward, Private Investigator
Cause of Death	Plane crash
Official Verdict	Accident
Inconsistencies	None apparent, except for the virtually impossible coincidence that every witness connected to the same aspect of the case had suddenly died just prior to their being sought in the investigation by District Attorney Jim Garrison; see text below.

Hugh Ward was a private investigator who worked directly with two people at the main nucleus of the JFK assassination: Guy Banister and David Ferrie. Banister and Ferrie were at the nexus of events that set up the assassination of President Kennedy and the set-up of Lee Harvey Oswald as the "apparent" assassin.

Deslesseps Morrison was the Mayor of New Orleans who was—as one would expect—involved in a large number of dealings. However, it's interesting to note that New Orleans was in many ways the center-staging location for the assassination in Dallas. New Orleans was home base to Mafia boss Carlos Marcello, David Ferrie, Dr. Mary Sherman, and Lee Harvey Oswald.

Although there is not much known about the deaths of New Orleans Mayor Deslesseps Morrison and Hugh Ward, it is known that the incredibly uncanny deaths of several key witnesses certainly stretches incredulity to a fair-minded investigator. The significance of those conveniently disappearing witnesses was not lost on District Attorney Garrison, or former FBI agent William Turner, who was on Garrison's investigative staff.

As William Turner noted in his book, *Rearview Mirror*, all roads investigating Lee Harvey Oswald seemed to lead to Guy Banister—and everyone connected to the two of them seemed to have died a recent and untimely death:

> I walked over to 531 Lafayette Place. There was no inscription on the door denoting it as Banister's business, only a realtor's shingle and a sticker of the then-nascent Republican Party of Louisiana. The door opened to stairs leading to a second-floor space that was unoccupied. Diagonally across the space was a second set of stairs, which led down to a door on Camp Street. The number over the door read "594." 594 Camp Street was the return address Lee Harvey Oswald had stamped on the first batch of pro-Castro literature he handed out on the streets of the Crescent City in August 1963—Subsequent batches bore a post office box number, suggesting that the use of the street address had been a lapse. What was Oswald's connection to Banister?[313]

Experience as an FBI agent helped William Turner focus the key players when he became an investigator for District Attorney Garrison:

> When I reported the Camp Street discovery to Garrison, I recommended that we assign priority to interviewing Banister. Too late, he said, Banister had been found dead in bed in June 1964, his pearl handled, monogrammed .357 Magnum revolver at his side. Although there was no autopsy, his demise was attributed to a heart attack. But Jerry Milton Brooks, who had done some clipping and filing for Banister in 1962, had identified his deputy, Hugh F. Ward, as also belonging to the Minutemen as well as an outfit called the Anti-Communism League of the Caribbean, which was headed by Banister after he came to New Orleans in 1955. Brooks credited the ACLC with helping the CIA overthrow the leftist Arbenz government in Guatemala, opening the way for a succession of rightist strongmen. The ACLC continued to act as an intermediary between the CIA and right-wing insurgency movements in the Caribbean, including Cuba after Castro gained power.[314]

Turner noted with concern that every witness he sought in connection to Banister had already been eliminated from the investigatory landscape:

> There was a chance that Ward would be willing to talk, but it turned out he was gone as well. On May 23, 1965, he was at the controls of a Piper Aztec chartered by former New Orleans mayor Deslesseps Morrison when the craft, engines sputtering, crashed on a fog-shrouded hill near Ciudad Victoria, Mexico, killing all on board. That left Maurice Brooks Gatlin, Sr.,

---

[313] Turner, *Rearview Mirror.*
[314] Ibid.

an attorney associated with Banister, on Brooks's list of key Minutemen in Louisiana. According to Jerry Milton Brooks, Gatlin served as legal counsel to the ACLC. In fact, Brooks had been a kind of protégé of Gatlin. The attorney's passport was stamped with visas of countries around the world. In Brooks's estimation, he was a "transporter" for the CIA. On one occasion Gatlin bodaciously told Brooks, "I have pretty good connections. Stick with me—I'll give you a license to kill." Brooks became a firm believer in 1962 when Gatlin displayed a thick wad of bills, saying he had $100,000 of CIA money earmarked for a French reactionary clique planning to assassinate General de Gaulle. Shortly thereafter Gatlin flew to Paris, and shortly after that came the Secret Army Organization's abortive ambush of the French president. But Gatlin as well was beyond Garrison's reach. In 1964 he fell or was pushed from the sixth floor of the Panama Hotel in Panama, dying instantly.[315]

Below, the crash of their Aztec model airplane is described in detail:

As the aircraft headed south, the weather worsened. By 6:00 p.m., pockets of rain storms dotted the area, and Ward had to detour his course slightly to avoid building thunderheads. Still, Ward was a capable pilot and there was plenty of fuel on board to divert his route of flight as needed.[316]

The important point above is that Craig Roberts, an *extremely* capable pilot who is very qualified to make that determination, just noted that Ward was a "capable pilot."

But something went wrong. The Aztec, flying south on instruments along the Gulf coast, was heard flying somewhere above by ranch hands at La Guajolote Ranch east of Ciudad Victoria—then change engine sounds as it flew overhead. According to the *caballeros*, the engines began to sputter and cough as the plane circled, apparently looking for a way down through the clouds. Fifteen minutes later, at approximately 6:15 p.m., the Aztec broke out through the low overcast and slammed into the ground, skipped, then skidded 200 feet to the edge of a small gorge. By the time rescuers could reach the wreckage, there was no one left alive to rescue.

The unusual factor to this "accident" is that *both* engines failed at the same time, with over three hours of useable fuel still on board.[317]

---

[315] Ibid.
[316] Roberts & Armstrong, *The Dead Witnesses*
[317] Roberts & Armstrong, *The Dead Witnesses*, emphasis in original.

20 | Maurice Gatlin, Esq., May 28, 1965

Victim	Maurice Brooks Gatlin, Attorney: Legal Counsel to "Minutemen"; also associated with Guy Banister.
Cause of Death	Heart attack and fall from sixth-story balcony.
Official Verdict	Natural Causes
Inconsistencies	1. While attending a meeting of the Inter-American Bar Association in San Juan, Puerto Rico, Mr. Gatlin reportedly suffered a heart attack and then fell over the ledge of a 6th floor balcony. No one is sure how exactly that happened and there is no other information available.[318] 2. Gatlin was another key witness sought by the investigation of District Attorney, Jim Garrison; see text below.

Maurice Brooks Gatlin was a well-connected attorney who was a fervent anti-Communist in league with private investigator Guy Banister and many others strongly associated with anti-Castro efforts.

Gatlin was legal counsel to the "Minutemen"—an extremely conservative group that was being investigated by New Orleans District Attorney Jim Garrison, because it was also suspected of being linked to the JFK assassination.

---

[318] *New Orleans Times-Picayune*, May 31, 1965, Page One: http://www.jfk-online.com/jpsgatobit.html

Another item of note we located was that—in addition to his association with Guy Banister, a man linked by many to the plotting of the JFK assassination, as well as the set-up of Lee Harvey Oswald as the patsy—Gatlin was also linked to others who have been mentioned as playing roles in the murder of JFK. Gatlin was also involved with the covert dealings of longtime CIA agent, E. Howard Hunt, and Mafia boss, Carlos Marcello:

> Hunt had extensive connections to organized crime, especially the national syndicate said to have been run by Seymour Weiss of the Standard Fruit Company (the sponsor of the Guatemalan coup) and Mafia kingpin Carlos Marcello. In 1958, Hunt organized an "anti-communist" conference in Guatemala. The conference chairman was Antonio Valladores, Marcello's attorney in New Orleans. Also present at the meeting was Maurice Gatlin, whose office at 544 Camp Street was, in the CIA shell-game investigated by Jim Garrison, a base of operations for the Kennedy assassination.[319]

> It was Gatlin who served as bag man for Banister, Clay Shaw—and the CIA—when the "transporter" carried a suitcase full of $100,000 in cash to Paris for the OAS. The money was to be used by the Organization to assassinate Charles de Gaulle on one of the many attempts the right-wing group of former French army and foreign legion officers made against the French president's life.

> Jerry Milton Brooks, a former Minuteman who worked for Banister, said that Maurice Gatlin often bragged about his dual life. "I have pretty good connections," Gatlin told Brooks, "Stick with me—and I'll give you a license to kill." Brooks later stated that he had seen Gatlin's passport, and that it "was filled with stamps of airports all over the world."

> Gatlin, due to his movements as a "transporter" for the CIA, and his intimate knowledge of the goings-on at 544 Camp Street, must have become a liability. For in May of 1964, before he could be located by the Warren Commission, he was pushed or jumped from the sixth floor of the El Panama Hotel in Panama City.[320]

When looked at in its full perspective, those pregnant words of that former FBI agent, William Turner, seem somewhat haunting:

> But the untimely deaths of Banister, Ward, and Gatlin gave me pause that there might in fact have been systematic elimination of people who knew too much.[321]

---

[319] Alex Constantine, *Psychic Dictatorship in the U.S.A.*, (Feral House: 1995): http://www.spartacus.schoolnet.co.uk/JFKcaddyD.htm
[320] Roberts & Armstrong, *The Dead Witnesses*
[321] Turner, *Rearview Mirror*

Victim	**Earlene Roberts, landlady at the rooming house in Dallas where Lee Harvey Oswald lived.**
Cause of Death	Heart Attack
Official Verdict	Natural Causes
Inconsistencies	1. As we report below, Mrs. Roberts was so harassed by the authorities that her relatives believed her health was ruined by it. So even if her heart attack was from natural causes, one might say it was still caused by her relationship to the JFK assassination.

Earlene Roberts was a nurse, but when she became diabetic, gave up her nursing career and began renting out rooms at her home in the Oak Cliff section of Dallas. She was an intelligent and confident woman, and a very good witness.

On October 14, 1963, she rented one of the rooms in her home to Lee Harvey Oswald; however, it was under a different name. Oswald rented the room under the name "O. H. Lee," a composite of his name.

Earlene Roberts was a very important witness, and the authorities were not happy about what she had to say. She testified that a friend called her at about 1:00 p.m. and informed her of the assassination of President Kennedy. She immediately turned on her television set in the downstairs room and then Oswald came through the door and rushed by her, going to his room in quite a hurry.

Earlene Roberts was sure she saw and heard a police car stop and honk outside Oswald's room, right after the assassination.

While Oswald was in his room, a police car from the Dallas Police Department pulled up outside the house and stopped in front of it. Mrs. Roberts was no "namby-pamby"—she was a confident witness whose testimony reveals with certainty *exactly* what she saw:

Mr. Ball: Did a police car pass the house there and honked?

Mrs. Roberts: Yes.

Mr. Ball: When was that?

Mrs. Roberts: He came in the house.

Mr. Ball: When he came in the house?

Mrs. Roberts: When he came in the house and went to his room, you know how the sidewalk runs?

Mr. Ball: Yes.

Mrs. Roberts: Right direct in front of that door—there was a police car stopped and honked. I had worked for some police-men and sometimes they come by and tell me some-thing that maybe their wives would want me to know, and I thought it was them, and I just glanced out and saw the number, and I said, "Oh, that's not their car," for I knew their car.

Mr. Ball: You mean, it was not the car of the policemen you knew?

Mrs. Roberts: It wasn't the police car I knew, because their number was 170 and it wasn't 170 and I ignored it.

Mr. Ball: And who was in the car?

Mrs. Roberts: I don't know—I didn't pay any attention to it after I noticed it wasn't them—I didn't.

Mr. Ball: Where was it parked?

Mrs. Roberts: It was parked in front of the house.[322]

Mrs. Roberts went on to testify that the number she saw on the police car was "106" and that shortly after the police car honked, Oswald then left the house. That posed a serious problem for authorities to explain, because the Dallas Police Department denied that they had any cars in that area, anywhere near the time of 1:00 p.m. on November 22, 1963.[323]

Her testimony posed further problems, because the time frame in which she placed Oswald leaving her home made it very difficult for him to have been at the scene of the murder of Officer J. D. Tippit a few minutes later. She saw Oswald waiting at the bus stop outside, after he'd left her house. A couple minutes later, Officer Tippit was shot dead and Oswald was accused of that crime. But the Tippit crime scene was over a mile away and it was established that no buses had come by during that time frame, in the direction of Officer Tippit's slaying.[324]

So what happened as a result of those disparities between her testimony and the "official version" of events, one might ask?

After testifying in Dallas in April of 1964, Mrs. Roberts was subjected to intensive police harassment. They visited her at all hours of the day and night, contacted her employers and identified her as the Oswald rooming house lady. As a result, she was dismissed from three housekeeping and nursing jobs in April, May, and June of 1964 alone; no telling how many jobs she lost after that.[325]

It's actually fair to say that Mrs. Roberts was probably driven to her death by all the harassment:

Relatives report that right up until her death a year and a half later, Earlene complained of being "worried to death'" by the police.[326]

As Earlene herself put it:

Every time I would walk out on the front porch somebody was standing with a camera on me—they had me scared to death.[327]

---

[322] *The Warren Commission*, "Testimony of Mrs. Earlene Roberts," Interviewed by Joseph A. Ball, April 8, 1964: http://jfkassassination.net/russ/testimony/robertse.htm
[323] John Simkin, "Earlene Roberts: Biography," accessed 22 Oct 2012: http://www.spartacus.schoolnet.co.uk/JFKrobertsE2.htm
[324] David Welsh, "In the Shadow of Dallas: The Legacy of Penn Jones, Jr.," *Ramparts Magazine*, November 1966, pp 39-50: http://www.unz.org/Pub/Ramparts-1966nov-00039
[325] Ibid.
[326] Ibid.
[327] Testimony of Mrs. Earlene Roberts to the Warren Commission, April 8, 1964, Dallas, Texas: http://www.history-matters.com/archive/jfk/wc/wcvols/wh6/pdf/WH6_Roberts.pdf

CONCLUSIONS BASED ON EVIDENTIARY INDICATIONS

- The case very clearly relates to the JFK assassination and was yet another very obvious case of The Powers That Be intimidating and harassing a key witness because their testimony did not fit the official version of events.
- As far as her death, it appears to have actually been a heart attack, so it's virtually impossible to determine the cause, but her relatives noted her deteriorating health as a direct result of the intense harassment from which she suffered.

CONCLUSION

Death: Probably the result of "natural" causes, but another clear case of obvious and intentional witness intimidation, which appears to have actually led to her death.

22 | Al "Guy" Bogard, February 15, 1966

Victim	**Al Bogard**
Cause of Death	Carbon monoxide poisoning
Official Verdict	Suicide
Actual Circumstances	Bogard witnessed "Oswald" where the "real" Oswald could not have been. He was subjected to harassment but appears to have been depressed and taken his own life.
Inconsistencies	None, yet many . . . see below.

Al Bogard was the car salesman who witnessed Lee Harvey Oswald—or an Oswald impersonator—test-driving a car at high speeds. That was significant because the "real" Oswald reportedly could not drive. It seemed like a set-up to establish something about Oswald's history—referred to in intelligence parlance as creating a "legend"—because the person also made the specific point of talking about Russia and telling Bogard, in no uncertain terms, that he could not afford the car at the moment but was expecting to come into a large sum of money in the very near future. He also specifically made the comment—loud enough for others to hear and recall—that maybe he would have to go back to Russia to get a car.

So Bogard remembered writing the name down on a business card: "Lee Oswald"— and when he heard Oswald's name on television as a suspect in the assassination, he was sure it was the same Oswald and he then tossed the card in the garbage. The FBI heard about that and was very interested, raising the question "WHY?"

> The real Bogard question is why did the FBI go thru a trash dumpster to find a Bogard business card on which HE wrote the name "Lee Oswald"? If Oswald had written it, maybe it would matter. But it just makes no sense, except that the FBI left no garbage dumpsters unchecked.[328]

We figured out why the FBI was probably so "interested" in that business card with Oswald's name on it. It was very clearly established that the "real" Oswald was somewhere else at that day and time. But the card was actual physical proof that someone impersonating Oswald was at the Downtown Lincoln-Mercury dealership at the same time. Historian Walt Brown offers a plausible explanation for what actually transpired:

> Oswald (the one with Marina and Ruth Paine) was clearly alibied for the afternoon of November 9, again shouting imposter. The business card that Bogard wrote the name of "Lee Oswald" on was the hard evidence of the impostor.

> And that is why Lawrence called it in. And it also explains why FBI agents combed through the dumpster in search of the card—it was "hard evidence."

> Without the card, (as we know from other instances where real evidence was flim-flammed or else people saw things but were wrong), it could easily have been stated that Bogard was wrong. He had actually waited on a customer named, for instance, "Lou Osborne," and in the confusion and tragedy of the moment, he mistook "Lee Oswald" for "Lou Osborne," who, amazingly, bore a striking resemblance to Lee Oswald.

> The card would prevent this, and therefore, Lawrence called it in and the FBI looked high and low.

> But they didn't find the card—or so they would have us believe, and Bogard was subjected to Nosenko-like interviews, including one in the cells of the Dallas jail, prior to his "suicide" in February of 1966.[329]

The mention of "Nosenko" was in reference to a brutal interrogation of a Russian spy, suspected of being a double agent. There was so much obfuscation and elimination of unwanted evidence that Walt Brown titled his book *The Warren Omission*, in reference to that.

> After the JFK assassination when the case obviously should have been investigated to determine what witnesses *actually* saw, instead, those interviews were obviously structured to *avoid* certain facts and are noteworthy for what they did *not* cover. There were "clearly-orchestrated interviews"

---

[328] Walt Brown, Ph.D., 26 Oct 2012, email to author.
[329] Walt Brown, Ph.D., "Jack Lawrence: A Patriot for All Seasons," *JFK/Deep Politics Quarterly*, Volume 15 #2, January 2010, page 10, emphasis in original.

conducted by the FBI (nobody asked where they thought the shots came from).[330]

Attempts by authorities to marginalize certain individuals should also be highly suspicious in their own right. For example, the FBI clearly attempted to marginalize the testimony of Arnold Rowland, who told them that, with certainty, he saw a man in the 6th floor window of the School Book Depository whom he <u>could not</u> identify as Oswald.

> What Rowland **did not see** was an identifiable Lee Oswald with the gun. . . . Because he didn't see that which had to BE seen, the FBI sent a bevy of agents scurrying to interview anyone who would state for the record that Rowland had a nasty habit of lying or making things up for the sake of getting attention.[331]

> Yet, if Rowland *had* wanted attention, he could have made himself instantly famous by simply telling the FBI what they had wanted to hear; that it was possible that it could have been Oswald whom he saw with the rifle. To his credit, he didn't—because he knew it was not true.

> I know of no other instance where the investigating agency, in this case, the FBI investigating a state crime, went to the trouble of checking out the honesty quotient of any OTHER witnesses—just the one who saw something he should not have seen.

> So he's a liar and he didn't see it.[332]

Bogard was maligned in much the same manner, albeit rougher and more blatant.

> Bogard was not asked to describe the man he saw, because he "positively identified him." He wasn't taken to a lineup, and subsequent to this, he was given a lie-detector test. He was also beaten severely by individuals unknown, and re-interviewed by the FBI several times, including an interview held in the Dallas Police Department jail cells, on the date of September 17, 1964, when the Warren Report was being printed.[333]

It's not clear what exactly drove Bogard to commit suicide. It is clear that he was bullied around by the FBI and that—as he himself put it—"people were out to get him."[334]

---

330 Walt Brown, Ph.D., "The 'Who's Who' of the Texas School Book Depository," *JFK/Deep Politics Quarterly*, Volume 15 #1, October 2009, page 36.

331 Walt Brown, Ph.D., "TMWMTM: (The Men Who Missed The Money: Parts I,II) Arnold Rowland and Albert Guy Bogard," *JFK/Deep Politics Quarterly*, Volume 15 #1, October 2009, page 21, emphasis in original.

332 Ibid, page 21, emphasis in original.

333 Ibid, page 24.

334 John McAdams' phone interview with Harper on June 1, 2001: "Dead in the Wake of the Kennedy Assassination, Albert Guy Bogard: Mysterious Death?": http://mcadams.posc.mu.edu/death14.htm

They searched high and low, like an episode of *CSI*, to find that business card, but they never found it.

Instead, they found Bogard by the side of the road. "Graveyard dead."[335]

CONCLUSIONS BASED ON EVIDENTIARY INDICATIONS

- It appears that Bogard did indeed commit suicide.
- Bogard's first cousin, Jimmy Harper, found the body. Although he did not provide information indicating death by something other than suicide, his cousin *did* say that Bogard "knew that people were out to get him, and may have taken his own life for that reason."[336]

CONCLUSIONS

Suicide: Possibly the result of being pursued and/or harassed by unknown parties.

---

[335] Walt Brown, Ph.D., "TMWMTM: (The Men Who Missed The Money: Parts I,II) Arnold Rowland and Albert Guy Bogard," *JFK/Deep Politics Quarterly*, Volume 15 #1, October 2009, page 24, emphasis in original.

[336] John McAdams' phone interview with Harper on June 1, 2001: "Dead in the Wake of the Kennedy Assassination, Albert Guy Bogard: Mysterious Death?": http://mcadams.posc.mu.edu/death14.htm

23 | Lee Bowers, August 9, 1966

Victim	**Lee Bowers**
Cause of Death	Wounds suffered in automobile crash
Official Verdict	Accidental
Inconsistencies	1. An eyewitness reported that Bowers' car was driven off the road by another car. 2. Bowers, who did not die immediately, is said to have reported to emergency personnel that he believed he had been drugged during his stop for coffee shortly before the crash.

Lee Bowers was a very important witness who was in a unique vantage point during the assassination and clearly reported seeing things that starkly contrasted with the official version of events.

> Lee Bowers' testimony is perhaps as explosive as any recorded by the Warren Commission. He was one of sixty-five known witnesses to the President's assassination who thought shots were fired from the area of the Grassy Knoll. (The Knoll is west of the Texas School Book Depository.) But more than that, he was in a unique position to observe some pretty strange behavior in the Knoll area during and immediately before the assassination.
>
> Bowers, then a tower man with the Union Terminal Co., was stationed in his 14-foot tower directly behind the Grassy Knoll. As he faced the assassination site, he could see the railroad overpass to his right front. Directly in front of him was a parking lot, and then a wooden stockade fence and a row of trees running along the top of the Grassy Knoll. The Knoll sloped down to the spot on Elm Street where Kennedy was killed. Police had "cut off" traffic into the parking area, Bowers said, "so that anyone moving around could actually be observed."[337]

What Bowers observed from that unique vantage point facing down upon the now infamous "grassy knoll" has fascinated JFK researchers for decades:

> Bowers made two significant observations which he revealed to the Commission. First, he saw three unfamiliar cars slowly cruising around the parking area in the thirty-five minutes before the assassination; the first two left after a few minutes. The driver of the second car appeared to be talking into "a mike or telephone"—"he was holding something up to his mouth with one hand and he was driving with the other." A third car, with out-of-state plates and mud up to the windows, probed all around the parking area. Bowers last remembered seeing it about eight minutes before the shooting, pausing "just above the assassination site." He gave detailed descriptions of the cars and their drivers.
>
> Bowers also observed two unfamiliar men standing on top of the Knoll at the edge of the parking lot, within 10 or 15 feet of each other . . ."one man, middle-aged or slightly older, fairly heavy-set, in a white shirt, fairly dark trousers. Another younger man, about mid-twenties in either a plaid shirt, plaid coat, or jacket." Both were facing toward Elm and Houston, where the motorcade would be coming from. They were the only strangers he remembered seeing.[338]

On August, 9, 1966, Lee Bowers was killed when his car left the road and crashed into a concrete abutment in Midlothian, Texas.

---

[337] Welsh, "In the Shadow of Dallas"
[338] Welsh, "In the Shadow of Dallas"

As it was reported in the book, *High Treason*:

> Lee Bowers was heading west on highway 67 from Midlothian down to Cleburne, and according to an eyewitness was driven off the road by a black car, sending him into a bridge abutment. He didn't die immediately; he held on for four hours, and during that time, was talking to the ambulance people and told them that he felt he had been drugged when he stopped for coffee back a few miles in Midlothian.[339]

According to the author, Penn Jones, Bowers began receiving death threats after testifying to the Warren Commission about what he had seen and after giving further evidence to attorney, Mark Lane.[340]

> Bowers widow at first insisted to Penn Jones that there was nothing suspicious about her husband's death. Then she became flustered and said: "They told him not to talk."[341]

Researcher David Welsh reported that the attending physician, who accompanied Bowers in the ambulance, "noticed something peculiar about the victim."[342]

> He was in a strange state of shock, a different kind of shock than an accident victim experiences. I can't explain it. I've never seen anything like it.[343]

There was no autopsy and, apparently, the body was cremated soon afterward.[344]

> Doctors saw no evidence that he had suffered a heart attack.[345]

The obvious question was asked by investigative reporter, Geraldo Rivera:

> But why would Lee Bowers have been killed when it seemed that he had already told all he knew?[346]

Well, there was, reportedly, a very good answer to that: The documentary stated that Bowers confided in his minister that he had seen "more than he had told publicly."

---

[339] Robert J. Groden & Harrison Edward Livingstone, *High Treason: The Assassination of JFK and the Case for Conspiracy* (Carroll & Graf: 1998)
[340] Penn Jones, Jr., "Disappearing Witnesses"
[341] Welsh, "In the Shadow of Dallas".
[342] Ibid.
[343] Ibid.
[344] Ibid.
[345] Ibid.
[346] Geraldo Rivera, "The Curse of JFK," May 6, 1992, *Now It Can Be Told*: http://www.youtube.com/watch?v=mcXJJsZs7LE

A friend of Bowers, Walter Rischel, told reporters that Bowers had been afraid to tell all that he actually witnessed during the JFK assassination. Rischel said that Bowers had confided him with information that was much more specific about the assassination, but that he was afraid to "go public" with it for some very good reasons.[347]

> Lee had disappeared for about two days—one night I know for sure—which was very uncharacteristic of him. And when he came back, one of his fingers was missing on one of his hands. So Lee gave Monty (his brother) some excuse for what had happened, which Monty didn't accept. So he called the local hospitals, the clinics, and some doctor's offices, and there was no record of anyone, certainly not Lee, going in and having that taken care of.[348]

Shortly afterward, he was killed in the mysterious auto accident.

Author Gerald Posner and researcher David Perry before him, have attempted to preclude the tale of Bowers' death as nothing more than sensationalism. As Posner put it, it was "conclusively proved" that Bowers' death was accidental.[349] Posner is apparently referring to the article by Mr. Perry, *Now It Can Be Told: The Lee Bowers Story*.[350] Posner and Perry are primarily referring to the criticisms of the investigatory work in a Geraldo Rivera documentary that investigates the death of Lee Bowers, and certain claims which were aired on the program.[351] Some of the criticisms of that program were very valid; others, in our opinion, were not. It is actually an excellent brief documentary that you can watch online: http://www.youtube.com/watch?v=mcXJJsZs7LE

There are contradictory claims concerning certain events related to the death which, at this point, seem irreconcilable. It is difficult, if not impossible, to now verify them either way with a sufficient degree of certainty. That's not all that unusual regarding a now relatively obscure event that occurred many decades ago. It is true and noteworthy that some of the claims surrounding the death are unsubstantiated and vague. Yet the fact that the truth apparently lies somewhere in the middle doesn't preclude Mr. Posner from stating that Mr. Perry "conclusively proved" that Bowers' death was accidental.[352] That would be convenient, but there's just one tiny little problem. It isn't actually true.

A former member of the Texas Highway Patrol, Charles Good, concluded that another car had indeed forced Bowers car off the road. He testified that eyewitness testimony confirmed that.[353]

Mr. Perry acknowledged that his investigation revealed that Charles Good was indeed a former member of the Texas Highway Patrol, "who claims to have investigated the accident" (apparently an attempt to minimize the investigatory skills of Mr. Good!),

---

[347] Ibid.
[348] Ibid.
[349] Gerald Posner, *Case Closed*
[350] David Perry, "Now It Can Be Told: The Lee Bowers Story," accessed 5 Nov 2012: http://mcadams.posc.mu.edu/bowers.txt
[351] Geraldo Rivera, "The Curse of JFK," May 6, 1992, *Now It Can Be Told*: http://www.youtube.com/watch?v=mcXJJsZs7LE
[352] Ibid.
[353] John Simkin, "Lee E. Bowers: Biography," accessed 5 Nov 2012: http://www.spartacus.schoolnet.co.uk/JFKbowers.htm

and did conclude that a car ran his friend, Lee Bowers, off the road.[354] But Mr. Perry couldn't dismiss the results of Charles Good's investigation, so he instead attempts to minimize them, stating that it is possible that Bowers had been driving the car in the rear and "If the driver in front wasn't looking in the rear view mirror he would not know the accident occurred."[355]

In fairness, here is the concluding paragraph of the folks on the "other side" of the issue:

> In the end, Monty Bowers (brother of Lee Bowers) concluded Lee's allergies contributed to his death. Both Monty and Lee had severe allergies and were prone to fits of sneezing. They took antihistamines that provided little relief. Monty told representatives of the insurance company his allergies bothered him that day. He assumed Lee experienced similar symptoms. Could it be, Lee took antihistamines, dozed off, and struck the abutment? Is it possible a sneezing fit caused him to lose control of the vehicle? In my view the answer is YES. I will modify my opinion when someone comes forward with verifiable facts to the contrary.[356]

As for us, frankly, there seems to be something a bit more sinister than a mere matter of sneezing here. So we'll stick with Mr. Good from the Texas Highway Patrol, who investigated the same case and concluded that his friend's car was forced off the road.

---

[354] David Perry, "Now It Can Be Told: The Lee Bowers Story," accessed 5 Nov 2012: http://mcadams.posc.mu.edu/bowers.txt

[355] Ibid.

[356] Ibid.

24 | Marilyn "Delilah" Walle, August 30, 1966

Victim	**Marilyn Walle (also known by her stage names "Delilah" and "Miranda" and as Marilyn Moon, Marilyn Magyar and April Walle), exotic dancer who was regular performer at Jack Ruby's *Carousel Club* in Dallas**
Cause of Death	Multiple Gunshots
Official Verdict	Murder
Actual Circumstances	Shot by her husband
Inconsistencies	None apparent

CONCLUSIONS BASED ON EVIDENTIARY INDICATIONS

As a dancer at Ruby's club, it was known that she witnessed Oswald's presence there on several occasions, as well as the fact that it was very apparent that Oswald and Ruby knew each other (a fact confirmed by various people at the *Carousel Club*). However, her murder appears to have been a domestic case, unrelated to the JFK assassination.

25 | Mary Pinchot Meyer, October 12, 1964

The body of Mary Pinchot Meyer is examined. It has been observed that, for a local Washington murder, a lot of "men in suits" and trench coats were certainly on the scene very quickly. A photographer at the crime scene made the following cogent observation: "The police kept us on the other side of the canal for a long time. I took the picture with a long-angle lens, and when I look at it now I wonder who all those men in the picture were."[357]

Victim	Mary Pinchot Meyer
Cause of Death	Two gunshots from a .38 at point-blank range; first, to the back of the head, second, straight through the heart, from the front.

[357] Nina Burleigh, *A Very Private Woman: The Life and Unsolved Murder of Presidential Mistress Mary Meyer* (Bantam: 1999), 294.

Official Verdict	Murdered indiscriminately while out for her morning run; Possible sex crime.
Actual Circumstances	Wife of high-level CIA officer; had a serious affair with President Kennedy; thought the would-be investigation of JFK assassination was a total whitewash and used her own high-level connections to research who really killed JFK. Her death caused a frantic search for her diary by the CIA's Counterintelligence Chief.
Inconsistencies	Numerous (see text below)

Mary Meyer was a gifted artist and had an aura of intelligence which men found very attractive.

She married Cord Meyer Jr. in 1945; he was a "rising star" in the CIA. Her husband became involved in the CIA's organized effort to sway public opinion through infiltration of the U.S. major media in a secret campaign known as *Operation Mockingbird*. According to Katharine Graham, publisher of the *Washington Post*, Cord Meyer was the principal "operative" of *Mockingbird*.[358]

Among Cord and Mary Meyer's best friends and companions in Washington was Ben Bradlee, Washington's bureau chief for *Newsweek*, who then became editor of the *Washington Post*. Mary's sister, Toni, was married to Ben Bradlee. So it was a very close-knit group at the peak of the Washington, D.C. press corps. Mary and her husband were also close friends with James Angleton and his wife; Angleton was the notorious head of Counterintelligence at CIA.

As Cord Meyer's politics drifted farther and farther to the right, it apparently alienated Mary and she filed for divorce in 1958. She cited "extreme mental cruelty" as her reason in court documents.[359] Mary became certain that she was under surveillance after leaving her husband. Her telephone and bedroom were bugged and she was sure that James Angleton was responsible.[360] On several occasions in the summer of 1964, she would come home and find that someone had been in her apartment while she was away.[361] She reported these incidents to the police and her friends were well aware that she was frightened by her circumstances.

It was known that Mary had an affair with President Kennedy and that, especially for *his* "track record," it was a much more serious relationship than typical.

While Kennedy had many affairs while in the White House, Angleton insisted that the President and Mary Meyer "were in love. They had something very important."[362]

---

[358] Deborah Davis, *Katharine The Great: Katharine Graham and Her Washington Post Empire* (Institute for Media Analysis: 1991).
[359] John Simkin, "Mary Pinchot Meyer: Biography," *Spartacus Educational*, accessed 2 May 2012: http://www.spartacus.schoolnet.co.uk/JFKmeyerM.htm
[360] Burleigh, *A Very Private Woman*
[361] Simkin, "Mary Pinchot Meyer: Biography"
[362] Joseph J. Trento, *The Secret History of the CIA* (Basic Books: 2005).

President Kennedy enjoyed her company and her intelligent conversation, and while it's not known how much of a political nature he shared with her, it's thought to be a great deal.[363]

Mary socialized closely with President Kennedy. At left are Ben and Toni Bradlee, Mary's sister.

Since Mary had been married to a CIA officer involved in media propaganda and was well-traveled in Washington political circles, it has been suggested that she had President Kennedy's confidence and that he probably shared a great deal with her. It is even reported that Mary and President Kennedy shared marijuana and took an LSD trip together.[364] The fact that Mary was also a close friend of CIA Counterintelligence Chief James Angleton has led to speculation that Mary knew a great deal about what actually happened in the JFK assassination and the reasons for the cover-up that followed. Many have speculated that Mary "put two and two together" from her various sources. It has been reported that she was upset about the absence of authentic information about the assassination contained in the Warren Report, which was published shortly prior to Mary's murder. She read it, was apparently furious about what it contained, and made it clear in statements to her Washington friends that the truth should be told instead of the "whitewash" contained in the official version of events. It has therefore been speculated that silencing her was the real reason for her murder.[365]

Mary left her home on the morning of October 12, 1964, to go out for her morning run. She was shot twice at point-blank range with a .38; the first shot was toward the back of the head and the second shot was to her heart. She died instantly.

A black man named Ray Crump was found nearby, arrested, and charged with the crime. He had no link to the shooting forensically; he was tested for nitrates and none were found on his hands; there was no blowback of blood on his clothing or person.[366]

---

[363] Peter Janney, *Mary's Mosaic: The CIA Conspiracy to Murder John F. Kennedy, Mary Pinchot Meyer, and Their Vision For World Peace* (New York: Skyhorse, 2012).

[364] Timothy Leary, *Flashbacks: An Autobiography* (J.P. Tarcher: 1983).

[365] Janney, *Mary's Mosaic*

[366] Zalin Grant, "Mary Meyer: A Highly Suspicious Death," *Zalin Grant's War Tales* (Pythia Press: 2011): http://www.pythiapress.com/wartales/Meyer.html

The case was big news all over Washington, as they could not find the murder weapon. A massive search came up empty even though an army of police officers and scuba divers searched every possible place nearby. Police even drained the water in the canal near the running path but came up with nothing.[367] They tried Raymond Crump for the crime anyway.

The newspaper reports hid the fact that Mary's ex-husband was a senior CIA officer; they described him as a government official or an author. The newspapers also reported incorrectly that Mary had been killed during a rape attempt—there was never any evidence of that, although it became the police "theory." The *Washington Post* reported that Mary was believed to be "victim of robbery attempt," for which there was actually little or no evidence. Cord Meyer reported that he supported the police version that the accused Ray Crump had attempted to sexually assault Mary and then killed her when she resisted. Cord Meyer's exact words were:

> I was satisfied by the conclusions of the police investigation that Mary had been the victim of a sexually motivated assault by a single individual and that she had been killed in her struggle to escape.[368]

Is it just us, or does that sound like it was written by a CIA attorney? To which we say *Hogwash,* **Mr. Meyer.** And we don't have to call him a liar; his own long-time personal assistant did that:

> Mr. Meyer didn't for a minute think that Ray Crump had murdered his wife or that it had been an attempted rape. But, being an Agency man, he couldn't very well accuse the CIA of the crime, although the murder had all the markings of an in-house rubout.[369]

It turns out that the whole case against Mr. Crump was an exceedingly obvious case of hogwash. It was a real smear job, right in the spirit of "Hey, don't let the facts get in the way of a good story." It could be said that the only problem with the charges against him was that there was absolutely no evidence supporting them.

The trial was a sham. President Lyndon Johnson's extensive influence (lest we forget, he became the new president due to the assassination) is a reoccurring common denominator of both the cover-up after the JFK assassination and the "clean-up" operation (control of exposure from witnesses like Mary Pinchot Meyer) that followed. For example, the judge who controlled the case was a political ally of Lyndon Johnson;[370] he ruled that the private life of Mary could not be mentioned in court.[371] All the links to the CIA—including the highly pertinent facts that she had been married to one and had traveled in those power circles for many years, circles which included President Kennedy himself—were never allowed to be spoken of in the courtroom.

It was well known among her friends that Mary kept a diary and an urgent search for it began after her death. When Ben and Toni Bradlee went to Mary's home to search for the diary, they found CIA Counterintelligence Chief James Angleton already there,

[367] Burleigh, *A Very Private Woman*
[368] Cord Meyer, *Facing Reality: From World Federalism to the CIA* (University Press of America: 1982).
[369] Janney, *Mary's Mosaic*, 346-347.
[370] Simkin, "Mary Pinchot Meyer: Biography"
[371] Burleigh, *A Very Private Woman*

looking for the same thing. Reports differ about what happened to the diary, but in any event, it was destroyed. Legally, it belonged to Mary's children, but hey—that's just legally. When you're dealing with the CIA, then all that's important is realistically—and realistically, Mary's children were never even allowed to view its contents.

Zalin Grant, an author and Army Intelligence veteran, did an excellent job of detailing most of the various inconsistencies of this case.[372] Peter Janney, who was very close to this story, has also amassed an incredible amount of important information.[373] We have added to those and provide below, in list form for the sake of clarity, the "big things wrong" with the case.

Key Points in the Assassination of Mary Pinchot Meyer:

The "unknown victim" (a point of importance later on) was pronounced dead at 2:05 p.m.. "Dr. Rayford observed that rigor mortis had not yet set in, which meant that she couldn't have been dead for more than two hours."[374]

The identity of the victim was not officially learned until after 6:00 p.m. Prior to 6:00 p.m., she was only known as an unidentified female murder victim.[375]

The killer either knew her or jogged up from behind on the exercise path to pass her, because both shots were point-blank range (six inches or less from her body) and Mary was strong, in good physical shape, and would not have let an attacker get that close without screaming for help, fighting him off, or both.[376]

The killing was, by all reports, an extremely professional job. She was shot "execution style"; one shot to the back of the head and one more straight through the heart to make sure she was dead after she went down. Both shots were lethal and quick, fired from a .38, with apparent precision. This was clearly not some casual shooting, but a cold-blooded, up-close-and-personal professional job:

> Mary appeared to be killed by a professional hitman. The first bullet was fired at the back of the head. She did not die straight away. A second shot was fired into the heart. The evidence suggests that in both cases, the gun was virtually touching Mary's body when it was fired. As the FBI expert testified, the "dark haloes on the skin around

[374] Janney, *Mary's Mosaic*, 48.
[375] Janney, *Mary's Mosaic*
[376] Grant, "Mary Meyer: A Highly Suspicious Death"

---

[372] Zalin Grant, "Mary Meyer: A Highly Suspicious Death," *Zalin Grant's War Tales* (Pythia Press: 2011): http://www.pythiapress.com/wartales/Meyer.html
[373] Janney, *Mary's Mosaic*

both entry wounds suggested they had been fired at close-range, possibly point-blank."[377]

Dr. Rayford not only agreed with, but amplified, concerns that the act was very professional, as he noted the presence of the precise "kill shot":

Things were not at all like they were supposed to be.

The second gunshot had been fired with particular precision: The bullet pierced the right lung and severed the aorta. Death would have been instantaneous. That bothered Rayford. The degree of expertise suggested the work of a professional.[378]

The fact that she was murdered when leaving her home for her regular exercise routine is also indicative of a professional hit because professional assassins seize upon just such a routine as the most opportune time to strike.[379]

The gun was never found despite a massive police search (another sign of a very professional job).[380] The search was "unprecedented in its scope and manpower" and even used a team of Navy scuba divers.[381]

The fact that she was murdered execution-style makes it highly likely that it was a professional hit. This was not a matter of a "crime of emotion" or a straight robbery or rape attempt; it was a cold-blooded killer who knew how to perform the deed seamlessly and without emotion.[382]

A former CIA "cleaner" (agent and assassin) later admitted that he had been instructed by the CIA, first to survey Mary Meyer, and then later to assassinate her after he received the "K" (contract) to "terminate" her. His name, officially, was William L. Mitchell, but that was his operational alias.[383]

A high-level CIA officer, Wistar Janney, exhibited clear foreknowledge of the assassination. Ben Bradlee wrote that Janney called him with the news "just after lunch," and Wistar Janney also informed Counterintelligence Chief James Angleton well before the victim had even been identified.[384]

---

[377] John Simkin, "Edward Grant Stockdale, Edwin Anderson Collins and Mary Pinchot Meyer: Three Deaths and the Assassination of John F. Kennedy," *Spartacus Educational*, accessed 12 Nov 2012: http://www.spartacus.schoolnet.co.uk/1Dallas.htm

[378] Janney, *Mary's Mosaic*, 55.

[379] Belzer & Wayne, *Dead Wrong*

[380] Grant, "Mary Meyer: A Highly Suspicious Death"

[381] Janney, *Mary's Mosaic*, 60.

[382] Belzer & Wayne, *Dead Wrong*

[383] Janney, *Mary's Mosaic*

[384] Janney, *Mary's Mosaic*

In an apparent effort to close the case quickly, an innocent man was railroaded into a murder charge by the police and prosecutor, with help from the *Washington Post* and Ben Bradlee of *Newsweek*, both of whom made it clear that the accused was guilty and her murder was an open-and-shut case; but the reality was far from it.[385]

The forensic evidence was highly contrary to a motive of robbery or one of sexual assault.[386] In fact—there was absolutely *zero* forensic evidence linking the accused to the crime.[387] The only thing he was guilty of was being in the vicinity of where the crime had taken place.

If we are to believe the official version, her diary was destroyed by the CIA—which is technically a felony, "obstruction of justice," in the case of a violent death.[388]

Angleton and Bradlee both lied about the diary.[389]

James Angleton and Ben Bradlee both even denied the *existence* of Mary's diary until it was revealed as true by other sources. They then admitted they had found the diary, but even then changed their stories about how it was discovered and destroyed. In a statement that defied credulity, Mr. Bradlee also said in an interview for a book that he had not been aware of Mary's affair with JFK until news of it came out after her murder.

Mary's blood-stained sweater also "disappeared" while in police custody, precluding advanced DNA testing.[390]

The case is still listed as an unsolved murder, and it had the same components as the JFK assassination: A self-contradictory crime scene with a "patsy," who could not possibly have committed the act, a rush to judgment, an obvious cover-up and an apparent unwillingness on the part of authorities to actually uncover the truth.[391]

---

[385] Janney, *Mary's Mosaic*
[386] Grant, "Mary Meyer: A Highly Suspicious Death" and Janney, *Mary's Mosaic*
[387] Janney, *Mary's Mosaic*, 60-61.
[388] Grant, "Mary Meyer: A Highly Suspicious Death"
[389] Grant, "Mary Meyer: A Highly Suspicious Death"
[390] Grant, "Mary Meyer: A Highly Suspicious Death"
[391] Janney, *Mary's Mosaic*

If one looks at the case of Mary's death in the context of more current revelations, the picture becomes clearer. The deathbed statement of longtime CIA officer E. Howard Hunt is highly relevant. Hunt had inside information on the JFK assassination and made a deathbed statement regarding the "chain of command" for the assassination. Vice President Lyndon Johnson was at the top of the chain and immediately beneath Johnson was Cord Meyer, Mary's ex-husband.[392] Mary was a very intelligent woman and was nobody's fool when it came to politics. Lyndon Johnson was President and

---

[392] Saint John Hunt, *Bond of Secrecy: My Life with CIA Spy and Watergate Conspirator E. Howard Hunt* TrineDay: 2012) and Saint John Hunt, "Chain of Command": http://www.saintjohnhunt.com/chain-of-command.html

actively covering up the links to the assassination. If Mary had finally put "two and two together" about her ex-husband's involvement, then a professional hit by a "cleanup" crew suddenly makes a great deal of sense.

Mary had access to the highest levels of information from various sources.[393] She was also a close friend of Bill Walton, a fellow artist.[394] That friendship with Walton was yet another link to the upper echelon of Washington power circles. Recall, for example, as far as high levels of information, that Walton was the special envoy sent to Moscow right after the JFK assassination, with the message from Robert Kennedy to the Soviet leadership that "We know that it was a domestic high level political conspiracy. . . ."[395] It doesn't get much higher than that.

Author Peter Janney thoroughly proves his points that the highest echelons of the CIA had foreknowledge of, and played a role in, the murder of Mary Pichot Meyer. After reading that book, you will no longer look at the case as an "unsolved murder."

As Mr. Janney notes, a woman as well-connected and intelligent as Mary posed some serious problems:

> **Mary was killed two weeks after the Warren Commission was released. She bought a paperback condensed version of the WC the day it was released and started reading it. She was furious. She knew it was a complete whitewash, and wasn't worth the paper it was printed on. She told friends that she was thinking seriously of coming out and revealing the truth of what she knew. Allegedly, she confronted Angleton and her former husband Cord about the absurdity of the WC. I think she knew at this point that certain people within the Agency had engineered the assassination. For the future of the CIA, she was definitely a big problem. And she was courageous enough to speak out.[396]**

Mr. Janney's book has established dramatic evidence that Mary was killed by the U.S. intelligence community and has documented the facts surrounding the matter.

For example, Mary was certain that she was under surveillance, that she was being stalked (for several weeks), and that her house had been broken into and searched, as though someone had been looking for something; she was very frightened by these events.[397]

Mary's Mosaic also establishes that Mary had indeed done some very serious research regarding how her lover and dear friend had been assassinated;[398] and had even obtained solid proof that there was substantial involvement in JFK's shooting by CIA-affiliated anti-Castro Cubans and the Mafia:

> **Meyer claimed to my friend that she positively knew that Agency-affiliated Cuban exiles and the Mafia were responsible for killing John Kennedy.[399]**

---

[393] Janney, *Mary's Mosaic*

[394] Janney, Peter, July 29, 2007, *The Education Forum: Mary Pinchot Meyer*

[395] Talbot, *Brothers: The Hidden History of the Kennedy Years,* emphasis added.

[396] Peter Janney, 29 July 2007 The Education Forum: Mary Pinchot Meyer. Accessed 23 Mar 2012 http:// educationforum.ipbhost.com/index.php?showtopic=3520&hl=janney&st=75

[397] Janney, *Mary's Mosaic*, 38, 311, 312.

[398] Janney, *Mary's Mosaic*, 282, 283.

[399] Janney, *Mary's Mosaic*, 314.

It established that high-level CIA officials, including his father, had definite pre-knowledge of Mary's murder. Mary's body was not even identified after her murder until "sometime after six o'clock in the evening."[400] Yet it was recorded that CIA officer Wistar Janney had informed both CIA officer Cord Meyer and newsman Ben Bradlee much earlier that day, with details about Mary's murder.[401] In the case of Bradlee, he specifically wrote that the call from Wistar Janney informing him about Mary's murder had been "just after lunch."[402]

Janney even uncovered direct evidence about the CIA's internal decision to "terminate" Mary Meyer.[403] Former killers who had been in the "cleaning business" for the CIA have openly talked about it and revealed that it was done exactly how it looks like it was done; that they "Had one of our cleaning men nail her down by the towpath while she was out for her daily jog."[404]

She was eliminated because she knew too much.[405]

The assassin was revealed by his operational codename, "William L. Mitchell":

> Damore then revealed that he had Mary's real diary in his possession (the diary found!) and that in the diary; Mary had made a connection between the Kennedy assassination and the CIA that involved "James Angleton." Mitchell, said Damore, had confessed to him a few hours earlier that morning: The murder of Mary Meyer had been "a CIA operation," in which Mitchell had been the assassin.[406]

"Mitchell" was a *real* professional too:

> It specifically identified a man by the name of "William Mitchell" as a member of "Army Special Forces kill teams" that operated domestically for the CIA and the National Security Agency (NSA).[407]

The shadowy intelligence operative, "William Mitchell," was contacted and identified and revealed some fascinating information too:

> "Mitchell" confirmed that his name, "William L. Mitchell," was an alias, and that he now lived under another alias in Virginia. He said his position at the Pentagon in 1964 had been just "a light bulb job," a cover for covert intelligence work. . . . It (Mary Meyer) had been "an operation," Mitchell disclosed. He had been "assigned" in September of 1964 to be part of a "surveillance team" that was monitoring Mary Meyer. . . . At some point— the precise date is unknown—the order was given to "terminate" her.

---

[400] Janney, *Mary's Mosaic*, 340-341.
[401] Janney, *Mary's Mosaic*, 340-341.
[402] Janney, *Mary's Mosaic*, 341.
[403] Janney, *Mary's Mosaic*, 314, 328, 329, 330, 355, 356, 384.
[404] Janney, *Mary's Mosaic*, 355.
[405] Janney, *Mary's Mosaic*, 384.
[406] Janney, *Mary's Mosaic*, 328.
[407] Janney, *Mary's Mosaic*, 324.

It was to be done in a public place, then made to look like something it wasn't.[408]

It doesn't get much clearer than that.

The "contract" was done "at the request of the Agency's Domestic K Office in D.C."[409]

It's quite a piece of work. If anything, Mr. Janney goes *too far*, attempting to marry the highly professional hit on Mary with the exact same type of highly professional operation aimed at JFK. But, as far as the fact that Mary was eliminated by the CIA in a job that—as Cord Meyer's personal assistant aptly put it, "had all the markings of an in-house rubout"[410]—it is now, at this late juncture, a proven point. The evidence is all there; one need simply look at the full facts of the case to reach that as its logical and inescapable conclusion.

And in conclusion, author Peter Janney sums it up quite succinctly:

The whole scene around Mary's murder was orchestrated by the CIA, and my father was part of the team.[411]

CONCLUSIONS BASED ON EVIDENTIARY INDICATIONS

National Security Assassination: Specifically linked to JFK assassination.

FURTHER RESEARCH

Mary's Mosaic: The CIA Conspiracy to Murder John F. Kennedy, Mary Pinchot Meyer and Their Vision of World Peace, Peter Janney, Skyhorse Publishing, 2012.

A Very Private Woman: The Life and Unsolved Murder of Presidential Mistress Mary Meyer, Nina Burleigh, Bantam, 1998.

"Mary Meyer: A Highly Suspicious Death," Zalin Grant, Pythia Press, 2011. http://www.pythiapress.com/wartales/Meyer.html

Bond of Secrecy: My Life with CIA Spy and Watergate Conspirator E. Howard Hunt, Saint John Hunt, TrineDay, 2012

"The Education Forum: Mary Pinchot Meyer," John Simkin, *Spartacus Educational,* 2005. http://educationforum.ipbhost.com/index.php?showtopic=3520

"CIA Executive's Son: Agency Murdered JFK & Lover," Andrew Kreig, 17 August 2012: http://www.opednews.com/articles/CIA-Executive-s-Son-Agenc-by-Andrew-Kreig-120817-298.html

---

[408] Janney, *Mary's Mosaic,* 328, 329, 331.
[409] Janney, *Mary's Mosaic,* 329.
[410] Janney, *Mary's Mosaic,* 346-347.
[411] Joseph P. Kahn, "One man's suspicion, obsession, and an unsolved murder," 26 May 2012, *Boston Globe:*http://www.boston.com/lifestyle/articles/2012/05/26/north_shore_author_peter_janney_makes_his_case_for_the_cia_plotting_to_murder_john_f_kennedy_and_jfk_mistress_mary_pinchot_meyer/?page=full

Victim	Lieutenant Commander William Bruce Pitzer
Cause of Death	Single Gunshot, Right Temple
Official Verdict	Suicide
Actual Circumstances	Pitzer had a prime role in the documentation of records from President Kennedy's autopsy and was reportedly well aware that the wounds had been altered. He died a few days before his retirement from the Navy, was looking forward to a high-paying job, and was said to be planning

to expose the problems with the JFK autopsy.[412] He was also *not* suicidal, according to all reputable accounts. US Army Special Forces Lieutenant Colonel Daniel Marvin was requested by the CIA to assassinate Pitzer for National Security purposes[413]:

> **He was getting close to retirement and it was his plan that when he retired was when that information would be released to the public, 'cause they'd prove that the President was hit with more than one bullet in the head and he was hit from a different direction than they said.[414]**

Inconsistencies	Dramatic and numerous; (refer to second chart in this chapter)

To understand why Lieutenant Commander Bill Pitzer had to be killed, it is first necessary to know what it was that he understood.

How and Why the Body of President Kennedy was Surgically Altered

One of the most amazing facts in all of American History is that after the assassination of President Kennedy, the wounds upon his corpse were surgically altered <u>prior to autopsy</u>. That's been verified by surgeons who were there at the death scene, both before and after the fact, and it actually did happen.[415]

In his 2010, exhaustive examination of every document ever available concerning the JFK assassination, Douglas Horne established conclusively that the alteration of President Kennedy's corpse did indeed take place.[416]

---

[415] David W. Mantik, M.D., Ph.D., "Inside the Assassination Records Review Board (AARB) by Douglas Horne: A Nearly-Entirely-Positive Review," 26 Feb. 2010. http://assassinationscience.com/HorneReview.pdf (accessed 3 Jan. 2012);
Douglas P. Horne, *Inside the Assassination Records Review Board: The U.S. Government's Final Attempt to Reconcile the Conflicting Medical Evidence in the Assassination of JFK* (Douglas P. Horne, 2009); David S. Lifton, *Best Evidence: Disguise and Deception in the Assassination of John F. Kennedy* (Macmillan:1980).
[416] Mantik, M.D., Ph.D., "Inside the Assassination Records Review Board (AARB) by Douglas Horne: A Nearly-Entirely-Positive Review"

---

[412] John Simkin, "William Pitzer: Biography," *Spartacus Educational*, accessed 21 Nov. 2012: http://www.spartacus.schoolnet.co.uk/JFKpitzerW.htm
[413] Lieutenant Colonel Daniel Marvin, US Army Special Forces (Retired), *Expendable Elite: One Soldier's Journey into Covert Warfare*, TrineDay, 2005; Lieutenant Colonel Daniel Marvin, US Army Special Forces (Retired), "The Unconventional Warrior Archives: Part Three—Orders to Kill," August 23, 2002,: http://www.expendableelite.com/UW_archives/UW_archive.0003b.html
[414] *JFK Assassination: 13 Version* (Documentary), 2003: http://www.youtube.com/watch?v=uWiMEQYt1n8

If that strikes you as a difficult set of facts to absorb, consider it a real-world example of Sherlock Holmes' irrefutable logic that "... when you have eliminated the impossible, whatever remains, *however improbable*, must be the truth."[417]

And in case that's not enough drama for you, get a load of this:

> Witnesses recall an audible gasp when the head was unwrapped, as the audience was shocked by the severe damage to the head; more damage, it seemed, than could have been caused by the rifle shots.[418]

It was Author/Researcher David Lifton who first made the astounding discovery that:

> An FBI report stating that the President's body had been surgically altered (in addition to the tracheotomy) prior to the Bethesda autopsy.[419]

The FBI report, describing the condition of the President's body *prior* to the beginning of the autopsy, read as follows:

> ... it was ascertained that the President's clothing had been removed and it was also apparent that a tracheotomy had been performed as well as surgery of the head area, namely, in the top of the skull.[420]

In addition to the FBI report, sworn testimony from FBI Special Agents James Sibert and Frank O'Neal also established that President Kennedy's corpse was surgically altered <u>prior</u> to autopsy. That alteration had to have taken place between the corpse's departure from Dallas and its arrival for autopsy at the Bethesda Naval Medical Center near Washington, D.C. (also known as the NNMC for National Naval Medical Center).

> The FBI agents who were present at the NNMC when the body arrived noted in a field report that the "first incision" was made at 8:15 p.m. They also noted, on the basis of comments made by one of the doctors present, that there had already been "surgery of the head area, namely, in the top of the skull." No such surgery had been performed in Dallas.[421]

The evidence itself made it necessary to control the autopsy:

> The severe damage done to the President's head, including the massive exit wound at the rear, made it obvious that he had been shot from the front ...[422]

---

[417] Sir Arthur Conan Doyle, *The Sign of the Four*, 1890: 111.
[418] Brian Rooney, "Burying The Truth—book review of Doug Horne's epic effort," April, 2010, *JFK: Deep Politics Quarterly*.
[419] Heiner, *Without Smoking Gun*
[420] Ibid.
[421] Ibid.
[422] Ibid.

That frontal wound made it obvious that at least one shot had been from the front. Combined with the known shots from the rear, that meant there had to be a conspiracy of multiple shooters. That conflicted with the official version of events and, hence, did not sit at all well with the Powers That Be.

So, practically at gunpoint by some accounts, and in blatant violation of the law, the Secret Service "kidnapped" the President's body from Texas authorities who actually had full legal jurisdiction and who vehemently protested the seizure and the countermanding of their legal authority in the case.

The President's body officially reappeared at Bethesda Naval Medical Center, where it was received for autopsy. However, the wounds to President Kennedy had been dramatically altered between the trip from Dallas to Bethesda.

By the time that President Kennedy's body reached Bethesda, it was demonstrably different. There were at least four dramatic irregularities in the state of the corpse between Dallas-to-Bethesda[423]:

1. When the body of President Kennedy left Parkland Hospital in Dallas, there was what doctors described as an entry wound in the right forehead and a massive blowout exit wound at the rear. At Bethesda, *pre*-autopsy, the wound in the right forehead was massive, appearing more like an exit wound.
2. Doctors said that fully two thirds of the President's brain was intact and secure in the skull cavity when it left Parkland. At Bethesda, the President's brain was almost completely absent and what was left of it oozed onto the table because it was not secure in the skull cavity (those present in the room at the time literally gasped in shock at the extent of the damage).
3. At Parkland, doctors saw a neat and clearly delineated entry wound in the front throat, through which they made a standard emergency tracheotomy incision. By the time the body reached Bethesda, the incision in the throat was demonstrably larger.
4. The President's body was placed aboard Air Force One in a bronze ceremonial casket. It has been verified that the body arrived at the morgue in a plain shipping casket and that the bronze casket delivered separately was empty.[424]

The documentation is incontrovertible and the testimonies are crystal-clear. And, of course, they were easily remembered because it was, after all, the President of the United States:

Over twenty-five witnesses who observed the President's wounds in Dallas remembered a wound approximately three inches in diameter

[423] Noel Twyman, *Bloody Treason: On Solving History's Greatest Murder Mystery, The Assassination of John F. Kennedy* (Laurel: 1997); Heiner, *Without Smoking Gun.*
[424] Ibid.

in the lower rear of the head. Not one of the Dallas doctors, nurses or hospital technicians has contended otherwise.[425]

But when the body arrived and was unwrapped at Bethesda, that wound that had measured three inches in diameter was a gaping hole measuring five inches by seven inches.[426]

Jerrol Custer says he was carrying X-rays of the dead President when he saw Mrs. Kennedy coming in through the front entrance. His account, combined with those of Dennis David and Donald Rebentisch, shows that the bronze ceremonial casket with which the Kennedys arrived did *not* contain the President's body.[427]

Dr. Humes, the surgeon in charge at the autopsy, is on-record admitting that the clandestine alteration took place. For the official record, at the beginning of the *official* autopsy, he described for the record what had already taken place on the body of the President as:

surgery . . . to the top of the head.[428]

Dr. Humes later attempted to withdraw that statement because the Powers That Be reportedly went berserk as soon as they learned of those words being uttered.[429] Nonetheless, Special Agents Sibert and O'Neal were present in an official capacity and countered that they were absolutely certain that they'd heard Dr. Humes officially state precisely those words.[430] And one would imagine that two FBI agents in their role of the Bureau's official presence at the autopsy of the President of the United States are going to be very good at remembering exactly what took place.

The brain was almost entirely gone. Paul O'Connor noted that the skull was nearly devoid of brain tissue and thought that the damage was remarkably severe for a bullet wound. "In most cases, we remove the brain for gross anatomy," he said. "But he didn't have any brains left . . . there wasn't anything to remove."[431]

Note, of course, that by <u>all</u> medical eyewitness accounts, at least two-thirds of the brain was secure in the skull at the moment that the body left Dallas, as doctors watched it being placed in the bronze casket. It was then loaded onto Air Force One bound for Bethesda.

Whether the brain had been removed by the time the body arrived at Bethesda (as stated by O'Connor and Custer), or whether it was first removed at the Bethesda autopsy, we can be certain that it had been

[425] Heiner, *Without Smoking Gun*
[426] Lifton, *Best Evidence*; Twyman, *Bloody Treason*.
[427] Heiner, *Without Smoking Gun*, emphasis in original.
[428] Horne, *Inside the Assassination Records Review Board*
[429] Ibid.
[430] Ibid.
[431] Heiner, *Without Smoking Gun*

subjected to surgery between its departure from Dallas and its arrival in Bethesda. The brain was present in Dallas and no small amount of gunfire could completely free the brain from its moorings in the skull. Several nerves and blood vessels hold the brain in place. These would have to be severed before the brain could be removed. At some point, Humes and Boswell must have realized that no bullet could have accomplished this feat, as evidenced by Humes' question regarding whether surgery had been performed at Parkland Hospital. Other indications of prior surgery are found in Humes' notes.[432]

The level of senior military control of the autopsy is well established. People were clearly "subordinated," to use the military term.

After the completion of the autopsy report, Admiral Burkley, the late President's personal physician, requested written confirmation from Dr. Humes that he had burned his original notes. All Naval hospital staff who had been involved in the autopsy were called into the commanding officer's office several days after and required to sign orders acknowledging their obligation to remain silent about what they had seen and heard, under penalty of court-martial.[433]

Elements of our government, in order to conceal evidence of a cross-fire that would have exposed a conspiracy to kill JFK, contrived an elaborate, if improvised, cover-up. The autopsists and other medical personnel were cowed by their military superiors into cooperating with the plot by fraudulent appeals to their patriotism (i.e., failure to go along would lead to World War III). The president's body was tampered with after being removed from the Dallas casket and spirited onto Air Force Two.[434]

Therefore, the "shell game" with the caskets was for a reason:

Meanwhile, the president's widow (and the rest of the nation) was being deceived by a brazen display with an empty coffin that was loaded onto Air Force One, flown to D.C., and taken in an elaborate motorcade to Bethesda Naval Hospital. The body was transported in haste . . . in a shipping casket to the Bethesda morgue and brought into the morgue by a group of sailors. Witnesses saw the body removed from such a casket.[435]

Then it gets even uglier:

At this point, Dr. Humes performed clandestine surgery on the head to enlarge the head wound to create "evidence" of a temporal/parietal exit and an incision was made to remove evidence of a right forehead entry. The scalp and skull were manipulated to conceal the size and

---

[432] Ibid.
[433] Ibid.
[434] Rooney, "Burying The Truth—book review of Doug Horne's epic effort"
[435] Ibid.

location of the occipital "blowout" and a "wound" was created to simulate a small entrance wound on the back of the head.[436]

Note that all of the above occurred <u>prior</u> to the autopsy.

The official autopsy then began. . . . The autopsists were continually interrupted and directed by the military brass in attendance. Photographs and X rays were taken by the "official" Bethesda personnel, and pictures that apparently did not conform to the cover-up plan were later "deemed" missing. The paper trail on these items was falsified as necessary.[437]

This was obviously <u>big stuff</u>! To accomplish those ends, records concerning the true nature of the autopsy had to be controlled:

There are many contradictions in the publicly available autopsy images. Some of the photographs which were finally released to the public are inconsistent with the X-rays, and neither the photos nor the X-rays agree with what eyewitnesses (who were doctors and law enforcement professionals) described in Dallas or Bethesda. Some of the X-rays and photos have been identified as forgeries by experts.[438]

The book *Without Smoking Gun* by Kent Heiner, is an excellent biography that concisely details the alteration of President Kennedy's body, the death of Lieutenant Commander Pitzer, and the testimony of U.S. Army Special Forces Lieutenant Colonel Dan Marvin, who was asked to assassinate Pitzer by the CIA for the stated purpose of National Security.[439]

---

[436] Ibid.
[437] Ibid.
[438] Heiner, *Without Smoking Gun.*
[439] Lieutenant Colonel Daniel Marvin, US Army Special Forces (Retired), "The Unconventional Warrior Archives: Part Three—Orders to Kill," August 23, 2002,: http://www.expendableelite.com/UW_archives/UW_archive.0003b.html

CIA veteran John Stockwell's investigation also confirmed Lifton's original claims of wound alteration upon the corpse of President Kennedy:

The evidence was extensively tampered with. The President's body was altered; the photographs of the autopsy were altered; and over 100 witnesses were killed or died mysterious and violent deaths.[440]

Learning exactly why that alteration took place is a matter of obvious importance—Lieutenant Commander Pitzer was at the heart of that issue, and the manner of his death is front-and-center in that drama.

---

[440] John Stockwell, *The Praetorian Guard: The U.S. Role in the New World Order* (South End Press: 1999).

If retrospect can reflect the true measure of a man, one could do no better than how a close friend summed up Bill Pitzer:

He was the finest man I ever met.[441]

The above quote summarizes the sentiment of those who were lucky enough to know Lieutenant Commander Bill Pitzer. He was, by all accounts, a man whose integrity beamed like a beacon; liked, admired and respected by most everyone in his circles.

Pitzer, who was an X-ray technician that filmed the Kennedy autopsy, told friends that after the autopsy, he was "debriefed" by persons unknown from the intelligence community, who basically threatened and intimidated him to remain silent about what he witnessed. He told friends that this experience was "horrifying," and stated that he was visited periodically by military personnel who reminded him repeatedly never to reveal—for reasons of National Security—what he saw while taking pictures.[442]

Evidentiary Inconsistencies in the National Security Assassination of Lieutenant Commander William Pitzer

1. Paraffin-tested negative for gunshot residue (GSR), strongly indicating that he had not fired a weapon. If he had committed suicide, then GSR would have been all over him, especially on the firing hand. Both Pitzer's right palm and the back of his right hand tested <u>negative</u>, the absence of nitrate indicating no exposure to gunpowder.
2. The government withheld the release of the autopsy report to the Pitzer family for many years, until they were finally forced to divulge its contents. After reviewing it, it's easy to see why they were so recalcitrant:

The paraffin tests of Pitzer's right palm and back of hand were negative, indicating the absence of nitrate, therefore no exposure to gunpowder. While false positives are not uncommon with this test due to contact with tobacco, cosmetics, certain foodstuffs etc., a negative result (as on Pitzer) is usually accepted as evidence of *no recent contact* with a discharged firearm.[443]

---

[443] Allan R.J. Eaglesham & R. Robin Palmer, "The Untimely Death of Lieutenant Commander William B. Pitzer: The Physical Evidence," January 1998, emphasis added: http://www.manuscriptservice.com/Pitzer/Article-1.html

---

[441] Heiner, *Without Smoking Gun.*
[442] Roberts & Armstrong, *The Dead Witnesses*, 35.

3. Paraffin tests conducted by the FBI also revealed that the revolver was held at a distance of over 3 feet away from victim. GSR testing showed that obvious gunshot residue (powder burns) would otherwise be present on right temple. This is a strong indication of a murder because a suicide quite obviously would not be at such a distance.

4. FBI files (not released until 1997, via a request under the Freedom of Information Act) revealed strong indications that Pitzer was murdered.

5. The autopsy of Pitzer's body revealed three wounds: an entry wound, an exit wound and an additional wound not related to the gunshot to his head.

6. The FBI was unable to locate any record of Pitzer acquiring live ammunition for the revolver that was signed out from the security office in his name.

7. A heel print obtained near Pitzer's corpse was <u>not</u> from the shoes that Pitzer was wearing, an indication that someone else was in the room with him when he was shot.

8. Even those who are sometimes skeptical about conclusions of assassination have examined the evidence of this case and reached the dramatic, yet inescapable conclusion that:

The physical evidence is inconsistent with suicide and indicates homicide.[444]

9. "According to his wife, William Pitzer was an inveterate note-maker, and this was evident when his body was discovered. Sheets of paper were scattered around, bearing the names of colleagues (even these are redacted from the FOIA-released photocopies) to whom messages were to be conveyed, written with a blue-crayon pencil found on a chair near the body. Therefore, if he took his own life, we must deduce that in his final hours and minutes he jotted down work-related items lest he forget them, but did not take a few seconds to explain his final act."[445]

10. Pitzer left a note in his office to remind himself to return the revolver that had been signed out from the security office. The note was found on an assistant's desk and it read:

Remind me to return gun to the sec. office.[446]

A person who was planning to shoot himself would obviously not be capable of returning the revolver, nor would it be necessary to return it.

---

[444] Eaglesham & Palmer, "The Untimely Death of Lieutenant Commander William B. Pitzer
[445] Ibid.
[446] Heiner, *Without Smoking Gun*

11. Lieutenant Commander Pitzer had been warned repeatedly by some extremely serious military personnel that he was never to reveal what he had witnessed during the autopsy of President Kennedy, for reasons of National Security.[447]

12. After his death, Lieutenant Commander Pitzer's wife was threatened with losing her benefits if she did not cooperate with the "official version" of events.[448] She "was instructed to keep her mouth shut."[449]

13. In addition to withholding the autopsy report from the family (and everyone else), the government would not even give Mrs. Pitzer her husband's wedding ring, and even lied about the reason, making up a story that his left hand had been too mangled from the shooting:[450]

When Mrs. Pitzer requested the return of her husband's wedding band, she was informed that his left hand was so mutilated that removal of the ring was impossible. She never did receive it. Yet, the autopsy report states that there were no wounds on the body other than those to the head. . . . Why did the US Navy apparently lie to a grieving widow and deny her most reasonable request?[451]

14. It is unclear whether Pitzer had an actual film he had made of the JFK autopsy, or had copies of professional photographs he had taken of the autopsy; Pitzer is gone and the testimony of others varies. But what *is* clear is that he possessed solid documentation of the altered JFK evidence, that he knew how to interpret that evidence, and that he apparently planned on divulging it in documentary form after his upcoming retirement.[452]

15. Special Forces Lieutenant Colonel Daniel Marvin, a decorated war hero, has testified and written extensively about how he was requested by the CIA to assassinate Lieutenant Commander Pitzer. Lieutenant Colonel Marvin had nothing to gain (and a lot to lose) by clarifying the historical record. A man of high character and loyalty, no one has been able to refute his account.

16. Friends were all in accordance that Pitzer had a tough, "can-do" personality, that he was the type to weather any storm and meet life's challenges head on, who would never opt for the easy way out by committing suicide.

---

[447] Heiner, *Without Smoking Gun*; Roberts & Armstrong, *The Dead Witnesses*, 35.

[448] Heiner, *Without Smoking Gun*

[449] Lieutenant Colonel Daniel Marvin, US Army Special Forces (Retired), in: Heiner, *Without Smoking Gun*.

[450] Heiner, *Without Smoking Gun*

[451] Eaglesham & Palmer, "The Untimely Death of Lieutenant Commander William B. Pitzer

[452] Heiner, *Without Smoking Gun*

17. *Nobody* told the Government that Pitzer was suicidal—that was literally an invention on their part[453]:

As stated in the Informal Board of Investigation's Report:

"Mrs. Pitzer could offer no explanation as to why Subject would take his own life and although appearing somewhat resigned to this fact, she still exhibited doubt that suicide was the true cause of death."[454]

He was looking forward to his upcoming retirement, which was only days away, and was excited about transitioning into a creative and high-paying job where he could utilize his expertise:

He was going to teach educational television. . . . He was quite enthused about it.[455]

Pitzer's family and friends believed that he had been murdered, that he had no reason to commit suicide, and had been badly frightened by repeated threats because of what he knew.[456]

18. Government agencies searched high and low for *anything* that could imply that Pitzer was depressed. All they could come up with was an old letter and some vague notes. The letter stated that he was having "trouble at home," but that was apparently in reference to his rocky marriage and he was handling that, not suicidal over it.[457]

19. If we view all of Lieutenant Commander Pitzer's actions on his final day as a "timeline" to discern his frame of mind, they are *dramatically* opposite to a troubled person contemplating suicide. Quite to the contrary, in fact, his final day was typical, even mundane. He was described as "very cheerful."[458] He made breakfast, raked leaves, got a haircut, stopped at the store, checked things at the office[459]—and was then shot in the head.

---

[453] Ibid.
[454] Eaglesham & Palmer, "The Untimely Death of Lieutenant Commander William B. Pitzer
[455] Heiner, *Without Smoking Gun,*
[456] Heiner, *Without Smoking Gun,* 92.
[457] Heiner, *Without Smoking Gun*
[458] Heiner, *Without Smoking* Gun, 32.
[459] Heiner, *Without Smoking Gun*

CONCLUSIONS BASED ON EVIDENTIARY INDICATIONS

National Security Assassination: Specifically linked to JFK assassination.

In one of the clearest cases of national security assassination in history, Lieutenant Commander William B. Pitzer was clearly murdered and his assassination was clearly the result of his special knowledge about the JFK autopsy materials.

FURTHER RESEARCH

Without Smoking Gun, Kent Heiner, TrineDay, 2004.

Expendable Elite: One Soldier's Journey into Covert Warfare, Lieutenant Colonel Daniel Marvin, US Army Special Forces (Retired), TrineDay, 2005.

"The Unconventional Warrior Archives: Part Three—Orders to Kill," August 23, 2002, Lieutenant Colonel Daniel Marvin, US Army Special Forces (Retired): http://www .expendableelite.com/UW_archives/UW_archive.0003b.html

"Bits & Pieces: A Green Beret on the Periphery of the JFK Assassination," Lieutenant Colonel Daniel Marvin, US Army Special Forces (Retired), May 1995 *The Fourth Decade*.

The Men Who Killed Kennedy – Episode VI. The Truth Shall Set You Free (Documentary), produced by Nigel Turner, A&E History Channel, 1995.

JFK Assassination: 13 Version (TV documentary accessible online), 2003: http://www. youtube.com/watch?v=uWiMEQYt1n8

27–28

Manuel Rodriguez Quesada, October, 1964
Gilberto Rodriguez Hernandez, September, 1964

Victims	**Manuel Rodriguez Quesada and Gilberto Rodriguez Hernandez**
Cause of Deaths	Gunshots
Official Verdict	Unsolved Murders
Actual Circumstances	Rodriguez Quesada and Rodriguez Hernandez were both heavily involved in gun-running operations, as well as high-level anti-Castro operations.
Inconsistencies	None—and we mean that in a *bad* way (the case is, unfortunately, very clear)

Manuel Rodriguez Quesada was a bodyguard for Rolando Masferrer (an upcoming chapter), who was an exile leader in one of the most powerful of the anti-Castro Cuban groups. Rodriguez Quesada apparently smuggled weapons and performed other activities for these groups, as well.

Gilberto Rodriguez Hernandez was Military Coordinator to the same Cuban government-in-exile groups. Many of the entries in this book—Carlos Prío Socarrás, Rolando Masferrer, and Eladio del Valle—are all linked inexorably to the violent anti-Castro groups active at that time.

It should be remembered that Eladio del Valle was an associate of David Ferrie and Guy Banister, and was murdered within hours of Ferrie's own death.[460]

---

[460] Roberts & Armstrong, *The Dead Witnesses*, 97.

It doesn't get much clearer than this one:

- Manuel Rodriguez Quesada and Gilberto Rodriguez Hernandez both had inside information on the setting up of the JFK killing in Dallas;
- Both were assassinated;
- Professional U.S. intelligence assassin, John O'Hare, admitted to performing both assassinations.

We find it very interesting that almost nobody even knows who they are—let alone what happened to them.

We even know the "who did it" on this one:

John O'Hare, according to Cuban exile sources and those who worked with him during the heady days of anti-Castro activity in south Florida, was one of the most dangerous men alive.[461]

Robert Morrow was a veteran CIA contract agent and, later, an author. He knew his way around the anti-Castro intelligence terrain quite well:

O'Hare, described as a "CIA mercenary and assassin" by Robert Morrow in *First Hand Knowledge*, admitted to Morrow that he killed both Quesada and Hernandez. These two were supposedly eliminated as a result of Eladio del Valle's fear that they would expose the identities of those responsible to the authorities.[462]

CONCLUSION

Both were assassinated, as a direct result of their knowledge of setting up the JFK assassination.

---

[461] Roberts & Armstrong, *The Dead Witnesses*, 98.
[462] Roberts & Armstrong, *The Dead Witnesses*, 98

Eladio del Valle,
February 22, 1967

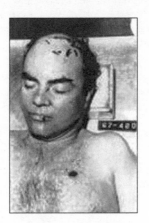

Victim	**Cuban Resistance Leader**
Cause of Death	Gunshot to heart; numerous machete wounds to head
Official Verdict	Unsolved murder
Actual Circumstances	Killed the same day that David Ferrie died, at the exact time that both were sought as key witnesses in the new Jim Garrison investigation of the JFK assassination.

On the **exact same day** that David Ferrie died—in fact, apparently even at the same hour—another key witness was also murdered in broad daylight, preventing his testimony from ever taking place. So here's some assassination "homework" for you: Ask yourself, realistically, what are the odds of this happening?

> On the day—at the same hour—that David Ferrie "committed suicide," one of Ferrie's closest friends and highly visible anti-Castro Cuban connections was murdered in Miami. Eladio del Valle, who was being sought by the Garrison investigation team, was found dead, his head split open with a machete and his body shot through the heart.[463]

Eladio del Valle was involved simultaneously with the anti-Castro movement, the CIA and organized crime, and one of the most important people linked to the JFK assassination. He was considered a leader of the anti-Castro groups. As we described in the preceding chapter, it was del Valle who apparently ordered the assassinations of Gilberto Rodriguez Hernandez and Manuel Rodriguez Quesada:

> These victims, Gilberto Rodriguez Hernandez and Manuel Rodriguez Quesada (killed September and October, 1964), were allegedly killed by O'Hare as part of a monumental government conspiracy invoked to provide a smokescreen to shield the real assassins.[464]

A couple years later, the tracks to these killers must have been getting clearer because, by the time of the Jim Garrison investigation, someone above del Valle made the same decision about him and sent the same professional assassin to do the job, as John O'Hare later admitted to author Robert Morrow:

> When del Valle became a liability later, due to the exposure of David Ferrie to the press in New Orleans and Garrison's interest in him, he was "neutralized."[465]

Eladio del Valle was a friend and associate of David Ferrie.[466] They were both sought for questioning by District Attorney Jim Garrison and they both died the same day. Ferrie had been questioned once and del Valle was killed before Garrison got to him, so it's all just way too coincidental:

> As early as 1960, del Valle was reportedly working with a New Orleans pilot, David Ferrie, in flying clandestine missions over Cuba. In January 1961, shortly before the Bay of Pigs invasion, del Valle told the New York *Daily News* that he had a fighting force of "8,500 men in Cuba and a skeleton force of about 200 working in Miami and Central America." By 1963, he was also a leader of the Committee to Free Cuba, or "Cuba Libre."[467]

---

[463] Roberts & Armstrong, *The Dead Witnesses*, 44.

[464] Ibid.

[465] Ibid.

[466] Michael Benson, *Who's Who in the JFK Assassination: An A to Z Encyclopedia* (Citadel: 2003), 109.

[467] Russell, *The Man Who Knew Too Much*, 182.

An investigator for the U.S. Senate Internal Security Subcommittee, who looked into the Cuban connections, had this to say about Eladio del Valle:

> Now there was a gun for hire. Anything that had to do with smuggling or gun-running, del Valle was with it. Both a bagman and a hitman; mainly involved with people from the Batista regime.

Tony Cuesta, another primary leader of the anti-Castro Cuban groups in Florida who admitted his own participation in the JFK assassination, also admitted that Eladio del Valle played a role in the conspiracy.[468] A friend of del Valle's also indicated that connection:

> Diego Gonzales Tendera, a close friend, later claimed that del Valle was murdered because of his involvement in the assassination of President John F. Kennedy.[469]

Here's another intelligence source who named del Valle as a key player in the conspiracy to kill JFK:

> According to "Harry Dean" (the "war name" of a man who claims to be a former CIA agent), as quoted by W. B. Morris and R. B. Cutler in *Alias Oswald*, the assassins were anti-Castro activists Hall and del Valle, who were hired by the John Birch Society.[470]

Author Anthony Summers also cites the fact that del Valle was the leader of Florida's Free Cuba Committee and, at the same time, had links to Florida Godfather, Santo Trafficante, who was also a key suspect in the JFK assassination.[471]

And it's also very interesting to note that del Valle was rumored to have been reporter Dorothy Kilgallen's source of information regarding David Ferrie, linking Ferrie to a key role in the whole conspiracy.

CONCLUSION

Assassination: Clearly related to Garrison's investigation of the JFK assassination. John O'Hare, the same professional assassin who admitted killing the above two "soldiers" at the instruction of del Valle, also admitted to then assassinating del Valle himself, when he became a "liability"—which was when District Attorney Jim Garrison publicly named David Ferrie as a prime suspect in the JFK assassination.[472] As we shall see in the next chapter and saw in the preceding two, these cases are much related—Ferrie told Garrison that he had just handed him a death sentence by naming him publicly and Ferrie was indeed dead a very short time later.

---

[468] Russell, *The Man Who Knew Too Much*

[469] *Reference Center for Marxist Studies*, "Eladio del Valle: Biography," accessed 27 Nov. 2012: http://marxistlibrary.org/eladio-del-valle-biography/

[470] Benson, *Who's Who in the JFK Assassination*, 109.

[471] Anthony Summers, *Not in Your Lifetime* (Marlowe & Co.: 1998), 319, 491.

[472] Ibid.

30 | David Ferrie,
February 22, 1967

Victim	**David Ferrie, anti-Castro covert operative, associate of New Orleans, Godfather Carlos Marcello**
Cause of Death	Brain aneurysm
Official Verdict	Natural Causes
Actual Circumstances	Victim had just been named as a defendant in District Attorney Jim Garrison's case for conspiracy in the JFK assassination; Ferrie told Garrison he had just signed Ferrie's death warrant and he was dead just a short time later.

Inconsistencies	Two typed notes were left behind "indicating suicide" and making it appear a rather odd coincidence that he died at the same time from natural causes; indicative of possible suicide staging.

Somebody was silencing key witnesses a lot quicker than New Orleans District Attorney Jim Garrison could get to them and ask them uncomfortable questions.

Eladio del Valle, Miami:

On the night of February 22, 1967, del Valle's body was discovered by Miami Police, sprawled across the floor of his flaming-red Cadillac. He had been brutally beaten, shot above the heart, and his head chopped open. He was being sought for questioning at the time by Jim Garrison's investigative staff.[473]

It was a busy day on February 22nd.

David Ferrie, New Orleans:

The same night del Valle died, so did his old friend, Ferrie. He had already been questioned once by Garrison about his possible knowledge of the assassination. Ferrie's body was found in his New Orleans apartment, alongside two typed notes, suggesting suicide. The coroner's ruling said '"natural causes," though Garrison suspected he had been poisoned.[474]

Ferrie was sought as a key witness because he seemed to be the man to whom all roads led:

- Ferrie knew Lee Harvey Oswald[475];
- He had worked closely with Jack Ruby[476];
- Ferrie and Oswald were frequent visitors to Guy Banister's office,[477]
- He had also worked closely with Clay Shaw[478];
- He was employed by Godfather Carlos Marcello as both his personal pilot and private investigator[479];

[475] Russell, *On the Trail of the JFK Assassins*, 254-255, 268-269.
[476] Ibid, 106.
[477] Jim Garrison, *On the Trail of the Assassins*
[478] Ibid, 106.
[479] Ibid, 98, 221.

[473] Russell, *The Man Who Knew Too Much*, 182.
[474] Ibid.

- He was reportedly slated as the pilot who was supposed to fly one of the assassins out of Dallas after the JFK assassination[480];
- Ferrie had clear links to the CIA, especially in its covert anti-Cuban operations[481];
- Ferrie was an expert hypnotist who extensively studied the limits of posthypnotic suggestion and had practiced his hypnosis skills on the boys in the Civil Air Patrol, one of whom was Lee Harvey Oswald[482];
- Ferrie had worked closely with Dr. Mary Sherman on a secret intelligence project developing cancer-causing super viruses and there were many strange circumstances surrounding Dr. Sherman's murder[483];
- Ferrie also knew Judyth Baker, who had also worked closely on the secret cancer project.

Almost immediately following President Kennedy's assassination, one of Garrison's assistants received a suggestion from Jack Martin, a local private detective with intelligence ties, to pick up and question a certain David Ferrie. Ferrie, a homosexual rumored to have CIA ties, was then employed as a private investigator and, probably, personal pilot by New Orleans reputed Godfather Carlos Marcello. At the moment of the assassination, he had been in a federal courtroom watching Marcello be acquitted of deportation proceedings that John and Robert Kennedy had instigated two years earlier.[484]

---

[480] Ibid, 98.
[481] Ibid, 85, 92, 98, 106-107.
[482] Ibid,, 254-255, 268-269.
[483] Haslam, *Dr. Mary's Monkey*, 64-65.
[484] Russell, *On the Trail of the JFK Assassins*, 98-99.

David Ferrie (second from left) was a leader in the Civilian Air Patrol for Lee Harvey Oswald (far right) when he was a young man.

It has been established that Ferrie was working big-time in anti-Castro covert military operations:

> As early as 1960, del Valle was reportedly working with a New Orleans pilot, David Ferrie, in flying clandestine missions over Cuba.[485]

As Jim Garrison wrote:

> The Banister apparatus . . . was part of a supply line that ran along the Dallas-New Orleans-Miami corridor. These supplies consisted of arms and explosives for use against Castro's Cuba.[486]

In addition to his proximity to del Valle and the other exiled Cubans working against Castro, Ferrie had also worked closely with both Jack Ruby and Clay Shaw, the CIA asset who was eventually indicted for the murder of President Kennedy.[487] Ferrie also knew Lee Harvey Oswald very well, going all the way back to Oswald's youth in the Civilian Air Patrol, and seems to have been closely involved in the process of setting up Oswald.[488] In fact, the links to the killers of President Kennedy seem to be deeply enmeshed in that same group of men—those who traveled back and forth seamlessly between organized crime and U.S. Intelligence; especially Ferrie, Ruby, and Roselli, who were deeply involved in the CIA's covert anti-Castro operations. It is from those same anti-Castro ops, based in South Florida, from which the process to set up Oswald was hatched.

To sum up the operational conclusions of Jim Garrison's investigative team at the New Orleans District Attorney's Office:

> As Garrison continued his investigation, he became convinced that a group of right-wing extremists, including Ferrie, Banister, and Clay Shaw were involved in a conspiracy with elements of the CIA to kill John F. Kennedy. Garrison would later claim that the motive for the assassination was anger over Kennedy's attempts to obtain a peace settlement in both Cuba and Vietnam. Garrison also believed that Shaw, Banister and Ferrie had conspired to set up Oswald as a patsy in the JFK assassination.[489]

So David Ferrie had some very strong linkage to the JFK assassination. Like Johnny Roselli, Jack Ruby, and Chauncey Holt, Ferrie traveled in two worlds at the same time. Ferrie was a trusted member of Organized Crime—he was actually Carlos Marcello's private pilot. But at the exact same time, he was also deeply involved in actions and even specific missions on behalf of U.S. Intelligence, primarily in anti-Castro intelligence operations.

[485] Russell, *On the Trail of the JFK Assassins*, 106.
[486] Jim Garrison, *On the Trail of the Assassins* (Sheridan Square: 1988), 44.
[487] Ibid, 106.
[488] Garrison, *On the Trail of the Assassins*; Russell, *The Man Who Knew Too Much*.
[489] Garrison, *On the Trail of the Assassins* and Garrison, *Playboy* interview, accessed 4 Dec. 2012.

It certainly appeared—to millions of suspicious-minded Americans, when it came to the crazy matters concerning the JFK assassination—that New Orleans District Attorney Jim Garrison was actually putting the pieces of the puzzle together and making sense of that intricate jigsaw puzzle as well:

> I have solid evidence indicating that Ruby, Ferrie, Oswald and others involved in this case were all paid by the CIA to perform certain functions: Ruby to smuggle arms for Cuban exile groups, Ferrie to train them and to fly counterrevolutionary secret missions to Cuba, and Oswald to establish himself so convincingly as a Marxist that he would win the trust of American left-wing groups and also have freedom to travel as a spy in Communist countries, particularly Cuba.[490]

And Garrison was colorful about his characterizations in the process:

> We have evidence linking Ruby not only to anti-Castro exile activities but, as with almost everyone else involved in this case, to the CIA itself. Never forget that the CIA maintains a great variety of curious alliances it feels serve its purposes. It may be hard to imagine Ruby in a trench coat, but he seems to have been as good an employee of the CIA as he was a pimp for the Dallas cops.[491]

So Americans—and the world—were suddenly paying close attention to what Garrison said about his investigation and its findings:

> . . . Ruby was up to his neck with the plotters. Our investigators have broken a code Oswald used and found Ruby's private unlisted telephone number, as of 1963, written in Oswald's notebook. The same coded number was found in the address book of another prominent figure in this case.[492]

Garrison was one sharp character. Listen to his words, as he eloquently dispenses with some of the typical nonsense he used to receive—and nonsense that is *still* widely disseminated in various media formats in very obvious attempts to marginalize Garrison's findings:

> First of all, let me dispose of this concept of the "temporarily deranged man." This is a catchall term, employed whenever the real motive of a crime can't be nailed down. In the overwhelming majority of instances, the actions of human beings are the direct consequences of discernible motives.

---

[490] *JFK Lancer*, "Jim Garrison's Playboy Interview, Part Three," accessed 10 Sept. 2012: http://www.jfklancer.com/Garrison4.html

[491] Ibid.

[492] Ibid.

> This is the fatal flaw of the Warren Report—its conclusion that the assassination of President Kennedy was the act of a temporarily deranged man, that the murder of Officer Tippit was equally meaningless and, finally, that Jack Ruby's murder of Oswald was another act of a temporarily deranged individual. It is, of course, wildly improbable that all three acts were coincidentally the aberrant acts of temporarily deranged men—although it's most convenient to view them as such, because that judgment obviates the necessity of relentlessly investigating the possibility of a conspiracy.[493]

District Attorney Garrison's legal logic was permeated with plain old common sense and the American people innately sensed it:

> In Jack Ruby's case, his murder of Lee Oswald was the sanest act he ever committed; if Oswald had lived another day or so, he very probably would have named names, and Jack Ruby would have been convicted as a conspirator in the assassination plot. As it was, Ruby made the best of a bad situation by rubbing out Oswald in the Dallas city jail, since this act could be construed as an argument that he was "temporarily deranged."[494]

In fact, to many millions, Garrison's eloquence was only surpassed by his logic:

> I do find it interesting that Jack Ruby died of cancer a few weeks after his conviction for murder had been overruled in appeals court and he was ordered to stand trial outside of Dallas—thus allowing him to speak freely if he so desired. I would also note that there was little hesitancy in killing Lee Harvey Oswald in order to prevent him from talking, so there is no reason to suspect that any more consideration would have been shown Jack Ruby if he had posed a threat to the architects of the conspiracy.[495]

The odd thing, as Garrison noted, is that if Ferrie's death had actually been natural, as the coroner concluded, then why was there a suicide note? In fact, there were two notes. Then, Garrison also famously stated, with some well-aimed sarcasm:

> I suppose it could just be a weird coincidence that the night Ferrie penned two suicide notes, he died of natural causes.[496]

So the self-proclaimed "conspiracy debunkers" had some work cut out for themselves and really had to go to work on those points. In the process, what they effectively "debunked" was the possibility that Ferrie had actually died from suicide. John McAdams wrote:

---

[493] Ibid.
[494] *JFK Lancer*, "Jim Garrison's Playboy Interview, Part Three," accessed 10 Sept. 2012: http://www.jfklancer.com/Garrison4.html
[495] Ibid.
[496] Ibid.

So, did Ferrie commit suicide? The last person to see him alive, George Lardner, Jr., reported him to be in good spirits. And several people who talked to him in the last week of his life reported that, in spite of his health problems, he was in a combative mood, intent on fighting Garrison's charges against him. Indeed, he was preparing to sue Garrison.

But one key piece of evidence was discovered by Blackburst in Garrison's own files. A bottle of Proloid tablets was found in Ferrie's apartment after his death, and it had seven tablets left in it. Why wouldn't somebody intent on suicide take the whole bottle?

Most likely, Garrison simply lucked out when Ferrie died the natural death the autopsy results showed.[497]

Aside from the observation that John McAdams has a pretty twisted notion of what "luck" would be to a man like District Attorney Jim Garrison, it also makes it apparent that Ferrie's death was probably not suicide *or* accident.

So what was it? A natural death from too much pressure, as some, even the medical examiner, suggested?[498] It was widely reported that Ferrie left behind two typed notes that "suggested suicide." But did they?

Both of those notes were typed, undated, and unsigned.[499] And, as Mr. McAdams correctly pointed out, the notes do not appear to actually be suicide notes. They appear, instead, to be two notes written by a man who knew he was leaving this world—they were more the words of a man who was making his final statements; of words that he wanted left behind.

One note to his best friend started out: "When you read this I will be quite dead and no answer will be possible."[500] It ended with the words: "As you sowed, so shall you reap."[501] The other letter started out: "To leave this life, to me, is a sweet prospect."[502] Then it complained about the justice system and ended "All the state needs is 'evidence to support a conviction.' If this is justice, then justice be damned." The letters can be accessed in their entirety online.[503]

So they, indeed, do not appear to actually be notes regarding a planned suicide. However, Mr. McAdams uses that point to refute Jim Garrison's claim, which was simply regarding the possibility that Ferrie, as Mr. McAdams puts it, "had killed himself to escape prosecution."[504] That's very interesting, but not at all what's actually important. And, in the process of trying to prove Garrison wrong, the case for things amiss in the field of foul play is actually expanded.

[497] *John McAdams' The Kennedy Assassination Pages*, "David Ferrie's 'Suicide Notes,'" accessed 3 Dec. 2012: http://mcadams.posc.mu.edu/death10.htm
[498] Ibid.
[499] "David Ferrie"
[500] John McAdams, "David Ferrie's 'Suicide Notes'"
[501] Ibid.
[502] Ibid.
[503] *John McAdams' The Kennedy Assassination Pages*, "David Ferrie's 'Suicide Notes,'" accessed 3 Dec. 2012: http://mcadams.posc.mu.edu/death10.htm
[504] Ibid.

The Portentous Prose and Proclamations of David William Ferrie

If it's extremely noteworthy that upon closer examination of the contents of those two notes, they do not sound like a man planning to commit suicide, then it would seem to not only refute Garrison, but to confirm Ferrie's own words and fears. It's very important to remember exactly what Ferrie said. After Ferrie was publicly named as an accused conspirator in the JFK assassination by the New Orleans District Attorney's office, Ferrie exploded at Jim Garrison's aide, Lou Ivon. Ferrie's exact words were the following:

You know what this news story does to me, don't you? I'm a dead man. From here on, believe me, I'm a dead man.[505]

Now, notice the similar sentiments in the words in Ferrie's two letters found in his apartment:

When you read this I will be quite dead and no answer will be possible.[506]

Keep in mind that Ferrie worked arm-in-arm with Mafia Godfather Carlos Marcello; he knew the machinations of the Mob, knew what they did to people who had to be eliminated, and had just seen one person whom he knew—Jack Ruby—do precisely that to another person whom he knew—Lee Harvey Oswald:

It doesn't take a genius to surmise from all this that Ferrie knew his days were numbered—and a very low number, at that.

---

[505] Garrison, *On the Trail of the Assassins*, 138.
[506] John McAdams, "David Ferrie's 'Suicide Notes'"

The conspiracy "refuters" also inadvertently rule out an accidental death, as well as suicide, by pointing out that the drug Proloid, found in Ferrie's apartment, "is too slow-acting to have killed Ferrie between the time he was last seen alive (by journalist George Lardner, Jr.) and the time he was found dead."[507]

And while it is true that the New Orleans Coroner, Nichols Chetta, eventually concluded that Ferrie died of a cerebral hemorrhage—technically what is known as a "Berry Aneurysm," which could, in simple terms, just be called a stroke—take note that the story does not end there. Not everyone believed that just because Ferrie had died of a stroke meant that he had not been murdered, and among that "not everyone" was none other than the Managing Director of the Metropolitan Crime Commission of New

---

[507] Ibid.

Orleans, Aaron Kohn, who still believed that Ferrie was murdered.[508] We think people should be pretty interested in his opinion, too.

Another witness related to the JFK assassination explained in a video interview how the specific type of cerebral hemorrhage from which Ferrie died can be intentionally inflicted; the assassin pierces the roof of the mouth with a smooth object like a nail file, leaving very little evidence of the tear.[509] The interview can be seen online at: http://jfkmurdersolved.com/film/ferrie.wmv

CONCLUSION
Unsolved—Possible assassination

FURTHER RESEARCH

On the Trail of the JFK Assassins, Dick Russell, 2008, Skyhorse Publishing

The Man Who Knew Too Much, Dick Russell, 2003, Carroll & Graf

Me & Lee: How I Came to Know, Love and Lose Lee Harvey Oswald, Judyth Vary Baker, 2001, TrineDay

Dr. Mary's Monkey: How the unsolved murder of a doctor, a secret laboratory in New Orleans and cancer-causing monkey viruses are linked to Lee Harvey Oswald, the JFK assassination and emerging global epidemics, Edward T. Haslam, 2007, TrineDay

Wim Dankbaar, "Judyth Vary Baker," *JFK Murder Solved*: http://www.jfkmurdersolved .com/judyth.htm

"DAVID FERRIE: WHY HE IS IMPORTANT IN THE KENNEDY ASSASSINATION— AND EFFORTS BEING MADE TO HIDE IT," Judyth Vary Baker, April 6, 2011, *James Fetzer: Exposing Falsehoods and Revealing Truths*: http://jamesfetzer.blogspot .com/2011/04/david-ferrie-why-he-is-important-in.html

"The Mystery of David Ferrie," John S. Craig, July, 1995, *Fair Play Magazine*: http:// acorn.net/jfkplace/09/fb.back_issues/05th_Issue/ferrie.html

---

[508] John S. Craig, "The Mystery of David Ferrie," July, 1995, Fair Play Magazine: http://acorn.net/jfkplace/09/ fb.back_issues/05th_Issue/ferrie.html
[509] Wim Dankbaar, "JFK Murder Solved," accessed 14 Sept 2012: http:jfkmurdersolved.com/film/ferrie.wmv

Rolando Masferrer,
October 5, 1975

Victim	**Rolando "El Tigre" Masferrer, Major Cuban Exile Resistance Leader based in South Florida**
Cause of Death	Dynamite-bombed in car
Official Verdict	Unsolved murder
Actual Circumstances	Like Jimmy Hoffa, Masferrer definitely had involvement in the JFK assassination, but was also involved in a lot of dirty deals with the Mafia. So he was clearly assassinated in a highly professional job, but the question is, by whom?

To give you an idea of this guy's clout, "El Tigre" financed a private army in support of Batista, the Cuban dictator who preceded Castro. The army was known as "Los Tigres"; which Masferrer was named after.

As author Dick Russell once observed, Masferrer was a powerful and ruthless anti-Castro leader among the Cuban "government in exile" fighting from ninety miles away in its Florida base of operations:

> Nicknamed "The Tiger" after his ruthless private army of the Batista era, Masferrer was an ex-Cuban senator and newspaper publisher who reportedly fled the island with as much as $10 million.
>
> "A guy who could slit your throat and smile while doing it," said one U.S. Senate aide.[510]

Colonel William C. Bishop was the senior military liaison to the Executive Action Assassination Program, and no stranger to some of the most dangerous killers on the planet—so it's noteworthy that he considered "El Tigre" right up there with the worst of the worst and as a man to be reckoned with. He described him as the "key bagman" for Alpha 66, an extremely violent anti-Castro movement; with strong ties to the Mafia via Trafficante's Mob people in Florida and elsewhere; and he also made this interesting connection:

> He also had different ties with Jimmy Hoffa. As far back as 1962, I think. But Rolando, from time to time when it came to large sums of money, had sticky fingers. I think that's why he was killed, eventually. Either that, or the Kennedy assassination. Because he knew about it.[511]

Colonel Bishop clearly confirmed that two of the participants in the JFK assassination were Rolando Masferrer and Tony Varona. And in an interview with Dick Russell, he elaborated on how the Kennedy Administration's Cuba policies had infuriated the anti-Castro Cubans:

> You take Tony Varona and Rolando Masferrer to name but two—and there were many, many more—when serious talk began to happen about the possibility of assassinating Kennedy.[512]

In an obviously professional operation, Masferrer was assassinated when dynamite exploded in his car.

> Rolando Masferrer, another Cuban exile employed by the CIA, was blown to bits when his car exploded on October 5, 1975. Masferrer had worked with "plumbers" Hunt, Sturgis, and Barker.

---

[510] Russell, *The Man Who Knew Too Much*, 333.
[511] Russell, *The Man Who Knew Too Much*, 333.
[512] Russell, *The Man Who Knew Too Much*, 333.

According to Miss Brussell:[513]

He would have been investigated for his activities in connection with assassination attempts on foreign leaders, had he not been killed.[514]

Military Intelligence operative Richard Case Nagell provided us with a picture of how it all fits together. Nagell described how Masferrer was:

- One of the individuals he was assigned to investigate;
- One of the individuals with known links to the JFK assassination;
- How he shared ties with other subjects of this book.

I conducted inquiries relative to "dissident" members of several Cuban refugee groups based in the United States; I checked out an alleged connection between a Miami resident named Eladio del Valle and New Orleans CIA informant Sergio Arcacha-Smith; I investigated an associate of the now deceased right-wing extremist David W. Ferrie of New Orleans . . . I conducted a surveillance on a man, said to have been an ex-CIA employee, observed talking to leader Manuel Artime and former Cuban senator/racketeer Rolando Masferrer.[515]

Dick Russell knew the significance of those statements when Nagell voiced them:

All of these people were prominent names in exile-related activities. All of them have also surfaced before—as having been involved in CIA-backed attempts to assassinate Fidel Castro, or even rumored connections to the assassination of President Kennedy.[516]

CONCLUSION

Assassination: Probable link to victim's knowledge of JFK assassination, but possibly Mafia retaliation killing as well.

---

[513] Assassination researcher and author, Mae Brussell
[514] Malcom Abrams, "30 Watergate Witnesses Have Met Violent Deaths," 12 July 1976, *Midnight Magazine*: http://www.maebrussell.com/Mae%20Brussell%20Articles/Watergate%20Deaths.html
[515] Russell, *The Man Who Knew Too Much*, 182.
[516] Ibid.

32 | Dr. Mary Sherman, July 21, 1964

Victim	**Cancer Researcher, Dr. Mary Sherman**
Cause of Death	Multiple stab wounds penetrating the heart, liver, stomach, labia minora, left arm and right leg. Extreme burns of right side of body with complete destruction of right upper extremity and right side of thorax and abdomen, exposing vital organs.[517]
Official Verdict	Unsolved murder

[517] Edward T. Haslam, *Dr. Mary's Monkey: How the unsolved murder of a doctor, a secret laboratory in New Orleans and cancer-causing monkey viruses are linked to Lee Harvey Oswald, the JFK assassination and emerging global epidemics* (TrineDay: 2007).

Actual Circumstances	Dr. Sherman was deeply involved in covert research, developing a "super-cancer" as a biological weapon. Dr. Sherman also knew both Lee Harvey Oswald and David Ferrie, both of whom were involved in the same research project.[518]
Inconsistencies	In addition to multiple stab wounds, virtually the entire right side of her upper body was absent, her apartment was set on fire after she was killed, _and_ her death occurred on the same day that the Warren Commission came to New Orleans to obtain testimony on the assassination of President Kennedy.[519] The victim's arm was literally disintegrated. The damage that her body sustained—with absolute certainty—cannot be explained by the official version of events, which maintained that she was murdered in her home and then set afire.[520] Various evidentiary consistencies were also apparent, which are examined in detail in the following text.

Dr. Mary S. Sherman was a gifted physician who was selected for a special cancer research project in New Orleans by Dr. Alton Ochsner, a prominent New Orleans physician; in fact, one of the nation's leaders in guiding the country's largest medical research projects.

> Dr. Mary Sherman was one of America's leading cancer experts and had all the credentials to prove it. The newspaper articles about her death refer to her as "an internationally-known bone specialist." She was an Associate Professor at a prominent medical school engaged in monkey virus research, director of a cancer laboratory at an internationally famous medical clinic, and Chairman of the Pathology Committee of one of the most elite medical societies in America. The medical articles she wrote were quoted for half a century.[521]

Her murder was front-page headlines in New Orleans. At first, the burglary angle was notably highlighted, being referenced approximately twenty times in just the first day of coverage by the two major New Orleans newspapers.

The murder of a famous female physician, especially with the apparent sexual angle of the killing, was the talk of the town:

---

[518] Judyth Vary Baker Me & Lee: How I Came to Know, Love and Lose Lee Harvey Oswald, (TrineDay: 2011), Haslam, _Dr. Mary's Monkey_
[519] Haslam, _Dr. Mary's Monkey_
[520] Haslam, _Dr. Mary's Monkey_
[521] Haslam, _Dr. Mary's Monkey_, 63-64.

Slashed with a knife, dismembered, and set on fire. It looked like a sexual killing, you know.[522]

The following was representative coverage in the New Orleans *States-Item*:

Homicide detectives said the front door to her apartment had been forced open, her wallet was empty, and her 1961 automobile was missing . . . Sam Moran, Special Investigator for the Orleans Parish Coroner's office, said the front door had been forced open and an unsuccessful attempt had been made to open a jewelry box.[523]

Well, that seemed pretty clear, didn't it? The cops were sure that it was a burglary job. Right?

Wrong!

Reconstruction of a Self-Contradictory Crime Scene

Deceased: Dr. Mary Sherman

July 21, 1964, New Orleans, Louisiana
The death scene at the home of prominent New Orleans physician, Mary Sherman, presented numerous apparent anomalies to investigators.

- No signs of forced entry;
- Burglar alarm in "off" position;
- Victim found in her home, but victim's car missing;
- A pair of "blood-soaked gloves" were found in the laundry hamper;
- Victim was found "upside down" in bed, i.e., feet at headboard, head at foot of bed;
- Clothing had been placed atop the victim and the clothing, as well as the mattress, were smoldering, but not ablaze;
- Two different sets of burns were present on victim's body: one set was pre-death and extreme in nature, one set was post-mortem and moderate in nature, neither set fatal (see text for description);
- Two different sets of knife cuts were present on victim's body: one set was pre-death, one set was post-mortem (refer to the accompanying text for description and discussion);
- Actual cause of death (COD): Heart pierced by knife that passed through the intercostal space near the sternum (breast bone), between the sixth and seventh ribs, directly over the heart;

---

[522] Haslam, *Dr. Mary's Monkey*, 49.
[523] Haslam, *Dr. Mary's Monkey*, 121.

- Neighbors heard absolutely nothing even though the walls were very thin and, for example, neighbors could usually tell when Dr. Sherman was home because they could ordinarily hear her footsteps quite easily;
- Smoke from the smoldering fire finally awakened a neighbor and emergency units were then called to the scene at 4:13 a.m.;
- Fire damage to the apartment and structure was very limited. "There was no structural damage to the wood-framed building."[524] In fact, the curtains in the bedroom—the same room in which the victim was found dead—had not even caught on fire;
- "Fire damage" to victim was extensive and far surpassed what could—by any stretch of the imagination—be logically expected from the fire damage in the apartment;
- No motive: Police could not discern any viable motive (burglary was ruled out), although homicide investigators implied a sexual motive, based on cuts to the genitals;
- As a result of the sexual slant in the homicide report, the newspaper reports then highlighted that aspect and people became convinced that it was a lesbian killing by a sexual psychopath, and one whom was known to the victim. That was an interesting theory—but one that was entirely wrong.

Material derived primarily from: Edward T. Haslam, *Dr. Mary's Monkey: How the unsolved murder of a doctor, a secret laboratory in New Orleans and cancer-causing monkey viruses are linked to Lee Harvey Oswald, the JFK assassination and emerging global epidemics*, 2007.

---

[524] Ibid, 227

Everyone in town was interested in the case and following details about her murder.

> It would not be until the next day, after a horrified city had literally millions of word-of-mouth discussions about the sensational murder/burglary, before the newspapers stated that the front door had not been forced open and her burglar alarm had been turned off. The press now reported that the homicide department, impressed by these facts, and the facts that "the intruder" knew which car belonged to Dr. Sherman and that a box full of jewelry which could have easily been carried off was left behind, ruled out burglary as a motive.[525]

The whole city followed the case with rapt attention. There were no signs of forced entry at Mary's apartment:

---

[525] Ibid, emphasis in original.

From Elmener Peterson, Mary's housekeeper, police learned that the burglar alarm was in the "off" position, that Dr. Sherman was "expecting visitors from out of town," and that she had laid out a polka dot dress, which they found lying on a chair in the bedroom. As to the issue of whether the intruder had forced the door open, the report says:

"The officers could find no signs of the door leading to the apartment patio or sliding glass door having been forced open."[526]

The Homicide Report also read that:

It appeared that no scuffle took place inside of said bedroom, and nothing appeared to be disarranged in the bedroom or throughout the apartment.[527]

Especially around Tulane Medical School, Dr. Sherman was well-known and well-respected, and professional people found the circumstances surrounding her death *extremely* suspicious:

But the grapevine said that whoever killed her knew what they were doing with a knife . . . maybe they even had a high level of medical knowledge, just judging by the way the cuts were done.[528]

However, the press coverage and the police reporting did not mesh well and people who were following the case sensed that something was awry:

Something didn't make sense. The explanations of Mary Sherman's murder didn't add up. The press coverage focused on an "intruder," yet there was no forced entry. The police investigation failed to determine any identifiable motive, but the homicide report strained to imply a sexual one. And why did they not want to say where the victim worked?[529]

The fact that no noises had been heard by the neighbors was another dramatically inconsistent aspect of the crime scene. The old building was of such type of construction that the neighbors were very used to hearing the footsteps of Dr. Sherman returning from work and, as a result, would usually be very aware of when she was home:

The crime scene was also bizarre. How could anyone inflict such massive destruction on another person in the still of the night in a flimsy apartment complex filled with other people, and not have anyone even hear anything?[530]

---

[526] Ibid, 127.
[527] *New Orleans Police Department*, "Homicide Report-Mary S. Sherman," October 29, 1964.
[528] Haslam, *Dr. Mary's Monkey*, 49.
[529] Ibid, 227.
[530] Ibid, 227, emphasis in original.

No one has spent more time researching the matter of Dr. Sherman's death than author Ed Haslam, who has literally devoted many years of his life trying to determine what actually happened. The first point of mystifying evidence which begged to be addressed, in Haslam's view, was the standpoint of fire damage.

There was obviously <u>no way</u> that a fire of the type in Dr. Sherman's apartment could have caused the extreme damage apparent in Dr. Sherman's body. In fact, clothing that was found atop the victim <u>had not even burned</u>.

The following is straight from the homicide report:

> **The body was nude; however, there was clothing which had apparently been placed on top of the body, mostly covering the body from just above to the pubic area to the neck. Some of the mentioned clothes had been burned completely, while others were still intact, but scorched.**[531]

So, being the solid researcher he is, Haslam did some intelligent checking of the matter, approaching it scientifically, from the standpoint of temperature.

Again, from the homicide report:

> **According to the criminologist, the mentioned clothes were composed of synthetic material which would have to reach a temperature of about 500 F before it would ignite into a flame; however, prior to this, there would be a smoldering effect.**[532]

It seemed fair to interpret the above excerpt from the homicide report as meaning that the fire—at least at the location of the clothing that had been placed atop the victim's body—had not reached a temperature of 500 F, as evidenced by the fact that it had smoldered, but had not ignited into flames.

Now, there were some actual numbers to work with. So Haslam did some checking, and here's what he learned:

- Even the professional incineration of human bodies in the process of cremation, most emphatically, <u>does not</u> result in the amount of destruction to the human body that was present in Dr. Sherman.
- An average cremation of human remains takes about two hours at a temperature of about 1,600 F; some as high as 2,000 F for a period of three hours—at the end of which, "you still have bones, or at least pieces of bones like joints, skull fragments, and knuckles."[533]
- The next step in the cremation process is to take those bone pieces and grind them up, and the final product is then bone dust.
- Hence, quite contrary to popular perception, the dust in the human "ashes" that is given to the families of the deceased is not actually the "ashes" of their cremated body—it is ground up bone dust.
- But the point to take away from all of the above is this:

---

[531] Ibid, 229.
[532] Ibid, 229.
[533] Ibid, 230.

Bones do not burn

Mr. Haslam's decades of study of this case have led to some amazing discoveries:

> Even the bodies of fighter pilots who crash and burn <u>do not</u> experience a level of fire and destruction capable of incinerating the bones. There is <u>always bone</u> left. Listen to the observations of someone who has been at those crash sites:

> Jet fuel burns at thousands of degrees, but there were still bones left. I also saw people who had been covered with napalm and the like. But there were still bones left.[534]

Analysis of Medical Evidence

Death of Dr. Mary S. Sherman

The medical facts of this case lead to some—very *necessarily*—dramatic conclusions.

1. There was intense charring of victim's body; charring is carbonization (like burning a steak) resulting from extremely high temperature burns:
   She was carbonized from the right side of her head down to her right hip.[535]
2. Yet, the damage was markedly localized and areas very near the extreme burns were virtually unharmed. For example, there were "intense high-heat burns on the scalp, immediately adjacent to the unburned hair."[536]
3. The damage was so intense that the right arm was completely missing, bone and all: "all that remained was a short piece of charred bone extending out from the shoulder."[537]
4. The "extensive destruction" was present through the "right half of her rib cage"; exposing the lung and other vital organs. "Exposure of the lung means massive destruction of both the rib cage and the chest wall." Bones in that region were, again, completely destroyed.[538]
5. There were *two* sets of burns sustained in victim's body: pre- and post-mortem.

---

[535] Haslam, *Dr. Mary's Monkey*, 234.
[536] Ibid.
[537] Ibid.
[538] Ibid, 235.

---

[534] Haslam, 231.

The first set of burns was from an extremely hot and very focused heat source, and occurred somewhere other than her apartment. The total destruction of her arm is evidence of a very powerful device capable of producing thousands of degrees of heat.[539]

Other burns on the victim were of a markedly more moderate nature and occurred as a result of the small fire in the apartment.

6. There were two sets of stab wounds: pre- and post-mortem. Dr. Sherman was stabbed "dead center in the middle of her heart"[540]—that was the wound that killed her:

Upon removal of the breast bone, there was found more than one quart of variously-clotted blood near the heart, evidence that she *was still alive* when she was stabbed in the heart.[541]

Other knife wounds were made *after* she was dead, evidenced by the absence of hemorrhaging:

The absence of hemorrhage around the liver wound means that the wound did not bleed, indicating that this wound to the liver was inflicted after death, during the second set of stab wounds.[542]

The death wound piercing the heart very precisely was apparently the "basis for the rumor that whoever killed Mary Sherman knew what he or she was doing, and may have had medical training."[543]

Additional knife wounds were determined to also be post-mortem. In fact, the knife wounds to the genitals were determined to be made not only post-mortem, but also through the clothing that had been placed atop the body. That nullifies the sexual aspect of the crime because the killer and/or crime scene stager was probably not even aware that the wounds had pierced the genitals.[544]

▶ **Conclusions Based On Medical Evidence:**

  • It is literally impossible that the severest aspects of the damage to Dr. Sherman's body were the result of the fire that occurred in her apartment.

---

[539] Ibid, 237.
[540] Ibid, 235-236.
[541] Ibid, 236, emphasis in original.
[542] Ibid, 236.
[543] Ibid, 236.
[544] Ibid, 237.

- Only an intensely focused and directed force of extremely high energy—such as a lightning bolt, or a beam of high-voltage electricity or radiation—would be capable of creating the extent of damage sustained in the victim. Therefore:
- Victim, necessarily, had to have sustained the first set of burns somewhere other than the official crime scene (her home), and at a time prior to being taken to her home and then set afire.
- Few devices capable of rendering such a directed beam of high-intensity energy were in existence in 1964:
  The partial charring of her scalp (without burning the rest of her hair) is evidence that this device focused its energy very precisely. Very few pieces of equipment would be capable of producing such a combination of burns. A linear particle accelerator is one.[545]

---

[545] Ibid, 237.

Therefore it seemed that the only possible logical solution to the crime would be to determine if Dr. Sherman had access to some type of highly advanced research equipment, such as a super-laser or a linear particle beam accelerator. Mr. Haslam's research established that not only did Dr. Sherman have access to a linear particle accelerator, but there was even concrete evidence of one having been used in her research. He determined and verified those points, in quite some detail.[546]

In summation of the above evidentiary points—and to a very high degree of probability—Dr. Mary Sherman apparently died in a laboratory accident of some type. However, the fact that she was intricately involved in matters of national security necessitated the masking of that accident. Therefore, it was staged to appear to be a murder that took place in her home.

There is also a link to the JFK assassination in this case that could not be more obvious:

. . . Warren Commission investigators started taking their testimony in New Orleans on the morning of July 21, 1964, several hours after Mary Sherman's murder. Some consider this coincidental timing suspicious, and have speculated that her death may have somehow been related to the Kennedy assassination or to her association with David Ferrie.[547]

---

[546] Ibid, 232-271.
[547] Ibid, 134, emphasis added.

Dramatic Inconsistencies Concerning the Death of Dr. Mary S. Sherman

1. It is impossible that the fire burned hot enough to cause the extreme damage to the right side of her body, literally disintegrating her entire right arm and the right portion of her chest and stomach. The hair on her body was unburned. The mattress was smoldering, but not burning, and clothing was singed, but not aflame ... but the right side of her body was totally vaporized, bone and all. No apparent cause could have inflicted such extreme damage. It has been suggested that her sensitive work with a linear particle accelerator was the actual source of the injury. No other viable explanation currently exists.[548]

2. Forensics revealed that the clothing was placed atop her body <u>after</u> death but prior to the arrival of emergency personnel.[549]

3. Most of the stab wounds were post-mortem, in what could be termed a bizarre case of "reverse staging"—the crime scene was intentionally staged to make her death appear to be a case of murder. But the victim was apparently already dead in a previous location, and brought to the staged scene at her home.[550]

4. Also reportedly recovered at the crime scene were "blood-soaked gloves."[551] Those gloves may have yielded valuable DNA information, especially with the new technologies available. However, they were destroyed—along with much other preserved evidence from the Mary Sherman case—during the flood disaster in New Orleans that followed Hurricane Katrina in 2005. The classic observation by author James DiEugenio bears repeating, regarding the "blood-drenched gloves" found in her apartment: "Think about that one."[552]

5. Dr. Sherman worked very closely with David Ferrie and Dr. Alton Ochsner, both of whom have been linked to Lee Harvey Oswald on a classified anti-Castro bioweapons project.[553]

---

[548] Haslam, *Dr. Mary's Monkey*
[549] Ibid.
[550] Ibid.
[551] Ibid, 9.
[552] James DiEugenio, "Posner in New Orleans: Gerry in Wonderland," *Citizens for Truth about the Kennedy Assassination*, accessed 11 Dec. 2012: http://www.ctka.net/posner_jd.html
[553] Baker, *Me & Lee*

6. Testimony for Warren Commission investigators began in New Orleans on the same day that Dr. Sherman was killed.[554]

7. Judyth Baker—who had worked on the cancer project with Dr. Sherman, Dr. Ochsner, David Ferrie, and Lee Harvey Oswald—was warned by David Ferrie, after Oswald was arrested, that she too would be killed if she told what she knew.[555]

8. Signs of a cover-up included:
   - Police classified it as a burglary, then issued a press blackout;[556]
   - The fact that her arm was missing was withheld from the public;[557]
   - Her FBI file revealed a letter from FBI Director J. Edgar Hoover directing his agents *not* to assist New Orleans Police with an investigation;[558]
   - Her body was cremated, precluding further forensic investigation.[559]
   - Police reports were withheld for almost thirty years.[560]
   - Author John Davis, in the book *Mafia Kingfish: Carlos Marcello and the Assassination of John F. Kennedy*, wrote that Dr. Sherman's death may have been related to Ferrie's death and that she was "David Ferrie's closest female friend."[561]
   - A "misinformation" job (and a sloppy one at that) was done by Gerald Posner in the book *Case Closed: Lee Harvey Oswald and the Assassination of JFK*. Mr. Posner made quite a few evidentiary errors regarding the Dr. Sherman crime scene in the section of his book very transparently entitled "The Non-Mysterious Mystery Deaths"; proving yet again that some people—as the old saying goes—just refuse to let the facts get in the way of a good story.[562]

---

[554] James DiEugenio, "Posner in New Orleans"
[555] Baker, *Me & Lee*
[556] Haslam, *Dr. Mary's Monkey*
[557] Ibid.
[558] Ibid.
[559] Ibid.
[560] Ibid.
[561] John H. Davis, *Mafia Kingfish: Carlos Marcello and the Assassination of John F. Kennedy* (McGraw-Hill: 1988).
[562] Haslam, *Dr. Mary's Monkey*, 135: citing Gerald Posner, *Case Closed: Lee Harvey Oswald and the Assassination of JFK* (Random House: 1993).

196 | Hit List

CONCLUSIONS

There is not yet sufficient evidence to conclusively prove a direct link between the death of Dr. Mary Sherman and the JFK assassination. *However*, Dr. Sherman was very clearly at work on a bioweapon that was ultra-secret in nature. Oddly, this is a case where an apparent medical accident, due to its nefarious and top-secret nature, had to be disguised, and the method chosen for that subterfuge was to disguise it as a murder. And it almost worked. Except for the fact that murderers could not disintegrate limbs with particle accelerators; at least not in 1964 they couldn't. It's possible that Dr. Sherman's death was intentional, hence murder. But for the time being, the preponderance of evidence actually leads to the following conclusion:

Death by medical accident accompanied by "euthanasic termination"; Crime scene was then staged as a murder in order to preserve the secrecy of the top-secret research project with which she was involved.

FURTHER RESEARCH

Dr. Mary's Monkey: How the unsolved murder of a doctor, a secret laboratory in New Orleans and cancer-causing monkey viruses are linked to Lee Harvey Oswald, the JFK assassination and emerging global epidemics, Edward T. Haslam, 2007, TrineDay

Me & Lee: How I Came to Know, Love and Lose Lee Harvey Oswald, Judyth Vary Baker, 2011, TrineDay

Mafia Kingfish: Carlos Marcello and the Assassination of John F. Kennedy, John H. Davis, 1988, McGraw-Hill

Wim Dankbaar, "Judyth Vary Baker," *JFK Murder Solved*: http://www.jfkmurdersolved. com/judyth.htm

David Ferrie: *Why He is Important in the Kennedy Assassination—And Efforts Being Made to Hide It*, Judyth Vary Baker, April 6, 2011, *James Fetzer: Exposing Falsehoods and Revealing Truths*: http://jamesfetzer.blogspot.com/2011/04/david-ferrie-why-he-is-important-in.html

The Mystery of David Ferrie, John S. Craig, July, 1995, *Fair Play Magazine*: http://acorn. net/jfkplace/09/fb.back_issues/05th_Issue/ferrie.html

33 | J. Edgar Hoover,
May 2, 1972

Victim	**FBI Director, J. Edgar Hoover**
Cause of Death	Heart attack
Official Verdict	Natural Causes

For an incredible span of forty-eight years, John Edgar Hoover maintained control of the FBI like a pariah, blackmailing politicians to the extent that even President Truman and President Kennedy were afraid to cross him because they deemed the political "cost" too high.[563] As one author aptly summed up his reign of power controlled by the fear of what was in his confidential files:

---

[563] Richard Hack, *Puppetmaster: The Secret Life of J. Edgar Hoover* (Phoenix Books: 2007).

Hoover does not have to exert pressure, he *is* pressure.[564]

Hoover's death has been regarded as suspicious by some members of the research community.[565] Though Hoover knew much about the assassination of President Kennedy (and much about just about everything) and was instrumental in the cover-up (he apparently helped engineer the suppression of information), his death does not appear to be the result of that. We researched the circumstances and, if anything, it appears to be more related to the events of Watergate, which took place in the same time frame of when Hoover died.

We obtained one report that was very interesting. Researcher extraordinaire, Mae Brussell, believed Hoover's death was indeed related to Watergate and the fact that Hoover possessed damaging information about the Nixon Administration:

> There is considerable evidence that he may have known about the White House "dirty tricks."
>
> An article in the *Harvard Crimson* quotes Felipe De Diego, a Cuban exile who took part in the break-in at psychiatrist Daniel Ellsberg's office, as saying:
>
> Two burglaries took place at Hoover's Washington home. The first was in the winter of 1972 to retrieve documents that might be used for blackmail against the White House.
>
> "After the first burglary," according to Diego, "a second burglary was carried out; this time, whether by design or misunderstanding, a poison, thyonphosphate genre, was placed in Hoover's personal toilet articles. Hoover died shortly after that."
>
> Thyonphosphate genre is a drug that induces heart seizures. Its presence in a corpse is undetectable without an autopsy. No autopsy was ever performed on the body of J. Edgar Hoover.[566]

Apparently, it would not have been the first time:

> In 1975, The *Washington Post* reported: "E. Howard Hunt, the former CIA agent who helped engineer the Ellsberg and Watergate burglaries, told associates that he was ordered to kill (Jack) Anderson with an untraceable poison obtained from a former CIA doctor, but that the scheme was dropped at the last minute."[567]

The history leading up to the Watergate scandal and Hoover's death are very interesting, as the two events clearly intersect:

---

564 Jan Knippers Black, *United States Penetration of Brazil* (University of Pennsylvania Press: 1977).
565 Malcom Abrams, "30 Watergate Witnesses Have Met Violent Deaths," 12 July 1976, *Midnight Magazine*: http://www.maebrussell.com/Mae%20Brussell%20Articles/Watergate%20Deaths.html
566 Abrams, "30 Watergate Witnesses Have Met Violent Deaths"
567 Michael Benson, *Who's Who in the JFK Assassination: An A to Z Encyclopedia* (Citadel: 2003), 208.

Nixon had instituted a White House intelligence unit in 1971, and Hoover had objected. It would have taken power and influence away from the FBI. It was only a short time later that Hoover suffered break-ins of his apartment (shared with Clyde Tolson, his longtime associate and reputed lover). These break-ins were sworn to by Felipe De Diego, past associate of E. Howard Hunt, under the direction of former FBI man G. Gordon Liddy. Hunt and Liddy were later connected with the Watergate break-in.

Prior to the Watergate burglary of the Democratic National Convention, Attorney General John Mitchell ordered the FBI to wiretap selected organizations and influential people. Hoover agreed to the task, but insisted that he keep the original transcripts of the tapes in his secret files so they could not be changed. Mitchell then asked his close friend, Robert Mardian, to get the transcripts from Hoover's secret vault and remove them to John Ehrlichman's safe in the White House. The man who was assigned this mission was a senior FBI official named William Sullivan. Sullivan was later killed in a strange "hunting accident."[568]

We cover the very strange and very self-predicted "accidental" death of William Sullivan in the following chapter.

By this time, Hoover was a marked man. The Nixon administration had already demonstrated the intention to remove anyone who got in its way, and Hoover was surely in the path of politics.

The Committee to Reelect the President (CREEP) set up its own intelligence operation, staffed with former CIA and FBI employees and other renegade mercenaries, who would shore up Nixon's empire against all future comers. One of those who posed a serious threat at this time was Hoover. It is speculated that he knew the truth about the Nixon/Kennedy Assassination connection and was prepared to take Nixon down in self-defense by revealing what he knew. It was at this critical time that Hoover died.[569]

Veteran researcher Pat Speer also noted the importance of the context in Hoover's death:

Over the next few months, both G. Gordon Liddy and Pat Buchanan wrote extensive analyses for Nixon, explaining why he had to sack Hoover, but Nixon kept backing down. In early '72, shortly after Hunt first contacted Bernie Barker, someone broke into the FBI office in Meridian Pennsylvania and began distributing documents to the media, which included the words COINTEL PRO. The revelations of FBI agents-provocateur targeting the anti-war movement among others spurred Hale Boggs to publicly criticize Hoover on the floor of Congress. Many thought this was the end of Hoover. But he somehow hung on. Then bam, he died in his sleep.

---

[568] Roberts & Armstrong, *The Dead Witnesses*, 77-78.
[569] Ibid, 78.

A month later the Watergate burglars were captured.

I've often wondered if Nixon didn't have Hoover killed, and if someone—maybe McCord, maybe the CIA—figured it out, and arranged for the Watergate bubble to burst.

I believe it's as likely Hoover was murdered as Sullivan.[570]

Researchers Craig Roberts and John Armstrong determined that the theory on the "mode of death" is not as outlandish as it may at first seem:

Hoover's cause of death is listed as "hyperactive cardiovascular disease." Basically, this is a heart attack. Yet no history of heart problems exists and no autopsy was performed to confirm the "findings."

On December 12, 1973, an article in the *Harvard Crimson* appeared, reporting that two burglaries of Hoover's apartment had occurred, and that during the second entry, Hoover's "toilet articles" were coated with a solution of thyon-phosphate poison, that, when touched, caused an immediate heart muscle seizure. Other sources mention the use of sodium-morphate, which accomplishes the same results.

It must be noted here that Hoover believed that separate bullets, fired from different locations, struck Governor Connally and President Kennedy. He also believed that the Oswald who defected to the Soviet Union was an imposter and that the real Lee Harvey Oswald was still running around loose somewhere.[571]

CONCLUSIONS BASED ON EVIDENTIARY INDICATIONS
Possible Murder: Not specifically linked to JFK assassination.

[570] Pat Speer, "Was William Sullivan Murdered?" 19 April 2005: http://educationforum.ipbhost.com/index.php?showtopic=3694&st=0
[571] Ibid, 78-79.

34–39

Six Top FBI Officials Linked to the JFK Assassination Who Died in a 6-Month Period, Prior to Their Scheduled Testimony

Victims	**Louis Nichols, Assistant FBI Director (Third in command of FBI)** **Alan Belmont (FBI Liaison to Warren Commission)** **James Cadigan (FBI document expert who examined evidence)** **Donald Kaylor (FBI fingerprint expert who worked case)** **J.M. English (Head of FBI Forensics Laboratory)** **William Sullivan (Head of Division Five, Domestic Intelligence)**
Official Cause of Death	Louis Nichols: Heart attack June, 1977
	Alan Belmont: "Long illness" August, 1977 James Cadigan: "Accidental fall at home" August, 1977 Donald Kaylor: Heart attack October, 1977 J.M. English: Heart attack October, 1977 William Sullivan: "Hunting accident" November 9, 1977
Official Verdict	Natural causes and accidents; no foul play in any cases.

1. Statistically, the odds of six top FBI officials—all with information directly related to the JFK assassination—dying within a six-month period and prior to their scheduled testimony as witnesses before a Congressional committee investigating the assassination, are sufficiently astronomical as to make their natural occurrence literally impossible.[572]

Inconsistencies

2. William Sullivan specifically predicted that he would be murdered and that it would be made to appear as an accident. It was not a casual or flippant remark, but rather a precise statement that occurred exactly as he had predicted it would.

The deaths of witnesses increased dramatically during the 1970s, when the House Select Committee on Intelligence Activities and the House Select Committee on Assassinations began scheduling witnesses to appear before their committees. Gangsters linked to the assassination started dropping like flies, and at exactly the same time too.[573] Among them were top Chicago crime boss Sam Giancana, his top hitman, Chuck Nicoletti, and their link to the CIA's Castro assassination program, Johnny Roselli. Other Chicago mobsters included Richard Cain and Dave Yaras, mobbed-up Jimmy Hoffa, LBJ-affiliated hitman Mac Wallace, Lucien Sarti, Carlos Prío Socarrás, Rolando Masferrer, and George de Mohrenschildt. It read like a *Who's Who* of the CIA's Mafia connections, especially as it related to the Agency's anti-Castro operations—and they were all conveniently dead.

Then the same "massive death of witnesses" syndrome apparently struck the CIA:

Several important figures in the Central Intelligence Agency died before they could give evidence to the House Select Committee on Assassinations.[574]

Lo and behold, they too were specifically linked to the Agency's anti-Castro operations. Among them were Sheffield Edwards, "Wild Bill" Harvey, William Pawley, Dave Morales, Thomas Karamessines, Win Scott, and John Paisley. When researchers noticed the "coincidences" piling up, they were called ridiculous "conspiracy buffs." To convey an idea of the *truly* ridiculous, merely consider this: As we reveal in the future chapter on his death, Spy-chief John Paisley was shot in the head, diving weights affixed to his body, and sunk in the ocean—and they *still* said that he committed suicide! Things were getting very strange indeed.

Then the same odd "bug" seemed to hit over at the FBI:

William Sullivan, the main figure in the FBI involved in the Executive Action program (the assassination program targeting Castro), was shot

---

[572] John Simkin, "Deaths of Witnesses Connected to the Assassination of John F. Kennedy," *Spartacus Educational,* accessed 9 Nov 2012: http://www.spartacus.schoolnet.co.uk/JFKdeaths.htm
[573] Ibid.
[574] Ibid.

dead near his home in Sugar Hill, New Hampshire, on November 9, 1977. Sullivan had been scheduled to testify before the House Select Committee on Assassinations.[575]

My, my, my—yet another incredibly uncommon coincidence. And you can then multiply that one by a factor of six.

Sullivan was one of six top FBI officials who died in a six-month period in 1977. Others who were due to appear before the committee who died included Louis Nichols, special assistant to J. Edgar Hoover and his liaison with the Warren Commission; Alan H. Belmont, special assistant to Hoover; James Cadigan, document expert with access to documents that related to death of John F. Kennedy; J.M. English, former head of FBI Forensic Sciences Laboratory where Oswald's rifle and pistol were tested, and Donald Kaylor, FBI fingerprint chemist who examined prints found at the assassination scene.[576]

Actually, most of the above men were even *more* related to events surrounding the assassination than the above info indicates. For example, Donald Kaylor was directly tied to the apparently falsely obtained palm print of Lee Harvey Oswald on the rifle that was supposedly used to kill Kennedy. The FBI went to the funeral home and the undertaker testified that they apparently obtained prints there from the dead Lee Harvey Oswald.[577] Alan Belmont played a particularly crucial role in the orchestration of the obvious government cover-up, forcing the ridiculous "lone assassin" scenario:

The review of the facts that follows shows that Alan Belmont, the number-three man in the formal hierarchy of the FBI, was the primary official in charge of the FBI activities following the assassination. It is Belmont, not Hoover, who ran the FBI cover-up.[578]

Authors Jim Marrs and Ralph Schuster summed up the incredible series of "coincidences" like this:

The year 1977 produced a bumper crop of candidates for listing under convenient deaths connected to the JFK assassination, including the deaths of six top FBI officials; all of whom were scheduled to testify before the House Select Committee on Assassinations.

Topping this list was former number-three man in the FBI, William C. Sullivan, who had already had a preliminary meeting with the investigators for the House Committee. Sullivan was shot with a high-powered rifle near his New Hampshire home by a man who claimed to have mistaken

---

[575] Ibid.
[576] Ibid.
[577] See testimony of mortician Paul Groody of Miller Funeral Home: "'Agents' fingerprinted Oswald corpse"; accessed 10 Nov 2012: http://youtu.be/P2W_-ID8RMI
[578] Donald Gibson, *The Kennedy Assassination Cover-Up* (Nova Biomedical: 2000). http://www.spartacus.schoolnet.co.uk/JFKbelmontA.htm

him for a deer. The man was charged with a misdemeanor—"shooting a human being by accident"—and released into the custody of his father, a state policeman. There was no further investigation into Sullivan's death.

Louis Nichols was a special assistant to J. Edgar Hoover as well as Hoover's liaison with the Warren Commission. Alan H. Belmont also was a special assistant to Hoover. James Cadigan was a document expert with access to many classified assassination documents, while J. M. English headed the FBI laboratory where Oswald rifle and pistol were tested. Donald Kaylor was the FBI fingerprint expert who examined prints found at the assassination scene. None of these six Bureau officials lived to tell what they knew to the House Committee.

Other key assassination witnesses, such as George de Mohrenschildt and former Cuban President Carlos Prío Socarrás —who died within weeks of each other in 1977—were also being sought by the House Committee.[579]

But no death was more dramatic than that of the head of Domestic Intelligence at the FBI, William Sullivan, who had almost come to blows with FBI Director, J. Edgar Hoover. He was forced to resign, was highly knowledgeable and privy to very confidential material regarding the assassinations of the 1960s and the freshly-brewing Watergate scandal of President Nixon, *and* was scheduled to testify the following week before the United States Congress. Now *that's* a convenient death.

The New York Times reported the story in a manner suggesting that Sullivan was actually out hunting in the middle of nowhere, although the wording was rather vague:

William C. Sullivan, former head of the Federal Bureau of Investigations Intelligence Operations, who broke in dramatic fashion with the late J. Edgar Hoover, was killed early yesterday in a shooting accident near his home in Sugar Hill, New Hampshire. He was sixty-five years old.

Major Mason J. Butterfield, law enforcement director of the New Hampshire Fish and Game Department, said that Mr. Sullivan, who had been on the way to meet two hunting companions shortly after daybreak, had been shot and instantly killed by another hunter, Robert Daniels, Jr., twenty-two, who had mistaken Mr. Sullivan for a deer.[580]

Mr. Daniels was fined $500 and also lost his hunting license for ten years; events which, quite fortunately, precluded him from conveniently shooting any other witnesses prior to their scheduled testimony. And besides, William Sullivan looked *nothing* like a deer. . . .

But *seriously*, folks—Mr. Daniels, as we shall see below, was actually quite a serious young man and a very experienced and cautious hunter. The chances of his mistaking William Sullivan for a deer are explored below, and they are *extremely* remote.

Author Richard Cibrano investigated the details and obviously suggests that Mr. Sullivan was murdered. After quoting the specific info in the very same *New York*

[579] Jim Marrs & Ralph Schuster, "A Look at the Deaths of Those Involved," 2002: http://www.assassinationresearch.com/v1n2/deaths.html
[580] *New York Times*, "William C. Sullivan, Ex-FBI Aide, 65, Is Killed In Hunting Accident," 10 Nov. 1977

Times article above, the author considers the unlikelihood of a very experienced hunter making very sophomoric mistakes:

> He met Bill Sullivan back in the 1950s when they were both working counterintelligence—Bill with the FBI and he with the CIA. He liked Bill from the start, believed him to be an honorable gentleman endeavoring mightily to keep a wayward FBI on course, despite the incessant raving of a self-motivated, dysfunctional director. Although an adversarial state of affairs dictated otherwise, the two men quietly advocated a policy of cooperation between the two agencies while maintaining an open line of communication with each other. With the passing years, their careers following dissimilar paths, they still managed to keep in touch, if with nothing more than a congenial note or an occasional phone call. . . .
>
> The very idea that Bill was mistaken for a deer and gunned down in cold blood is utterly preposterous. He was an experienced hunter who went strictly by the book. Bill would never take risks—never expose himself to the carelessness of rank amateurs. So profound was his concern, he placed himself in the minds of these "Elmer Fudds" and followed the necessary precautions. Rule number one: He would never hunt in the predawn hours. The article did note that the shooting occurred after daybreak, thereby eliminating darkness as an excuse. Finally, with a growing sense of indignation, the man arrives at the unavoidable conclusion.[581]

Veteran CIA officer, Leutrell Osborne, also investigated the matter.

> Leutrell "Mike" Osborne, twenty-six-year veteran CIA Case Officer and Counter Intelligence expert like many African-Americans are somewhat familiar with the now deceased Director of Domestic Intelligence for the FBI, William Sullivan. Most of those who know of him also know that he was killed a week before he was to testify before the House Select Committee on Assassinations in 1977. . . .
>
> William Sullivan's goal was to testify before the public HSCA hearings and lay his cards on the table, so to speak. He was going to give the committee and the American people the truth about J. Edgar Hoover's hatred of Martin Luther King, Jr., as well as his hatred for John F. Kennedy and Presidential Candidate Robert F. Kennedy.[582]

Gary Revel was a Special Investigator commissioned for the official investigation into the Martin Luther King Jr. assassination:

> Mr. Revel says he is still trying to unravel the bizarre happenings of that year. His brother, his cousin's husband, William Sullivan, and five other FBI or former FBI officials, who could have been valuable to his investigation

---

[581] Richard Cibrano, *Dead Reckoning* (Xlibris: 2009).
[582] "Deadly Business of a King's Murder," 28 Feb. 2006: http://www.leutrellosborne.50megs.com/whats_new.html

died mysteriously or were simply killed during that year. Sullivan and the other five were scheduled to testify before the committee. Donald Kaylor was a fingerprint expert who had worked on the JFK assassination evidence. Alan Belmont and Louis Nichols were both special assistants to J. Edgar Hoover. JFK assassination document examiner and expert James Cadigan was another. J. M. English, an expert on the rifle that supposedly killed President John F. Kennedy and was head of the FBI Forensic Sciences Laboratory, was also dispatched. Those who travel to a place beyond reason and continue to try to defend the official stories of lone assassins and thorough investigations simply haven't gotten it yet. When there are so many coincidences, any reasonable person will just know that something is amiss.[583]

Special Investigator Revel warned that the series of deaths were even more sinister than they initially appeared:

Revel said deaths of these FBI SAs (Special Agents) could be more significant than what many realized because all six of these FBI SAs were identified to Revel as being important witnesses for the HSCA. "Is it likely that the stress of the planned testimony really brought on heart attacks to three of these people?" questioned Revel.

One FBI Special Agent, Alan Belmont, died of an illness. People do die of illnesses, but the prolific coincidences of 1977 make even that death start to look bizarre.... James Cadigan died from an accidental fall in his home. Normally, this would not be suspect. However, for Revel, there were too many accidental deaths that year.[584]

The definitive investigation of the actual circumstances surrounding William Sullivan's supposed accidental death is the *Special Report: The Death of "Crazy Billy" Sullivan*, by Jeff Goldberg and Harvey Yazijian. That study determined that, upon closer examination, the substance of the case for it being an accident was completely unsubstantiated:

The official version of the accident rest on two conclusions:

Daniels' view of Sullivan was obscured and fleeting. Sullivan's clothing, in a sense, made him look like a deer. These are the basics of the case. But on closer examination, neither can be judged now as certain.[585]

The above story then goes on to detail specifically why those two points are not true; they are too long to fully convey here, but we recommend you access the full article, as it's very well-written and illuminating.[586]

---

[583] Ibid.

[584] "Leutrell Osborne Finds Disturbing New Details Investigating Martin Luther King Jr. Assassination," 22 March 2006: http://www.leutrellosborne.50megs.com/whats_new.html

[585] Jeff Goldberg & Harvey Yazijian, "Special Report: The Death of 'Crazy Billy' Sullivan," *New Times*, 24 July 1978:

[586] Goldberg & Yazijian, "The Death of 'Crazy Billy' Sullivan": https://groups.google.com/forum/?fromgroups#!topic/alt.conspiracy.jfk/Rx4o-wYym18

The incident occurred right after daybreak, so there was sufficient light and alcohol was not a factor. Note Mr. Daniels' experience and rationality, from his own statements:

> **"During the year before the accident, I saw about fifteen or twenty deer,"**
> **he said. "I didn't shoot at any of them because I didn't think it was the**
> **right shooting time. I consider myself a sportsman, not a person who**
> **goes out to kill as many deer as he can."[587]**

The larger point, as other residents observed, is that hunters know what they know—and they don't forget it—under any normal circumstances. Put simply, they *learn* cautious, and they *remain* cautious.

In fact, it was the first fatal hunting accident to occur in that area in over twenty years.[588] That's the basis of the very well-earned reputation they had as serious hunters.

> **"I'm really suspicious of the hunting accident," one Lisbon resident said,**
> **"not just because Sullivan was involved, but because this guy (Daniels)**
> **knows how to hunt, and I don't care what they say, he knows how to hunt.**
> **Local hunters don't make mistakes like that."[589]**

Now, add to all that, the fact that William Sullivan, a highly intelligent man, specifically and precisely predicted his own death. And it was not a vague reference, or some general statement that anyone might have made. He specifically stated to a friend that he would be murdered, that it would be made to look like an accident, and to not believe it. He told his friend, Robert Novak, something that Novak was never able to forget:

> **Someday you will read that I have been killed in an accident, but don't**
> **believe it; I've been murdered.[590]**

Historian John Simkin, a long-time investigator of contemporary events in general, and the death of William Sullivan in particular, concluded that it was actually a case of murder:

> **On the surface it seemed to be an accident. However, I believe it was**
> **murder.[591]**

So that's the story of the death of William Sullivan. Much less is known about the specific circumstances of the deaths of the other five senior FBI officials. However, as the odds of probability prove out—if even one of those deaths is suspicious, then they *all* should be. Because it is mathematically impossible for six senior FBI officials to die naturally in one six-month period, precisely at the time they are being scheduled to give

---

[587] Ibid.

[588] Ibid.

[589] Ibid.

[590] John Hawkins, "Right Wing News," 20 Aug 2007. Robert D. Novak, *The Prince of Darkness: 50 Years Reporting in Washington* (Crown Forum: 2007).

[591] John Simkin, "Was William Sullivan Murdered?" 19 April 2005: http://educationforum.ipbhost.com/index.php?showtopic=3694&st=0

testimony on their specific knowledge regarding the JFK assassination. The odds that the moon is actually made of green cheese are higher than the aforementioned. Find a mathematician and examine the laws of probability in great detail. He or she will conclude the same.

CONCLUSION

It did not happen naturally.

Richard Cain,
December 20, 1973

Victim	**Richard Cain, high-ranking Chicago police official; well-connected to Chicago mob; worked directly with Sam Giancana**
Cause of Death	Gunshot; one blast from a sawed-off shotgun, under chin.
Official Verdict	Gangland murder
Actual Circumstances	Cain reportedly played a role in the JFK assassination (that's direct from the Giancana Family) and he was also involved in covert anti-Castro operations.
Inconsistencies	None Apparent

Overview

▶ **The Murder of Richard Cain**

High-level police official in Chicago who was actually a member of the Chicago Outfit. He reported directly to Chicago mob boss Sam "The Man" Giancana.

- Killed execution-style in a Chicago delicatessen on the afternoon of December 20, 1973.
- Two assassins entered Rose's Sandwich Shop on Chicago's West Side and lined the customers and employees up with their faces to the wall. They made Richard Cain turn around and fired a sawed-off shotgun directly into his head at point-blank range.
- Linked directly to the JFK assassination by:
- Fabian Escalante: at the time of the assassination, Escalante was head of Counter-Intelligence for G2 (Cuban Intelligence, formally known as Cuban Department of State Security); he then became Director of the Cuban Security Studies Center and conducted an extensive re-examination of the JFK assassination, utilizing a wealth of sources and materials retained by Cuban Intelligence.
- The Giancana Family of Chicago claimed, in print, that Richard Cain was actually one of the shooters in Dallas.
- Author Claudia Furiati examined, in detail, the informant reports to G2 Cuban Intelligence, linking Cain to the assassination.
- Professor Peter Dale Scott implicates Cain (and Johnny Roselli, also Chicago Outfit) to the assassination via their anti-Cuban activities and further states that they both also "later professed knowledge about the assassination."

Richard Cain was what's known as a "dirty cop," and he was exceedingly good at it. He made it all the way up to Chief Investigator for the Cook County Sheriff's Department (which covered Chicago) and was on the payroll of Sam "The Man" Giancana, leader of the Chicago Mob the whole time . . . the very people Cain was supposed to be going after.

Cain was so "good" at his job that he became a "made member" of the Chicago Outfit—an untouchable member of the strongest crime family in the country. For the book *The Godfather* by Mario Puzo, Cain was actually the model used for the character of Frank Neri—a vicious Mafia contract killer with a police badge.

The Giancana family implicated Cain as one of the shooters of JFK and there are many links between Cain and efforts to assassinate Castro on behalf of the CIA. The

Tangled Web (written by Cain's brother) is an amazing recent addition to the literature that offers a rare "inside glimpse" to the world of the Mob.

We investigated the circumstances of his murder and here's what we learned:

CONCLUSIONS BASED ON EVIDENTIARY INDICATIONS

- Case has all the signs of a classic Mafia hit.
- Cain apparently did have sensitive knowledge that was highly pertinent to the JFK assassination, and was an informant to the FBI.
- However, the hit appears to be unrelated to the JFK cover-up. It was apparently the result of Cain's efforts to take over the lucrative gambling operations on the South Side (there were rumors that he wanted to take over the whole Chicago Crime Family), internal mob disagreements over a robbery, and his inability to come to terms with old-school Chicago mobster, Marshall Caifano. Cain's brother also obtained reliable eyewitness testimony that Richard Cain was in Chicago on November 22, 1963.
- The fact that Cain was a regular informant to the FBI does not appear to be the reason for his murder, because the Mob apparently did not learn of Cain's talking to the FBI until after his death.
- The murder was apparently the result of an internal decision by mafia leadership. Cain was a made member of the mafia and, therefore, could not be murdered by renegade action of mobsters. Like Jimmy Hoffa, it had to be "sanctioned" from the top.

    Chicago mobster Marshall Caifano appears to have set up the well-executed hit on Cain. It was Caifano who set up the "meet" at Rose's Delicatessen (one of his regular hangouts) to discuss the matter of their "business problems."

FURTHER RESEARCH

The Tangled Web: The Life and Death of Richard Cain- Chicago Cop and Mafia Hitman, Michael J. Cain, Skyhorse Publishing, 2009.

Double Cross: The Explosive, Inside Story of the Mobster Who Controlled America, Sam Giancana & Chuck Giancana, Skyhorse Publishing, 2010.

JFK and Sam, Antoinette Giancana, John R. Hughes, DM OXON, MD, PHD & Thomas H. Jobe, MD, 2005.

ZR Rifle: The Plot to Kill Kennedy and Castro, Claudia Furiati, 1994.

Richard Cain: Biography, John Simkin, *Spartacus Educational*: http://www.spartacus. schoolnet.co.uk/JFKcainR.htm

Bringing It All Together: The New Releases and How They Help Us Converge On The Heart Of The Case, Peter Dale Scott, *The Fourth Decade*, Vol. 4, #1, November, 1996.

Who Killed Richard Cain?, Chicago Tribune, 23 December 1973, section 2, page four.

Cain played mob game and lost big, Chicago Tribune, 21 December 1973, page one.

Cain was on move with big schemes, Chicago Tribune, 28 December 1973, page sixteen.

Ex-Cop Cain shot to death, Chicago Tribune, 21 December 1973, page one.

Police seeking mystery woman in Cain slaying, Chicago Tribune, 22 December 1973, page one.

Cain bugged hood's home, Chicago Tribune, 22 December 1973, page three.

41 | Sam "The Man" Giancana, June 19, 1975

Victim	**Sam Giancana, nationally powerful mobster headquartered in Chicago, with huge business interests in Nevada, Miami Beach, Hollywood, and Latin America**
Cause of Death	Multiple gunshots to head
Official Verdict	Mob retaliation killing
Actual Circumstances	Giancana's murder was directly linked to the fact he was being forced to testify (as we detail below, granting him immunity would have forced his testimony) and those with "exposure" in the JFK assassination could not allow that testimony to take place.

Giancana was called "The Man" for one very simple reason: Because everybody knew that he was. Let's put it this way: Even the most notorious hitman in the country, Chuck Nicoletti, differentiated from an ordinary hit and a contract "from 'The Man' himself."[592] The first was somewhat negotiable; the second was referred to as if it was chiseled onto a stone tablet and hand-delivered by no less than Moses himself.

And allow us make a very frank point here at the onset—it's not just us that noted the important timing of Sam Giancana's murder—it was the United States Congress:

> **The Church Committee found that one very important witness had been murdered a few days before he was to testify.**
>
> **—Sam Giancana**[593]

It is also extremely relevant that, due to a change in the law, which was basically a trick forcing mobsters to testify by granting them immunity when they refused to incriminate themselves, thereby eliminating the potential for self-incrimination and, hence, also eliminating any right to *not* answer questions—Giancana would have been compelled to testify: Due to a clever change in U.S. laws enacted by Congress in 1970, mobsters were forced into testifying by granting them immunity from prosecution when they attempted to "take the Fifth"—refuse to answer on the grounds that responding may tend to incriminate them, which is a protection granted by the Fifth Amendment to the United States Constitution. The act of granting them immunity compelled them to answer since they were no longer subjecting themselves to incrimination. Therefore, Giancana could not have used "taking the Fifth" to avoid questions as mobsters had typically done—he would have been compelled to answer all questions put to him or be guilty of contempt.[594]

> The timing of the Church Committee was crucial, as was the fact that the laws regarding testimony had changed so that one could no longer take the Fifth Amendment if one were given immunity. In other words, one could either assert one's Fifth Amendment rights or have immunity, but not both. If Sam were given immunity, he would be compelled to testify. Giancana's assassination occurred after the CIA discovered that he would be accepting immunity to talk to the Church Committee.[595]

> Information gained by the 1975 Church Committee on CIA Activities led to the 1976 House Committee on Assassinations, which then drew important conclusions about Carlos Marcello. The Senate committee, chaired by Frank Church, was the first to reveal the dirty secrets of the CIA and the Mafia plot to murder Castro. John F. Kennedy had clearly ordered the CIA to kill Castro, and he and his brother had given their approval for a plot, called the AM/LASH plan, against Castro in 1963. According to a 1988 television interview with Judith Campbell, the president was clearly aware of the CIA-Mafia

---

592 Wim Dankbaar, *Files on JFK* (Trine Day: 2008), "Interview of James Files by Jim Marrs and Wim Dankbaar"
593 Antoinette Giancana, John R. Hughes, DM OXON, MD, Ph.D.& Thomas H. Jobe, MD, *JFK and Sam: The Connection Between the Giancana and Kennedy Assassinations*, (Cumberland House: 2005), 144.
594 Bruce G. Ohr, "Effective Methods to Combat Transnational Organized Crime in Criminal Justice Processes," 2000-2001, page 54: http://www.unafei.or.jp/english/pdf/PDF_rms/no58/58-05.pdf
595 Giancana, Hughes, DM OXON, MD, Ph.D.& Jobe, MD, *JFK and Sam*, 78.

plot, and the Church Committee found that this plot had never been reported by the FBI, CIA, or Robert F. Kennedy to the Warren Commission.[596]

As the old expression goes, the plot thickens:

> This same committee discovered the affairs between Campbell and John
> F. Kennedy, and between Campbell and Sam Giancana. These discoveries
> led to a subcommittee study of the relationship of the FBI and CIA to the
> John F. Kennedy assassination, resulting in a collapse of the public's faith
> in the Warren Report. Senators Richard Schweiker and Gary Hart report-
> edly found that the FBI and the CIA had misled the Warren Commission to
> prevent the truth about the assassination from coming to light.[597]

It has been widely reported that help from the Chicago mob in general, and Giancana in
particular, were recruited by Joseph Kennedy and that help was largely responsible for
delivering the very close presidential election to JFK in 1960:

> Many historians believe that ballot stuffing in Chicago (then under the
> control of old-school Democrat Mayor, Richard Daley) helped ensure Ken-
> nedy's election in 1960. Giancana himself reportedly claimed that he had
> helped run a vote-stealing scam in Cook County, Illinois, a district that
> had been the deciding factor in Kennedy's victory. On the other hand,
> there are also persistent rumors of Mafia involvement in JFK's 1963 assas-
> sination, perhaps as revenge for what they saw as the ingratitude of the
> Kennedys in the form of RFK's crusade against organized crime.[598]

Hence, the logic goes, Giancana and the mafia were double-crossed by the Kennedy
Administration's war on organized crime:

> Giancana was next called to testify before a United States Senate com-
> mittee investigating Mafia involvement in a failed CIA plot to assassinate
> Castro. Before he was scheduled to testify, Giancana flew to Houston,
> Texas, and underwent gall bladder surgery. He returned to his Oak Park
> home on June 17, 1975. Two days later, Sam Giancana was shot once in
> the back of the head and several more times up through the chin with
> a .22-caliber pistol while cooking in his basement. Though theories
> abounded as to who killed him (rival mafiosi, CIA operatives nervous
> about his future testimony, one of many former girlfriends), no one was
> ever arrested in connection with the murder.[599]

> Antoinette Giancana believes that John F. Kennedy double-crossed
> her father by not giving him the protection he needed after Kennedy's

---

[596] Ibid.

[597] Ibid, 144.

[598] "Sam Giancana: Biography," accessed 11 Nov 2012, *bio. True Story*, A+E Networks, http://www.biography.com/
people/sam-giancana-9542088?page=2

[599] "Sam Giancana: Biography," accessed 11 Nov 2012, *bio. True Story*, A+E Networks, http://www.biography.com/
people/sam-giancana-9542088?page=3

election in 1960. It is her strong belief that the mob helped to kill Kennedy and the government (CIA) killed her father.[600]

Giancana, who was directly connected to Jack Ruby (who was originally from Chicago), is said to have provided a linkage between the New Orleans mob under Carlos Marcello (who hated the Kennedys because of prior attacks by Bobby Kennedy as Attorney General), the Dallas assets, who would come into play in 1963, and Trafficante, with his JM/WAVE (CIA station in Florida that was base for its anti-Castro operations) connections. It was Giancana who, after manipulating of the Illinois ballot boxes during the 1960 election, swung Kennedy's victory over Nixon. Now that Bobby Kennedy was attacking the Mafia—even though J. Edgar Hoover insisted there was no Mafia inside the U.S.—Giancana (as did the other Mafia bosses) felt betrayed.[601]

Congressional investigators knew that Giancana was linked to the JFK assassination and ordered him to testify. On June 19, 1975, very shortly before that testimony would have taken place, Giancana was gunned down in the basement kitchen of his quiet suburban Chicago home while frying sausages.

In addition to a massive wound at the back of the head, Giancana was also shot six times, in a circle, around the mouth. That has been interpreted as a very obvious message that the same fate awaited anyone who talked.

The perplexing part of the case is that even the police say that "it didn't look like a mafia hit."[602] Yet few mob bosses were more careful than Sam Giancana and, as many have noted, he never would have opened his door and let his killer in unless it was someone whom he knew and trusted.

Giancana's home was also under surveillance:

Attorney General Robert Kennedy had Giancana's home in Oak Park placed under twenty-four-hour surveillance in 1963.[603]

Plus, the Oak Park enclave was commonly referred to as an "impenetrable fortress":

That night, while cooking in the kitchen of his Chicago home—which was described by many as a "fortress" or "bunker"—Giancana came under the gun. According to both his daughter and the police, who stated that Giancana was invulnerable in his own home due to the security systems and impregnability of the structure, only someone he knew or trusted could have gotten to him. Giancana would have to have let them in, gone back to cooking, and then been surprised when the assailant—or assailants—pulled a .22 pistol.[604]

---

[600] Giancana, Hughes, DM OXON, MD, Ph.D.& Jobe, MD, *JFK and Sam*, 78.
[601] Roberts & Armstrong, *The Dead Witnesses*, 104.
[602] Malcom Abrams, "30 Watergate Witnesses Have Met Violent Deaths," 12 July 1976, *Midnight Magazine*: http://www.maebrussell.com/Mae%20Brussell%20Articles/Watergate%20Deaths.html
[603] "Sam Giancana: Biography," accessed 11 Nov 2012, *bio. True Story*: http://www.biography.com/people/sam-giancana-9542088?page=2
[604] Roberts & Armstrong, *The Dead Witnesses*, 105.

Others associated with Giancana's anti-Castro efforts in concert with the CIA, also began to die convenient deaths. The closest two were Johnny Roselli and Chuck Nicoletti, Giancana's top lieutenant and most notorious hitman, "respectively."

> Johnny Roselli was the next to die. Roselli met with Schweiker and other committee members in the Carroll Arms Hotel in Washington D.C. He indicated that he had good reason to believe that Cuban associates of Castro and Trafficante (Florida mafia boss who was also part of the CIA-mafia plot to assassinate Castro) were involved in the Kennedy assassination and that he would testify to these facts. Ten days after a dinner with Santo Trafficante, Roselli was murdered, presumably on a yacht belonging to a Trafficante associate; his dismembered body was dumped into the ocean in an oil drum.[605]

> Giancana's close associate Chuckie Nicoletti was murdered in 1977, immediately after the House Select Committee determined he would be called for testimony. George de Mohrenschildt, adviser to the CIA and the mob and a friend of Oswald, had also been scheduled to testify in 1977, but he died on the day he was to be questioned regarding the murder of John F. Kennedy.[606]

The incredible "timeliness" of the convenient deaths was not lost on the United States Congress:

> The sudden deaths of Sam Giancana and Johnny Roselli and the alleged heart attack of the CIA's William Harvey, the official in charge of the CIA-mafia plot against Castro, helped to stimulate the formation of a committee to reinvestigate the Kennedy assassination. The Ninety-fourth Congress in September 1976 put together the House Select Committee on Assassinations to reinvestigate the John F. Kennedy and Martin Luther King assassinations. The committee's final report indicated that Carlos Marcello had "probable complicity above all others."[607]

Take a gander at the dates laid out in the following timeline to get a better grip on the dramatic goings-on that took place within a very narrow time window:

▶ **April 7, 1975**
Nelson Rockefeller chairs hearings on the CIA's involvement in assassinations.

---

[605] Giancana, Hughes, DM OXON, MD, Ph.D.& Jobe, MD, *JFK and Sam*, 144.
[606] Ibid, 80.
[607] Ibid, 145.

▶ **June 9, 1975**

The U.S. Senate's Church Committee takes testimony on the CIA's use of the mafia for assistance with assassinations.

▶ **June 19, 1975**

The CIA plot to assassinate Cuba's leader, Fidel Castro, is made public in both the *Chicago Tribune* and *New York Times*.

▶ **June 19, 1975**

Members of the U.S. Senate's Church Committee arrive in Chicago for the purpose of escorting Sam Giancana to Washington for his appearance before the committee.

▶ **June 19, 1975, 9:00 p.m.**

Two "law enforcement officers" are observed outside Sam Giancana's home by his neighbors in Oak Park, a wealthy suburb of Chicago.

▶ **June 19, 1975, 11:15 p.m.**

Three surveillance cars reportedly leave the area of Sam Giancana's home.

▶ **June 19, 1975, 11:30 p.m.**

Sam Giancana is murdered inside his home.

▶ **June 20, 1975**

The *Chicago Tribune* reports the murder of Sam Giancana. Allegations are made that the murder was sanctioned by the CIA.

▶ **June 21, 1975**

The *Chicago Tribune* reports that Giancana's house was under surveillance on the night that he was killed.

▶ **June 24, 1975**

Johnny Roselli testifies to the Church Committee. June 24, 1975, was also the day that Sam Giancana had been scheduled to testify.

▶ **July 30, 1975**

Jimmy Hoffa disappears. Several reliable sources indicated that Hoffa had been involved with national mob bosses Carlos Marcello and Santo Trafficante in the plot to assassinate President Kennedy.

▶ **1976**

Information obtained by the Church Committee leads to an expansion of the investigation. The House Select Committee on Assassinations is formed and authorized to fully investigate the new leads in the assassination.

▶ **July 27, 1976**

Johnny Roselli is warned to leave Miami.

▶ **July 28, 1976**

Roselli is murdered.

▶ **Winter, 1976–Spring, 1977**

The House Select Committee on Assassinations continues its investigation. Two of the witnesses that the Committee determines will be called to testify are Giancana associate, Chuck Nicoletti, and George de Mohrenschildt.

▶ **March 29, 1977**

Chuck Nicoletti is murdered. George de Mohrenschildt reportedly "commits suicide" on the exact same day, which is also the day he was scheduled to give testimony; however, the circumstances of de Mohrenschildt's death also point to murder.

Information in the above chart derived primarily from:

Antoinette Giancana, John R. Hughes, DM OXON, MD, Ph.D.& Thomas H. Jobe, MD, *JFK and Sam: The Connection Between the Giancana and Kennedy Assassinations*, (Cumberland House: 2005);

Charles Brandt, *I Heard You Paint Houses: Frank "The Irishman" Sheeran and the Inside Story of the Mafia, the Teamsters, and the Last Ride of Jimmy Hoffa* (Steerforth Press: 2005)

John Simkin, *Jimmy Hoffa: Biography*,
http://www.spartacus.schoolnet.co.uk/USAhoffa.htm

Whatever Sam Giancana knew about the Cuban operations, assassination attempts against Fidel Castro, and the assassination of John F. Kennedy, he took them to the grave. For as disbelief mounted in the American people regarding the lone-gunman prognosis of the Warren Commission and the Senate Intelligence Committee was preparing to question him, Giancana was himself murdered.

From the crime scene, it appeared that Giancana had turned his back on the gunman, whereupon the assassin produced his pistol, shot him in the back of the head six times, then rolled his body over, reloaded, and shot several bullets around his mouth. The M.O. matched that of a standard mafia hit, and the message sent by the mouth shots was quite clear: Giancana had already said too much—and would never talk again; especially to the Senate Intelligence Committee. The murder weapon, a silenced Duramatic semi-auto .22 pistol, was later found snagged in the brush on a bank of the Des Plaines River. The last recorded sale of the gun was traced to a Miami gun dealer in 1965.[608]

The message, in any case, was exceedingly clear:

All other organized crime witnesses took note of Giancana's fate. Most remained silent.[609]

CONCLUSIONS BASED ON EVIDENTIARY INDICATIONS

Murder: Silenced witness testimony specifically linked to JFK assassination.

[608] Roberts & Armstrong, *The Dead Witnesses*, 105.
[609] Ibid, 105.

42 | Johnny Roselli,
August, 1976

Victim	**Johnny Roselli, the Mafia liaison to CIA, in the CIA's efforts to recruit mobsters to assassinate Cuban leader Fidel Castro.**
Cause of Death	Garroted (strangled with a wire from behind), stabbed, shot, legs sawn off, stuffed into oil drum, and sunk into ocean.
Official Verdict	Mafia retaliation killing
Actual Circumstances	Roselli was scheduled to testify before Congress. He was apparently silenced to preclude that testimony.

Johnny Roselli began his criminal career with Al Capone and was sent to Hollywood by Capone in 1924 "to develop gambling, extortion and vice rackets" for the Chicago Mob.[610] He eventually became a close associate of the leading mafia members of his era, including Meyer Lansky, Sam Giancana, and Santo Trafficante. His charming demeanor and Hollywood-style looks, usually accompanied with sunglasses, got him nicknamed "Handsome Johnny." That, combined with his love of the sun and boating, made him a natural for what he smoothly dovetailed into. He was "Chicago's Man" in Las Vegas, Hollywood, and Miami Beach, acting as the Chicago Mob's liaison for lucrative business interests in those locations. For example, he was involved in the multi-million dollar extortion of movie studios, and also oversaw the extremely lucrative "skimming" operation on the Las Vegas Strip (taking millions in cash from the daily "take" at the big casinos and keeping it "off the books" for accounting and would-be tax reporting purposes), ensuring that Chicago got its fair share of the skim.[611] Those were huge "responsibilities" in the world of the mob.

Roselli was also connected to billionaire Howard Hughes. Hughes was one of the richest and most influential people in the world at the time, sharing the mutual interest with the mob and CIA of "eliminating" Fidel Castro by any means available:

> Las Vegas mafia figure, Johnny Roselli, served as a hinge pin between the Hughes organization (via Robert Mayheu), the three mafia families of Giancana, Marcello and Trafficante, and the CIA. It was Roselli who provided the main mafia action connection to hitmen, money laundering, and weapons.[612]

In 1961, the CIA approached Roselli to enlist help from the mafia in assassinating Fidel Castro. Roselli went through Sam Giancana of Chicago, to enlist the help of Trafficante of Florida, because it was Trafficante's Cuban connections that would be a valuable resource in the enterprise.

> On March 12, 1961, William Harvey (of the CIA's Executive Action assassination program) arranged for CIA operative, Jim O'Connell, to meet Sam Giancana, Santo Trafficante, Johnny Roselli, and Robert Maheu (Howard Hughes's go-between for the CIA and mafia) to meet at the Fontainebleau Hotel (in Miami Beach). During the meeting, O'Connell gave poison pills and $10,000 to Roselli to be used against Fidel Castro.[613]

The plan failed, but its ultimate purpose succeeded, because, as author Richard Mahoney points out, the alliance between the mob and CIA was what ultimately made the cover-up following the JFK assassination a guaranteed event:

> Late one evening, probably March 13, Rosselli passed the poison pills and money to a small, reddish-haired Afro-Cuban by the name of Rafael "Macho"

---

[610] John William Tuohy, "Johnny Hollywood: Part One," April, 2002: http://www.americanmafia.com/Feature_Articles_202.html

[611] FBI Files on John Roselli, http://www.vault.fbi.gov/John (Handsome Johnny) Roselli.

[612] Roberts & Armstrong, *The Dead Witnesses*, 114.

[613] John Simkin, "John Roselli: Biography," *The Education Forum*, (parenthetical comments added), accessed 13 Nov 2012: http://www.spartacus.schoolnet.co.uk/JFKroselli.htm

Gener in the *Boom Boom Room*, a location Giancana thought to be "stupid." Rosselli's purpose, however, was not just to assassinate Castro, but to set up the mafia's partner in crime, the United States Government. Accordingly, he was laying a long, bright trail of evidence that unmistakably implicated the CIA in the Castro plot. This evidence, whose purpose was blackmail, would prove critical in the CIA's cover-up of the Kennedy assassination.[614]

In 1976, the House Select Committee on Intelligence Activities was very interested in taking testimony from Johnny Roselli:[615]

In late July 1976, Roselli made a dinner date. He was seen with his old friend Santo Trafficante at The Landings, a restaurant in Fort Lauderdale. Two days after dining with Santo, Roselli disappeared.[616]

It was a very gruesome case of "over-kill" that was obviously intended to send a message. Roselli's dismembered body was found floating in a 55-gallon oil drum off the coast of Florida:

He had been garroted. Roselli's legs had been sawed off and squashed into the drum with the rest of his body.[617]

That's the thing about working for the mob—they have good benefits for a few years, but then the retirement plan really stinks.

They buried him in the classic style. His body was sealed in an empty 55-gallon oil drum. Heavy chains were coiled around the container and holes were punched in the sides. Then the drum was dumped in the waters off Florida. It might have stayed on the bottom indefinitely—except that the gases caused by the decomposing body gave the drum buoyancy and floated it to the surface.[618]

As *Time Magazine* put it, it was "Deep Six for Johnny":

The manner of Roselli's death also fit a mafia pattern: He was beguiled to his death by someone he trusted. The dumping of his body in the bay was another message.[619]

Another reason Trafficante should have been a suspect was because of the point that, of the three nationally prominent mobsters known to be working directly with the CIA on eliminating Fidel Castro, *only* Trafficante was left. Giancana and Roselli were both murdered before their scheduled testimony.

[614] Richard D. Mahoney, *Sons and Brothers, The Days of Jack and Bobby Kennedy* (Arcade: 1999).
[615] Simkin, "John Roselli: Biography"
[616] Frank Ragano & Selwyn Raab, *Mob Lawyer* (Random House: 1996).
[617] Simkin, "John Roselli: Biography"
[618] "Deep Six for Johnny," *Time Magazine*, August 23, 1976: http://www.time.com/time/magazine/article/0,9171,945646,00.html
[619] Ragano & Raab, *Mob Lawyer*

One fact, however, was indisputable: Santo Trafficante was the only survivor of the three mobsters recruited by the CIA to kill Castro.[620]

Covert operations veteran Tosh Plumlee was very active in such matters; he even flew Roselli and Chuck Nicoletti to certain locations on "company" business. In fact, Roselli was so active in intelligence ops that many operatives thought Roselli actually was Military Intelligence. He even had a codename for Military Intel ops, "Colonel Ralston"; and was so commonly known that some operatives simply referred to him as "The Colonel."[621]

Mr. Plumlee agrees that Roselli was killed to keep him from testifying about what he knew about the mafia's involvement in the anti-Castro operations of U.S. Intelligence, and how it led to the JFK assassination.

Here's how he answered the question, "Why do you think Johnny Roselli was killed?"

Mainly, because he was getting ready to testify and we have to understand that the Kennedy assassination was one of many, many black-op operations that were going on at that particular time and Roselli was up to his neck in making liaison with the members of Organized Crime for elements within CIA and Military Intelligence.[622]

Plumlee knew what he was talking about. Although acknowledging that intel was intentionally compartmentalized and that he was not privy to where the intel on the JFK assassination attempt was picked up (resulting in the "Abort Team" being flown into Dallas), Plumlee certainly *was* aware of the talk and rumors circulating among his fellow operatives, which is, of sorts, a form of raw intelligence gathering as well. That intel was quite clear in that it generally conformed to the source of the JFK-targeting for assassination as being the Texas Mafia and anti-Castro Cubans.

In the early stages of the Kennedy assassination, there were many, many, many reports that Kennedy was going to be "hit" and many, many reports that Kennedy was going to be "hit" by organized crime; so this was all investigated. That's why I don't feel that any direct involvement on a high level from our government was involved in the Kennedy assassination, but I certainly believe that there were rouges within the CIA, rouges within the Military Intelligence, rouges within the mafia, and rouges within the high-ups in the National Security Council that were certainly aware that an attempt was going to be made. The mechanics of the attempt, I don't think that they were aware, and I think that they launched an extensive intelligence gathering investigation to find out if the rumors that were circulating around Southern Florida were true, that Kennedy was

---

[620] Ragano & Raab, *Mob Lawyer*
[621] Belzer & Wayne, *Dead Wrong*
[622] Wim Dankbaar, "Robert 'Tosh' Plumlee Interview 6/4/92 Dallas," accessed 2 Nov 2012: *http://www.jfkmurdersolved.com/TOSHTRANS1.htm*, expanded and clarified in: Tosh Plumlee, emails to author, 12-15 Nov. 2012.

going to be "hit"; first in Austin, Texas; later it was West Palm Beach as the location; then Austin, Texas, and then it turned out to be Dallas.[623]

And the source of the hit on JFK was apparently the mafia's connection to the CIA attempts to assassinate Cuba's Fidel Castro:

> On the point about the information regarding a JFK assassination attempt in late 1963, there were a lot of rumors circulating around MI (Military Intelligence) and CIA, as well as FBI and their Cuban connections within organized crime in Havana. There was a lot of talk that it was the Texas Mafia that was going to do the job, and also talk that Cubans were involved.[624]

And Roselli knew so much about the JFK assassination that it was certainly intimidating to those who were closely involved:

> Roselli also claimed that a CIA hit team that had been dispatched to Cuba had been "turned" and used to kill Kennedy.[625]

That point gels precisely and quite chillingly with a very specific quote from the CIA's David Atlee Phillips:

> I don't know why he killed Kennedy, but I do know he used precisely the plan we had devised against Castro.[626]

That's some pretty big stuff there, folks.

CONCLUSIONS BASED ON EVIDENTIARY INDICATIONS
Murder: Silenced witness testimony specifically linked to JFK assassination.

---

[623] Ibid.
[624] Tosh Plumlee, email to author, 14 Nov 2012.
[625] Simkin, "John Roselli: Biography"
[626] David Atlee Phillips, The AMLASH Legacy (unpublished manuscript), in Belzer & Wayne, Dead Wrong, 146.

43 | Chuck Nicoletti,
March 29, 1977

Victim	Charles Nicoletti, hitman, Chicago Mob
Cause of Death	Three .38 gunshots to rear of head
Official Verdict	Mafia retaliation killing
Actual Circumstances	Nicoletti was the premier mob hitman in the country, was known to be in Dallas at the time of the JFK assassination, and was named as a shooter by many with inside knowledge. Nicoletti was also known to be unhappy about the recent assassination of his benefactor, Sam "The Man" Giancana. Like Giancana before his murder, Nicoletti was scheduled to soon testify before the House Select Committee on Assassinations. He was apparently silenced to preclude that testimony.

It is not at all surprising that Nicoletti was shot from the back. He was as tough a customer as they come, and if he had seen even a glimpse of it coming, the shooter would not have lived to talk about it.

Since Chuck Nicoletti was the premier hitman in the country in 1963, and "contracted" his work directly with Chicago's Sam Giancana, it should be asked where he was on November 22, 1963, when JFK was shot. The answer to that question is that he was in Dallas. In fact, Nicoletti's "work book" entry for that date is stark and chilling. It simply states:

Dallas–JFK.[627]

A number of sources confirm that Nicoletti was present in Dealey Plaza when the shots were fired, and even how he arrived there and departed.[628] Wim Dankbaar's book, *Files on JFK*, and the work of former FBI veteran Zack Shelton clearly document how Chauncey Holt drove Nicoletti into Dallas and how he was taken into and out of Dealey Plaza. The events of November 22, 1963 were certainly one of the things that the House Select Committee on Assassinations was planning to ask Nicoletti about. But he was murdered before that testimony took place.

March 29, 1977, was a day that two key witnesses were brutally killed: Nicoletti was shot three times in the back of the head while he sat in his car; George de Mohrenschildt, subject of a later chapter in this book, died from wounds sustained from a shotgun blast to the head on the same day. "Both men were due to appear before the House Select Committee on Assassinations where they were to be asked about their involvement in the assassination of John F. Kennedy."[629]

Apparently, Nicoletti was on-record as being unhappy about the earlier hit made on his boss, Sam Giancana. It makes sense, therefore, that the same parties who silenced Giancana also found it in their obvious best interest to silence Nicoletti. A "cover story" about mob retaliation was put forward, but the real reason was apparently to keep Nicoletti away from testifying:

> On the date of his death, Nicoletti received three .38 slugs to the back of his head, in what seems to be an effort to silence his disdain for the slaying of Sam Giancana and any other possible relevant issues. The hit was seen as retaliation for a hit on a Milwaukee mob leader, but that is a reported cover. During his career as a hitman, he was involved in as many as twenty mob hits, and is alleged to have been involved with the assassination of John F. Kennedy.[630]

CONCLUSIONS BASED ON EVIDENTIARY INDICATIONS
Murder: Silenced witness testimony specifically linked to JFK assassination.

---

[627] Wim Dankbaar, *Files on JFK*. Zack Shelton, Interview with author, 2006.
[628] Dankbaar, *Files on JFK*. Zack Shelton, Interview with author, 2006, Belzer & Wayne, *Dead Wrong*.
[629] John Simkin, "Charles Nicoletti: Biography," accessed 12 Nov 2012: http://www.spartacus.schoolnet.co.uk/JFKnicoletti.htm
[630] *La Cosa Nostra Data Base*, "Charles Nicoletti," accessed 12 Nov 2012: http://www.lacndb.com/Info.php?name=Charles%20Nicoletti

Victim	George de Mohrenschildt (sometimes known as Baron de Mohrenschildt, although actually he was descended from the Baron Hilienfelt)
Cause of Death	Shotgun blast
Official Verdict	Suicide
Actual Circumstances	George de Mohrenschildt was the key link between Lee Harvey Oswald and the CIA, as well as connecting him to extremely conservative Texas oil millionaires rumored to be involved in the JFK assassination.
Inconsistencies	Numerous and dramatic (see text that follows)

Decades after his death, the story of George de Mohrenschildt is still so explosive that Vincent Bugliosi, author of *Reclaiming History*, ordered the TV camera operators to immediately stop filming the second that Jesse Ventura calmly mentioned that de Mohrenschildt was a part of the CIA. You can watch it online: "Jesse Ventura vs. Vincent Bugliosi."[631] It's a pretty short match, proving quickly that Ventura can still wrestle.

Mr. Bugliosi is the type of author who can wipe out large portions of our forests with a 1,648-page book on the JFK assassination, yet reach the ridiculous conclusion that Oswald acted alone. And that's not just our opinion; it is the opinion of a vast majority of Americans—bringing to mind the words of flamboyant attorney, Dean Andrews (portrayed memorably by John Candy in Oliver Stone's film, *JFK*):

He's got the right *ta-ta*, but the wrong *ho-ho*.[632]

George de Mohrenschildt was a sophisticated businessman, descended from Russian royalty, who was a CIA asset used for various tasks. One of those tasks, as attorney Mark Lane puts it, was that "he was the babysitter for Lee Harvey Oswald for the CIA."[633] A CIA Case Officer named J. Walton Moore was apparently de Mohrenschildt's "handler" from the CIA.[634]

Jackie Kennedy, wife of JFK, was also very close to George de Mohrenschildt; in fact, she called him "Uncle George."[635]

CIA business assets operate in much the same way as their media assets; they provide raw intelligence on matters of interest to the Agency. As de Mohrenschildt himself put it, the CIA helps him "win" an oil contract in Turkey, he then later reports back to the CIA about everything he knows about the business people and leaders whom he met while doing business there.[636]

George Herbert Bush knew de Mohrenschildt well, too . . . yes, *that* Bush. George de Mohrenschildt was the uncle of Bush's roommate at Andover, and then Bush and de Mohrenschildt were members of the same clubs in Texas.[637] In fact, Bush's phone number was found in de Mohrenschildt's address book. Gaeton Fonzi, Special Investigator for the House Select Committee on Assassinations, verified that de Mohrenschildt's address book contained entries for "Bush, George H.W. (Poppy)" and also for "Zapata Petroleum, Midland," Texas.[638] Bush was one of the founders of Zapata, and many FBI and CIA veterans have substantiated that Zapata provided help to the CIA for its anti-Castro intelligence operations.[639]

---

[631] "Jesse Ventura vs. Vincent Bugliosi"; excerpted from *Conspiracy Theory with Jesse Ventura*, "The JFK Assassination", 2010, Episode 5, *TruTV*: http://youtu.be/I7P9z5Hcp8U

[632] "1967 INTERVIEW WITH DEAN ANDREWS"; the clip is an obvious "hatchet job," a thinly veiled attack on Jim Garrison, but one worth enduring to see Andrews in action and can be viewed at: http://youtu.be/cD3CdA7Ad-I, excerpted from "THE JFK CONSPIRACY: THE CASE OF JIM GARRISON" (Documentary), *NBC Television*, 1967.

[633] Mark Lane, in: "G. de Mohrenschildt–The Security Alarm," excerpted from *Inside Edition* (with Bill O'Reilly), *CBS Television*, accessed 26 Nov. 2012: http://youtu.be/37dtEpvyUJU

[634] Russ Baker, *Family of Secrets* (Bloomsbury Press: 2009).

[635] John Simkin, "George de Mohrenschildt: Biography," *Spartacus Educational*, accessed 26 Nov. 2012: http://www.spartacus.schoolnet.co.uk/JFKdemohrenschildt.htm

[636] John Simkin, "George de Mohrenschildt: Biography"

[637] Ibid.

[638] Gaeton Fonzi, *The Last Investigation* (Thunder's Mouth Press: 1993); Baker, *Family of Secrets*.

[639] Fabian Escalante (2004), *The Cuba Project: CIA Covert Operations Against Cuba 1959–1962*.

U.S. Army Brigadier General Russell Bowen wrote that there was a cover-up of Zapata's CIA connections:

> Bush, in fact, did work directly with the anti-Castro Cuban groups in Miami before and after the Bay of Pigs invasion, using his company, Zapata Oil, as a corporate cover for his activities on behalf of the agency. Records at the University of Miami, where the operations were based for several years, show George Bush was present during this time.[640]

As far as things held in common, Bush and de Mohrenschildt also shared oil wealth and the CIA. Before he became President, Bush was Director of the CIA, and before becoming CIA Director, was involved in supporting anti-Castro intelligence operations on behalf of the Agency. Like de Mohrenschildt, the oil business was a perfect "cloak" for those intelligence activities:

> The CIA was using companies like Zapata to stage and supply secret missions attacking Fidel Castro's Cuban government in advance of the Bay of Pigs invasion. The CIA's codename for that invasion was "Operation Zapata." In 1981, all Securities and Exchange Commission filings for Zapata Off-Shore between 1960 and 1966 were destroyed. In other words, the year Bush became Vice President, important records detailing his years at his drilling company disappeared. In 1969, Zapata bought the United Fruit Company of Boston, another company with strong CIA connections.[641]

It has also been established that de Mohrenschildt provided intel to Military Intelligence; specifically the 112th MIG (Military Intelligence Group) in San Antonio, Texas—the same 112th from which Colonel Robert Jones, the afternoon of the same day as the assassination of JFK, immediately provided files on "Lee Harvey Oswald/Alek Hidell"; an act which precipitated war planes being launched against Cuba until they were called back hastily.[642]

James Southwood was a U.S. Military Intelligence veteran with a Top-Secret security clearance. Two months before the assassination of President Kennedy, Southwood received "a very important assignment" at the 502nd Military Intelligence Battalion: to provide all documentation possible on "Lee Harvey Oswald, a.k.a. "Harvey Lee Oswald" and "Alek James Hidell." The request also sought "any/all information on Jeanne and George de Mohrenschildt."

And, as Southwood explained it to author, Dick Russell:

> All the information I had about Oswald had been given to the 112th by George de Mohrenschildt.[643]

---

[640] Russell S. Bowen, *The Immaculate Deception: The Bush Crime Family Exposed* (America West: 2000)
[641] Ken Biggs, "George H. W. Bush," accessed 27 Nov. 2012: http://famoustexans.com/georgebush.htm
[642] James P. Hosty Jr. & Thomas Hosty, *Assignment Oswald: From the FBI agent assigned to investigate Lee Harvey Oswald prior to the JFK assassination* (Arcade Publishing: 1997).
[643] Dick Russell, *The Man Who Knew Too Much: Hired to Kill Oswald and Prevent the Assassination of JFK* (Carroll & Graf: 2003).

We researched this case in detail and we found three highly relevant tracks of information that have been completely ignored in mainstream media:

- CIA agent Hugh Huggins' did "special work" for the Kennedys.[644] We paid close attention to his revelations about the little "visit" he paid to de Mohrenschildt right after the assassination of President Kennedy and at the specific direction of Attorney General Robert Kennedy;
- His close friend, Willem Oltmans, revealed that de Mohrenschildt admitted to him—in detail—that he had been the "go-between" for the assassination, between big Texas oil millionaires, unhappy CIA agents, and Lee Harvey Oswald; and, of dramatic significance;
- A tape recording was made of the killing.

Taking them one at a time, here's a quick outline of what Hugh Huggins, a CIA agent used by the Kennedy brothers for very special assignments, had to say about it.

- Huggins also stated he knew George de Mohrenschildt to be a veteran CIA contract agent.
- Huggins obtained information for his investigation by using a variety of methods, which apparently included breaking two of George de Mohrenschildt's fingers to inspire the level of cooperation he demanded.[645]
- Huggins concluded that planning and organization for the assassination were clearly performed by George de Mohrenschildt and David Ferrie, both of whom were veteran CIA players; and that George de Mohrenschildt was actually present in Dallas on the day of the assassination, even though his alibi states otherwise.[646]
- Huggins stated further that the death of George de Mohrenschildt by shotgun was actually murder, not suicide.[647]

Most research on the matter has been about whether or not (or how closely) de Mohrenschildt was in cahoots with the CIA. Few have dared venture into the realm of his actual involvement in the assassination. Yet the evidence leads in that direction and Huggins may have been right about de Mohrenschildt's involvement. Willem Oltmans, a friend of de Mohrenschildt, clearly implied there was a link. What Oltmans said was startling, in that de Mohrenschildt had "confessed to being involved in the assassination of John F. Kennedy."[648]

> Oltmans claimed that de Mohrenschildt had admitted serving as a middleman between Lee Harvey Oswald and H. L. Hunt in an assassination plot involving other Texas oilmen, anti-Castro Cubans, and elements of the FBI and CIA.[649]

---

[644] Bill Sloan, *JFK: Breaking the Silence* (Taylor Publishing: 1993).
[645] Sloan, *JFK: Breaking the Silence*
[646] Ibid.
[647] Ibid.
[648] Simkin, "George de Mohrenschildt"
[649] Ibid.

So, according to a direct source, George de Mohrenschildt said he acted as the go-between for the setting up of the JFK assassination as the liaison between Texas billionaires (H. L. Hunt) and renegade CIA agents. That's a pretty big bombshell. As his mental health declined rapidly, de Mohrenschildt then denied that—Oltmans said he just changed his story.

> I am responsible. I feel responsible for the behavior of Lee Harvey Oswald . . . because I guided him. I instructed him to set it up.[650]

As one might imagine, there were a *lot* of people who wouldn't be too thrilled about hearing him say that to a Congressional committee.

> On March 29, de Mohrenschildt gave an interview to author Edward Jay Epstein, during which he claimed that in 1962, Dallas CIA operative J. Walton Moore had given him the go-ahead to meet Oswald. "I would never have contacted Oswald in a million years if Moore had not sanctioned it," de Mohrenschildt said. "Too much was at stake."[651]

RAPID DEMISE

There's more than one way to silence a witness. And when we looked into the rapid demise of George de Mohrenschildt, what we found was *extremely disturbing*; including electroshock "treatments" and injections of drugs that a suspicious doctor refused to identify—even to de Mohrenschildt's wife—when she noticed the dramatic and rapid decline of her husband and the accompanying mental delusions he began suffering, Jeanne de Morenschildt attempted to intervene. But the doctor refused to allow her to see what he was doing and even began yelling at her for questioning him.[652]

For such a suave and sophisticated socialite, de Mohrenschildt's mental and physical decline was so incredibly rapid that it bears further examination. To the disbelief of old friends, he went from a solid, extremely confident man to virtually a human "vegetable"; and it didn't take long, either.

> I couldn't believe my eyes. The man had changed drastically . . . he was nervous, trembling. It was a scared, a very, very scared person I saw.[653]

The change in de Mohrenschildt's demeanor was 180 degrees different; diametrically opposed to the man he had been:

> The wife of de Mohrenschildt, Jeanne, put all the blame for her husband's sudden decline on a very suspicious doctor. It all apparently started with a bout of bronchitis. George de Mohrenschildt suffered from chronic bronchitis and, in the spring of 1976, had a case of it that was worse

---

[650] Ibid.
[651] Edward Jay Epstein, *The Assassination Chronicles* (1992).
[652] Marrs, *Crossfire*
[653] Simkin, "George de Mohrenschildt"

bronchitis and, in the spring of 1976, had a case of it that was worse than usual. From some friend or acquaintance—Jeanne could not recall whom—George had heard about a doctor who was newly arrived in Dallas that was supposed to be good, and went to see him for an office visit. It was then that his real troubles began.[654]

Jeanne said after several trips to the new doctor, Charles Mendoza, by late spring or early summer, the bronchitis was gone but she noticed abrupt and dramatic personality changes in her husband. He became paranoid and began making wild claims. And instead of getting better, it seemed to be getting rapidly worse, until finally she confronted George's new doctor:

> When I confronted (Mendoza) with this information, as well as asking him exactly what kinds of treatments and medications he was giving George, he became very angry and upset. By then, I had become suspicious and started accompanying George on each of his visits to the doctor. But this physician would not allow me to be with George during his treatments. He said George was gravely ill and had to be alone during treatments.[655]

Dr. Mendoza was apparently giving George some type of special injections—he refused to say what they were—as well as some expensive drug prescriptions.

George's condition deteriorated so rapidly that he was checked into a mental hospital and given electroshock therapy.

> I have become convinced that this doctor, in some way, lies behind the nervous breakdown George suffered in his final months.[656]

Not much is known about the mysterious Dr. Mendoza:

> The doctor is indeed mysterious. A check with the Dallas County Medical Society showed that Dr. Mendoza first registered in April 1976, less than two months before he began treating de Mohrenschildt, and at the same time the House Select Committee on Assassinations was beginning to be funded.[657]

And just as quickly as the mysterious Dr. Mendoza had appeared, he vanished:

> Mendoza left Dallas in December, just a few months after de Mohrenschildt refused to continue treatments at the insistence of his wife. Mendoza left the society a forwarding address that proved to be nonexistent. He also left behind a confused and unbalanced George de Mohrenschildt.[658]

---

[654] Marrs, *Crossfire*
[655] Ibid.
[656] Ibid.
[657] Ibid.
[658] Ibid.

It is known, though, that George de Mohrenschildt was never the same again—he never recovered mentally. Something clearly happened to him and no one knew what that something had been.

> I was absolutely shocked, because I knew de Mohrenschildt as a man who wins tennis matches, who is always suntanned, who jogs every morning, who is as healthy as a bull.[659]

HIGHLY SUSPICIOUS DEATH

George de Mohrenschildt was subpoenaed to testify before the Congressional committee investigating the assassination, and died the day before he was scheduled to testify.

There is plenty of evidence that de Mohrenschildt was being *seriously* harassed and felt very threatened:

> Oltmans told the HSCA: "He begged me to take him out of the country because they are after me."[660]

George de Mohrenschildt felt he was being "hounded" by federal agents and feared for his life.

On September 5, 1976, de Mohrenschildt wrote a polite but panicked letter to his old friend, George H. W. Bush, who was Director of the CIA at the time. He asked Bush for his assistance "to remove the net" of the surveillance nightmare surrounding his life. These were his exact words:

> You will excuse this hand-written letter. Maybe you will be able to bring a solution to the hopeless situation I find myself in. My wife and I find ourselves surrounded by some vigilantes; our phone bugged; and we are being followed everywhere. Either FBI is involved in this or they do not want to accept my complaints. We are driven to insanity by the situation. I have been behaving like a damn fool ever since my daughter Nadya died from (cystic fibrosis) over three years ago. I tried to write, stupidly and unsuccessfully, about Lee H. Oswald, and must have angered a lot of people—I do not know. But to punish an elderly man like myself and my highly nervous and sick wife is really too much. Could you do something to remove the net around us? This will be my last request for help and I will not annoy you anymore. Good luck in your important job. Thank you so much.[661]

For whatever it's worth—or *not* worth—Bush answered back with a vague, formal letter that basically said he didn't know what de Mohrenschildt was even talking about.

The House Select Committee on Assassinations became very interested in taking testimony from George de Mohrenschildt. Robert Tanenbaum, Committee Counsel,

---

[659] Ibid.
[660] Simkin, "George de Mohrenschildt"
[661] Baker, *Family of Secrets*

listened intently to what Willem Oltmans told him about de Mohrenschildt's connections to the case and where he could be located. Tanenbaum, to his credit, responded with urgency, telling Oltmans:

We will have an investigator there tomorrow.[662]

And true to his word, Tanenbaum did. Special Investigator Gaeton Fonzi appeared the next day to try to interview him for the Committee. George's daughter had been staying at a luxurious villa near Palm Beach, Florida, and George had been staying there also.

> **On the morning of March 29, 1977, Gaeton Fonzi, the committee's Miami-based investigator, arrived at the villa in Manalapan. He was told by de Mohrenschildt's daughter that her father was meeting with journalist Edward Jay Epstein at a Palm Beach hotel, but would be back that night. At 1:00 p.m., de Mohrenschildt left by car and returned to his temporary residence. By 2:21 p.m., he was dead. Authorities determined the time by listening to a tape on which de Mohrenschildt's daughter was recording a TV soap opera while she was at work.**[663]

Author Dick Russell investigated the circumstance of de Mohrenschildt's death and learned from Jeanne de Mohrenschildt that there was much there to be investigated. Instead, it was quickly and officially ruled a suicide. He asked her, point blank, if she thought her husband had taken his own life:

> **Nobody that knew him does, that's my answer.**[664]

Dick Russell tried to get the story out of her, but here is all that she would say:

> **I have a few other little facts that prove he didn't.**[665]

And here's what Jeanne was apparently referring to: Attorney Mark Lane attended the Coroner's Inquest in Florida, because the untimely death was far too coincidental. What he learned was amazing. There was a tape recording of George de Mohrenschildt's murder—a maid had been instructed to make an audio tape of a television soap opera and had done so. So the tape recorder was running and audio recorded the shooting death of George de Mohrenschildt The shotgun blast can be clearly heard. Attorney Mark Lane heard it as it was played for the Grand Jury at the Coroner's Inquest.

But there are also some other sounds on the tape recording that are extremely pertinent to the manner of his death. Lane describes them:

> **They claimed he committed suicide. But if you listen to the tape, you hear this: You hear a little noise, then you hear silence and then you hear**

---

[662] Russell, *The Man Who Knew Too Much*, 173.
[663] Ibid.
[664] Ibid.
[665] Ibid.

'Beep-Beep-Beep-Beep-Beep,' a little more noise, and then you hear the shot. The 'Beep-Beep-Beep-Beep-Beep' was a security system, on medium mode. One mode is—if it's on fully armed—if anyone opens a door or window, a siren goes off and the police are notified. On another mode, it's off entirely. But on the *medium* mode, it goes 'Beep-Beep-Beep-Beep' to show that someone has opened the door and come into the house. Just before de Mohrenschildt was shot, that's what happened.[666]

It's a game-changer piece of evidence—and you can listen to it yourself—it's available on the Internet.[667]

I talked to the District Attorney when I listened to that tape. I was down there just before the Coroner's Inquest. And I said, "Does that sound like someone came into the house?" He said, "We're not going to go into that." And I said, "Why?" He said, "You understand why. This is bigger than all of us. We have to do what we have to do." I said, "I don't understand that." And he said, "Well, listen, you can't speak at the Coroner's Inquest, you're just gonna be a spectator." I said, "I know that." And so he played the tape and told the Coroner's Jury—a cross-section of the folks in the area—that this was a suicide, etc. And this woman on the Coroner's Jury said, "That 'Beep-Beep-Beep-Beep,' that sounds like my security system! Somebody apparently went into the house!" And he said "We're not going into that!" And so they ruled that it was a suicide, and that was the end of that. But I think there are some very serious questions as to whether he was murdered.[668]

Another thing to consider with seriousness is this: George de Mohrenschildt, by all accounts, was a suave, debonair, extremely sophisticated gentleman who moved seamlessly through the higher social strata. It is rather preposterous to presume that he would:

A. Choose a shotgun as a means of committing suicide, and
B. Leave his shotgunned corpse and the easily predictable accompanying bloodbath of a mess for his daughter and their host to return home to find.

On May 11, 1978, Jeanne de Mohrenschildt gave an interview to the *Fort Worth Star-Telegram,* where she said that she did not accept that her husband had committed suicide. She also said that she believed Lee Harvey Oswald was an agent of the United States—possibly of the CIA—and that she was convinced he did not kill John F. Kennedy. She then went on to say:

They may get me too, but I'm not afraid.[669]

---

[666] Mark Lane, in: "G. de Mohrenschildt—The Security Alarm," excerpted from *Inside Edition* (with Bill O'Reilly), *CBS Television,* accessed 26 Nov. 2012: http://youtu.be/37dtEpvyUJU

[667] "G. de Mohrenschildt—The Security Alarm": http://youtu.be/37dtEpvyUJU

[668] Ibid.

[669] Simkin, "George de Mohrenschildt"

We agree with Jeanne de Mohrenschildt, and as she also said:

It's about time somebody looked into this thing.[670]

CONCLUSIONS BASED ON EVIDENTIARY INDICATIONS

It cannot be stated to a degree of complete certainty, but incongruities at crime scene indicate that George de Mohrenschildt was probably murdered and that his murder was to prevent his testimony regarding the true nature of Lee Harvey Oswald.

CONCLUSION

Probable national security assassination, *directly* linked to JFK assassination.

---

[670] Ibid.

President Carlos Prío Socarrás, April 5, 1977

Victim	Carlos Prío Socarrás, President of Cuba (1948–1952)
Cause of Death	Gunshot wounds
Official Verdict	Suicide
Actual Circumstances	Found shot outside his home in Florida, just as he was being sought to testify before the House Select Committee on Assassinations.
Inconsistencies	1. There is a dearth of information on this particular case. 2. Victim played a key role in anti-Castro operations.

3. He knew Jack Ruby and Frank Sturgis; had many links to mafia.
4. Was a witness of special interest to Congress, and;
5. Was shot before he could testify about what he knew.

Another witness sought by the House Select Committee on Assassinations was former Cuban President, Carlos Prío Socarrás. He was murdered less than a week after George de Mohrenschildt and Chuck Nicoletti were eliminated.

Prío Socarrás was Cuba's last elected President, serving from 1948–1952. He reportedly never kept his campaign promise of removing the mafia from Cuban politics and, in fact, reportedly had links to the mafia himself. It has also been noted that he apparently gained noticeable wealth during his presidency. General Fulgencia Batista ousted Prío Socarrás in 1952, and Prío Socarrás fled to the U.S. Then, in 1953, Castro ousted Batista and remained in power for many decades.[671]

Apparently, the reason Batista, whom history denounces as a dictator, found it so easy to throw a military coup against Prío Socarrás, was because he was even more corrupt than the dictators:

> The 'Cuban Democracy' tenure of Carlos Prío (1948–1952) has often been described as the most corrupt in the island's history, a time when political gangs (and some American counterparts) ran rampant.[672]

The legendary gunrunner, Robert McKeown, put it this way about the former President, an old buddy of McKeown's:

> Prío got out of Cuba with a helluva lotta money, and he didn't give a damn how he spent it either. I carried $100,000 in cash in my goddamn inside coat pocket a lotta times.[673]

Prío Socarrás was found dead from gunshot wounds outside his Miami Beach home on April 5, 1977. The official ruling was suicide, but little is known about the incident. Author David Miller in his article, "Did the CIA Kill Carlos Prío?" suggested that Prío Socarrás had been murdered to keep him from testifying.[674]

---

[671] *The Cuban History*, "Pres. Prío Socarrás (1948-1952)," accessed 29 Nov. 2012: http:www.thecubanhistory .com/2011/12/president-carlos-prio-socarras/

[672] Russell, *On the Trail of the JFK Assassins*, 136.

[673] Ibid, 136-137.

[674] *The Cuban History*, "Pres. Prío Socarrás"

Prío Socarrás had already been linked in testimony to both Jack Ruby and Frank Sturgis, both persons of "keen interest" to the Committee, and had also apparently been involved in the CIA's bungled Bay of Pigs intelligence operation that attempted and failed to wrestle back control of Cuba from Fidel Castro.[675]

---

[675] Ibid.

I may have faults, but being wrong ain't one of them.

—*Jimmy Hoffa, 1961 Teamsters' Convention*

Jimmy Hoffa always managed to make his opinions known, even under fire at a Government hearing. The above "finger" was reportedly directed at Robert Kennedy, who had been grilling Hoffa on his connections to Organized Crime. Hoffa could not use the 5th Amendment as a shield because he was the President of a labor union. So instead, he claimed a poor memory, in exchanges that became increasingly heated— and led to the above gesture.

Victim	**Jimmy Hoffa, top labor leader in country; major connections to mafia; arch-enemy of Attorney General Bobby Kennedy**
Cause of Death	Disappeared; missing person; presumed dead
Official Verdict	Declared "legally dead" on July 30, 1975 (after seven years). Law enforcement agencies still (as recently as early 2013) investigate the matter as an open case.

Actual Circumstances	In typical mafia fashion, Hoffa was lured to his death by two people whom he thought he could trust: Frank "The Irishman" Sheeran and Russell "The Old Man" Bufalino.
Inconsistencies	Contrary to the popular media notion that we do not know what happened, Sheeran's verified "deathbed testimony" revealed *exactly* what happened to Hoffa.

Overview

▶ **The Disappearance of Jimmy Hoffa**

Labor leader; very popular President of the powerful two-million member Teamsters Union, with its billion-dollar pension fund that was used to make "sweet loans" to mafia "fronts," such as casinos and hotels in Las Vegas. Strong ties to mafia (nationally, but his actual power center was Detroit and Chicago). Bitter enemy of the Kennedys, especially Bobby (they openly despised each other).

- Disappeared and presumed murdered.
- Last seen at *The Red Fox* restaurant outside of Detroit, after lunchtime on Wednesday, July 30, 1975.
- Team of over 200 FBI agents conducted a massive search and investigation—for years—but never solved the crime.
- Body was never found. The most massive search in modern history never determined what happened to Hoffa's body.
- The FBI was confident of the identity of Hoffa's killers. Their "certain suspects" list was:
  - Frank "The Irishman" Sheehan (hitman)
  - Chuckie O'Brien (stepson of Jimmy Hoffa)
  - Salvatore "Sally Bugs" Briguglio
  - Gabriel "Gabe" Briguglio
  - Stephen "Steve" Andretta
  - Thomas "Tom" Andretta
  - Anthony "Tony Pro" Provenzano
  - Anthony "Tony Jack" Giacalone
  - Russell "The Old Man" Bufalino (boss of the Bufalino Crime Family of Pennsylvania and large parts of New York, New Jersey, and Florida for thirty years; 1959–89)
- "Deathbed testimony" of long-time hitman Frank Sheeran revealed that Hoffa had asked mob leaders Carlos Marcello and Santo Trafficante to get rid of JFK and that, shortly after that request, Sheeran was directed to deliver high-powered

rifles to David Ferrie (Marcello's private pilot) to be used in Dallas.
- One of the first things that Bobby Kennedy did after his brother's murder was direct his top assistant at the Justice Department, Walter Sheridan, to check for the involvement of Jimmy Hoffa.

He was referred to by everyone—including himself—simply as "Hoffa"—and Hoffa was one tough cookie. Believe it or not, at one time, Jimmy Hoffa was as famous as The Beatles or the President of the United States—and, in some ways, was possibly more influential and powerful than both of them put together. He was the nation's most prominent labor leader during decades of battle—waged openly and fiercely—between big business and millions of working-class Americans. Hoffa was a hero to the millions, but was the openly declared enemy of big business. Even Attorney General Bobby Kennedy, Hoffa's arch-enemy, acknowledged Hoffa's lofty status:

He's not just the most powerful man in labor; he's the most powerful man in the country, next to the President.[676]

And he earned that reputation the hard way—by proving it. He started out unloading trucks at a pay of 32 cents-per-hour under horrendously unfair working conditions. Then, one hot afternoon, when loads of fresh strawberries came in on the trucks, young Hoffa gave the signal and the men sat down instead of unloading them. As the strawberries sat there ripening in the hot sun, the company was only left with two choices: let them rot or listen to the workers' demands. What came to be known as the big gamble of The Strawberry Boys paid off and a new union was born that day.

During the years of union organizing that followed, strikes and knock-down-drag-out brawls were just another day at work for these guys. Hoffa had his skull cracked open dozens of times by tough "Union-busters" and "Strike-breakers"; tough thugs hired by the big companies to come in and break heads. Hoffa took it. . . . The men followed him. The cops were on the side of the companies, so arrests were part of the game. Arrests were so expected that Hoffa would line up a Magistrate to approve bail for his boys on an immediate basis. During one free-for-all, Hoffa's right hand man was arrested twenty-six times during a twenty-four-hour period; he just kept fighting and getting collared by police—then he'd post bail and go right back to the picket line, jumping back into the ongoing brawl.

He grew up hard and tough and stayed that way, developing a reputation for fearlessness that cemented itself into the Hoffa legend. If a gang of union toughs and mob guys went marching off to have lunch or a few beers, you could bet the ranch

---

[676] Arthur A Sloane, *Hoffa* (MIT Press: 1991), 134-135.

that it was Hoffa marching out in front of the pack. He was short and stout, but was solid as a rock and took quick, frantic steps right up to his dying day. Hoffa was packed with a powerful, confident energy that screamed "I lead—you follow, or get the hell outta my way." He had a mouth that would tell you exactly what he thought of you before you were halfway through a sentence. You might mess with the U.S. Government—you might mess a little bit with the mob—but you did not mess with Hoffa or his union.

His union was the International Brotherhood of Teamsters and represented over two million hard-working truck drivers, warehouse workers, and others crucial to maintaining the steady flow of daily business in America. Teamsters were synonymous with Hoffa—he lived and breathed it, and the rank and file union members loved him back in return. And if your company needed trucks to pick up or deliver anything at all, then you needed the Teamsters. So if a truck brought it, Hoffa controlled it. And he could shut down your whole business quicker than you could say "Labor Dispute" or "Informational Picket Line."

So, suffice to say that Hoffa knew his way around and was not afraid of trouble. But the Teamsters weren't always that strong—Hoffa built it. For two decades he organized workers and consolidated small unions into stronger regional groups. Membership increased tenfold. Then he transformed the regions into one huge national group, leveraging the new "strength in numbers" to secure rights for workers.

Against all odds—and incredible hostility from the big companies—Hoffa managed to engineer a national umbrella contract covering every driver—the National Master Freight Agreement—that guaranteed every driver in the union a decent wage under decent conditions. That achievement, as well as the pension to add to their Social Security for retirement, made Hoffa a hero to millions of working-class Americans.

But the Teamsters Union was also synonymous with the Mafia. For years, the mob used the billion-dollar union pension fund as their own private cash register, making very cozy loans to shell companies for mob bosses nationwide, with very lucrative "points" given as bonuses to the mob guys who handled the loan deals. And nobody was better at it than Hoffa; in fact, he invented the whole enchilada. It was loans from the pension fund that developed Las Vegas in the 50s and 60s. They financed a string of huge, expensive casinos that were the largest of their era, including Caesar's Palace, Circus Circus, the Dunes, the Desert Inn, and the Stardust.

The mob influence with the union led to the attention of Attorney General Bobby Kennedy and his war on organized crime. Hoffa and Kennedy became bitter enemies, squaring off against each other in televised committee hearings, where their hatred for each other was so thick in the air that you could just sit there and watch it smolder. In 1960, Bobby Kennedy said:

But there was no group that better fits the prototype of the old Al Capone syndicate than Jimmy Hoffa and some of his lieutenants.[677]

---

[677] Robert F. Kennedy, *The Enemy Within* (Harper: 1960).

No one has described the actual context of the Hoffa-Kennedy war better than longtime mobster and Hoffa associate, Frank Sheeran:

> You see, you've got to keep in mind that when Bobby Kennedy came in as Attorney General, the FBI was still basically ignoring so-called organized crime. . . . For years and years since Prohibition ended, the only thing that the so-called mobsters had to contend with was the local cops, and a lot of them were on the pad (bribed; on the payroll). . . . Then Bobby Kennedy gets in and a bad dream turns to everybody's worst nightmare. All of a sudden everybody that's going along minding their own store starts getting indicted. People are actually going to jail. People are getting deported. It was tense.
>
> Now in that Nashville trial on the Test Fleet case at the end of 1962, Jimmy's taking a stand against Bobby, in what was shaping up like a major war ever since Bobby got in as attorney general.[678]

It became clear that Kennedy was intent on sending Hoffa to prison—the Justice Department literally had its own "Get Hoffa Department," and Hoffa, of course, knew it. So there was motivation for Hoffa to get the Kennedys before he was nailed by them, and it was also apparent that the best way to "beat the heat" was by getting rid of JFK, which would ultimately diffuse Bobby. The matter was actually discussed in just such a way: If they got Bobby, JFK was still President and would retaliate fiercely; but if they got the President, Lyndon Johnson would become President. LBJ had his own ties to the mob, particularly with Carlos Marcello, and he hated Bobby almost as much as Hoffa did. So the best way to get Bobby was actually to take out JFK.

Deathbed testimony from hitman Frank Sheeran, a close friend (and killer) of Hoffa's for many years, reveals that the mobsters followed through on that plan—Hoffa had implored mob bosses Carlos Marcello and Santo Trafficante to "get" JFK—and eventually they did precisely that. Sheeran delivered rifles to Dave Ferrie, pilot for mob boss Carlos Marcello, to be used in the assassination. Ferrie was also linked to Lee Harvey Oswald and was involved in setting up the assassination, and like Hoffa, Oswald, and Ruby, Ferrie was also murdered in the ensuing "clean-up" following the murder of President Kennedy. The Hoffa link to the JFK assassination was also substantiated by attorney Bill Bonanno, son of the legendary New York Godfather, Joe Bonanno.

Confirmation of that also came later when the boss of an East Coast crime family warned Hoffa to back off on making mob matters public (when Hoffa had been talking too much in his bid to get back the presidency of the Teamsters). Frank Sheeran was sitting right there during that conversation, with his boss, Russell Bufalino and Jimmy Hoffa. Bufalino was a quiet Godfather who more resembled the character of Don Corleone in the film, *The Godfather*, than any of his fellow bosses. He was boss of the Bufalino Crime Family, respected as one of the wisest (and fairest) mafiosos for over thirty years. His territory was technically northern Pennsylvania and upstate New York, but had stretched to New Jersey and Florida. And the respect he'd gained actually gave

---

[678] Charles Brandt. *I Heard You Paint Houses: Frank "The Irishman' Sheeran and the Inside Story of the Mafia, the Teamsters and the Last Ride of Jimmy Hoffa*, (Steerforth Press: 2005), 147.

him tremendous influence nationwide. Here's how Sheeran remembered it and it wasn't the kind of thing that was easy to forget:

Russell turned to Jimmy and was now facing Jimmy and me both.

"There are people higher up than me that feel you are demonstrating a failure to show appreciation," and then he said so softly that I had to read his lips, "for Dallas."

After the above comment, when Hoffa had left, Sheeran told Bufalino that Hoffa seemed so powerful that he was almost untouchable. But Bufalino knew better and coolly responded:

You're dreaming, my friend. If they could take out the president, they could take out the president of the Teamsters.[679]

Eventually, the FBI pressure that was put on Hoffa in the following years came up with enough to get him sentenced to prison. Hoffa installed Frank Fitzimmons into the leadership role of the Teamsters while Hoffa was in "school" (Mafia slang for prison). Fitzimmons seemed loyal, reliable, and safe—though it turned out not to be the case.

Hoffa only served five years of a thirteen-year prison sentence because he was pardoned by President Nixon. The pardon was "married" to a string of huge cash payments to Nixon's re-election committee—appropriately named CREEP, for Committee to Re-Elect the President (you couldn't make this stuff up if you tried).

And, in exactly the same manner—a suitcase stuffed with cash handed over to the Attorney General of the United States (John Mitchell)—Hoffa also engineered a way around the clause in the pardon that restricted him from running for President of the Teamsters again. And, next thing you knew, Hoffa challenged Fitzimmons for the Presidency. With the rank and file union members right behind him, as usual, it looked like it was all his for the taking.

A war ensued for leadership of the Teamsters. Hoffa wanted the presidency back and made it clear he was going to do anything to get it, but the mob was comfortable with the easygoing Fitzimmons who could be easily controlled, as they feared the explosive Hoffa's return to leadership.

Threats were made. Control was contested. Nobody looked safe. A "meet" was set up to make one last attempt at peace. Hoffa agreed to meet in a public place with the head of the enemy faction in the Teamsters, "Tony Pro" (Tony Provenzano). The meeting would be brokered by a friend of both, whom they could both, within limitations, have some trust: "Tony Jack" (Anthony Giacalone). The meet was for 2:30 p.m. on a Wednesday afternoon at the Red Fox restaurant just outside of Detroit; after the lunchtime crowd, but with still enough people to make it a safe, public meeting.

Officially, Jimmy Hoffa was last seen outside that restaurant shortly after the appointed time. He left an outdoor phone booth and then walked over to a car in the parking lot, got into it, and the car drove away. Officially, he was never seen again.

---

[679] Charles Brandt. *I Heard You Paint Houses: Frank "The Irishman" Sheeran and the Inside Story of the Mafia, the Teamsters and the Last Ride of Jimmy Hoffa*, (Steerforth Press: 2005).

Under these highly explosive circumstances, Hoffa would never have gotten into a car with his most bitter enemy. Therefore, it is quite logically presumed that he must have been lured into the car by the presence of associates whom he trusted in true Mafia tradition.

Unofficially, we do know what happened. He called his wife from the pay phone (Hoffa always used pay phones for sensitive calls) to see if his friend had called the house because his "insurance" was late. Frank Sheeran had agreed to drive to the restaurant and be there with Hoffa, a half hour prior to the set meet. If he had Sheeran and Giacalone there, Hoffa knew he'd be safe.

"Tony Pro" had no intention of showing up for the meeting. He was back in Detroit in a public place, making sure he had a highly visible alibi. The same was true for "Tony Jack." It had already been decided by "higher forces" in the mob that it was time to take care of the Hoffa problem.

> I was supposed to be sitting there in the restaurant when the two Tonys showed up for their 2:30 appointment with Jimmy. Only Tony Jack was getting a massage at his health club in Detroit. Tony Pro, meantime, wasn't even in Michigan. He was in New Jersey at his union hall playing Greek rummy, with the FBI no doubt sitting across the street from the union hall keeping an eye on him.[680]

The hit on Hoffa was "sanctioned" by Detroit and Chicago. The man, who made the hit, Frank Sheeran, explains:

> New York had turned it down. They didn't sanction it, but they didn't oppose it either. "If you did it you were on your own"-type of thing. It couldn't have been done without Detroit's sanction, because it was their territory. Same for Chicago, because they were close by and there was a lot of tie-in between Chicago and Detroit.[681]

Frank Sheeran, who was even Hoffa's own shooter on many occasions throughout the years, was his close and trusted friend. But Sheeran was really given no choice. He knew that being told to make the hit on Hoffa meant that he was actually being spared his life, due to his close connection with Russell "The Old Man" Bufalino. Putting out a contract on Hoffa meant that the Mob—at the top level of leadership—had decided to go with the "Tony Pro" faction on the battle for control of the union. So they were "cleaning house" and, typically, since Sheeran was a "Hoffa man," that meant he'd get his house painted too. Offering him the hit was sparing his life. So, in Sheeran's defense, if he'd declined or even tried tipping off his friend to run for it, then he was a dead man too.

Frank Sheeran was one of the top hitmen in history: He shot Crazy Joey Gallo, head of the Gambino Crime Family in New York City (in a restaurant in Little Italy in 1972), "Sally Bugs" Briguglio (on a New York street in broad daylight), and a number of other high-profile hits for the mob.

---

[680] Ibid.
[681] Ibid, 259.

"Deathbed confessions" carry a lot of weight in a court of law because the confessor can finally free their conscience without fear of reprisals. When Sheeran was nearing the end, he "came clean" to attorney Charles Brandt, who recorded every word of it. Sheeran got his orders for the hit directly from Russell "The Old Man" Bufalino, and he explained, very specifically, how the hit was made. After describing exactly how and where he drove there, street-by-street, with precise detail and descriptions, Sheeran also conveyed the broader context:

> The whole thing was built around the wedding. Bill Bufalino's daughter was getting married on Friday, August 1, 1975. That was two days after Jimmy disappeared. People would be coming in from all the (mafia) families around the country. There would be over 500 people there. . . . Because of the wedding, Jimmy would be inclined to believe that Tony Pro and Russell Bufalino would be in the Detroit area so they could meet with him in the afternoon he disappeared. The thing with Tony Pro wanting his million-dollar pension was a decoy. They just used the pension beef to get Jimmy to come out.[682]

The car that pulled up was another part of the plan. It was driven by Chuckie O'Brien, Hoffa's foster son who still called Hoffa "Dad"; and it was a car familiar to Hoffa too—the maroon Mercury of Tony Jack's son. Tony Jack was pals with Hoffa and he knew the car well; it was just the type of car that would be used for such a meeting, because it wasn't flashy and just blended in.

> Jimmy Hoffa's foster son, Chuckie O'Brien, and I were going to be part of the bait to lure Jimmy into a car with Sally Bugs, Tony Pro's right-hand man. . . . Without being told, I knew that there was no reason for Sally Bugs to get in Chuckie's car other than to keep an eye on me. To make sure I didn't spook Jimmy not to get in the car. Jimmy was supposed to feel safe with me in Chuckie's car so he'd go to this house with brown shingles and walk right in the front door with me as his backup.[683]

So there were two people Hoffa trusted inside that car: Frank "The Irishman" Sheeran and Hoffa's stepson, Chuckie. He never would have gotten into the car if they weren't there. Sheeran explains:

> Everybody being at ease was an important feature, because Jimmy was as smart as they come at smelling danger from all his years in bloody union wars and knowing the people he was dealing with. He was supposed to meet Tony Jack and Tony Pro in a public restaurant with a public parking lot. Not many people change a public meeting place to a private house on Jimmy Hoffa—even with me in the car. Even with his "son" Chuckie driving.[684]

---

[682] Brandt. *I Heard You Paint Houses*
[683] Ibid.
[684] Ibid.

The setup for the hit had to be picture-perfect because Hoffa was a very cautious man under any circumstances, and particularly so for this meeting. Sheeran continues:

> The psychology of the matter was played to perfection. They knew how to get under the man's skin. Jimmy Hoffa had been forced to wait for me for a full half-hour, from 2:00 to 2:30, only because he was stuck waiting for the 2:30 meeting. And then he waited his standard fifteen minutes for the two Tonys besides. Waiting forty-five minutes made Jimmy nuts like it was supposed to and then to compensate for all the bull he put out, he got cooperative like he was supposed to.[685]

Hoffa trusted Frank "The Irishman" Sheeran, a longtime friend and professional hitman. Because of this, Sheeran was forced into the murder plot.

Sheeran told Hoffa that McGee—their code name for Russell Bufalino, also known as "The Old Man"—had changed the setup. Hoffa was told that Bufalino had decided to broker the meeting—and hopefully to settle the score—and that McGee was waiting at a nearby home, along with "Tony Pro." They knew that Hoffa would buy that story because Bufalino was known nationwide as a formidable peace broker for finding solutions to problems when possible, rather than simply opting for bloodshed.

> Sally Bugs said "His friend wanted to be at the thing. They're at the house waitin."[686]

They knew that Hoffa seeing Sheeran sitting in the front passenger seat would help the set-up to pass.

> Seeing me there, Jimmy instantly would believe Russell Bufalino was already in Detroit sitting around a kitchen table at a house waiting. My friend Russell wanting to be there would explain the sudden last-minute change in plans in Jimmy's mind. Russell Bufalino was not the man to conduct a sit-down in a public place he didn't know like the Red Fox. Russell

---

[685] Ibid.
[686] Ibid.

> Bufalino was old school. He was a very private person. He'd only meet you in public in places he knew and trusted.[687]

Out of respect for "The Old Man," Hoffa basically had to go along with the new setup.

> Russell Bufalino was the final bait to lure Jimmy into the car. If there was going to be any violence, anything unnatural, Russell would not be there.[688]

With that story, combined with the presence of his stepson behind the wheel of the car, and his old friend, Frank "The Irishman" in the passenger seat, Hoffa got into the car.

They drove a couple minutes to a nearby house they had gotten as a "loaner" (a previously set up arrangement where a person who was "in" with the Mob lent them short term use of the house). Sheeran's car, a Ford, was in the driveway and was also a "loaner" (stolen off a long-term parking lot so that it wasn't traceable back to him). Another car was also in the driveway, a brown Buick. It actually belonged to the "cleaners" (the guys who get rid of the dead body and the shooter's gun) who were waiting inside the back of the house. But as far as appearances, it looked just like the type of nondescript car that Bufalino would arrive in (the intelligence community reference to "cleaners" is as assassins, but the Mob refers to them as the people who deal with the dead body). Everything looked "legit" to Hoffa. The logical assumption was that The Old Man was waiting inside to try to broker a deal with Hoffa and Tony Pro.

> The house and the neighborhood were not threatening in the least. It was a place you'd want your kids to grow up in. The garage in the rear was detached, which was a nice touch. Nobody was asking Jimmy to go in that house in secret through an attached garage. Jimmy and I were walking right in the front door in broad daylight with two cars parked right there in the driveway.[689]

Hoffa's stepson parked the car in the driveway. Hoffa got out of the back and Sheeran got out of the passenger seat. Hoffa walked into the house for the "meeting" thinking that Sheeran, the man walking in right behind him, was his protection. The moment Hoffa entered, he knew "what it was."

> When Jimmy saw that the house was empty, that nobody came out of any of the rooms to greet him, he knew right away what it was. If Jimmy had taken his piece with him, he would have gone for it. Jimmy was a fighter. He turned fast, still thinking we were together on the thing, that I was his backup. Jimmy bumped into me hard. If he saw the piece in my hand he had to think I had it out to protect him.[690]

Then his friend did the dirty deed he'd been forced into doing.

> He took a quick step to go around me and get to the door. He reached for the knob and Jimmy Hoffa got shot twice at a decent range—not too

[687] Brandt. *I Heard You Paint Houses*
[688] Ibid.
[689] Ibid.
[690] Ibid.

close or the paint splatters back at you—in the back of the head behind his right ear. My friend didn't suffer.[691]

The "cleaners" had put linoleum tiles down in the vestibule of the house to make it easier to get rid of the blood. The Andretta brothers were Tony Pro's people.

They were there as cleaners to pick up the linoleum they had put down in the vestibule and to do any clean-up that might be necessary and to remove any jewelry and take Jimmy's body in a bag to be cremated.[692]

Sheeran also knew that the FBI's initial claim on DNA was wrong. The FBI claimed that hair found in the trunk of that car had been analyzed for DNA and was a match to Jimmy Hoffa. Sheeran knew better, and he knew it as a fact:

Jimmy was never in the trunk, dead or alive.[693]

Later testing revealed that a hair recovered from the rear passenger's side seat (where Sheeran placed Hoffa) was being DNA-tested. The FBI revealed on September 7, 2001, that the hair was matched to Jimmy Hoffa.

Further confirmation of Sheeran's confession came from comparing the forensic evidence and Sheeran's specific descriptions. Dr. Michael Baden is a nationally respected forensic expert who was formerly Chief Medical Examiner of New York City. Dr. Baden examined the evidence and concluded that:

Sheeran's confession that he killed Hoffa in the manner described in the book is supported by the forensic evidence, is entirely credible, and solves the Hoffa mystery.[694]

CONCLUSIONS BASED ON EVIDENTIARY INDICATIONS

- Jimmy Hoffa was definitely murdered, even though the body was never found.
- Case has all the signs of a classic Mafia hit.
- Hoffa did have sensitive knowledge that was highly pertinent to the JFK assassination, and he was at a point in his life when he was talking too much and too publicly.
- However, the hit appears to be unrelated to the JFK cover-up. It was the result of Hoffa's maniacal quest to regain his Presidency of the Teamsters Union, at any cost.
- The murder was the result of an internal decision by mafia leaders. The hitman "came clean," so we know a great deal about the case.

---

[691] Brandt. *I Heard You Paint Houses*
[692] Ibid.
[693] Ibid.
[694] Ibid.

- The hit on Hoffa wasn't sanctioned (formally authorized) by the New York mafia, but they didn't block it either. The hit was sanctioned by the Detroit Outfit, with the blessings of the Chicago Crime Family as well.
- FBI's suspect list was right on target. The "house was painted" by Frank Sheeran. The "cleaners" (according to Sheeran himself) were the Andretta brothers, associates of Anthony "Tony Pro" Provenzano, a "made" member of the Genovese Crime Family of New York. The bosses authorizing and masterminding both the hit and the clean-up were Tony Pro, and East Coast Crime Boss Russell Bufalino (Sheeran's boss).
- In Sheeran's defense, if he had warned his friend Jimmy Hoffa, or had asked not to make the hit, he too would have definitely been murdered. In mafia tradition, he was being spared in exchange for making the hit himself. He also knew that Hoffa was a dead man whether Sheeran was the trigger man or it came from someone else. As Sheeran put it:

In the end, they made the decision to spare me out of respect for Russell.[695]

- Hoffa's body was cremated by the Andretta brothers who were the "cleaners" on the hit (they worked for the Tony Pro faction).
- As East Coast Crime Boss Russell Bufalino whispered to his top hitman Frank Sheeran:

There won't be a body. Dust to dust . . .[696]

See: *I Heard You Paint Houses: Frank "The Irishman" Sheeran and the Inside Story of the Mafia, the Teamsters and the Last Ride of Jimmy Hoffa*, Charles Brandt, 2005

CONCLUSION
Murdered by the mafia for internal mob reasons. However, *do* take note of what Crime Boss Russell Bufalino tried to explain to Jimmy Hoffa:

There are people higher up than me that feel that you are demonstrating a failure to show appreciation, for Dallas.[697]

FURTHER RESEARCH
I Heard You Paint Houses: Frank "The Irishman" Sheeran and the Inside Story of the Mafia, the Teamsters and the Last Ride of Jimmy Hoffa, Charles Brandt, 2005

Bound By Honor: A Mafioso's Story, Bill Bonanno, 2000

Richard Nixon's Greatest Cover-Up: His Ties to the Assassination of President Kennedy, Don Fulsom, October 5, 2003, *CrimeMagazine.com*

[695] Brandt. *I Heard You Paint Houses*
[696] Ibid.
[697] Ibid.

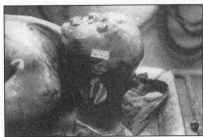

Victim	**CIA Officer John Paisley**
Cause of Death	Shot in the head execution-style, diving weights affixed to his body and thrown into the ocean.
Official Verdict	Suicide
Actual Circumstances	Assassination
Inconsistencies	Numerous (see text)

One of the most fascinating aspects of all contemporary history is the absolutely *frantic* search for a "mole" (a foreign intelligence agent disguised as a loyal employee) known to exist at the highest level of U.S. Intelligence, at the height of the Cold War between the world's two superpowers.

> **For almost twenty years, a quiet but ominous fear has haunted the corridors of the Central Intelligence Agency. It is the specter of a "mole"—an American official somewhere in the upper echelons of the CIA who is really a Soviet agent planted by its own spy network, the KGB.[698]**

That fear turned out to be well-founded, because it was learned that very sensitive information was being obtained by the Soviets in some unknown manner—so the search for the mole was on.

As far as how "big a deal" that was, here's how one CIA source put it:

> **If there is a mole inside the CIA hierarchy, this means that every particle of our intelligence is suspect and possibly contaminated. It means the Soviets have detailed knowledge of our verification capability and can circumvent it. It changes the world power balance.[699]**

No one knew who that mole was, and John Paisley, as Deputy Director, was right in the thick of the search. Extremely sensitive intelligence was known to be "leaking" out of the CIA and going directly to the Soviets—but no one knew how. And—just like a movie—it turned out that the mole was quite probably Paisley himself.

Paisley was one of the CIA's highest-ranking officers, serving as Deputy Director in the highly sensitive Office of Strategic Research. That high-level position made him privy to many secrets.

The search for the mole was one of the highest priorities in the history of U.S. Intelligence. And to James Angleton, the CIA's Chief of Counterintelligence, the search became an obsession that was driving him crazy.[700]

Veteran CIA officer Victor Marchetti testified that Paisley had extensive knowledge about the JFK assassination and was murdered during the investigation of the House Select Committee on Assassinations because he was "about to blow the whistle."[701] A CIA memo stated that "Coast Guard personnel found some papers dealing with the Cuban crisis" aboard his boat.[702] Counterintelligence Operative Richard Case Nagell revealed that Paisley was the Soviet mole the CIA had been trying to identify for several years.

---

[698] Russell, *On the Trail of the JFK Assassins*, 167.
[699] Ibid.
[700] Ibid, 177.
[701] John Simkin, "Deaths of Witnesses Connected to the Assassination of John F. Kennedy," *Spartacus Educational*, accessed 9 Nov 2012: http://www.spartacus.schoolnet.co.uk/JFKdeaths.htm
[702] John Simkin, "John Paisley: Biography," accessed 30 Nov. 2012: http://www.spartacus.schoolnet.co.uk/JFKpaisley.htm

It is not yet clear if Paisley was assassinated by agents acting on behalf of U.S. Intelligence, or if Russian Intelligence agents assassinated him because they knew that their mole had been found. But it is clear that John Paisley was assassinated.

Evidentiary Inconsistencies in the Assassination of CIA Officer John Paisley

1. Kill-shot was behind victim's left ear. Paisley was right-handed.
2. No weapon, expended cartridge, blood or brain tissue was found aboard the boat; clearly indicating that the victim was killed elsewhere and then dumped into the ocean.

Investigator Bernard Fensterwald summed up some more of the evidence, point-by point:

- There's no sign that anybody fired a shot aboard that vessel.[703]
- No gun was ever found.[704]
- There wasn't any suicide note.[705]
- He had talked to a number of people that day, in person and by (ship) radio, and certainly didn't seem depressed or like anything was wrong with him.[706]
- He apparently was in the process of eating a meal when whatever happened occurred.[707]

3. Thorough investigations have concluded that Paisley was murdered. It is quite unbelievable to suppose that a person committed suicide by putting diving weights around their waist, jumping off a boat, and shooting themselves in the head before they hit the water—yet that is what John Paisley would have had to do to even come *close* to the official government version. *Not possible.* As the authors of the book intelligently concluded:

Although the physical evidence defies that conclusion, the police determined that Paisley had wrapped two nineteen-pound weight belts around himself, jumped from *Brillig* (his boat), and shot himself in the head in midair.[708]

---

[703] Russell, *On the Trail of the JFK Assassins*, 172.
[704] Ibid.
[705] Ibid.
[706] Ibid.
[707] Ibid.
[708] William R. Corson, Susan B. Trento & Joseph J. Trento, *Widows: The Explosive Truth Behind 25 Years of Western Intelligence Disasters* (BDD: 1989).

Nothing is more unlikely than that preposterous official version:

- According to the official theory, he jumped in the water with the gun and then blew his head off, having put two diving weights on to begin with.[709]

Right, we believe *that.*

The reason police "concluded" the above insanity was because it was literally the only way that the assassination could be officially framed as a "suicide."

---

[709] Russell, *On the Trail of the JFK Assassins*, 172-173.

CONCLUSION

Unless and until further information comes to light regarding linkage between Paisley and the JFK assassination, Paisley's murder clearly appears to be the result of his nefarious intelligence associations: National Security Assassination or Assassination by Soviet Intelligence.

Although some linked Paisley to the JFK assassination via knowledge to which he was privy, his assassination instead appears to be directly related to the issue of the high-level mole in U.S. Intelligence. The CIA had the obvious motive: Paisley apparently turned out to be the high-level mole the Agency had been deceived by for many years.

FURTHER RESEARCH

On the Trail of the JFK Assassins, Dick Russell, 2008, Skyhorse Publishing

The Man Who Knew Too Much, Dick Russell, 2003, Carroll & Graf

Widows: The Explosive Truth Behind 25 Years of Western Intelligence Disasters, William R. Corson, Susan B. Trento & Joseph J. Trento, 1989, BDD

The CIA and FBI Suppression of Information, Alan Weberman; 2004

John Simkin, "John Paisley: Biography," *Spartacus Educational:* www.spartacus .schoolnet.co.uk/JFKpaisley.htm

48 | Gary Powers, August 1, 1977

Victim	Gary Powers, CIA pilot
Cause of Death	Helicopter crash
Official Verdict	Pilot Error: Poor Fuel Management
Actual Circumstances	Powers was flying a news helicopter for a Los Angeles TV station, covering a story on large fires in the area. The National Transportation Safety Board report attributed the probable cause of the crash to pilot error (poor fuel management).[710] To us, like many others, that does not seem very likely, with a pilot of the caliber as Gary Powers.

[710] *Check-Six.com*, "The Francis Gary Powers Helo Crash," accessed 7 Nov. 2012: http://www.check-six.com/ Crash_ Sites/Powers-N4TV.htm

Inconsistencies	*Tons* of them (see below).

As far as his "claim to fame":

> Gary Powers was an American pilot whose Central Intelligence Agency U-2 spy plane was shot down while flying a reconnaissance mission over Soviet Union air space, causing the 1960 U-2 incident.[711]

As we detailed in our book, *Dead Wrong*, the "U-2 incident" of Powers' shoot-down mushroomed into a huge crisis, torpedoing international peace talks and extending and expanding an extremely expensive and protracted "Cold War" between the Superpowers; leading many to speculate that it was planned and executed for *precisely* that reason.[712]

As we also established, CIA agent Gary Powers was one cool customer: calm and collected, and used to performing with perfect poise under intense pressure. For example, when reporters asked him how high he was flying in his U-2 when he was shot down, Powers calmly responded:

> **Not high enough.**[713]

Therefore, his death bears close examination, especially since it relates to pilot error under pressure. Powers was a highly decorated pilot, earning the Silver Star, the Distinguished Flying Cross, the CIA Intelligence Star, the National Defense Service Medal the Prisoner of War Medal, and "the CIA's coveted Director's Medal for extreme fidelity and extraordinary courage in the line of duty."[714] To put it plainly, if you had a problem airborne, he was your man—the guy you knew could get you out of it.

Powers flew a Bell 206 Jet Ranger helicopter for a Southern California TV news station. Covering some large fires in the area on August 1, 1977, he reportedly ran out of fuel and crashed his helicopter in the Sepulveda Dam Recreation Area.

However, many have speculated that a pilot with the skills of Gary Powers should have been able to put the helicopter down with no problem at all. Lieutenant Colonel Craig Roberts was a very experienced helicopter pilot. Here's his take on it:

> **Powers, an experienced and very professional pilot, ended his life in a very incredible—and not very believable way. He supposedly died in a helicopter crash after running out of fuel.**[715]

At the scene, however, things seemed very much under control:

---

711 Ibid.
712 Belzer & Wayne, *Dead Wrong*
713 Ibid.
714 "Francis Gary Powers"
715 Roberts & Armstrong, *The Dead Witnesses*, 125-126.

Powers radioed Van Nuys airport control tower that he was returning for fuel and asked for a direct approach, indicating to the news reporters after the crash that he must have been dangerously low on fuel. He then radioed the KNBC news room and advised that after he took on a load of fuel he would be ready for the next assignment. The news room told Powers that he and his cameraman, George Spears, would probably be assigned to cover a brush fire nearby.[716]

Then something very dramatic obviously happened very quickly and it all went to hell in a hurry:

As Powers approached the airport, something happened that caused him to lose control of the Bell Jet Ranger helicopter. As any helicopter pilot can relate, engine failure for any reason is hardly a reason for a helicopter to crash out of control. Unknown to the general public is the fact that when an engine stops in a helicopter, it does not simply fall out of the sky. The pilot enters a maneuver called "autorotation," and by lowering the collective stick, which places the main rotor blades into a negative angle of attack, glides the aircraft back to earth by using the spinning blades, driven by the upwards flow of air, as a "parachute." A normal "auto" gives a pilot at least a forty-five degree angle of glide—and in the Jet Ranger, a very forgiving helicopter, a much longer range to find a safe landing area. Autorotations are a totally controlled maneuver, and every helicopter pilot practices many of them before being awarded a commercial helicopter pilot's license.[717]

We checked with our covert operative friend, Tosh Plumlee, who was, for many years, a CIA pilot and a very experienced helicopter pilot. He agreed with Lieutenant Colonel Roberts:

Powers was noted as being a very safe pilot and lack of fuel would not be one of his weak points in flying the Ranger. His autorotation skills were exceptional according to his flight reports and FAA check rides. At 1,500 feet over L.A., he would have had at least a two-mile radius to maneuver to a safe landing, even if he landed on the "freeways." However, the loss of a tail rotor at very low altitude and at low forward speed would make the chopper very hard to control because of the main rotor torque. The spin encountered and loss of collective control would cause rapid loss of altitude; and if at low altitude would be deadly combinations, as the record and witnesses indicated at the time of the accident. Why this concept was not addressed by the safety board at the time of the investigation is beyond me.[718]

---

[716] Ibid.
[717] Roberts & Armstrong, *The Dead Witnesses*, 125-126.
[718] Tosh Plumlee, email to author, 7 Nov. 2012.

Lieutenant Colonel Roberts confirmed Plumlee's suspicions:

> The true story of Power's death might lie in the statement of one witness who told firemen at the scene that he had witnessed the crash, and that it appeared that the helicopter's tail rotor came off. This would be a more plausible explanation for the death of an experienced pilot.
>
> Though tail rotor failure, or "catastrophic severance," would make Powers' situation much more serious than a mere engine failure, all helicopter pilots are trained to handle such an event with other emergency procedures. By maintaining his forward air speed at sixty knots, Powers could have accomplished what is known as a "run-on landing" at Van Nuys. It will never be known if Powers diagnosed his problem at the time of failure, and if not, he would have encountered severe control problems if he slowed the aircraft to see what was wrong. This would be a more plausible answer to what happened that day.
>
> Whether Gary Powers knew anything of importance concerning the Kennedy assassination is unknown. But his ties to the CIA, the U-2 projects at Atsugi, Japan—where Oswald was based—and the fact that he spent a year in Russia while Oswald was in the Soviet Union might provide a clue. Powers was forty-seven.
>
> Cause of death: Helicopter crash—possibly due to sabotage.[719]

Plumlee investigated the specifics of the crash and also concluded that it was sabotage:

> I have always believed the Jet Ranger was sabotaged involving the tail rotor assembly."
>
> That was a weakness of the Jet Ranger, to begin with, making it the weakest point for sabotage:

There was "a known fault of the Jet Ranger, or 'Death Ranger', as it was known in some circles, because of the tail rotor failures on some early models of the Ranger. The Long Ranger was a later modification of the Jet Ranger and the tail rotor assembly was strengthened and modified at that time."[720]

An eyewitness to the crash said he heard a popping noise, looked up, and "saw the back prop fall off." That too sounds like sabotage, not like running out of fuel, does it not?

That eyewitness report of the prop flying off also seems to be substantiated by the final radio transmission received from Gary Powers, which was the following:

> TV-4 (his handle)—Just lost—[721]

---

[719] Roberts & Armstrong, *The Dead Witnesses*, 126.
[720] Tosh Plumlee, email to author, 7 Nov. 2012.
[721] *Check-Six.com*, "The Francis Gary Powers Helo Crash," accessed 7 Nov. 2012: http://www.check-six.com/Crash_Sites/Powers-N4TV.htm

The official explanation also sounds very weak. They had to address the point of how a pilot as experienced as Powers—a guy who was shot down at 70,000 feet over enemy territory and *survived* to talk about it—could run out of fuel on a simple little news sortie. Here's how they addressed it:

> **Many have wondered or speculated on how an experienced pilot such as Powers could have allowed the aircraft to run out of fuel. Powers had reported a fuel gauge error to the mechanics. When the plane's fuel gauge indicator displayed "Empty," he actually had enough fuel for thirty more minutes of flight time. Apparently, the aviation mechanic fixed the fuel gauge in the KNBC helicopter, but did not tell Powers of the correction.[722]**

Now please read the above statement again and ask yourself this: A mechanic isn't going to tell a news celebrity and war hero like Gary Powers about something as important as changing his fuel gauge before letting him go airborne over Los Angeles with a fuel gauge that has been altered? *You gotta be kidding.*

The official version also makes it sound as though Powers was desperately searching around for a safe place to land, where there were no children who might have been harmed by his crash landing. Here are some representative statements of that perceived quandary, as far as where, in a huge recreational area, to put it down:

> **Popular with locals as a spot to exercise, play, or simply be outdoors, the park features numerous facilities, including several baseball diamonds.[723]**

---

[722] *GaryPowers.org*, "The 1962 Spy Exchange of Powers for Abel," accessed 7 Nov. 2012: http://garypowers.org/1962-spy-exchange-of-powers-for-abel/

[723] *Check-Six.com*, "The Francis Gary Powers Helo Crash," accessed 7 Nov. 2012: http://www.check-six.com/Crash_Sites/Powers-N4TV.htm

But, if one believes the official version, our heroic combat veteran pilot who never cowered under pressure just couldn't find a place to put it down, not even on one of the "several baseball diamonds."[724]

> At 12:35 p.m., Powers had the park in sight, and flew the helicopter downwards in an effort to crash-land the helicopter without injuring anyone. However, at the last moment, he saw several teenagers playing baseball on the diamonds below. . . . Powers intentionally banked to avoid children on the fields and ultimately crashed the helicopter into an adjacent agricultural field, resulting in the aircraft rolling and the occupants' deaths.[725]

NEWS FLASH, FOLKS: Gary Powers was a highly skilled pilot; he could have put that bird down just about anywhere, *and* he would've known that if there were any kids around, they'd have gotten out of the damn way.

Here's how our covert intel vet described how the sabotaged craft actually crashed:

> I see another possibility which I have not found mentioned in any of the accident safety reports and that is called "main rotor stall"; equals "flat pitch," collective forward—blades in flat pitch. BUT must maintain forward movement and glide speed (45-65kts preferred) 10-15 degree slope . . . normal autorotation with collective forward, down. All would be normal like a falling leaf, UNLESS something else happens that would impede your forward speed, such as tail rotor failure (TRF). At this point, the torque of the main rotors would take over the loss of the counteracting tail rotor and cause the aircraft to suddenly spin and lose forward airspeed. Pulling up on the collective would not help because the rotor blades had stalled in flat pitch and, not having enough forward speed to maintain blade lift, the blades had nothing to bite into, like airflow over blade surfaces. The aircraft would drop like a rock spinning into the ground with high G force (objects flying out of chopper—perhaps due to spinning G forces as witnesses described). The pictures I've seen indicated high impact—twisted, mangled, wreckage—something not usually seen after a failed autorotation attempt.[726]

Plumlee also describes how he sees the "big picture" of the event:

> I think Powers knew of Oswald's role in going to Russia. We wanted to see what the range in altitude and radar capabilities of the Soviets were at the time. We Americans sent Oswald into Russia to give the Russians the secret codes and other necessary information that would cause the Russians to be able to shoot down our U-2. It was to test their capabilities to reach the altitude of our U-2's , to see if they could reach and destroy the target at that high altitude. Powers was set up to be the fall guy for this experiment. At the time, we did not expect the Soviets to be able reach the Powers U-2's altitude, let alone blow it out of the sky. And if they did

---

724 Ibid.
725 Ibid.
726 Tosh Plumlee, email to author, 7 Nov. 2012.

shoot it down, then the pilot would have been expected to be killed, not captured. Powers proved them wrong and proved to be an embarrassment. However, we did find out that the Soviets did have the capabilities to reach the altitude and the pay load of explosives to knock the U-2 out of the air. What did Powers know and when did he know it? If I remember right, I think he accused the government of covering up something in reference to his shoot down over Russia. Powers paid the price for this knowledge in 1977 in a helicopter crash in L.A.[727]

CONCLUSIONS BASED ON EVIDENTIARY INDICATIONS

- First off, it is extremely unlikely that a pilot as good as Gary Powers would reach "Fuel-Critical" in a news helicopter;
- Secondly, even if he *had* run out of fuel, he was fully capable of putting a Bell 206 Jet Ranger safely down on the ground with zero fuel;
- The conclusion of sabotage reached by the two helicopter experts (above) meshes with the eyewitness report that he heard a popping noise, looked up, and "saw the back prop fall off."

CONCLUSION

Probable sabotage, though not specifically linked to JFK assassination.

---

[727] Tosh Plumlee, email to author, 7 Nov. 2012, emphasis in original.

49 | Jim Reeves,
July 31, 1964

Photo Courtesy of Larry Jordan

Victim	**Country singing legend, Jim Reeves, was an international star, known to millions of his fans as simply, "Gentleman Jim."**
Cause of Death	Plane Crash
Official Verdict	Pilot Error
Actual Circumstances	Possible Sabotage
Inconsistencies	Numerous (see text below)

Famous singing artist, "Gentleman Jim" Reeves has never been included on the various lists of suspicious deaths over the years (as far as we know). He was used to making an entirely different type of "hit list," but we have learned important information indicating that he *should be*. He apparently did have a link to the JFK assassination, which—from the standpoint of mathematical probability calculations alone—should place him on the list.

Jim's connection to the JFK assassination was established by his biographer, Larry Jordan, author of the excellent biography, *Jim Reeves: His Untold Story*, which details how Reeves knew *both* Jack Ruby and Lee Harvey Oswald.[728] When in Dallas, Reeves and his band would perform at *The Longhorn Ballroom*, which was owned by Dewey Groom.[729] Jack Ruby knew both Dewey Groom and Jim Reeves, and Reeves frequently saw Jack Ruby—as well as Lee Harvey Oswald—around the Dallas nightclub scene.

Reeves—as is well-documented—had an amazing photographic memory. It was of the type that people were stunned by his uncanny memory tricks, and suspected that it must be a magic "trick" of some type. It wasn't. It was simply that Jim Reeves actually had a real and true photographic memory. For example, a casual autograph-seeker would come up to Jim and ask him for his autograph. Jim would ask her where she was from and her name, and would then write her a line or two on that along with his autograph on a record that she had brought. *Years later,* if Jim saw the person again, he would recall the information, walk by them and say something to the effect of "Well *hi* there, Doris from Wichita."[730] The person would be absolutely stunned—and who *wouldn't*?

Now, back to the JFK assassination . . . but keep note of his photographic memory. Jim and his band performed at a big nightclub in Dallas the night before the assassination of President Kennedy. The band traveled on to Amarillo the next morning, but, for some reason that was never satisfactorily explained, Jim "got hung up in Dallas" that next day and did not travel with his band. So he was still in Dallas when the assassination took place, and it's not completely clear how he eventually caught up with the band. But after the President was shot and Lee Harvey Oswald was arrested, *the second that Oswald's face was flashed on television,* Jim immediately told the group of friends he was with that he knew Oswald and had seen him often. That point is quite noteworthy: Reeves registered immediate recognition, instantly telling his friends who were watching television with him that he was very familiar with the man and had, in fact, just seen him recently.[731]

It also became apparent that Jim was apparently acting as a high-level courier of some type, possibly in an intelligence capacity. Though that may seem odd, it is not unprecedented—international stars can move in circles that others cannot and it would not have been the first time that one was used as an "intel" courier. Jim was also closely "hooked up" with some military brass. As Larry Jordan notes:

> **He made various tours for the U.S. Military and also had the uncanny knack of being able to get some of his band members furloughed for**

---

[728] Larry Jordan, *Jim Reeves: His Untold Story* (Page Turner Books International: 2011).
[729] Larry Jordan, emails to author, 28 November 2012.
[730] Larry Jordan, telephone interview with author, 29 Nov. 2012.
[731] Ibid.

unscheduled leave whenever it suited his fancy. Who has that kind of clout?[732]

Jim was able to land at military airports (and often did so) as a general aviation (private) pilot, which was unheard of. Jim also always insisted that his plane be watched 24/7, even at rural airports. At one of the small airports, it is established that they had to hire a special guard just to watch his plane. What was Jim so concerned about this for?[733]

That aspect links up to Jim's death and, possibly, to the JFK assassination:

- Reeves was a very good pilot in an excellent aircraft—a Beechcraft Debonair—but he flew into bad weather, a fact that, in a small craft, can bring any pilot down.
- However, the thing about Jim Reeves's death that is suspicious from an investigatory standpoint is not so much the plane crash itself—even expert pilots can be brought down when flying into serious weather—and it's not even a witness report that lends itself to the possibility of sabotage having brought down the plane. What is so suspicious in this particular case is what transpired *after* the crash. In some very strange developments, it was all too apparent that, for some reason, the official search was diverted to an area entirely different from where the control tower had pinpointed the crash site; apparently to allow some "independent" searchers first access to the crash site. And, in a seemingly related aspect, that a great emphasis was placed on finding the briefcase that was known to be on that plane.

The *Nashville Tennessean* reported in Sunday's edition that more than 2,000 persons were in the search effort, still without success. Included were 300 Civil Defense units, metropolitan police, Williamson County sheriff's officers, members of the Donelson Citizens Band Radio Service, forty National Guardsmen, and sixty airmen from Sewart Air Force base. Red Cross rescue units served coffee and donuts. Jeeps, wagons, and private cars were used in the search, along with twelve airplanes and two military helicopters. They combed a 20-square-mile area, checking out a multitude of false leads. On Sunday, day three of the search, Mary Reeves recalled thinking, "This is ridiculous. They can't have just vanished."[734]

The crash happened at 4:52 p.m., just off a main thoroughfare that was busy with rush-hour traffic. While it was still daylight, a search team assembled at the corner of Franklin Road (a main thoroughfare running north and south) and Baxter Lane, which intersected it. This team was organized by the Civil Defense and included a member of Black Ops in Southeast Asia (Bob Newton, who ultimately is credited with finding the plane). Ironically, this spot was within sight of the woods into which Reeves crashed. It strains credulity that nobody looked in that woods.

[732] Larry Jordan, email to author, 29 November 2012.
[733] Sara Jordan, email to author, 14 January, 2012.
[734] Jordan, *Jim Reeves*, 628.

In fact, one of the participants in the search—a well-known piano player, Bill Pursell—recalled having suggested the team look in the woods, but was told by a law enforcement official that the plane was reported down over toward Radnor Lake, well northwest of that location![735]

- It was established that Jim definitely took a briefcase onto the small plane in which he flew. Multiple witnesses verified that Reeves' briefcase <u>was</u> indeed taken onto that airplane; and never "officially" located in the wreckage, or, for that matter, anywhere else.
- It was established that it was an extremely high priority of the search team to *locate* that briefcase.

This misinformation continued to be given out. Moments after the Reeves plane disappeared from radar, Bill Larson got airborne and was vectored by tower controller John Hetish—the last to speak to Reeves by radio—who vectored Bill to the exact location. However, since the plane penetrated the tree canopy at a steep angle, it was not visible from the air. Later that night, when Bill was asked by Highway Patrolman Truman Clark to accompany him on a helicopter sweep of the area, both men were puzzled to see searchers on the opposite side of Franklin Road. Truman radioed headquarters and was told the search should be concentrated in that area and not over the woods.[736]

Eyewitness Wiley Tombs dismissed the assertion that searchers didn't find the wreckage until Sunday. Interviewed in his home, Wiley gestured and said, "Down this road to [Baxter Lane], and down Hill Road, it was full of cars. And [people] were ... jumping out of them and running ... over to talk to me. ... Somebody's got it down that they didn't find the plane until [Sunday] but hell, *they found it that evening.*'" Was the wreckage actually discovered Friday night? Did authorities want a chance to get to the crash site first in order to find what they were looking for—a suitcase full of money or perhaps something more sensitive in nature?[737]

- It was established that the official search was intentionally diverted to a known false location, so that authorities could get to the crash site first.

It remains a mystery as to why, when airport authorities precisely pinpointed the crash location as being on the *east* side of Franklin and just south of some high voltage power towers (based on the last radar sighting of Jim's plane), searchers were misdirected to the *west* side of the road.[738]

- When the search was eventually "re-targeted" to the *actual* known coordinates of the crash (days later), the briefcase was already gone. Puryear Mims,

[735] Larry Jordan, email to author, 14 January, 2012.
[736] Ibid.
[737] Jordan, *Jim Reeves*, 636-637 emphasis in original.
[738] Ibid, 623.

a U.S. intelligence veteran, knew the plane was down because he actually heard it crash. But he did not report any of this to authorities for two days, until he finally reported it to Bob Newton, another "black ops" guy.

Bob Newton, who was a veteran of "black ops" (covert operations) in southeast Asia for two years—having been in Laos and Cambodia before the Vietnam conflict exploded—was credited with finding it. Thus he became the second important figure in the Jim Reeves plane crash saga to have worked for military intelligence (the other being Puryear Mims).[739]

- Therefore, what the crash instigated as far as priorities was a frantic search for that briefcase. It seemed that too much emphasis was placed on finding Jim's briefcase. The top priority *should* have been looking for survivors—and instead, it was apparently the briefcase.

The crash site was not properly secured by the FAA and although there were police lines up, over 100 people assembled, moving wreckage before the investigation had even been concluded.[740]

Tower supervisor Halmond Adkins was asked to go to the scene to identify the plane from its N number. "The highway patrol come and escorted me out there. It was exactly the same spot we had been vectoring everybody."[741]

- In the days and weeks just prior to the crash, Jim had been involved in some "land deals" of a suspicious nature. For example, he was going off to a remote location to look at property supposedly being sold for development. But the deal was with some very shady people, which was out-of-character for Jim, who was a very straight-forward guy—and the so-called "properties" were investments no one in their right mind would seriously be interested in—which was *very* out of character for him. It raises questions. Why would a busy international star fly off to a different state to supposedly look at property that was not the least bit enticing and was being touted by a suspected criminal?[742] The man was out on bail and was being prosecuted for having shot a husband and wife in cold blood, and then attempting to burn their remains.

It strains credulity that rescue workers—who assembled Friday night within sight of the woods—never searched them. Or did they? Strangely, there is also a dearth of documentation in federal agency files regarding this accident, even though paperwork on crashes far longer ago than Jim's is still available. It's as if the files regarding the Reeves mishap have been sanitized. Retired police officials in Nashville speculate the reason

---

[739] Jordan, *Jim Reeves*, 629.
[740] Larry Jordan, email to author, 14 January, 2012.
[741] Ibid. 630.
[742] Jordan, *Jim Reeves: His Untold Story*

for this may involve some security issues. The FBI came and visited the wife of Reeves' piano player/road manager, who also died in the crash.[743]

Bobbi Manuel added to the intrigue when she revealed that soon after her husband's death, "Two FBI agents came to question me. . . . This was all a shock to me!" They wanted to know about Dean and whether or not he had any connections to organized crime "because Dean had been seen on the same elevator with some of Jimmy Hoffa's men. I told them I didn't believe Dean knew them." In response to inquiries from this author, the FBI searched their files for anything pertinent to Jim or Dean. While nothing turned up on Manuel, they indicated that files on Reeves had been recently destroyed for undisclosed reasons, on the order of a judge in Washington, D.C.[744]

Crash site: The Medical Examiner had pape[r] in his hand as he examined the scene. It wa[s] officially denied that he took any notes and h[is] notes disappeared, just as Jim's briefcase did.

From Larry Jordan's book, *Jim Reeves: His Untold Story*

- Even though an FOIA request was issued, every scrap of information—from the FAA accident report to report of the medical examiner in the case—have vanished.

Over and over I have had people in official capacities—ranging from current members of the FAA, to the NTSB, to Nashville area law enforcement, and even the man credited with finding the wreckage—tell me they felt there was a lid placed on the crash investigation due to an intelligence link.[745]

A CIA source directly informed author Larry Jordan that, for his own safety, he should maintain a high level of visibility if he continued researching the very sensitive matter of Jim Reeves' death. That source reminded him that it was a "a very volatile time in history." That CIA source also confirmed to Jordan that Jim Reeves had indeed served the U.S. Military and others

---

[743] Ibid, 636-637
[744] Jordan, *Jim Reeves*, 637.
[745] Larry Jordan, email to author, December 19, 2012.

as a high-level courier, that he'd had a briefcase and that the searchers knew about the briefcase. That briefcase, another source informed Jordan, contained "something no one is supposed to see."[746]

- One investigator hinted at the possibility of sabotage—due to the fact that one of the small plane's wings was seen coming off.
- Reeves' biographer has reported that he was pointedly warned not to get too inquisitive about the matter in the process of investigating the case for his book.

Author Larry Jordan received a phone call that made him shake his head in disbelief:

It is just astonishing to me that I received an unsolicited phone call from a man who works for metro Nashville law enforcement, who put his "friend"—who supposedly had worked in U.S. intelligence—who warned me not to probe too deeply into the Reeves crash.[747]

Ann McDuffee worked at the airport/general store at the tiny Batesville, Arkansas, airport, from which Jim Reeves' plane took off on its fatal voyage. Ms. McDuffee died just days after the crash of Reeves' plane from a suspicious car accident. Her family believed she was run off the road. If anyone could have witnessed any tampering of Jim's plane it was her, because she had overseen the comings and goings at the small airport that day. When authorities learned that the Reeves plane was missing, it was Ann McDuffee who took the call from the FAA the night of the day the Reeves plane disappeared, asking her to go out and check the N numbers of all the planes to make sure the Reeves plane wasn't still sitting there on the ground. She had direct links to that plane/airport and knew the significance of her family providing services for such a big star. Ann would have been in a position to have observed anyone around Reeves' plane had it been sabotaged before his fateful flight home. The victim's family insists there was evidence that she was run off the road because debris from another car was found at the scene.[748]

A veteran Nashville detective who had been close to U.S. Army Special Forces also explained that the Reeves case had "an intelligence overlay."[749]

CONCLUSION
Possible Sabotage, currently unclear if linked to JFK assassination

---

[746] Larry Jordan, email to author, 14 January, 2012.
[747] Larry Jordan, email to author, December 19, 2012.
[748] Larry Jordan, email to author, 14 January, 2012 and Sara Jordan, email to author, 14 January, 2012.
[749] Larry Jordan, email to author, 14 January, 2012.

Victim	**Robert F. Kennedy, Senator from New York, who had just won the Democratic Primary in California, and was thought to be well on his way to being elected the next President of the United States.**
Cause of Death	Gunshots at point-blank range; from one-to-three inches behind the victim's right ear.
Official Verdict	Murdered by Sirhan Bishara Sirhan, a "lone nut"; no co-conspirators involved.
Actual Circumstances	The accused literally could not have killed the Senator, for reasons delineated below.

1. Ballistics-testing by veteran ballistics expert, William W. Harper, determined that the bullets that hit Senator Kennedy did <u>not</u> come from Sirhan's gun.
2. Sirhan was <u>not</u> at any point close enough to Senator Kennedy to have fired the kill shot. Coroner determined that the shot was fired from within one to three inches away from left ear. About the only thing that everybody in that room agreed with was that Sirhan was <u>never</u> that close.
3. Bullet trajectories indicate that primary shooter was at close range, behind target, and to his right. Sirhan was in front of Senator Kennedy and to his left, walking towards him. So it is not possible for bullets fired from his gun to have entered Senator Kennedy from behind and then traversed back-to-front.
4. Sirhan held his gun parallel to Senator Kennedy; therefore, the trajectories traversing upwards are also totally contradictory to his actual position.
5. Sirhan's gun held only eight bullets but <u>fourteen bullets were fired</u>, necessitating at least two shooters. *At least* fourteen shots were identified.

Inconsistencies

6. Psychiatrists determined that Sirhan was the most easily hypnotizable subject they'd ever seen; his notebooks contained repetitious entries such as "RFK must die," that were determined to have been written as post-hypnotic suggestion; conditions indicate that he was in a trance state during the murder.
7. Investigators from the Los Angeles Police Department acknowledged that they were completely unable to document any of Sirhan's actions during a six-week period prior to the assassination which they labeled his "White Fog" period. They also acknowledged that such a complete disappearance was extremely unusual.
8. Therefore, Sirhan Bishara Sirhan has been imprisoned since 1968 for a crime he did not commit because he was convicted of "Murder in the First Degree," and did not meet the requirements of that charge; he did not possess conscious intent at the moment of the crime; therefore, the act was not premeditated, nor did he possess malice aforethought. The evidence proves conclusively that the defendant was never at any point close enough to the victim to have fired the fatal shot. It has also been proven that the trajectories of the shots that hit Senator Kennedy could not have come from the defendant's gun. Those

facts mandate a verdict of "Not Guilty" when a person is accused of "Murder in the First Degree." Therefore he should be a free man and, technically, never should have been convicted on that charge in the first place (see *Dead Wrong* for a more thorough examination of the above and other evidence).[750]

We still do not know with absolute certainty who murdered Senator Robert Kennedy—but we *do* now know with absolute certainty who *did not*. The accused killer, Sirhan Bishara Sirhan, was never close enough to have fired the kill shot, was never at the correct angle to have fired the kill shot, and as that other evidence very clearly illustrates upon proper examination, he indeed did <u>not</u> fire the kill shot.

Probably no one in the world knew more—and had intentionally *learned* more—about the assassination of President Kennedy than did his brother, Robert.

Additionally, the fact that it was rumored that one of the primary reasons Robert Kennedy sought the Presidency was to re-open (some might say "begin" would be a better choice of words) serious investigation into the true circumstances of his brother's death, certainly makes him strongly linked to that assassination as far as a witness.

He was linked in other ways, too. It was apparently from the anti-Castro operation in Florida that the plan to kill President Kennedy was hatched. Robert Kennedy oversaw that program. That's why Robert Kennedy registered immediate recognition of the name "Lee Harvey Oswald"—because he knew Oswald was part of the anti-Castro operation.[751]

Alexander Haig didn't turn out to be a Kennedy ally—he became Secretary of State under the very conservative Reagan Administration—but in the early 1960s, Haig was a military assistant in the Army and was in charge of assimilating Cuban exile veterans from the failed Bay of Pigs invasion into the United States. That program was at the personal direction of President Kennedy, since he felt a genuine responsibility to the Cuban exiles and, as a result, Haig was privy to very sensitive intelligence regarding Cuba.

In his memoirs he states that:

> Under the personal leadership of Robert Kennedy, at least eight efforts were made to eliminate Castro himself, the earliest involving Mafia figures recruited by the CIA soon after the inauguration. These attempts continued until the day President Kennedy was himself assassinated in Dallas. The secret of this deadly enterprise was so closely held that not even John A. McCone, Director of Central Intelligence from 1962–1965, knew that some of his men were involved until he read about it in a newspaper story."[752]

That anti-Castro intelligence operation was an odd mixture of conservative CIA agents, mafia members, anti-Castro Cubans, and other names that keep popping up continually

---

[750] Belzer & Wayne, *Dead Wrong*.
[751] Lamar Waldron & Thom Hartmann, *Ultimate Sacrifice* (New York: Carroll & Graf, 2005).
[752] Alexander Haig, *Inner Circles: How America Changed the World: A Memoir* (Warner Books: 1992), 112.

in the investigation of the assassination: Jack Ruby, Lee Harvey Oswald, David Ferrie, and Guy Banister.

That's why Robert Kennedy immediately called the Director of the CIA after learning of his brother's death, and blurted into the phone:

"Did the CIA kill my brother?"[753]

And that's why another of his first reactions to the assassination was to call a contact at the anti-Castro Florida camp and shout into the telephone:

"One of your guys did it!"[754]

Alexander Haig summarized the end result as follows:

> In any case, the key fact that a secret group headed by the President's brother had been plotting to kill Castro was kept from the Warren Commission and from the American people. That was the seed of the real cover-up . . .'[755]

Haig was apparently right about the point above, although he was also a stated believer in the obvious "smokescreen" sent up by President Johnson that Castro had been behind the JFK assassination in retaliation.[756] As Robert Kennedy himself concluded, the real blame for his brother's murder was quite a bit closer to home. Many have inferred that Robert Kennedy was actually referring to President Johnson when he sent an emissary to Moscow with a message that included the following blockbuster information:

> We know that it was a high-level domestic political conspiracy.[757]

So Robert F. Kennedy certainly knew a lot about the JFK assassination. Whether that was a factor in his murder is not clear. But this much is very clear:

He too was silenced.

CONCLUSIONS BASED ON EVIDENTIARY INDICATIONS

The man convicted of the crime could not possibly have committed it. Furthermore, he was obviously programmed, as experts have determined.

Chief Psychiatrist Bernard Diamond:

"Let me specifically state that it was immediately apparent that Sirhan had been programmed."

CONCLUSION

Murdered by a conspiracy that set up the accused killer, Sirhan Bishara Sirhan. Currently unclear whether or not directly linked to the JFK assassination.

---

[753] Waldron & Hartmann, *Ultimate Sacrifice*
[754] Ibid.
[755] Haig, *Inner Circles*, 115.
[756] Haig, *Inner Circles*, 112-116.
[757] David Talbot, *Brothers: The Hidden History of the Kennedy Years* (Free Press: 2007).

CONCLUSION

We learned a great deal from our work on this project and we sincerely hope that you have as well. We investigated "only" fifty cases for this study out of hundreds, and our findings were fair and unbiased; we found that some cases clearly *were* national security assassinations, that many cases were *not*, and in some cases, the waters are still too cloudy to tell.

It was treacherous ground, as might be expected. Even veteran investigators in the JFK research community have been reticent and leery about the claims of too many convenient or coincidental deaths. It's a sobering topic. It had taken on the texture of an "urban legend" at this point, and one that was approached with much caution. As historian Walt Brown put it:

> **With but a few exceptions, I'm not a strong subscriber to the "300 dead witnesses" story. There was never any guarantee of immortality because someone was in proximity to a JFK event.[758]**

Well, we researched the specifics of the cases, and here's what we learned. We don't need to be afraid of vague claims and sweeping statements, as we can investigate them instead . . . and we did for this book. We learned that many of the deaths were, indeed, *too* convenient. They were murders; many of which were the direct result of the victim's linkage to the JFK assassination.

Likewise, we don't need to be frightened by large numbers; we can simply ensure that they are calculated correctly. We did that for this book also, and the numbers clearly indicate that all of those witness deaths, indeed, were *too* coincidental; the math literally proves it. One needn't wonder whether it's thirty deaths that reaches the threshold of "too coincidental" mathematically, or whether it's three hundred unnatural deaths that does so. One simply needs to verify the correct math. There were over seventy unnatural deaths out of approximately 1,400 witnesses during a fourteen-year period. Note that:

> **The correct odds of that occurring are 1-in-715 million trillion trillion.**

That's not our *opinion*; that's the *mathematical reality*. That, in itself, conveys the obvious need for taking a closer look at the specifics of these deaths. In *Dead*

---

[758] Walt Brown, Ph.D., 26 Oct 2012, email to author.

Wrong, we substantiated that Lyndon Johnson, 36th President of the United States, was one of the most corrupt "leaders" (using the term very loosely) in contemporary history, which—as one might imagine—is really saying quite a "mouthful" these days, folks![759] In fact, he wasn't just corrupt; he was even corrupt in the classic Shakespearean sense—plotting the overthrow of his predecessor, John F. Kennedy, a man whom he despised in every way imaginable. To posit that political motivations are a primary influence in crimes of a power-shifting nature is a dramatic understatement. For example, it was recently determined that—contrary to the "official" historical version for the past several *thousand* years—King Ramses III, the "Last Great Pharaoh" of ancient Egypt, was actually murdered in a conspiracy to seize power, in a succession plot involving his own son.[760] So this has been going on for a *long* time, people. And when it came to plotting for power and dirty dealing that even involved the murders of his political enemies under very incriminating circumstances, JFK's own Vice President was the leader of that wolf pack.[761] In fact, let's put it this way—when you look up the word "corrupt" in a dictionary, there should be a picture of Lyndon Baines Johnson smirking back at you and accompanying the definition.

At the other end of the spectrum, when one looks up the word "integrity" in the dictionary, there should be a photo of Lieutenant Colonel "Dangerous Dan" Marvin, U.S. Army Special Forces, accompanying that definition. Lieutenant Colonel Marvin has testified at length for the historical record that, while an assassin with Special Forces, the CIA requested of him to assassinate Lieutenant Commander William Pitzer to preclude his release of items considered being a threat to national security. Lieutenant Colonel Marvin, who passed away in 2012, dedicated the final decade of his life to trying to set the record straight on cases like Lieutenant Commander Pitzer. You can still watch him speak online, in clips that capture his compassion, humanity, and integrity. Lieutenant Colonel Marvin was also featured in Part Six, the most-often censored episode of the *The Men Who Killed Kennedy*.[762] In a blatant example of apparent censorship, the compelling documentary was purchased by the *Arts & Entertainment Network* for its History Channel, aired once and was then shelved for good after the company caved in to political pressure.[763] However, it is currently accessible online and is a real eye-opener too. Lieutenant Colonel Marvin vividly details the assassination procedures which were in place for U.S. intelligence during the early 1960s, as well as the specifics regarding the national security assassination of Lieutenant Commander Pitzer.[764]

[759] Belzer & Wayne, *Dead Wrong*, 17-23. Douglas Caddy, Esq., "Letter to Mr. Stephen S. Trott, Assistant Attorney General, U.S. Department of Justice," August 9, 1984, *The Estes Documents*: http://home.earthlink.net/~sixthfloor/estes.htm

[760] Catherine Hornby & Robin Pomeroy, "King Ramses III's throat was slit by assassins: experts," December 18, 2012, *Reuters*: http://www.reuters.com/article/2012/12/19/us-egypt-ramses-idUSBRE8BH19U20121219

[761] Belzer & Wayne, *Dead Wrong*, 17-23.

[762] *The Men Who Killed Kennedy: The Truth Shall Make You Free* (Documentary), Episode Six, 1995, Produced & Directed by Nigel Turner, in association with *The History Channel* (a nine-part series originally developed for UK ITV): http://youtu.be/VI07govlUqI

[763] *The Men Who Killed Kennedy: The Truth Shall Make You Free*: http://youtu.be/VI07govlUqI

[764] *The Men Who Killed Kennedy: The Truth Shall Make You Free*: http://youtu.be/VI07govlUqI

We can draw some clear conclusions:

- The tremendous odds against all of these deaths being "coincidental" does indeed bear out. Many of these deaths clearly were the result of a clean-up operation, eliminating witnesses with "uncomfortable" knowledge before they could testify before the pertinent investigating committees. As the old saying goes in the intelligence community: "Twice is coincidence, but three times is enemy action."[765]

- A national security cover-up *did* indeed take place.[766] It is evidenced not only by the silencing of key witnesses such as the honorable Lieutenant Commander William Pitzer, U.S. Navy (a case in which we even have the man who was asked to assassinate him), but by the ludicrously obvious and numerous instances of government lies and obfuscation that took place in the years following the assassination of President John F. Kennedy.

- A component of that cover-up was the national security murders of those individuals who were considered dangerous to maintenance of the cover story.

- In fairness, we should state that investigation also revealed that some deaths were not suspicious or even directly linked to the JFK assassination. The results of our investigations did reveal that some of the many deaths were actual suicides or from natural causes. For example, the death of former Ambassador William Pawley is often cited as suspicious due to the fact that it occurred just prior to testimonies in the investigation by the House Select Committee on Assassinations. However, his death does appear to be coincidental to that investigation. Therefore, his and other deaths were not included as entries in this volume and, unless and until new information comes to light, they do not rightfully qualify as mysterious deaths.

- Our research *has* determined, however, that—even in some of those cases—there is much that is officially incorrect. CIA official John Paisley was murdered—he did not commit suicide as the U.S. Government has continually alleged (in a prime example of continuous lies and obfuscation). On the other side of that coin, contrary to the official finding in the case, Dr. Mary Sherman was *not* murdered; she apparently died accidentally in a laboratory. But the secret nature of that laboratory necessitated a murder scenario. So that's why and how they covered that one up.

It should also be noted that there were some cases of "coincidental deaths" related to the JFK assassination which we did not have space to include in this book. We focused instead on what we considered to be the primary cases. However, fair examination of the foregoing facts in this book leads to some logically necessary conclusions. There *is* substantiated evidence that many of these deaths *were* indeed linked directly to a clean-up operation of "loose-ends" and problems that surfaced regarding the cover-up.

---

[765] Ian Fleming, *Goldfinger* (Jonathan Cape: 1959): "Once is happenstance. Twice is coincidence. Three times, it's enemy action."
[766] Belzer & Wayne, *Dead Wrong*, 128-131.

Beyond Potential Coincidence:

To convey a sense of the implausibilities which become all too apparent here, consider this:

David Ferrie and Eladio del Valle were the two key witnesses being sought by a fresh new investigation of the staff of New Orleans District Attorney Jim Garrison. They both died extremely violent deaths—on the same day—*before* those investigations could be properly conducted.

Likewise, just as a Congressional investigation was gearing up to take important testimony, three of their most important witnesses died extremely violent deaths within the same week: Hitman Chuck Nicoletti, George de Mohrenschildt, Oswald's CIA "overseer" who was shot the same day as Nicoletti—just as a Committee investigator was literally on the way to interview him—and anti-Castro Cuban politician Carlos Prío Socarrás, who was a prime component of the whole nexus in South Florida from which the JFK assassination was hatched. Others from that same nexus—like Sam Giancana and Johnny Roselli—were murdered shortly thereafter, just as their testimony, too, was being sought by Congress.

William Sullivan, a high-ranking FBI officer, explained to a close friend that he would be killed soon and that it would be made to look like an accident, but not to believe it; that it would actually be murder. A short time later, he died in a mysterious "hunting accident." *Coincidence*? This was an intelligent individual making a precise prediction, so do not even utter such a naïve word, *please*.

Mobster Jack Zangetty *specifically* predicted that:

A man named Ruby will kill Oswald tomorrow and in a few days a member of the Frank Sinatra family will be kidnapped just to take some of the attention away from the assassination.

Both of those specific predictions came true; Zangetty was then murdered. These examples are not even calculable for potentially being coincidence; they are mathematically impossible. They are demonstrative of knowledge, not conjecture.

▶ **National Security Assassination Deaths:**

Lee Harvey Oswald
Jack Zangetty
Dorothy Kilgallen
Lieutenant Commander William Pitzer
Mary Pinchot Meyer
Gary Underhill
Eladio del Valle (same day as Ferrie)
Rolando Masferrer

Chuck Nicoletti
George de Mohrenschildt (same day as Nicoletti)
Carlos Prío Socarrás (shot same week as Nicoletti)
Mac Wallace
Sam Giancana
Johnny Roselli
William Sullivan

As another old saying goes, the mafia "takes care of their own," and it was quite obviously no coincidence that those with detailed knowledge of the anti-Castro intelligence operation which was apparently "turned" and used against President Kennedy were murdered near the time they would been forced to testify before the Congressional committee investigating the assassination. Among those very clear cases are: Sam Giancana, Chuck Nicoletti, Johnny Roselli, Eladio del Valle, and Rolando Masferrer.

The elimination of witnesses by the government or those acting on its behalf—and apparently emanating from the office of the President of the United States (since Lyndon Johnson had a *lot* of tracks to cover up)—seems to have been executed in several of the more complicated and high-profile cases. Mary Pinchot Meyer, Lieutenant Commander William Pitzer, Dorothy Kilgallen, Gary Underhill and—if he was right about the method of his death—Jack Ruby, appear to have been eliminated due to their actions and intentions regarding specific information they possessed.

It is also much worth mentioning that we know that witnesses such as Grant Stockdale, Hank Killam, and Gary Underhill were in extreme fear for their lives from some form of government assassination because they specifically expressed those fears to friends who left a clear record of it. But who knows how many of the other witnesses possessed similar fears, but left no record of them?

The CIA's supporters in mainstream media—and they have many[767]—maintain the preposterously silly notion that all this is just some pipedream from the "camp" of what they make a point of calling "conspiracy buffs" (as opposed to *real* researchers such as themselves, apparently), with no basis in reality whatsoever. *Baloney*, boys and girls!

As an example:

> Journalist Tim Weiner, who covered the CIA for twenty years and wrote *Legacy of Ashes: The History of the CIA*, is even more skeptical.
>
> "You could fill a five-foot shelf with books theorizing the CIA played a role in Kennedy's assassination," Weiner said, calling such efforts "hearsay, innuendo, gossip, and nonsense."
>
> In fact, says Weiner, there are legitimate reasons to question the Warren Report and its findings about Oswald—but not, he says, to accuse the CIA of conducting domestic assassinations.
>
> The bottom line is, there's not a shred of evidence—none—that the CIA ever killed anyone in this country.[768]

Mr. Weiner is right. The CIA probably never has *intentionally* assassinated anyone on U.S. soil. They contracted it out, through the mob or in the case of Lieutenant Commander William Bruce Pitzer, to a Special Forces assassin who was willing to volunteer for the

---

[767] Carl Bernstein, "The CIA and The Media: How America's Most Powerful News Media Worked Hand in Glove with the Central Intelligence Agency and Why The Church Committee Covered It Up," October 20, 1977, *Rolling Stone Magazine*: http://www.carlbernstein.com/magazine_cia_and_media.php and John Simkin, "Operation Mockingbird," *Spartacus Educational*, accessed 19 Dec. 2012: http://www.spartacus.schoolnet.co.uk/JFKmockingbird.htm

[768] Joseph P. Kahn, "One man's suspicion, obsession, and an unsolved murder," 26 May 2012, *Boston Globe*: http://www.boston.com/lifestyle/articles/2012/05/26/north_shore_author_peter_janney_makes_his_case_for_the_cia_plotting_to_murder_john_f_kennedy_and_jfk_mistress_mary_pinchot_meyer/?page=full

mission. In the case of Mary Pinchot Meyer, it was apparently contracted through a man with the operational codename William L. Mitchell, who was from some dark government agency connection so shielded that no one could even figure out where he really worked![769]

In other cases, it has been very clearly established that the mafia was used for domestic assassinations which—as Army Special Forces veteran Lieutenant Colonel Marvin has testified—was standard operational procedure during that historical time frame.[770]

And the thing that's clearest of all is that, if we rely on mainstream media, this information would never seem to get to us!

Fresh New Evidence: On the Points Responsible for the Murder of President Kennedy

Contrary to common perceptions, much *is* now known about how President Kennedy was actually assassinated. There have been major developments in the last few years that mainstream media, in its inimitable way, has managed to virtually conceal from public awareness:

- The motorcade security of President Kennedy was *structurally changed* in Dallas, from the highly-protective wedge formation (which was used by JFK and was even considered *standard* dignitary protection), to a highly *in*secure motorcycle formation, thereby enabling the assassination;[771]
- It was also the route-change of the motorcade in Dallas that enabled the assassination and the responsibility for that has been established also;[772]
- Less protection than was normal for JFK was quite apparent in Dallas;[773]
- Quite contrary to the officially sanitized version, JFK <u>did not</u> order Secret Service agents off the bumper of the limousine in which he was riding. Vince Palamara has substantiated that JFK <u>never interfered with Secret Service protocol</u>;[774]
- The responsibility for the route change and the reductions in motorcade protection appears to lead directly to allies and associates of Vice President Lyndon Johnson.[775]

---

[771] Al Carrier, 2003 "The United States Secret Service: Conspiracy to Assassinate a President," *Dealey Plaza Echo*, Volume 7, Issue 1, March 2003, 36-48: http://www.maryferrell.org/mffweb/archive/viewer/showDoc.do?absPageId=389290

[772] Vince Palamara, *Survivor's Guilt: The Secret Service and the Failure to Protect the President,* 2006: http://www.assassinationresearch.com/v4n1.html

[773] Ibid.

[774] Ibid.

[775] Ibid.

---

[769] Janney, *Mary's Mosaic*

[770] *The Men Who Killed Kennedy: The Truth Shall Make You Free*: http://youtu.be/VI07govlUqI

- The freshly sworn-in President Johnson even "used conspiracy to preclude conspiracy."

Top LBJ aide, Cliff Carter, sent the new President's message throughout Washington and Dallas, slamming the door on the mere *mention* of conspiracy:

Dallas District Attorney "Henry Wade described three calls from Cliff Carter on Friday night (mere hours after JFK was murdered). Carter said that:

'any word of a conspiracy—some plot by foreign nations—to kill President Kennedy would shake our nation to its foundation. President Johnson was worried about some conspiracy on the part of the Russians … it would hurt foreign relations if I alleged a conspiracy—whether I could prove it or not … I was to charge Oswald with plain murder.'

In addition to Wade, Police Chief Curry and Texas State Attorney General Carr also received similar calls from Cliff Carter, instructing them to avoid any charges or remarks indicating conspiracy."[776]

So one might say that there was a second conspiracy to make it look like there was no conspiracy at first; and directed by a man who was apparently a major player in both!

Summarized simply, it is now known that the following actions enabled the assassination of President Kennedy:

1. Motorcade formation change from the standard dignitary protection "Wedge formation" to a wide-open formation that made the President an open target;
2. Motorcade route change, taking it by the dog-leg turn and into the open shooting fields of Dealey Plaza;
3. Agents being ordered off the bumpers of the limo, which was <u>not</u> at the direction of the President.

---

[776] Larry Hancock, *Someone World Have Talked: The Assassination of President John F. Kennedy and the Conspiracy to Mislead History* (JFK Lancer: 2010), Chapter 19: http://www.larry-hancock.com/excerpts.html

Secret Service protection was visibly reduced even though it was known that the threat-level in Dallas was high:

The Secret Service men were not pleased because they were in a "hot" city and would have preferred to have two men ride the bumper of the President's car with two motorcycle policemen between him (JFK) and the crowds on the sidewalks.[777]

---

[777] Jim Bishop, *The Day Kennedy Was Shot* (HarperCollins Canada: 1992), 134.

The Many Roads Leading to Vice President Lyndon Johnson: As the motorcade leaves the airport in Dallas, mere minutes before President Kennedy is ambushed, US Secret Service Agent Don Lawton openly questions his superiors about being ordered off the riding bumper of the car of the President whom he is trying to protect. The order came from Emory Roberts, Special Agent-In-Charge of the Vice-Presidential Secret Service Detail, in the car toward which SA Lawton is gesturing.

Formula for Murder:

▶ **Motorcade Formation Change Enabling JFK Assassination**

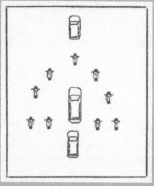

Standard Formation

The **"Wedge Formation"** is standard textbook procedure for established Dignitary Protection and Motorcade Security Standards and was used in other 1963 motorcades of President Kennedy (in second car).

Security Breach: This **non-secure** formation—reportedly at the direction of the LBJ team at Dallas airport—had the President needlessly exposed. (Charts by Al Carrier, 2003)[778]

Security Expert Al Carrier immediately recognized the above-diagrammed wedge formation "as the motorcycle positioning in the 1962 Berlin Kennedy motorcade and the November 14, 1963, Tampa, Florida motorcade."[779]

The procedure was in place at the time of the assassination. For some reason, it was not followed on November 22, 1963.[780]

Dallas Formation

[778] Carrier, "The United States Secret Service: Conspiracy to Assassinate a President"
[779] Ibid.
[780] Ibid.

With the Secret Service follow-up car directly behind the President's limo in the wedge formation, the President had secured protection. Note specifically that the five units being placed ahead of the pilot car rather than the President's car in Dallas placed them in a completely ineffective position:

> There is an obvious problem with the positioning of these five units. Why would they be placed in front of the lead car when they were needed in front of the President's limo, especially on Main Street, where the heavy crowds closed in to the degree that the four units to the rear of the limo could not move forward to keep the crowds back?[781]
>
> Why were the five lead motorcycles ahead of the lead car? Why were the four motorcyclists with the presidential limo ordered to stay back?[782]

The motorcade formation employed in Dallas had the President so exposed that the driver of the President's limo, U.S. Secret Service Special Agent William Greer, literally kept his door held slightly open with his left hand to keep spectators at least at arm's length away.

> The late Jean Lollis Hill, who witnessed the assassination in Dealey Plaza and was dating one of the motorcycle officers assigned to the

[781] Ibid.
[782] Ibid.

limo, reported in *JFK: The Last Dissenting Witness* that she was told that Johnson's Secret Service Agents had changed the orders and advised the remaining four motorcyclists not to advance beyond the back tires of the limo.[783]

As Al Carrier also notes:

It is clear that there were enough Dallas Police Department motorcycle officers present to provide ample security to the President and his party. (There were eighteen two-wheeled motorcycles in the motorcade.)[784]

The LBJ team also attempted to change the passenger configuration of the Dallas motorcade in order to get Governor Connally, a longtime LBJ ally, out of the limousine in which Kennedy was riding. Unlike the other changes, this redirection of plans was overruled by President Kennedy's people. Since the purpose of the President's trip to Dallas was to mend political fences, it was important to the President that the much more conservative Governor Connally ride with Kennedy, and that the much more liberal Texas Senator Ralph Yarborough be seen riding with the more conservative Lyndon Johnson, as originally planned. The attempted change is very noteworthy, as the prestige position is always to be seated with the President, yet Johnson attempted to remove his close ally from that honor and place a political enemy there instead.

Contrary to misinformation, "the interviews conducted by Vince Palamara with agents involved in the motorcade security clearly show that the agents were not hampered in their duty. They all describe the President and his advisors as being easy to work with and who did not interfere with their duties of protection."[785] Former Secret Service agents expressed to Palamara that JFK would never have ordered an agent off the bumper of his car; quite to the contrary, he respected their decisions on protection and deferred those matters to their judgment.[786]

A further and little-known point is that, when it comes to security, the Secret Service has full authority to overrule even the President of the United States—and has been known to do so. For example, after the attacks on September 11, 2001, President Bush insisted on returning to Washington and issued that order. The Secret Service countermanded that order and redirected *Air Force One* to Offet Air Base in Nebraska because that is what their security protocol dictated.[787]

Analysis reveals that other standard protection protocols were also blatantly absent. Typically, in any Presidential motorcade—even in 1963—Secret Service agents ensured that manhole covers along the parade route are bolted shut, that open windows in buildings are closed, that all overpasses along the route are completely cleared of civilians, and that tall buildings are monitored for possible shooters. Those standard precautions were visibly absent from the protection in Dallas.

The responsibility for the security stripping on the Dallas trip does not appear to lead directly to the Secret Service, but rather to Vice President Lyndon Johnson and

[783] Ibid, citing Bill Sloan & Jean Hill, *JFK: The Last Dissenting Witness* (Pelican: 1992).
[784] Carrier, "The United States Secret Service: Conspiracy to Assassinate a President"
[785] Carrier, "The United States Secret Service: Conspiracy to Assassinate a President"
[786] Palamara, *Survivor's Guilt: The Secret Service and the Failure to Protect the President*
[787] Carrier, "The United States Secret Service: Conspiracy to Assassinate a President"

those under his immediate control. Decisions that weakened security were made by Assistant Dallas Police Chief George Lumpkin, top Lyndon Johnson aide (and "hatchet man") Cliff Carter, Democratic National Committee (DNC) advance man Jack Puterbaugh, Emory Roberts, the Secret Service agent in charge of Johnson's protection detail, and Floyd Boring, a higher ranking member of the Secret Service. Those are the individuals reportedly responsible for the choice of the parade route (which took the President into the long slow turn and left him exposed in Dealey Plaza), the weak motorcycle formation, the absence of agents on the riding bumpers of the President's car, and the inadequate protection along the parade route in general.

Professor James Fetzer's extensive study in 2000 concluded that:

> **Secret Service policies for the protection of the President were massively violated during the motorcade in Dallas.[788]**

The procedural deviations were numerous:

> **More than a dozen Secret Service policies for the protection of the President seem to have been violated during the motorcade in Dallas, including no protective military presence; no coverage of open windows; motorcycles out of position; agents not riding on the Presidential limousine; vehicles in improper sequence; utilization of an improper route, which included a turn of more than 90 degrees; limousine slowed nearly to a halt at the corner of Houston and Elm; the limousine came to a halt after bullets began to be fired; agents were virtually unresponsive; brains and blood were washed from the limousine at Parkland, even before the President had been pronounced dead; the limousine was stripped down and being rebuilt already Monday, the day of the formal state funeral; a substitute windshield was later produced as evidence; and so on—discoveries that are strengthened and extended by Vincent Palamara and Douglas Weldon, J. D., in this book.[789]**

MOTORCADE ROUTE

Vince Palamara's many years of research and communication with former U.S. Secret Service personnel assisted him in learning who, as Palamara puts it, "was actually to blame for the slow 120-degree turn, the Main-Houston-Elm juncture, which was a violation of Secret Service protocol and common sense."[790] The evidence, as far as pushing for the route change (which *did* occur) taking the motorcade into the dangerous dog-leg turn route, leads primarily to Dallas Assistant Chief of Police, George Lumpkin, with probable assistance at the approval level from senior Secret Service member, Floyd Boring.[791]

---

[788] James H. Fetzer, Ph.D., 2001, "'Smoking Guns' in the Death of JFK": http://www.jfkresearch.com/prologue.htm
[789] James H. Fetzer Ph.D., *Murder in Dealey Plaza: What We Know Now that We Didn't Know Then* (Open Court: 2000).
[790] Vince Palamara, *Survivor's Guilt: The Secret Service and the Failure to Protect the President*, 2006
[791] Ibid.

George L. Lumpkin, Assistant Police Chief of Dallas in 1962, recommended the route to the Secret Service. He stated that the alternative route (reaching the Trade Mart by avoiding the slow 120-degree turn) was rejected because "it was filled with winos and broken pavement," and because Kennedy wanted exposure and there would not have been large crowds there (nor were there many in Dealey Plaza which was past the downtown portion of the motorcade where they had experienced the largest crowds).[792] Lumpkin was also a Colonel in Army Intelligence and rode in the pilot car of the Kennedy motorcade that day; he was also the officer who ordered that the Texas School Book Depository Building to be sealed off after the assassination, as well as the man who specifically chose Ilya Mamantov to be Marina Oswald's Russian interpreter following the assassination.

Aides to Vice President Johnson apparently approved that route and also authorized its publication in the newspapers.

It was apparently Texas Governor John Connally who had pushed for the Trade Mart to be the site of President Kennedy's luncheon/speech, even though Connally himself conceded that it was a security nightmare. Had the speech been scheduled at one of the other sites that were being seriously considered, the motorcade would never have taken the dog-leg turn onto Elm Street into Dealey Plaza.

The Dallas Police Department also told the Secret Service that they would secure whatever route was selected. They clearly did not secure the route adequately, nor did the Secret Service. As former Secret Service agent Lynne Meredith wrote:

> I have always believed that the following adverse situations all contributed to the unfortunate and unnecessary death of President Kennedy. . . . No Secret Service agents riding on the rear of the limousine. . . . Inadequate security along the entire ten-mile motorcade route from the airport to downtown Dallas that day, particularly in the buildings along the route of travel. . . . The motorcade route published several days in advance . . .[793]

Revelations of recent years have cast deep doubts on even the *possibility* of the government's official version of the JFK assassination being valid:

- It has been substantiated that high-ranking CIA officers had pre-knowledge that Mary Pinchot Meyer would be murdered;[794]
- CIA officer E. Howard Hunt made "deathbed testimony" that CIA officer Cord Meyer (ex-husband of Mary Pinchot Meyer) and Vice President Johnson organized the JFK assassination;[795]
- It has been substantiated by author Ed Haslam that a covert cancer laboratory in New Orleans linked Lee Harvey Oswald, Jack Ruby, David Ferrie, Guy Banister, Dr. Mary Sherman and Judyth Baker;[796]
- Judyth Baker's book, *Me & Lee*, has not only confirmed the cancer laboratory and the involvement of the above individuals, but documented that

[792] Ibid.
[793] Palamara, *Survivor's Guilt: The Secret Service and the Failure to Protect the President*
[794] Janney, *Mary's Mosaic*
[795] Hunt, *Bond of Secrecy*
[796] Haslam, *Dr. Mary's Monkey*

its purpose was to develop a rapid-onset cancer to be used as a bioweapon against Fidel Castro.[797]

Covert anti-Castro efforts in the early 1960s were much more prevalent than most Americans realize. The U.S. embargo was crippling Cuba economically:

> Add to that years of U.S.-sponsored covert warfare waged against Cuba (from blowing up Cuban oil refineries to infecting Cuban livestock with viruses), and it is amazing Castro's government survived at all.[798]

> Then the inevitable discussion of how to assassinate Castro started. No one even suggested that the U.S. had not been trying, despite the fact that assassinating a foreign head of state was explicitly illegal.[799]

A New Orleans District Attorney discovered that the plot to assassinate President Kennedy originated within the womb of the plans to assassinate Castro. He also learned that the nucleus of the conspiracy was in New Orleans and that Lee Harvey Oswald's false "defection" to the Soviet Union, as well as his connections to former FBI man Guy Banister, tied Oswald in to the U.S. intelligence community, especially its epicenter in Lafayette Square in New Orleans:

> In the blocks surrounding Lafayette Square were the local offices of the FBI, the CIA, and the Secret Service. Across the square from Banister sat Chairman Herbert of the Armed Services Committee of the U.S House of Representatives, whose job it was to prepare the U.S. military's budget for Congress' approval and to hide the CIA's budget from both Soviet and American scrutiny.[800]

Lee Harvey Oswald, our so-called "lone-nut assassin," was operating right in the middle of this intelligence center. It has been established that he worked closely with Banister—and was seen often in Banister's office—and also worked nearby as a "cover" job at a coffee company with Judyth Baker.

> One block away was the Reilly Coffee Company where Lee Harvey Oswald worked. The address stamped on the famous "Hands Off Cuba" flyers that Oswald handed out that hot August day in 1963, was 544 Camp Street: The Newman Building. Banister's wife found similar flyers in her husband's office after his death.[801]

It's noteworthy that Banister and Reilly were two of the most conservative anti-Castro members of the whole New Orleans community. The fact that they both assisted Lee Harvey Oswald in acts that appeared to be pro-Communist is highly suspicious. With

---

[797] Baker, *Me & Lee*
[798] Haslam, *Dr. Mary's Monkey*, 144.
[799] Ibid.
[800] Haslam, *Dr. Mary's Monkey*, 148.
[801] Haslam, *Dr. Mary's Monkey*, 148-149.

the benefit of hindsight, the technique was obviously a method of setting up Oswald's intelligence "legend" so that he could be used operationally.

> Garrison concluded that Oswald was involved with both Banister and Ferrie during the summer of 1963, and that Banister was Oswald's "handler" who arranged events, such as the trip to the mental hospital, to make Oswald later appear to be a convincing political assassin.[802]

It has also become quite apparent, with the benefit of newer information, that those connections were *exactly* what "needed to be covered up" in the confusing aftermath of the assassination and its would-be investigations. In fact, the footprints of federal agents had been all over the case:

> Garrison related how he had tried to find Guy Banister's files in 1966, several years after Banister's death in September 1964. His investigators sought out Banister's wife, who told them that upon her husband's death, his files had been promptly removed from his office before she got there. She was told they were removed by federal agents.[803]

> What Garrison had figured out that was so dangerous was the existence of "a right-wing medical-political alliance at work in New Orleans in the 1960s, and that Dr. Alton Ochsner was at the center of it."[804] It was all related to anti-Castro intelligence activities and that was the missing factor in the equation to ". . . explain the extreme manner in which the New Orleans Police Department shut down the investigation into Mary Sherman's murder and sanitized the reports . . ."[805]

Investigative author Ed Haslam confirmed the worst of District Attorney Garrison's suspicions. Haslam identified a secret laboratory that had been used by David Ferrie and Dr. Mary Sherman for developing a "galloping" (rapid-onset) cancer. He also discovered the existence of a linear particle accelerator at a separate laboratory, but also in New Orleans, being used for a secret anti-Castro research project at that time, involving Lee Harvey Oswald that was probably responsible for the intense destruction to Dr. Sherman's body.[806]

This was a true bombshell discovery, as it was a real game-changer in the "big picture" of the JFK assassination. Imagine the potential consequences: "What would have happened to the 'lone-nut' theory if the public began to suspect that Lee Harvey Oswald had been spying on a top-secret U.S. Government laboratory?"[807]

Mr. Haslam's grisly discoveries continued when his investigation of the gruesome death of Dr. Sherman led him to author-investigator Judyth Baker, who had been a prime witness in those very events in which Dr. Sherman had been involved. The

---

[802] Haslam, *Dr. Mary's Monkey*, 149.
[803] Ibid, 158.
[804] Ibid, 166.
[805] Ibid, 244.
[806] Haslam, *Dr. Mary's Monkey*, 243-271.
[807] Ibid, 269.

amazing history was pieced together into the puzzle: "She and Lee Harvey Oswald stood side-by-side in an underground medical laboratory located in David Ferrie's apartment on Louisiana Avenue Parkway in New Orleans, and that she was the laboratory technician that handled the cancer-causing monkey viruses which were being used to develop a biological weapon for the purpose of killing Fidel Castro."[808]

> Judyth (Baker) reports that Lee (Oswald) secretly worked as a team member on Ochsner's bioweapons project, that Oswald met with Ochsner personally, and that it was actually Oswald who requested that Dr. Ochsner set up his media coverage to help position him as a pro-Castro activist, so that he could get into Cuba more easily and develop their bioweapon to sympathetic doctors, who would use it to kill Castro.[809]

According to Judyth Baker, Dr. Mary Sherman displayed "to her a collection of microscope slides of a 'galloping cancer' that Mary had developed by exposing the cancer-causing monkey viruses to radiation."[810]

The development of that biological weapon was successful:

> Furthermore, she said, after successfully killing numerous monkeys with their new biological weapon, this group had tested it on a human subject in a mental hospital, killing the human.[811]

The success of the bioweapon project—which involved Jack Ruby—had major implications in Ruby's well-expressed allegations that he had been injected with cancer cells.[812] It was not some vague notion that came from nowhere. He knew that a "super-cancer" had been developed as a weapon to be used covertly and that someone like himself would also make an excellent candidate for its use.

The implications of all these were quite dramatic in themselves:

> Like the cover-up which dumped Mary Sherman's burned and mangled corpse at her apartment, Lee's murder was deemed a "necessity" to protect the underground medical laboratory and its sponsors. Thus was silenced the man who could have explained what really happened (or perhaps, what did not happen) in Dallas on November 22, 1963.[813]

Baker testifies to the historical record—and backs it up with documentation—that while she and Lee Harvey Oswald were together in New Orleans, it was very clear that he was working "penetration" on behalf of U.S. intelligence and was not only infiltrating, but attempting to preclude, a plot against the life of President Kennedy. That information coincides with the testimony of veteran Military Intelligence operative,

---

[808] Haslam, *Dr. Mary's Monkey*, 284, citing Judyth Baker, *Me & Lee*.
[809] Ibid, 337, citing Judyth Baker, *Me & Lee*.
[810] Ibid, 322, citing Judyth Baker, *Me & Lee*.
[811] Ibid, 285, citing Judyth Baker, *Me & Lee*.
[812] Ibid, 307, citing Judyth Baker, *Me & Lee*.
[813] Ibid, 301, citing Judyth Baker, *Me & Lee*.

Richard Case Nagell who—as a double agent for the U.S.—was also tracking Oswald for Soviet Intelligence.[814] Baker concludes that "Lee infiltrated the plot to kill President Kennedy, was set up as the patsy, and was then murdered to protect the real assassins by silencing him."[815]

As Ed Haslam observed, the fact that the secret research project was linked to leaders in American medicine of the stature of Dr. Alton Ochsner and Dr. Mary Sherman, practically *necessitated* a cover-up:

> Connecting Ochsner to Oswald not only rules out "lone nut" as a realistic description of Oswald, but it helps us understand how convenient "lone nut" was for protecting Ochsner (and others) from inconvenient questions about both the bioweapon project and the JFK assassination.[816]

That was apparently the need for the whole cover-up—they were all involved together: Oswald, Ruby, Ferrie, Banister, Dr. Ochsner, Dr. Sherman—all tied inextricably together in the whole sordid story:

> Jack Ruby visited David Ferrie's apartment one day when Judyth and Lee (Oswald) were there. Ferrie introduced him to Judyth as Sparky Rubenstein. Judyth was surprised that Ferrie briefed Ruby on their bioweapon project. (Why not? They all worked for Marcello.) Ruby recognized Lee, and said that he used to see him at parties when he was a boy.[817]

In *that* context, Jack Ruby's fears for his safety—clearly expressed to Chief Justice Earl Warren—suddenly take on very clear meaning and dire implications:

> This means that Jack Ruby knew about Oswald's connection to the underground medical laboratory when he shot him, and he knew about the cancer cocktail that could be used to silence him as he awaited trial for Oswald's murder. It is no wonder he wanted to get out of Dallas. And it is no wonder that the Warren Commission did not accept his offer to talk in exchange for safer accommodations.[818]

As we detailed in a portion of the introductory material in this book—death by medical "accident"—the circumstances related to the injections Ruby received while in Dallas Police custody are cloudy at best. Ruby was visited there by psychiatrist Louis Jolyon "Jolly" West, reportedly a top expert in the CIA's MKULTRA program, a project involving special drugging and mind-control techniques that included programming individuals to kill.[819] When that factor is added to the context that Ruby had also been

---

[814] Russell, *The Man Who Knew Too Much.*
[815] Haslam, *Dr. Mary's Monkey,* 328, citing Judyth Baker, *Me & Lee.*
[816] Haslam, *Dr. Mary's Monkey,* 335.
[817] Ibid, 307, parenthetical comments in original.
[818] Ibid, 307
[819] Greg Parker, "Jack Ruby Timeline" (note 12), 23 Nov. 2004, *The Education Forum,* http://educationforum.ipbhost. com/index.php?showtopic=2342

well-aware of the project to use a type of rapid-onset cancer as a biological weapon, the circumstances become quite suspicious, to say the least:

> **Jack Ruby told Al Maddox (his Dallas police guard) that he had been injected with cancer cells. Maddox has said that the doctor that gave Ruby injections came from Chicago. Maddox was present at Parkland Hospital when Ruby died of an embolism caused by galloping lung cancer.**[820]

People on both sides of the issue often fail to look at key points and the solution to a puzzle sometimes rests in asking the right questions. The right question is rarely asked regarding the JFK assassination—but here it is:

> **If you're planning to shoot Jack Kennedy in the head with high-powered rifles in broad daylight, you'd better spend some time thinking about his brother. His brother is Bobby Kennedy, the Attorney General, and he has the power and the resources to come after you. In order to get away with killing Jack, you must neutralize Bobby at the critical moment . . .**
>
> **The question:**
> *How do you paralyze Bobby at the critical moment?*
>
> **The answer:**
> *By publicly accusing one of his agents of the crime!*[821]

It has become pretty obvious at this point that Oswald was set-up to "take the fall" for the assassination of President Kennedy, even though he was set up as a component of the conspiracy.[822] In one way or another, he seemed to be connected to all the players in the drama:

> **Far from being a "lone nut," Oswald was connected to so many powerful and/or corrupt people that no one wanted him to get into a courtroom and start talking. Not even the Attorney General.**[823]

The perfect patsy. From that perspective, it all makes perfect sense, and that scenario also explains the National Security cover-up that followed the assassination of JFK:

> **When you see who the players were, and how unwelcome such an investigation would have been to them, you will understand why it was not done.**[824]

---

[820] Haslam, *Dr. Mary's Monkey*, 307, parenthetical comments in original.
[821] Haslam, *Dr. Mary's Monkey*, 344, emphasis in original.
[822] Belzer & Wayne, *Dead Wrong*, 110-153.
[823] Haslam, *Dr. Mary's Monkey*, 344.
[824] Ibid, 340.

Some of the most important statements related to the JFK assassination suddenly make a lot more sense when looked at freshly and in the new context of:

- A secret laboratory in New Orleans involving Lee Harvey Oswald, Jack Ruby, David Ferrie, and Guy Banister;
- Oswald's affiliations with U.S. Intelligence and Robert Kennedy's knowledge of that fact;
- Robert Kennedy's suspicions concerning the involvement of both Carlos Marcello and Vice President Lyndon Johnson in the assassination.

They're going to find out about Cuba. They're going to find out about the guns, find out about New Orleans, find out about everything.—Jack Ruby[825]

This was spoken to a visitor while Ruby was in jail, but note the fact that these were his *real* concerns and were much more stressed than the fact that he had even been filmed committing first degree murder inside of a police station!

When I saw the phone records of all the people Jack Ruby was calling before Dallas, before the assassination, it looked like my witness list for the Senate Rackets Committee.—Attorney General Robert F. Kennedy[826]

This was spoken to his Press Secretary.

If I told you what I really know, it would be very dangerous to this country. Our whole political system could be disrupted.—FBI Director J. Edgar Hoover

This was spoken in response to the question from a friend's son, "Do you think Lee Harvey Oswald did it?"[827]

One of your guys did it.—Attorney General Robert F. Kennedy[828]

This was spoken telephonically in a phone call he made immediately upon learning that the name of the alleged assassin was "Lee Harvey Oswald"; the call was to his "anti-Castro" group in Florida, verified and

---

[825] Peter Dale Scott, *Deep Politics and the Death of JFK* (University of California Press: 1993), 179: http://www.ctka.net/pr795-ruby.html

[826] Anthony Thorne (citing David Talbot, May 24, 2007 interview on *Fresh Air*, NPR), May 26, 2007, "David Talbot's New Book Brothers," *The Education Forum*: http://educationforum.ipbhost.com/index.php?showtopic=9824&st=150

[827] John Simkin, "Theory: CIA," *Spartacus Educational*, accessed 21 Dec 2012: http://www.spartacus.schoolnet.co.uk/JFKinvestCIA.htm

[828] Richard D. Mahoney, *The Kennedy Brothers: The Rise and Fall of Jack and Bobby* (Skyhorse Publishing: 2011), 178.

witnessed by both Harry Ruiz Williams and Haynes Johnson.[829] "Robert Kennedy was utterly in control of his emotions when he came on the line and sounded almost studiedly brisk as he said, 'One of your guys did it.'"[830] Historians interpret that remark as meaning that Robert Kennedy "clearly was referring to embittered Cubans deployed by elements in the CIA. Asking (CIA Director) McCone if the CIA was involved in such a way that 'he could not lie' suggested that Kennedy thought the CIA operatives were acting at a deniable distance."[831]

It is also now known that it was Bobby Kennedy's very own Attorney General's Office which actually *originated* the cover-up, via the memo from Kennedy's Deputy Attorney General and staunch ally, Nick Katzenbach.[832] That may very well have been the "dark beauty" of the hijacked "black op" in that it forced the victims into covering up the crime. Thus, the sinister brilliance of the method in which the assassination of President Kennedy took place, also assured its secrecy.

> I was one of the two case officers who handled Lee Harvey Oswald... we gave him the mission of killing Fidel Castro in Cuba ... I don't know why he killed Kennedy. But I do know he used precisely the plan we had devised against Castro.—David Atlee Phillips, CIA, Director, WHO (Western Hemisphere Operations)

> In 1963, Phillips was one of the CIA officers responsible for planning anti-Castro operations. Phillips had personal knowledge of Lee Harvey Oswald, who was known to Phillips as part of the U.S. Intelligence anti-Castro operational apparatus.[833]

To say that Fabian Escalante was no stranger to complex covert intelligence maneuvers would be quite an understatement. Escalante was head of Cuba's elite G2 Intelligence unit which oversaw counterintelligence at the most complex point of East-West relations. Those complex cat-and-mouse games of the "James Bond world" of counterintelligence were his specific field of expertise. Escalante summarizes the conclusions of the investigation by Cuban Intelligence:

> Oswald was an Intelligence agent of the US—CIA, FBI, military, or all of these, we don't know. He was manipulated, told he was penetrating a

[829] Talbot, *Brothers*; David Talbot, May 26, 2007, "David Talbot: The Kennedy Family and the Assassination of JFK," *The Education Forum*: http://educationforum.ipbhost.com/index.php?showtopic=10049

[830] Mahoney, *The Kennedy Brothers*, 178.

[831] Ibid.

[832] Belzer & Wayne, *Dead Wrong*, 128-130.

[833] David Atlee Phillips, unpublished manuscript, 1977; Morley, *Our Man in Mexico*, 238.

group of Cuban agents that wanted to kill Kennedy. But from the very beginning, he was to be the element to blame Cuba.[834]

- There were two objectives to the plot—to kill Kennedy and to blame Cuba for the crime.[835]
- We believe Kennedy became an obstacle to US military aggression against Cuba.[836]
- Not less than fifteen persons took part in the assassination.[837]
- At the same time, knowing a little about CIA operations, we see how they used the principle of decentralized operations— independent parties with a specific role, to guarantee compartmentalization and to keep it simple.[838]

Robert Kennedy also told several of his own staff members that he strongly believed Carlos Marcello and other mafia members were responsible for his brother's death, but that he could do nothing about it. He also harbored a deep sense of guilt, saying that he felt responsible for the tragedy.

- It has been publicly known only since 1992, that Robert Kennedy told a few close advisers that New Orleans Mob Boss Marcello was behind JFK's assassination, as we confirmed with Kennedy aide Richard Goodwin. *Salon* received additional confirmation of mafia involvement from Robert Kennedy's former Press Secretary, Frank Mankiewicz, who conducted a secret investigation of JFK's death for Robert.[839]
- Robert Kennedy had a fear that he had somehow gotten his own brother killed, and that his "attempts to prosecute the Mob and to kill Castro backfired in some terrible way."[840]

We know that it was a domestic high level political conspiracy that killed the President, and Bobby Kennedy intends to run for President at some point, and when he does, if he succeeds, he will resume the policies of President Kennedy's—of détente towards the Soviet Union.
—Message from Attorney General
Robert F. Kennedy and Kennedy family[841]

[834] Russell, *The Man Who Knew Too Much.*
[835] Ibid.
[836] Ibid.
[837] Ibid.
[838] Ibid.
[839] Waldron & Hartmann, *Ultimate Sacrifice*, citing interviews with Pierre Salinger (April 3 and 10, 1998) and interview with confidential source (April 14, 1998): http://www.buzzflash.com/contributors/05/12/con05463.html
[840] Waldron & Hartmann, *Ultimate Sacrifice*, citing ABCNEWS.com, November 20, 2003, "A Brother's Pain," Interview with Evan Thomas: http://www.buzzflash.com/contributors/05/12/con05463.html
[841] Talbot, *Brothers.*

> This was in a message sent to Moscow from the Kennedy family, via special envoy, right after the assassination. As author David Talbot observed: "this is the height of the Cold War, and at this point it indicates that Bobby Kennedy and the family are placing more trust in the Soviet government than in their own government."[842]
>
> If the American people knew the truth about Dallas, there would be blood in the streets.[843]
>
> —Attorney General Robert F. Kennedy
>
> This was spoken to an old family friend, in the context that his brother had been the victim of a domestic political conspiracy.[844]

---

[842] Talbot, *Brothers*; Anthony Thorne (citing David Talbot, May 24, 2007 interview on *Fresh Air*, NPR), May 26, 2007, "David Talbot's New Book Brothers," *The Education Forum*: http://educationforum .ipbhost.com/index.php?showtopic=9824&st=150

[843] Talbot, *Brothers*.

[844] Talbot, *Brothers*; David Talbot, May 26, 2007, "David Talbot: The Kennedy Family and the Assassination of JFK," *The Education Forum*: http://educationforum.ipbhost.com/index .php?showtopic=10049

Many other cases should rightfully be investigated, in addition to further investigating the cases we covered. Some of those cases bearing special mention are:

- **Mac Wallace** was Lyndon Johnson's "professional assassin of choice"—at least, prior to becoming President.[845] After reaching the post of President of the United States, Johnson certainly had more sophisticated means at his disposal for the purpose of "eliminating" his enemies. As Commander-in-Chief, he could direct the darkest aspects of the covert forces of the U.S. intelligence community at his own personal whim. Mac Wallace was then a liability because he "knew where all the bodies were buried"—and, in some cases, probably *literally*, as well as figuratively. Therefore, the death of Mac Wallace certainly warrants a great deal of examination and, in reality, very little is known about his death and not very much information seems to be available.
- **Roger Craig** was a Dallas County Deputy Sheriff who *swore* repeatedly that the rifle he found in the Book Depository building was <u>not the same rifle</u> they framed Oswald with. Craig's case is fascinating and could fill a book in itself (and *should*).

---

[845] Belzer & Wayne, *Dead Wrong*, 17-23. Douglas Caddy, Esq., "Letter to Mr. Stephen S. Trott, Assistant Attorney General, U.S. Department of Justice," August 9, 1984, *The Estes Documents*: http://home.earthlink. net/~sixthfloor/estes.htm

- **Dallas Police Officer Roscoe White** was apparently part of the same Dallas Police Department Tactical Team of which J. D. Tippit was a member. That Dallas Police Department unit had substantial liaison with U.S. Military Intelligence and operated as support for sensitive intel operations. White also served at the Atsugi Air Base with Lee Harvey Oswald and also knew Jack Ruby very well. Yet the story from family members that he was directly involved in the assassination of President Kennedy does not appear to be authentic.

A member of the Military Intelligence team sent to Dallas on November 22, to attempt to abort the assassination of President Kennedy, had this dramatic observation regarding Dallas Police Officers J. D. Tippit and Roscoe White. It was a "game-changer" piece of intelligence that hardly anybody who investigated the case actually knew:

> **Tippit and White both had Military intel and CIA fingerprints, all over Dallas and Fort Worth, before the assassination of Kennedy. They both knew about the "Abort Team," and why and how they were dispatched to Dallas that day.**[846]

- **Cliff Carter** has been included by some researchers but, stated simply, there is no evidence he was murdered—though he clearly seems linked to the assassination. Carter reportedly died of pneumonia in September of 1971 when—*seriously*, folks, we kid you not—it was reported that no penicillin could be found in time . . . in Washington, D.C.! That was reported as the cause of death.[847] Others may, no doubt, dispute that claim. And if they do, we say, "*Fine.*" Maybe his death has not been proven suspicious, but <u>his career certainly was</u>. As Lyndon Johnson's "hatchet man," Cliff Carter was reportedly involved in a lot of dirty work, including arranging murders by hitman Mac Wallace and other acts which covered the many trails leading to Lyndon Johnson, the man who became President of the United States as a result of the JFK assassination.[848]

There is virtually no doubt at this point that individuals like John Martino and David Morales were clearly involved—to some extent—in the planning and operational support of the JFK assassination, yet very little is actually known about the circumstances of their deaths.

Regarding **David Morales**, historian John Simkin wrote that "Morales began to worry about his own health during the HSCA investigations." He "made his last trip to Washington in early May, 1978." Then—after a friend told him that he wasn't looking well—Morales replied:

> **I don't know what's wrong with me. Ever since I left Washington I haven't been feeling very comfortable.**[849]

[846] William Robert "Tosh" Plumlee, Email to author, 18 Sept 2012
[847] Penn Jones, Jr., "Disappearing Witnesses," Jan 1984, *The Rebel* magazine: http://www.maebrussell.com/Disappearing%20Witnesses/Disappearing%20Witnesses.html
[848] Douglas Caddy, Esq., "Letter to Mr. Stephen S. Trott, Assistant Attorney General, U.S. Department of Justice," August 9, 1984, *The Estes Documents*: http://home.earthlink.net/~sixthfloor/estes.htm
[849] John Simkin, "David Sánchez Morales: Biography," *Spartacus Educational*, accessed 11 Dec. 2012: http://www.spartacus.schoolnet.co.uk/JFKmorales.htm

The same friend found out that Morales wound up in the hospital that night, so the next morning, he went to see him.

> They wouldn't let anyone in. They had his room surrounded by sheriff's deputies.

That same day, Morales was taken off life support and died. There was no autopsy.[850]

- **John Martino** apparently died of natural causes. But before dying, he admitted his involvement in the JFK assassination to several people and clearly had established foreknowledge that it was going to happen. Don't think so? Here's what he told his wife on the morning of November 22:

> Flo, they're going to kill him. They're going to kill him when he gets to Texas.[851]

Another death that should be investigated is the case of **Manuel Artime**, who died on November 18, 1977. Gaeton Fonzi, Special Investigator to the U.S. Congress' House Select Committee on Assassinations, was highly professional and not one to make wild claims. Yet, Fonzi concluded that Manuel Artime might have been a double agent working for Cuban Intelligence,[852] and also included Artime's death, specifically, as being of a suspicious nature:

> There are some, what I call mysterious deaths. Artime fits into that category—he got cancer awfully fast.[853]

Artime died from rapid-onset cancer just as he was preparing to testify before the 1977 Congressional Committee. It should be noted David Ferrie and Dr. Mary Sherman had been working on rapid-onset cancer to be used as an assassination technique targeting Fidel Castro. Notes about methods of inducing cancer were found in Ferrie's apartment after his death. Artime was apparently playing both sides of the fence in the secret anti-Castro intelligence operations; working with Bobby Kennedy's team but also passing info to the mob.[854] Rolando Masferrer, a killer associated with Mobster Santo Trafficante's organization, was brought into the anti-Castro operations through Johnny Roselli or Manuel Artime.[855] Note that all the aforementioned witnesses died prior to, or during, the Congressional Committee that was specifically investigating links between the assassination and anti-Castro operations: Rolando Masferrer, Manuel Artime, Johnny Roselli, Sam Giancana, and George de Mohrenschildt.

---

[850] Ibid.
[851] John Simkin, "John Martino: Biography," *Spartacus Educational*, accessed 11 Dec. 2012: http://www.spartacus .schoolnet.co.uk/JFKmartino.htm
[852] John Simkin, "Manuel Artime: Biography," *Spartacus Educational*, accessed 12 Dec. 2012: http://www.spartacus .schoolnet.co.uk/JFKartimeM.htm
[853] Ibid.
[854] Waldron & Hartmann, *Ultimate Sacrifice*: http://www.ultimatesacrificebook.com/documentation.html
[855] Ibid.

- **Win Scott** was the CIA Station Chief in Mexico City during the time period that Lee Harvey Oswald's intelligence legend was being established in Mexico. He retired in 1969, and wrote a manuscript about his career and its adventures. The CIA's Counterintelligence Chief, James Angleton, quickly confiscated many sensitive materials upon Scott's death on April 26, 1971, reportedly of a heart attack. Angleton took a manuscript and three cartons of files, containing tape recordings of Lee Harvey Oswald. His son fought to get the materials back but was only partially successful; everything regarding his father's life after 1947, was removed for reasons of "National Security."[856]

Michael Scott was also told by a CIA source that his father had not died from natural causes.[857]

- **Desmond Fitzgerald** was in charge of all Clandestine Operations at CIA and reportedly died of a heart attack on July 23, 1967.[858] But note what was written about that death by veteran Military Intelligence covert operative, Richard Case Nagell:

Now *there* is a corpse that should be exhumed and examined by a qualified pathologist.[859]

If you wonder what Mr. Nagell meant by the above statement—so do we. In fact, we should *all* probably be curious about that one.

- The death of **Ed Voebel** is another case of interest, primarily due to the fact that Voebel was a witness whose testimony actually *proved* that there had to be an intelligence "double" for Lee Harvey Oswald. Decades of research by author John Armstrong has substantiated that there had to be <u>at least two</u> "Oswalds" being used in the spy games of the U.S. intelligence community before, during, and after his staged defection to the Soviet Union. That so-called "defection" was an obvious intelligence maneuver and a very transparent one, at that.[860]

  Voebel's testimony documented the existence of the Oswald double because it proved, via documentation in dental history, that the Oswald *he* knew in school had a tooth knocked out—but the Oswald who was buried had no missing or crowned teeth. That really nails it down, because dental records never lie. It's a fascinating story, from John Armstrong's seminal

---

[856] John Simkin, "Deaths of Witnesses Connected to the Assassination of John F. Kennedy," *Spartacus Educational*, accessed 13 Dec. 2012: http://www.spartacus.schoolnet.co.uk/JFKdeaths.htm

[857] Ibid.

[858] John Simkin, "Desmond Fitzgerald: Biography," *Spartacus Educational*, accessed 13 Dec. 2012: http://www.spartacus.schoolnet.co.uk/JFKfitzgeraldD.htm

[859] Russell, "Richard Case Nagell: The Man Who Knew Too Much," http://www.dickrussell.org/articles/richard.htm

[860] Belzer & Wayne, *Dead Wrong*, 116-125.

study of the matter, in the book, *Harvey and Lee*, portions of which are accessible online.[861]

SOCIAL CONTEXT

In a larger sense, the witness deaths in general—and the national security assassinations in particular—are indicative of a greater problem regarding the difficult maturation process of the American "experiment in Democracy."

We are reminded of the timeless words of relentless District Attorney, Jim Garrison, reminiscing about the haunting events witnessed in *his* experience. It's an admittedly long excerpt—and frankly, we should all study every syllable of it. Because precisely what Jim Garrison was worried about happening to the United States of America seems to be exactly what has happened. This is from a man who witnessed the fresh and horrific remains of Nazi concentration camps and it speaks from and to the heart of the whole human drama:

> I was with the artillery supporting the division that took Dachau; I arrived there the day after it was taken, when bulldozers were making pyramids of human bodies outside the camp. What I saw there has haunted me ever since. Because the law is my profession, I've always wondered about the judges throughout Germany who sentenced men to jail for picking pockets at a time when their own government was jerking gold from the teeth of men murdered in gas chambers. I'm concerned about all of this because it isn't a German phenomenon; it's a human phenomenon. It can happen here, because there has been no change and there has been no progress and there has been no increase of understanding on the part of men for their fellow man.
>
> What worries me deeply, and I have seen it exemplified in this case, is that we in America are in great danger of slowly evolving into a proto-fascist state. It will be a different kind of fascist state from the one of the Germans evolved; theirs grew out of depression and promised bread and work, while ours, curiously enough, seems to be emerging from prosperity. But in the final analysis, it's based on power and on the inability to put human goals and human conscience above the dictates of the state. Its origins can be traced in the tremendous war machine we've built since 1945, the "military-industrial complex" that Eisenhower vainly warned us about, which now dominates every aspect of our life. The power of the states and Congress has gradually been abandoned to the Executive Department, because of war conditions; and we've seen the creation of an arrogant, swollen bureaucratic complex totally unfettered by the checks and balances of the Constitution.[862]

---

[861] Armstrong, *Harvey And Lee: The Magic Tooth*: http://www.mindserpent.com/American_History/books/Armstrong/Tooth/Tooth.htm

[862] *JFK Lancer*, "Jim Garrison's Playboy Interview, Part Three," accessed 4 Dec. 2012: http://www.jfklancer.com/Garrison4.html

Mr. Garrison is, unfortunately, no longer with us, and therefore incapable of responding to his detractors, those self-proclaimed "conspiracy debunkers." We are honored though, to close this book by responding to them on his behalf, and in his own words:

> In a very real and terrifying sense, our Government is the CIA and the Pentagon, with Congress reduced to a debating society. Of course, you can't spot this trend to fascism by casually looking around. You can't look for such familiar signs as the swastika, because they won't be there. We won't build Dachaus and Auschwitzes; the clever manipulation of the mass media is creating a concentration camp of the mind that promises to be far more effective in keeping the populace in line. We're not going to wake up one morning and suddenly find ourselves in gray uniforms goose-stepping off to work. But this isn't the test. The test is: What happens to the individual who dissents? In Nazi Germany, he was physically destroyed; here, the process is more subtle, but the end results can be the same.

> I've learned enough about the machinations of the CIA in the past year to know that this is no longer the dream world America I once believed in. The imperatives of the population explosion, which almost inevitably will lessen our belief in the sanctity of the individual human life, combined with the awesome power of the CIA and the defense establishment, seem destined to seal the fate of the America I knew as a child and bring us into a new Orwellian world where the citizen exists for the state and where raw power justifies any and every immoral act. I've always had a kind of knee-jerk trust in my Government's basic integrity, whatever political blunders it may make. But I've come to realize that in Washington, deceiving and manipulating the public are viewed by some as the natural prerogatives of office. Huey Long once said, "Fascism will come to America in the name of anti-fascism." I'm afraid, based on my own experience that fascism will come to America in the name of national security.[863]

---

[863] Ibid.

The following are the case-by-case conclusions for the fifty deaths investigated for this book.

Investigatory Results of Fifty Deaths Related To JFK Assassination

Victim	Date	Relationship	Determination
Officer J. D. Tippit	November 22, 1963	Dallas Police Department officer gunned down during the confusing exit of the JFK kill-team and the ex-filtration of a Military Intelligence "abort team" from Oak Cliff section of Dallas.	**UNSOLVED MURDER: Was <u>not</u> shot by Lee Harvey Oswald as alleged.**
Lee Harvey Oswald	November 24, 1963	U.S. Intelligence operative conducting simultaneous penetration of pro- and anti-Castro Cuban organizations, framed for assassination of JFK via "hijacked" anti-Castro intelligence operation.	**MURDER: National Security Assassination that was brokered by the mafia.**
Jack Ruby	January 3, 1967	Mob-affiliated nightclub owner who shot Oswald and was known to just about everyone connected to the JFK assassination; from Oswald to CIA and most points between. Worked on periphery of a top-secret "weaponized" cancer project and suspected it was used to terminate him after he was finally granted a new trial.	**RAPID-ONSET CANCER: Possible National Security Assassination.**

Victim	Date	Relationship	Determination
Jack Zangetty	Late November, 1963	Correctly predicted that Jack Ruby would eliminate Oswald and that the son of Frank Sinatra would be kidnapped to divert the public's attention. Both took place just as he predicted and he was promptly murdered thereafter.	**OFFICIALLY UNSOLVED MURDER: Eliminated by Mafia for knowing and talking too much.**
Rose Cheramie (Melba Christine Marcades)	September 4, 1965	Officially classified as "accident victim," she was a drug courier associated with Jack Ruby. She correctly predicted assassination two days prior to murder of JFK. She clearly possessed accurate foreknowledge and the fact that the victim was found on the property of the Chief of Security for Texas oilman H. L. Hunt is extremely relevant.	**MURDER: Directly linked to JFK assassination.**
Karyn Kupcinet	November 28, 1963	Did not place the mysterious phone call predicting the JFK assassination, but her murder may have been to divert the public's attention (as the Sinatra kidnapping was), especially insofar as Chicago focus on Ruby and Chicago Mob.	**OFFICIALLY UNSOLVED MURDER: Only relation to JFK assassination is as possible "shock crime."**
Grant Stockdale	December 2, 1963	Close friend of President Kennedy who supposedly jumped from his 13th-floor office because he was depressed. But the actual circumstances do not suggest suicide.	**PROBABLE MURDER: Directly linked to JFK assassination.**
Jim Koethe	September 21, 1964	Newspaper reporter who had been in Jack Ruby's apartment the day Ruby shot Oswald. Killed by a karate chop to the neck. Officially ruled as a burglary and killed by the burglar. But all his notes for a book on JFK case were taken and never found.	**OFFICIALLY UNSOLVED MURDER: Possible linkage to JFK assassination.**

Victim	Date	Relationship	Determination
Bill Hunter	September 11, 1964	Also a newspaper reporter who also had been in Jack Ruby's apartment the day Ruby shot Oswald. Victim was shot by police officer. Shooting appears accidental, but something of evidentiary importance may have occurred at Jack Ruby's apartment on the day that he killed Oswald.	ACCIDENT, No apparent linkage to JFK assassination except victim's presence at Ruby's apartment.
Dorothy Kilgallen	November 8, 1965	Famous reporter who was the only one granted an interview by Jack Ruby. She vowed she would soon break the JFK case "wide open" and died of an overdose soon thereafter. Ruled Suicide or Accidental Overdose. But the crime scene was very clearly staged and her notes for her JFK book—as well as her "back-up" copy of them—completely vanished.	MURDER: Probable National Security Assassination— Direct linkage to JFK case.
Florence Pritchett Smith	November 9, 1965	Friend of Dorothy Kilgallen who had been entrusted with a back-up copy of Kilgallen's notes and died the day after Dorothy. Cause of death was a cerebral hemorrhage, apparently as a result of leukemia. But the notes were never found.	ILLNESS: No apparent linkage to JFK assassination except the disappearance of evidence.
Betty McDonald	February 13, 1964	Former dancer at Jack Ruby's nightclub who provided the alibi for the shooter of another witness—Warren Reynolds. Although Reynolds was a clear case of witness intimidation, McDonald's death in the Dallas jail appears unrelated.	SUICIDE OR MURDER: No apparent linkage to JFK assassination except clear case of witness intimidation upon Warren Reynolds.

Victim	Date	Relationship	Determination
Eddy Benavides	February, 1964	Domingo Benavides, the look-alike brother of the victim, eyewitnesses the murder of Officer Tippit (right after the JFK assassination) and was certain that his killer was <u>not Oswald</u>. His brother Eddy was then killed in a Dallas bar.	**MURDER: No apparent linkage to JFK assassination except clear case of witness intimidation upon Domingo Benavides.**
Bill Chesher	March 31, 1964	Auto mechanic who did have information about some of the links between Jack Ruby and Lee Harvey Oswald, but appears to have died from natural causes.	**HEART ATTACK: No apparent linkage to JFK assassination.**
Hank Killam	March 17, 1964	Victim had known both Jack Ruby and Lee Harvey Oswald and was clearly in fear for his life, which he reported to anyone who would listen. Died from slit jugular vein and went crashing through the plate glass window of a store. Official determination was "suicide," which was later changed to "accident." But crime scene analysis clearly indicates homicide.	**MURDER: National Security Assassination— Direct linkage to JFK case.**
Gary Underhill	May 8, 1964	Veteran CIA agent who told friends he had direct knowledge of who was responsible for JFK's murder. Like Killam, Underhill was *also* running for his life, *also* predicted his own murder, and *also* was murdered shortly after predicting it.	**MURDER: National Security Assassination— Direct linkage to JFK case.**
Guy Banister	June 6, 1964	Former head of FBI Chicago office who was a key handler of Oswald , the construction of Oswald's intelligence "legend" and—in the opinion of District Attorney Garrison—the set-up of Oswald as the fall guy. His extensive filing system then vanished.	**HEART ATTACK: No immediate linkage to JFK assassination except the disappearance of evidence.**

Victim	Date	Relationship	Determination
Hugh Ward	**May 22, 1964**	Hugh Ward and New Orleans' Mayor Deslesseps Morrison died in the crash of the small plane piloted by Ward. Both men were connected to the whole New Orleans/Guy Banister apparatus at the heart of the conspiracy to kill JFK. New Orleans District Attorney Jim Garrison was very interested in the actions of both men.	**PLANE CRASH, POSSIBLE SABOTAGE: Double engine failure (concurrently) with fuel on board.**
Deslesseps Morrison	**May 22, 1964**	No apparent inconsistencies, except for the virtually impossible coincidence that every witness connected to the Guy Banister aspect of the case had suddenly died just prior to their being sought in the investigation by District Attorney Jim Garrison.	**PLANE CRASH, POSSIBLE SABOTAGE: Double engine failure (concurrently) with fuel on board.**
Maurice Gatlin	**May 28, 1965**	Legal Counsel to the Minuteman group who was bag man (money transporter) for Guy Banister and CIA, and went off the 6th floor balcony of a hotel in Panama while Gatlin had been on a business trip.	**HEART ATTACK + FALL FROM 6th FLOOR BALCONY: Possible linkage to JFK assassination.**
Earlene Roberts	**January 9, 1966**	Witness who testified that shortly after the JFK assassination, a Dallas police car pulled up and stopped in front of Oswald's rooming house—while Oswald was inside the home—and honked, as though it was a signal, which also put Oswald in a specific place and time that conflicted with the official version. She was then virtually driven to her death by harassment from authorities, in the opinion of family members.	**HEART ATTACK: No direct correlation to JFK assassination but another clear case of witness intimidation.**

Victim	Date	Relationship	Determination
Al Bogard	February 15, 1966	Car salesman who witnessed an Oswald impersonator (setting up Oswald's intelligence "legend") test-drive a car and maintained his story, even after clear harassment by the FBI. Bogard was on record that "people were out to get him."	SUICIDE: But was being pursued by unknown parties and is another clear case of witness intimidation.
Lee Bowers Jr.	August 9, 1966	Bowers was a unique witness, having seen suspicious people and activity at the Grassy Knoll. Official death ruling was "Accident"—but an investigator (former member of the Texas Highway Patrol) concluded that another car had run Bowers' car off the road, causing his death.	AUTOMOBILE CRASH: MURDER OR HIT-AND-RUN, possibly linked to JFK assassination.
Marilyn "Delilah" Walle	August 30, 1966	Exotic dancer at Jack Ruby's nightclub who had direct knowledge that Ruby and Oswald indeed knew each other. But her death was apparently a domestic murder.	MURDER: No apparent linkage to JFK assassination.
Mary Pinchot Meyer	October 12, 1964	OFFICIALLY UNSOLVED MURDER, but contrary to the official version and well-orchestrated cover-up, the very professional assassination of JFK's mistress had direct linkage to a clean-up operation with CIA foreknowledge.	NATIONAL SECURITY ASSASSINATION: Directly linked to JFK assassination.
Lieutenant Commander William Pitzer, U.S. Navy	October 29, 1966	Lieutenant Commander Pitzer had autopsy evidence proving that President Kennedy had been shot from the front and reportedly planned on releasing it after his upcoming retirement. His death was officially ruled suicide, but had direct linkage to a clean-up operation with specific CIA foreknowledge.	NATIONAL SECURITY ASSASSINATION: Directly linked to JFK assassination.

Victim	Date	Relationship	Determination
Manuel Rodriguez Quesada	October, 1964	Militant member of powerful anti-Castro group who had inside information on the setting up of the JFK killing in Dallas. Professional assassin John O'Hare admitted executing the contract on the victim.	NATIONAL SECURITY ASSASSINATION: Directly linked to JFK assassination.
Gilberto Rodriguez Hernandez	September, 1964	Military Coordinator for anti-Castro group who had inside information on the setting up of the JFK killing in Dallas. Professional assassin John O'Hare admitted executing the contract on the victim.	NATIONAL SECURITY ASSASSINATION: Directly linked to JFK assassination.
Eladio del Valle	February 22, 1967	OFFICIALLY UNSOLVED MURDER—Shot the same day that David Ferrie was also eliminated from Jim Garrison's witness list. Eladio del Valle was a militant anti-Castro leader and also linked to CIA and the mafia in their united anti-Castro efforts. Like David Ferrie, he was being sought as a witness by Jim Garrison. Professional assassin John O'Hare stated that del Valle ordered the contracts on Quesda and Hernandez, then had to be "neutralized" himself because he became a liability as Garrison's investigation was getting closer. O'Hare also admitted to assassinating del Valle.	NATIONAL SECURITY ASSASSINATION: Directly linked to JFK assassination.
David Ferrie	February 22, 1967	Victim had just been named as a defendant in Jim Garrison's case for conspiracy in the JFK assassination. Ferrie told Garrison he had just signed Ferrie's death warrant and Ferrie was indeed dead, just a short time later. As documented, the way that Ferrie died can be intentionally inflicted as a murder technique.	UNSOLVED: POSSIBLE MURDER that appears directly linked to JFK assassination.

Victim	Date	Relationship	Determination
Rolando Masferrer	October 5, 1975	The dynamite-bombing of the car of Cuban Exile resistance leader Rolando "El Tigre" Masferrer is still officially an unsolved murder. Like Jimmy Hoffa, Masferrer definitely had some involvement in the pre-assassination planning for JFK's murder, but was also involved in a lot of dirty deals with the mafia. So he was clearly assassinated in a highly professional job, but it is currently unclear by whom.	ASSASSINATION: Probable link to victim's knowledge of JFK assassination, but possibly Mafia retaliation killing.
Dr. Mary Sherman	July 21, 1964	Officially an unsolved murder, but the preponderance of evidence indicates that Dr. Sherman actually was killed as a result of a laboratory accident involving a linear particle accelerator. Because the lab was part of a secret bioweapon anti-Castro project, it had to be disguised. So the victim was brought to her home—the evidence proves that although her body was devastated by a major event, she was still alive—and the crime scene was then staged as a murder and her apartment set on fire, in a desperate attempt at plausibility for her death.	DEATH BY MEDICAL ACCIDENT ACCOMPANIED BY "EUTHANASIC TERMINATION."
FBI Director J. Edgar Hoover	May 2, 1972	The sudden death of the longtime FBI Director occurred as he was vying for power with President Nixon in a crucial pre-Watergate period, and one source suggests that Hoover was eliminated with chemicals capable of inducing death and leaving the appearance of cardiac arrest.	HEART ATTACK: POSSIBLE MURDER but not specifically linked to JFK assassination.

Victim	Date	Relationship	Determination
Louis Nichols, FBI	**June, 1977**	Assistant Director at FBI (third in command). The odds against six top FBI officials dying from *any* causes—with all six close to evidence matters in the JFK assassination and all six dying in less than a six-month period just before they were scheduled to testify before Congress—are so astronomically high that they can be considered mathematically impossible.	**HEART ATTACK: But six deaths of six FBI officials (who were scheduled to testify) in a six-month period literally defies mathematical possibility .**
Alan Belmont, FBI	**August, 1977**	Alan Belmont was the FBI's Liaison to the Warren Commission.	**"LONG ILLNESS": But six deaths of six FBI officials (who were scheduled to testify) in a six-month period literally defies mathematical possibility.**
James Cadigan, FBI	**August, 1977**	James Cadigan was an FBI document expert who examined key evidence related to the JFK assassination.	**"ACCIDENTAL FALL IN HOME": But six deaths of six FBI officials (who were scheduled to testify) in a six-month period literally defies mathematical possibility.**
Donald Kaylor, FBI	**October, 1977**	Donald Kaylor was an FBI fingerprint expert who examined key evidence related to the JFK assassination.	**HEART ATTACK: But six deaths of six FBI officials (who were scheduled to testify) in a six-month period literally defies mathematical possibility.**

Victim	Date	Relationship	Determination
J.M. English, FBI	**October, 1977**	J. M. English was head of the FBI Forensics Laboratory.	**HEART ATTACK: But six deaths of six FBI officials (who were scheduled to testify) in a six-month period literally defies mathematical possibility.**
William Sullivan, FBI	**November 9, 1977**	The Director of the Domestic Intelligence Division at the FBI, Bill Sullivan specifically predicted that he would be murdered and that it would be made to appear as an accident. It was not a casual or flippant remark—it was a precise statement that occurred exactly as he had predicted it would.	**"HUNTING ACCIDENT": But six deaths of six FBI officials (who were scheduled to testify) in a six-month period literally defies mathematical possibility.**
Richard Cain	**December 20, 1973**	High-ranking Chicago law enforcement official who actually answered to Sam Giancana, head of the Chicago Mob. Was also involved in anti-Castro operations and had sensitive knowledge about the plot to kill JFK. But Cain was killed in a classic mafia hit, apparently for internal reasons (power struggle in Chicago).	**Murdered by mafia for internal mob reasons, apparently unrelated to JFK assassination.**
Sam Giancana	**June 19, 1975**	OFFICIALLY UNSOLVED MURDER, but the head of the Chicago Mob and—according to many—a key conspirator of the plot to kill JFK, was gunned down execution-style in his fortress-style suburban home right before he was to testify to Congress. It's not clear if it was Government-sanctioned or simply a "mob job," but it was very professional, even sending a message about not testifying, via bullet wounds circling the mouth of victim.	**ASSASSINATION TO PRECLUDE WITNESS TESTIMONY: Clearly linked to JFK assassination.**

Victim	Date	Relationship	Determination
Johnny Roselli	August, 1976	OFFICIALLY UNSOLVED MURDER but Johnny Roselli knew a great deal about the JFK assassination and was being sought for testimony before Congress and his murder was no coincidence—that much is very clear. His knowledge about the relationship between the CIA's anti-Castro operations, the Mafia and the plan to kill JFK, was too sensitive to ignore.	**ASSASSINATION TO PRECLUDE WITNESS TESTIMONY, clearly linked to JFK assassination.**
Chuck Nicoletti	March 29, 1977	OFFICIALLY UNSOLVED MURDER—Top mafia hitman Chuck Nicoletti was in Dallas at the time of the JFK assassination, and was named as a shooter by many with inside knowledge. Nicoletti was also known to be unhappy about the recent assassination of his benefactor, Sam "The Man" Giancana. Like Giancana before his murder, Nicoletti was scheduled to soon testify before the House Select Committee on Assassinations.	**ASSASSINATION TO PRECLUDE WITNESS TESTIMONY: Clearly linked to JFK assassination.**
George de Mohrenschildt	March 29, 1977	Shot the same day as Nicoletti, George de Mohrenschildt was a main link between the CIA and Lee Harvey Oswald. He stated that he was being hounded and harassed and that he was in fear for his life. He was shot the day before he was scheduled to testify—in fact, a Committee investigator was literally on his way to his home when he was shot.	**PROBABLE NATIONAL SECURITY ASSASSINATION TO PRECLUDE WITNESS TESTIMONY: Clearly linked to JFK assassination.**

Victim	Date	Relationship	Determination
Jimmy Hoffa	July 30, 1975	OFFICIALLY UNSOLVED MURDER: Hoffa was the top labor leader in the country, very much in with the Mob (who loved his multibillion dollar pension fund), was the arch enemy of the Kennedys, and reportedly involved in the pre-assassination planning. But it was Hoffa's efforts to regain control of the Teamsters Union that actually got him killed.	**Murdered by mafia for internal mob reasons, not directly linked to JFK assassination.**
John Paisley	September 24, 1978	Top-level CIA officer who claimed to have knowledge regarding the true nature of the JFK assassination. Paisley was also suspected of being the high-level "mole" known to have penetrated the U.S. intelligence apparatus. Ruling of "suicide" was preposterous: the right-handed Paisley was shot behind the left ear, diving weights affixed to his waist and thrown into the ocean. He apparently turned out to be the mole that the Agency had been deceived by for many years.	**NATIONAL SECURITY ASSASSINATION or ASSASSINATION BY SOVIET INTELIGENCE: But apparently unrelated to JFK assassination.**
Gary Powers	August 1, 1977	Gary Powers was a veteran CIA agent who was shot down in his spy plane in Russian air space in 1960, triggering a cancellation of a World Peace Summit. Powers believed the Soviets shot him down from information that Oswald had provided them. His helicopter crash in 1977 was classified as Pilot Error, but circumstances suggest otherwise.	**HELICOPTER CRASH: POSSIBLE SABOTAGE, not directly linked to JFK assassination.**

Victim	Date	Relationship	Determination
Jim Reeves	**July 31, 1964**	Country singer, who may have been a special courier and knew Lee Harvey Oswald. Died in crash of small plane. It has been substantiated that the search for the crash site was diverted, apparently for the purpose of allowing authorities to get to the site first. The briefcase that Reeves was known to have carried onto the plane was then missing from the wreckage.	**PLANE CRASH: POSSIBLE SABOTAGE and elimination of evidence, but not directly linked to JFK assassination.**
Senator Robert F. Kennedy	**June 6, 1968**	Told associates that he would investigate JFK's death if could get into the nation's highest office, and then murdered just as he appeared to be well on his way to attaining the Presidency.	**ASSASSINATED: By a conspiracy that set up the accused killer, Sirhan Bishara Sirhan—currently unclear whether or not directly linked to the JFK assassination.**

As we proved in the Introduction, there is substantial mathematical evidence to the contrary of these deaths being coincidental. There is also substantial cited evidence that heart attacks can be induced as an assassination technique. But because heart attacks are *generally* perceived to be natural (at least those not induced by the CIA), even if we excluded those two "first-year deaths" (Bill Chesher and Guy Banister) from the equation, they can be replaced by several *other* first-year deaths which should be added.

Added to the names on the first year of the original list should be:

Officer J. D. Tippit, November 22, 1963
Lee Harvey Oswald, November, 1963: Murdered by Jack Ruby in an extremely obvious case of silencing a very important witness

Grant Stockdale, December 1963
Captain Michael D. Groves, December 3, 1963: Commander of the Honor Guard for JFK funeral which, oddly, began practicing for a presidential funeral three days prior to the assassination. Died very suddenly at dinner table; cause of death: Unknown; possible food poisoning.[864]

---

[864] Roberts & Armstrong, *The Dead Witnesses*

Jim Reeves, July, 1964

Gilberto Rodriguez Hernandez, September, 1964

Manuel Rodriguez Quesada, October, 1964

Warren Reynolds should, for all intents and purposes, also be added to the list and his case duly noted. He owned a car dealership and witnessed the shooting of Officer J. D. Tippit, and even gave chase to the man who escaped. However, he stated that the man was *not* Oswald, and he refused to be browbeaten into changing his testimony that it *may* have been a man looking like Oswald. Reynolds was shot in the head with a rifle on January 23, 1964, but, miraculously, he survived. Blatant intimidation continued and his ten-year-old daughter was almost kidnapped, but the abduction attempt failed; he received threats on his life and other intimidations, such as trespassers nosing around outside his home at night. Finally, Reynolds had become a nervous wreck and told the FBI he had changed his mind and would identify Oswald as the shooter. After reversing his testimony, his harassment suddenly halted—but *surely*, that's just *one more incredible coincidence . . .*

The following witnesses can also be added to Richard Charnin's list of witness deaths within fourteen years of the assassination:

Officer J. D. Tippit
Captain Michael D. Groves
Jim Reeves
Gilberto Rodriguez Hernandez
Manuel Rodriguez Quesada
Harold Russell, February, 1967
Salvatore Granello, December, 1970
Roscoe White, September 24, 1971
Jimmy Hoffa
Joseph Ayres, August, 1977
Herminio Diaz Garcia, 1966
Charles William Thomas
Ed Voebel—1971
Manuel Artime November 18, 1977

Artime apparently died of rapid-onset cancer just as he was preparing to testify before the 1977 Congressional Committee. As we noted, David Ferrie and Dr. Mary Sherman had been working on rapid-onset cancer, to be used as an assassination technique targeting Fidel Castro. Notes about methods of inducing cancer in victims were found in Ferrie's apartment after his death. Artime was apparently playing both sides of the fence in the secret anti-Castro intelligence operations, working with Bobby Kennedy's team but also passing info to the mob. Rolando Masferrer, a killer associated with Mobster Santo's organization, was brought into the anti-Castro operations through Johnny Roselli or Manuel Artime. Note that all the aforementioned witnesses died prior to or during the Congressional committee that was specifically investigating links between the assassination and anti-Castro operations of Rolando Masferrer, Manuel Artime, Sam Giancana, Johnny Roselli, etc.

Also added to the overall list should be:

Alan Dorfman
David Morales
Cliff Carter
Senator Robert F. Kennedy

General C. D. Jackson reportedly died of cancer, just as an update to the original list of deaths, which listed his fate as "unknown." General Charles Douglas Jackson was Managing Director of the same *Time-Life International* that quickly purchased the very controversial film of the assassination by Abraham Zapruder, and then promptly kept it under lock and key, lest the public actually learn what happened. His death would also seem to merit some attention. General Jackson was also an expert in PsyOps (Psychological Warfare) for the OSS (which later mutated into the CIA), and a Special Assistant to President Eisenhower on Psychological Warfare. Jackson was also a key member in the establishment of the highly secretive *Bilderberg Group*, which many associate with development of the original plans for a "New World Order." The General was also a CIA agent for the last 16 years of his life and played an active role in *Operation Mockingbird* and the successful penetration of U.S. media by CIA operatives placed in roles as journalists. *No wonder he made the original list!*

Below is the portion of the original list from Jim Marrs and Ralph Schuster pertaining to the period of one year post-assassination:[865]

Date	Name	Connection with Case	Cause of Death
11/63	Karyn Kupicinet	TV host's daughter who was overheard telling of JFK's death prior to 11/22/63	Murder
12/63	Jack Zangetty	Expressed foreknowledge of Ruby shooting Oswald	Gunshot
2/64	Eddy Benavides	Lookalike brother to Tippit shooting witness, Domingo Benavides	Gunshot to head
2/64	Betty McDonald	Former Ruby employee who alibied Warren Reynolds shooting suspect.	Suicide by hanging in Dallas Jail

Date	Name	Connection with Case	Cause of Death
3/64	Bill Chesher	Thought to have information linking Oswald and Ruby	Heart attack
3/64	Hank Killam	Husband of Ruby employee, knew Oswald acquaintance	Throat cut
4/64	Bill Hunter	Reporter who was in Ruby's apartment on 11/24/63	Accidental shooting by policeman
5/64	Gary Underhill	CIA agent who claimed Agency was involved	Gunshot in head, ruled suicide
5/64	Hugh Ward	Private investigator working with Guy Banister and David Ferrie	Plane crash in Mexico
5/64	Deslesseps Morrison	New Orleans Mayor	Passenger in Ward's plane
8/64	Teresa Norton	Ruby employee	Fatally shot
6/64	Guy Banister	Ex-FBI agent in New Orleans connected to Ferrie, CIA, Carlos Marcello & Oswald	Heart attack
9/64	Jim Koethe	Reporter who was in Ruby's apartment on 11/24/63	Blow to neck
9/64	C.D. Jackson	*Life* magazine senior Vice-President who bought Zapruder film and locked it away	Unknown
10/64	Meyer, Mary Pinchot	JFK "special" friend whose diary was taken by CIA chief James Angleton after her death	Murder

ALSO AVAILABLE

Dead Wrong

Straight Facts on the Country's Most Controversial Cover-Ups

by Richard Belzer with David Wayne
Afterword by Jesse Ventura

Have you ever heard a news story of a politician being "found dead" or "committing suicide" and thought it strange, as if there's something they're not telling us? After you read Dead Wrong, you'll realize that your instincts were correct. For years the government has put out hits on people that it finds "expendable" or who it felt were "talking too much." David Wayne is here to show you that not only were these people murdered, but that it was done by our own government!

Find out how Marilyn Monroe was murdered, who really shot Martin Luther King Jr., and many other cover-ups throughout our country's history. Dead Wrong gives you the extensively researched straight facts on some of the most controversial cases this country has ever seen. You'll learn that what the government tells you is not always to be believed.

$14.95 Paperback • ISBN 978-1-62087-870-5

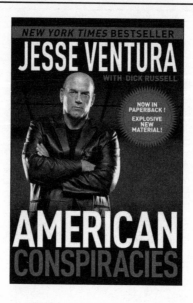

American Conspiracies
Lies, Lies, and More Dirty Lies That the Government Tells Us

by Jesse Ventura with Dick Russell

In this explosive account of wrongful acts and ensuing cover-ups, Jesse Ventura takes a systematic look at the wide gap between what the government knows and when the government knows it, and what is revealed to the American people and when it is revealed. The media is complicit in these acts of deception, often refusing to consider alternate possibilities and dismissing voices that diverge from public opinion. In *American Conspiracies*, Ventura looks closely at the theories that have been presented over the years and examines the truth, as well as the lies.

The assassinations of Abraham Lincoln, the Kennedys, and Martin Luther King Jr.—these cases and more need to be re-examined in Ventura's eyes. Was Watergate presented honestly, or was the CIA involved? Did the Republican Party set out to purposefully steal two elections? Has all of the evidence on 9/11 been presented, or is there another angle that the media is afraid to explore? And finally, is the collapse of today's financial order and the bailout plan by the Federal Reserve the widest-reaching conspiracy ever perpetrated? Nothing gets by Jesse Ventura in *American Conspiracies*.

$14.95 Paperback • ISBN 978-1-61608-214-7

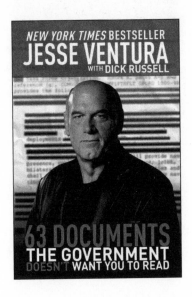

63 Documents the Government Doesn't Want You to Read

by Jesse Ventura with Dick Russell

The official spin on numerous government programs is flat-out bullsh*t, according to Jesse Ventura. In this incredible collection of actual government documents, Jesse Ventura, the ultimate nonpartisan truth-seeker, proves it beyond any doubt. He and Dick Russell walk readers through sixty-three of the most incriminating programs to reveal what really happens behind the closed doors. Witness as he breaks open the vault, revealing the truth about:

- The CIA's top-secret program to control human behavior
- Operation Northwoods—the military plan to hijack airplanes and blame it on Cuban terrorists
- Potentially deadly health care cover-ups, including a dengue fever outbreak
- What the Department of Defense knows about our food supply—but is keeping mum
- Homeland Security's "emergency" detention camps
- Fake terrorist attacks planned by the United States

$14.95 Paperback • ISBN 978-1-61608-571-1